Composing Our Future

Composing Our Future

PREPARING MUSIC EDUCATORS TO TEACH COMPOSITION

Edited by
Michele Kaschub
and
Janice P. Smith

OXFORD
UNIVERSITY PRESS

OXFORD
UNIVERSITY PRESS

Oxford University Press is a department of the University of Oxford.
It furthers the University's objective of excellence in research, scholarship,
and education by publishing worldwide.

Oxford New York
Auckland Cape Town Dar es Salaam Hong Kong Karachi
Kuala Lumpur Madrid Melbourne Mexico City Nairobi
New Delhi Shanghai Taipei Toronto

With offices in
Argentina Austria Brazil Chile Czech Republic France Greece
Guatemala Hungary Italy Japan Poland Portugal Singapore
South Korea Switzerland Thailand Turkey Ukraine Vietnam

Oxford is a registered trade mark of Oxford University Press
in the UK and certain other countries.

Published in the United States of America by
Oxford University Press
198 Madison Avenue, New York, NY 10016

Library of Congress Cataloging-in-Publication Data
Composing our future: preparing music educators to teach composition / Michele Kaschub and
Janice P. Smith, editors.
    p. cm.
  Includes bibliographical references and index.
  ISBN 978-0-19-983228-6 (alk. paper) — ISBN 978-0-19-983229-3 (alk. paper)
  1. Music—Instruction and study. 2. Composition (Music). I. Kaschub, Michele, 1967–
II. Smith, Janice, 1952–
  MT40.C715 2013
  781.3071—dc23
                                                    2012011006

9 8 7 6 5 4 3 2 1

Printed in the United States of America
on acid-free paper

This book is dedicated to music teachers and their students so that together they may find their compositional voices.

CONTENTS

SECTION } I

Introduction

1 }

Embracing Composition in Music Teacher Education

Michele Kaschub and Janice P. Smith

Opportunities to compose, listen to music, and engage in both traditional and technologically-mediated performance have never been as readily available to so many people as they are today. This phenomenon has led many music education professionals to consider what the nature of music in schools can become, and by extension, where music teacher education programs should focus their efforts. Do music teacher preparation programs enable pre- and in-service teachers to develop the skills and understandings necessary to empower their students to take advantage of this multiplicity of venues, materials, and possibilities for musical expression? Are pre- and in-service teachers prepared to engage students in the types of learning experiences that will lead them to continue their interactions with music once they leave formal schooling? Are music teacher-educators responsively engaged with the shifting realities of music's role in society? It is from within these challenging realities that a new focus on composition education emerges.

Music educators readily acknowledge the importance of composition. Writings that focus on composition resources and pedagogy appear with increasing frequency in a variety of e-media formats, music teacher magazines, research journals, and books. An abundance of workshops and sessions devoted to composition are regularly featured at state, divisional, and national level conferences across the sub-specialties of music education. Moreover, acknowledgement of this rapidly growing interest and attention was made in 2011 as the National Association for Music Education inaugurated the Council for Composition to further advance research, teaching, and learning in this area of music education.

Teachers, most of whom have had no previous experience with creating music as composers or training in how to teach composition, have been steadily exposed to a rapidly growing dialogue about composition and its potential value as a tool for teaching music. They seek materials, tools, techniques, and the support that will enable them to successfully engage their students in music composition. Additionally, some teachers are now beginning to develop their own compositional capacities so that they can more effectively guide young composers. Consequently, music teacher education programs must consider what assistance they can offer at both undergraduate and graduate levels of study.

As music teacher-educators contemplate the curricular modifications necessary to address composition within existing programs, apt questions arise concerning why such change is needed and what specific changes should be made. These questions should not be taken lightly. Curricular change is a reflection of philosophical evolution met by the boundaries of institutional contexts. The realities of practice—costs, credit hour limitations, efficiency of content delivery, faculty-student ratios, scheduling and a multitude of other institutionally nuanced factors—impact change. A strong philosophical stance and substantive rationale for change is imperative if such challenges to practice are to be overcome.

Evolutions in Musical Experience

There are, at minimum, three critical shifts in how music is experienced that make curricular change imperative. The first shift is in the area of autonomous access. Whether the role is that of creator, performer, or listener, access to music is instant, all-pervasive, and no longer bound by place or time. Musical freedom of such latitude has never been experienced by humanity. However, gains in freedom are equally met with shifts in responsibility. It is now the individual who selects an interaction mode (singing, playing, composing, listening, improvising), makes musical choices, develops preferences, and constructs artistic musical human understandings. This emerging individualized musical independence heralds the need for equally distinctive and personalized educational opportunities.

The second shift is found in the area of experiential context. Much of music's history has required group experience. People sang and played together and sometimes listened to the live performance of music as part of an audience. Over time and with technological innovation, focus has shifted toward the experience of the individual. More often than not, music is experienced through earbuds where the interaction between the music and the creator, performer, or listener is mediated by an electronic device. In fact, the roles of creator, performer, and listener can often merge in such interactions. Individuals are connected to others, but as part of an unfolding storyline rather than as a concurrent participant within a musical experience bound by place and time. This evolution in musical experience suggests that simultaneity of experience and concomitant group-focused instruction needs to be balanced with instruction that recognizes musical interaction as a means of constructing self.

The third shift is found in the area of participant population. For the most part, school music offerings typically draw a very specific, performance-oriented population, while students with interests in other areas of music are often left underserved. Though the training of musical performers filled a vital societal need at a time when music could only be experienced if performers were present, this period has long since passed. Accelerating advances in technology have ushered in new possibilities for musical experiences for an increasingly large population with eclectic interests. More and more people seek a wide range of musical engagements. These engagements are not limited by the strictures associated with performance as has been the western musical traditional. Rather, a diversification of access points and a multiplicity of experience-types hold collective appeal for many musical populations.

Technology's allure stems from the fact that, for many, it facilitates each individual's capacity to explore and develop personal creative potentials across an assortment of music-making activities and engagements. It can be tailored to self-interest. Instead of thinking about musical learning opportunities in the historically-bound performance versus non-performance dichotomy, music education should allow for commensurate and complementary musical opportunities that allow individuals to fully explore creating, performing, and listening. Within these expanded educational spaces, individuals will often seek connections to a larger community as a natural outgrowth of their experiences. The format presented by institutions that conserve the traditional—but limiting—dichotomy of performance and non-performance no longer meets the need of creative individuals.

Composition Aligned with Contemporary Musical Practices

Composition is particularly attractive to people who seek musical autonomy. Access, compositional context, and the very definition of who can be a composer all have been expanded by technological means. Current ways of crafting and controlling musical experience provide a freedom of time and place that allows people to focus on their own musical pursuits and their individual creativity. Whether or not a choice is made to share these adventures with others is of lesser concern because a group of performers is no longer necessary for music to be heard. Much like writing, composing is now available to anyone who wishes to compose.

Composition is aligned with a modern rebalancing of individual and group music experiences. Throughout history, composers often have had to rely on others to bring their musical ideas to life. However, what was once reliance is now choice. Technological innovations now allow composers to overcome the challenges that have historically limited compositional engagement. The challenges of notating and preserving musical ideas, securing performers, locating venues, and attracting audiences, have been substantially reduced by the advent of highly accessible tools.

Composers have always struggled to transfer musical ideas from the imagination to external notations so their musical intentions might be preserved and possibly shared. Software for notating and recording music, iconographic interfaces, and sound manipulation programs have made the exploration, generation, and manipulation of musical ideas available to anyone who cares to imagine in sound. While craft and creativity still are required, the means of sonifying ideas and of sonic manipulation are readily available.

Composers once needed to secure performers to bring compositions into the acoustical present so that notational accuracy and the sonic intentions could be verified. Performers were also needed so that audiences could hear the musical work. Technologies now exist that expand the composer's palette. Composers may choose to pursue acoustic or electronically mediated sound sources, or combinations of the two for performance. The ensemble needed to perform music may be just a click away.

Performance venues once came at great cost in terms of both time and monetary investment. Compositions created or recorded through electronic media are exceptionally easy to share via social networks or other digital media. While concert halls, houses of worship, and stadiums are still available, websites, blogs, and online purveyors of digital recordings are increasingly viable options for sharing one's music. Again, composers have an expanded palette of choices as they identify the venues most appropriate for their works.

Composers once had to work very hard to promote their works or have their works promoted to attract audiences to performances. Media outlets, web-based and mobile technologies, and social media now allow for greater dispersion of concert announcements and of the musical works themselves. Further, these media substantially shift the direction of the experience. Rather than an audience always attending a live event, the audience may choose when to engage digitally with a performance. Listeners may also actively enter into dialogue about the music, the musicians, or the composer. Moreover, the audience and the composer may even choose to interact with each other. Composers can choose to have much—or little— to say about their works and the audience's reaction to them. All of this can enhance the experiential context for everyone involved.

The journey from composer's initial inspiration to public performance once required a cast of many players filling distinctive roles with limited overlap. As technological innovations have unfolded in a manner that allows one person to fill the role of composer, conductor, performer, producer, and consumer, the nature of individual and collective interactions with musical compositions has been substantially altered. Whether the composer is working alone or in partnership with others, interaction among, between, and with other musicians has assumed new dimensions.

The advent of social media has substantially altered the way in which composers, performers, and audience members interact with music. Instant messaging, Internet forums, microblogs, podcasts, wikis and other formats have made access to information and opinion instant, continuous, and ubiquitous. These social media are shifting our culture away from one of discrete ownership toward one that also acknowledges, seeks, and welcomes collaborative participation.

At any point in the compositional process, composers may share their work, make recommendations, detail their musical passions, connect with personal contacts, empathize with others facing similar challenges, or offer resources to others. Through social media-based communications, composers may attract followers, influence others, and engage in conversations that provide opportunities to learn within a community of musicians that quite possibly spans the globe. As participants engage in interactions with other composers facing similar challenges, they are able to frame their level of expertise in relation to others. These observations contribute to their perception of themselves as composers.

Above all, composition attracts a broad participant base. It fascinates those who perform, create, and listen, but it can appeal to each of these for different reasons. People with a particular passion for performance are often eager to create original works that are a unique projection of their own musical understandings and experiences as mediated by their instrument. Conversely, some performers feel limited in what they can express musically because they are bound to a specific instrument. Composition provides access to the exploration of other musical voices.

For people who invest great time and energy in absorbing music through listening, composition can provide a means for making sense of musical ideas and their inherent or constructed relationships. Intuitive understandings of how music works can lend breadth and depth to initial attempts at composition. Imitative works are often first to emerge. These are soon followed by compositions that reveal the composer's voice. These are influenced by the range of expressive gestures that are familiar from music listening experiences.

The opportunity to express through sound the ineffable "knowings" that emanate from the realm of feeling is a powerful and desirable experience. Were words, numbers, colors, and movement sufficient for capturing human experience, music would not exist. To provide every student—not just those who pursue performance—an opportunity to explore and expand the intuitive and feelingful understanding of what it is to be human through music composition is the responsibility of every music teacher. Therefore, music composition must be strategically positioned within music teacher education and music teachers must be provided the opportunity to acquire the tools to facilitate children's compositional development.

Beliefs about Learning and Teaching Composition

Composition represents a unique form of knowing that both reveals and constructs an understanding of one's self and others. It provides an opportunity for creating meaning and making sense of the world. Students learn to write to clarify and share their thinking. Similarly, the process of composing allows students to clarify and share feeling. Composing, when well-taught, develops musical thinking that "requires the interweaving of *knowledge about* and *know-how*. When combined synergistically, composers are able to create pieces that represent their *knowing within* and *of* music" (Kaschub & Smith, 2009, p. 1). This leads to a deeper and broader understanding of music, and by extension, of the composer. The process of composing produces both a musical product and an expanded self-knowledge for the composer.

People can learn to compose. Just as most people learn to speak, read, and write, most people can imagine and organize sounds so that they can be shared with others. While great novels and epic poems may be rare creations, nearly every person can create a story that holds personal meaning and which may intrigue or amuse others. Similarly, there are few Pulitzer Prize–winning compositions, but everyone can create music which captures the essence of a special event or meaningful experience in their lives.

Like many skills, practice with composing improves the ability to compose. The more one attempts to sonify feeling, the more one learns what gestures work, what sounds express, and what brings musical satisfaction. Simple compositional etudes constructed to develop a specific compositional device or notational skill do not usually allow for this type of feelingful engagement. Neither do random compositions based on phone numbers or thrown dice. Rarely is feeling sonified by chance. It is only when there is a felt need—an expressive intent—that compositions come to life and mean something to the composer, and, by extension, to a listener.

Learning communities are vital to the musical growth of composers. These communities can consist of everyone who interacts with the composer and the compositions or may be limited to a smaller group with whom the composer chooses to share a work. They may be comprised of people of varying skill levels or simply a trusted mentor and a composer. However, when there is a larger community of practice, composers are able to hear works by more advanced composers. They can also exercise their analytical listening skills and then provide feedback to peers. Most importantly, composers can ascertain how successfully their feelingful intentions were artistically crafted into sound from the feedback provided by their "peer audience."

One of the most necessary aspects of music education in the twenty-first century is an emphasis on using sound—regardless of its source—expressively. Students should be helped to organize and share their musical intentions with the world. While there will always be different degrees of compositional skill and artistic expression, these are likely to be normally distributed across the population and are present in some degree in everyone. The purpose of music education should be to develop and refine these skills.

Teachers can help students to become better composers. Those who focus on the compositional capacities of intention, expressivity, and artistic craftsmanship are likely to find inspiring expressive potential within young composers (Kaschub & Smith, 2009). However, this can be obscured by exercises dominated by notational demands or over-attention to music's elements. Further, educators who encourage students to balance music's principle relationships—motion/stasis, unity/variety, sound/silence, tension/release, stability/instability—help students focus on the expressive use of technique rather than simply on the techniques themselves. To facilitate this type of learning, teachers need preparation that expands their own compositional capacities as well as provides models and practice in guiding compositional work with students.

Foundational Experiences in Teacher Preparation

There are three critical components to music teacher preparation in composition. Teachers must compose, form a foundation of pedagogical knowledge, and participate in active composing communities comprised of professional composers, teachers, and students. Educators who have participated in these three types of experiences will be able to readily access the personal knowledge and skills they have gained.

Teacher education programs must provide their students with access to a wide variety of personal experiences with composition in an equally varied number of contexts. This means pre- and in-service teachers need to compose individually and collaboratively to explore the processes unique to each setting. They need to engage in creating music in multiple styles, idioms, and genres, utilizing an expansive palette of sounds, including acoustic and electronic instruments, as well as other sources. They also need to work with invented notations, graphic and iconic symbol systems, and traditional notation, as each of these preservation systems reflects a different understanding of the representation of musical ideas. Throughout these experiences, educators must critically examine the work of other composers and composition teachers to gain insight into additional techniques and approaches. These strategies become part of a repertoire of specialized knowledge that will inform their future practice and pedagogy.

All music educators need to have direct experience with planning, implementing, assessing, and reflecting upon composition lessons. Ideally, this happens in a setting that provides opportunities to interact and reflect on their work with other composer-educators. Such models may be available in school-based settings or more likely may need to be approximated in college classrooms until partnerships with school-based composition teachers can be developed. Once foundational skills have been established, teachers benefit from opportunities to lead composition activities, acquire feedback from others, and reflect on their own approaches. Careful reflection allows teachers to consider how lessons may be modified to enhance student learning.

Teaching composition, like any other specialized branch of teaching, is best learned within a community of practitioners who share similar values and goals. Educators need not work in isolation. Contemporary democratic practices in composition contradict the prevalent myth of the solitary great composer. Even the historical geniuses of the past participated in informal composing communities through correspondence and concert attendance as they sought to hear the works of their predecessors and contemporaries. Participation in a composing community provides teachers and teacher-educators an opportunity to hear and learn from the work of their peers.

Providing valuable feedback to peers requires the use of analytical and critical observation skills that can be developed and refined with practice. Similarly, willingness to accept feedback from others and make use of such comments and suggestions to improve instruction ensures continued growth in pedagogical expertise. The ability to engage in constructive dialogue with others in a manner that honors their ideas and artistic autonomy without stifling either one should be practiced. It is critical to the success of any teacher-facilitated composition activity.

Situating Composition in Teacher Education

Composition pedagogy is a powerful topic within any music teacher education program. Educators must engage in analytical, creative, and critical listening as well as interpretive score study and performance. This allows them to be effective communicators of musical ideas and of information about those ideas.

As teachers engage deeply with the intentions of the composer and the craftsmanship brought to bear on the creation of musical works, they glimpse music's true expressive capacity. And yet, even with the value of composition so readily apparent to all those who engage it, finding a space for composition within already overburdened teacher preparation programs remains a daunting challenge.

This problem must be met with a multitude of solutions. While certain commonalities of approach undoubtedly will emerge, individual programs will likely launch context-specific pathways for the study of composition pedagogy. Indeed, some programs already include stand-alone composition methods courses focused on K–12 instruction, but these still are exceptionally rare. This needs to change if teachers are going to be prepared to respond to the shifts in musical experiences enumerated at the beginning of this chapter.

Topics relevant to composition pedagogy often are already embedded to some degree within existing courses. Studies that focus on masterworks easily can be modified to include an additional examination of the compositional techniques used by the composer. Another broad topic that arises in many music courses is the question of how creativity is sparked and how musical ideas emerge and evolve from that impetus. This, too, corresponds directly to a critical, creative point in the process of composition. Likewise, courses in history, theory, conducting, literature, and performance, as well as general, choral, and instrumental methods and techniques all offer opportunities to address composition pedagogy.

Modeling appropriate feedback and responsive teaching can occur in many classes, but few college-level faculty outside of education have the background and expertise to effectively demonstrate these interactions. It is unfortunate that many faculty lack specific training in teaching and logically resort to teaching as they were taught. In order for students to gain an understanding of these concepts and practices, music teacher-educators will need to utilize new models of best practice emphasizing their applicability to most educational settings.

Programs that choose to offer classes in composition pedagogy must realize that such courses differ from other methods classes. At present there are few resources to share, let alone multiple methods books to compare and evaluate. Absence of such material allows for an important conversation about why so few resources currently exist for composition. Most importantly, the absence of composition lesson books organized by grade and level number allows teachers to learn that their most important pedagogical tool is the ability to develop materials that are purposefully and specifically tailored to the students being taught. After all, even with hundreds of years of documented compositional practice, no single pedagogy of composition has emerged. There are as many approaches to teaching composition as there are potential composers waiting to be taught.

What Composition Educators Need to Be Able to Do

Teachers must be able to organize experiences that allow others to interact with materials and ideas that lead to the construction of knowledge. This is the crucial curricular parameter for arts educators. The very path that leads to meaningful artistic engagement lies in conflict with curricular mandates that are bound by that which can be easily tested. These types of educational initiatives, forged in the intemperate fires of politics, are inherently doomed to fail because they restrict educational innovation to what can be efficiently measured. At the same time, highly structured and test-driven curriculum schemes also deny students the support they need to develop skills in critical thinking, creativity, collaboration, and communication that are—and will continue to be—in such high demand in the twenty-first century workplace. All four are central to the processes of teaching and learning in music composition.

Educators must be prepared to build programs that invite students to think critically about how music is created and crafted. More importantly, students must be encouraged to examine the meanings that they have discovered, constructed, and experienced in the process of composing, as this additionally evidences critical feeling. In order to develop critical thinking skills (conceptual knowledge) and critical feeling skills (perceptual knowledge) pertinent to artistic endeavors, teachers must model reflection on the work at hand and provide constructive commentary. They need to encourage students to similarly critique their own work and the work of others in ways that enhance the students' critical thinking skills. Comparing and contrasting musical ideas, expanding musical gestures, measuring the expressive capacity of the work, and many other thought processes can be very helpful to the practice of composing.

Students must be engaged in transformative experiences that allow them to create feelingful compositions. Creativity apart from meaning can be entertaining and freeing, but creativity in the service of expressive communication expands the students' sense of self. Teachers who foster this type of creative activity, with attention to expressive communication, connect their students with experiences, challenges, joys and struggles that are common in the larger world around them. Composing brings structure to creativity. It is purposeful and intentional yet, at the same time, it is intensely personal. Teachers who encourage students to create must guard the students' sense of ownership of their work, as it is one aspect of the self-constructed identity that composition evokes.

Teachers must help students develop two distinct types of communication skills. The first is evidenced in the ability to make meaningful sounds that project an artistic intention. This is the craft of composition and is revealed in the composer's ability to sonify feeling. This also often reveals the composer's "voice"—the specific manner and gesture of musical ideas that can be recognized as the work of a particular person. The second skill is equally critical. It is the ability to use words, in speech or writing, to explain features and nuances of a composition that might impact a performer's or listener's experience. Words about music are necessary when subtleties developed by the composer are difficult for others to discover. In such cases, composers—or others who have critically analyzed the work—employ words about music to point the way.

Finally, teachers must help students develop skills of collaboration. This is best accomplished as teachers themselves engage in collaborative work with students. It is often assumed that collaboration occurs within large ensembles. This, however, is rarely the case. True collaboration requires an equality of participation and personal artistic contribution and investment. Co-laboring implies working together to accomplish something. In composition settings, composers may choose to collaborate with peers to create their work. They may decide to collaborate with other musicians to have the work performed. If there is to be a live performance, they may seek to collaborate with a variety of other persons involved in providing a venue and the publicity necessary to draw an audience. These collaborations differ significantly from the ability to follow the conductor's baton.

Toward the Future

Our mission is to take music education into the twenty-first century. It is not enough to say that we are already living there when our practices are still firmly fashioned after nineteenth-century models. Twenty-first century teacher preparation must be bold. It must break free from its traditional conservatory strictures and be flexible, creative, and complex. It must stride the landscape of a rapidly changing world brimming with new challenges and opportunities as well as new possibilities. The "one-size-fits-all" teacher preparation of the past, full of courses and requirements that no longer suit the education environments of the present, fails to acknowledge the future of a musical world outside of schools and academe. Our world is diverse, globalized, and media-saturated. Life unfolds at a hectic pace. These very issues both enable and lead to a need for students who can think, create, and work differently than we have in the past.

Words that once had very specific meanings—school, teacher, learner, curriculum—are in a state of rapid evolution. In vibrant learning environments, the roles of teacher and learner are temporary and shift seamlessly within that context. Educators are no longer the sole repository of knowledge. There is simply too much to know and more efficient ways to access information than to wait for one person to relay what he or she knows to another. Learning, once thought of as happening primarily at school, is now an all-pervasive behavior that beckons engaged learners to pursue their passions. While schools and educational institutions may change radically in the twenty-first century, the human impulse to make and share music will continue to be a defining aspect of what it is to be human.

As teacher-educators, we can work to compose a future for music education that re-connects contemporary music practices and school music. The shifts observable in how humans encounter and interact with music can provide direction for our actions. If we examine current trends, we see that students will continue to have greater and greater access to music. Will this be matched by an equal access to their own creative artistic power? Personal autonomy will continue to play a significant role in musical experiences. Will these experiences be interactive and based in a community of learners who seek to expand and refine musical understandings? More and more people will interact with music across a range of varied experiential contexts. Will these experiences help them construct personal meaning representative of the diversity of their engagements? Music composition can provide the opportunity for students to seek, find, and develop their unique artistic voices by using sound expressively to construct highly personal and meaningful understandings of themselves and the world around them.

It is our responsibility and our privilege to make sure they have the opportunity to do so.

Reference

Kaschub, M., and Smith, J. P. (2009). *Minds on Music: Composition for Creative and Critical Thinking*. Lanham, Maryland: R&L Education—A Division of Rowman & Littlefield Publishers, Inc.

SECTION } II

Foundations and Futures

SECTION } II

Foundations and Futures

As we consider what the future may hold for composition in music education, it is important to examine the foundational work that has brought us to our current level of understanding. One way of approaching this topic is to consider the research exploring music creativity and composition. These areas of inquiry have a substantial history spanning a range of topics that reveal core compositional processes as well as emerging practices. Insights gained from these perspectives may suggest future directions for music teacher education in composition.

Peter Webster opens this section with an analysis of musical intelligence and how such intelligence might be related to composition and creativity. He asserts that composing contributes to the development of musical intelligence and musical creativity and that these attributes exist to some degree in all humans. In reviewing the definitions of musical intelligence, Webster highlights the work of Howard Gardner and Bennett Reimer as he discusses what might be meant by compositional intelligence. He then relates these concepts to his model of creative thinking in music.

Maud Hickey presents a summary of current research that examines teaching music composition in (or related to) school music. She groups the studies into the following themes: eminence; university composition students; differing perspectives and circumstances (teacher/student); ensemble classrooms; technology, and pre-service teacher education. She concludes with practical suggestions for music teacher educators to use when introducing this literature to pre- and in-service teachers.

Randall Allsup provides a philosophical foundation for a new vision of teaching composing. He begins by redefining composition and explores the ideas of "composing" and "composition" as open and closed forms respectively. The pedagogical implications of these definitions and suggestions for new ways of participating in music are offered. The chapter concludes with a prediction for what music education could look like in the near future.

2 }

Music Composition Intelligence and Creative Thinking in Music

Peter R. Webster

This book is designed to address the difficult topic of teaching music composition in today's schools. Building on their excellent previous work on this topic (Kaschub & Smith, 2009), our editors ask music teachers to broaden their perspectives and consider preparing students for a lifetime of music-making and listening through music composition. This is, for many teachers in North America, a radical idea. We know from years of experience that teachers can help students learn to perform with instruments and their voices at high levels of achievement; we know too that they can be helped to listen to music more carefully and even improvise in some-what limited contexts. But can they also think in sound well enough to compose original music? Isn't that such a specialized skill that it would be impossible to be taught in schools and better left for other contexts? And isn't this kind of creative thinking unlikely to be a realistic objective given our busy schedules with students in today's schools? Some might further question if such work with students is intel-lectually possible, especially in early years of elementary schools.

Certainly the emerging literature on student composition in the last thirty years has provided multiple examples that compositional thinking is not only possible, but that students have achieved astoundingly high levels of compositional sophis-tication when done in nurturing school environments. Students can think in sound and are highly motivated to do so without much insistence from music teachers; students find the activity immensely enjoyable and teachers who have experimented with even the simplest approaches to composition have found that the payoffs for music learning by a wide variety of students to be well worth the time. Not only is composition in the schools intellectually possible for students of all ages, but also it enhances other music experiences such as performance and listening. Evidence for all this can be found in this very book and in many other publications (e.g., Wiggins, 2009; Younker, 2000).

This chapter will suggest, in a fundamental way, at least two reasons why com-positional thinking by students is vitally important: it increases musical intelligence and increases the likelihood of creative achievement. I argue here, as others have before me, that students have a natural capacity for thinking in sound for compositional purposes and that this capacity is not just a talent for "gifted" individuals but *a natural part of what we might consider a musical intelligence that is present to some extent in all*. Further, I claim that a musical intelligence that involves composition is intimately connected to my model of creative thinking in music.

Newer Perspectives on Intelligence

Psychological views of intelligence in the present era are complex and defy short descriptions (Sternberg & Detterman, 1986). Schools of thought are influenced by evidence from psychometrics, neuroscience, sociology, and educational theory. One aspect of most modern views of this difficult construct is that definitions of "intelligence" should include room for multiple ways of knowing.

In Howard Gardner's landmark book, *Frames of Minds* (1983/1985),[1] and in many of his publications that followed (1999, 2006), the case is made for music as one of at least seven specialized intelligences that form human mental capacity. Gardner argues for specialized intelligences based on several criteria; these include: (1) identification of such intelligences by the presence of brain damage, (2) the existence of exceptional people that exemplify the intelligence, (3) psychometric, experimental, and historical data, (4) existence of some type of symbol system, and—important for this chapter—(5) the notion of a set of core abilities. For Gardner, an intelligence is the ability to solve problems and create products that are valued in cultural settings and that abilities such as these are not exemplified just in domains where logical and linguistic abilities are dominant (Gardner, 1983/1985, p. x).

This particular perspective on human cognitive ability has been highly valued by music educators in part because it reinforced and gave credibility to the importance of music as part of what makes us human (Fowler, 1990). Interestingly, the scholarship that represents the perspective of multiple intelligences and its focus on musical thinking and ability has not been as celebrated in music education literature in recent times as much as advocacy positions that grow from music's role in teaching other subjects such as mathematics, language, science, and human traits such as motivation, leadership, and self-efficacy (Elpus, 1997).

The notion of multiple facets of human intelligence was, of course, not new with Gardner's significant publication. Concerns about one-dimensional assessments of intellectual potential can be traced back to the earliest days of intelligence testing with the work of Binet and Simon (1916) in France. Binet himself was uncomfortable with an assessment tool that provided only one "score" and had serious doubts that any psychometric instrument could assess completely the complexity of human capabilities (Kamin, 1995). Nevertheless, the notion of a single psychometric instrument that might provide a convenient and cost-effective way of labeling students' potential for learning was attractive to many. Binet's instrument was made popular in following years in the United States by the work of Terman at Stanford University and his famous Stanford-Binet assessment tool is still in use after many revisions. The Weschler Adult Intelligence Scale (WAIS) (Weschler, 1958) was developed with the idea of expanding the reporting structure by including more than one score and by using reference groups that were age appropriate in reporting results. The WAIS is seen as useful in identifying certain learning disabilities (Kaufman, 1990), but most agree still falls far short in helping us identify the mosaic of human capacity.

Guilford (1967) felt this way as well when developing his famous Structure of Intellect model, which theorized over 150 separate abilities, including dimensions for divergent and convergent thinking across several content areas and products. In doing so, he ushered in a renewed interest in creative thinking and its assessment as part of a number of human capabilities worthy of psychological study. Since the work of Guilford, the history of attention to creativeness and creative thinking in psychology and related fields has been largely driven by the idea of multiple facets of mind and brain.

GARDNER'S CORE ABILITIES IN MUSIC

It is in this context of multiple facets of human ability that we find a conceptual home for the notion of music composition intelligence. Gardner's writing on music has focused largely on a more general view of musical ability, and not specifically on compositional thinking. However, in staking out his claims for music as one of several intelligences, Gardner used examples from the writings of adult composers when first establishing his core abilities (Gardner, 1983/1985, pp. 101–108).

> There are several roles that musically inclined individuals can assume, ranging from the avant-garde composer who attempts to create a new idiom, to the fledgling listener who is trying to make sense of nursery rhymes (or other "primer level" music). There may well be a hierarchy of difficulty involved in various roles, with performing exacting more demands than listening does, and composing making more profound (or at least different) demands than performing. It is also probable that certain kinds of music—such as the classical forms under discussion here—are less accessible than folk or musical [*sic*] forms. Yet there is also a core set of abilities crucial to all participation in the musical experience of a culture. (p. 104)

Core abilities in music for Gardner center on the ability for individuals to manipulate and/or perceive the elements of pitch, rhythm, and timbre. To these more perceptual, acoustical aspects of music, he adds the dimension of feeling:

> In alluding to affect and pleasure, we encounter what may be the central puzzle surrounding music. From the point of view of "hard" positivistic science, it

should seem preferable to describe music purely in terms of objective, physical terms: to stress the pitch and rhythmic aspects of music, perhaps recognizing the timbre and the permissible compositional forms . . . Yet hardly anyone who has been intimately associated with music can forbear to mention its emotional implications: the effects it has upon individuals; the sometimes deliberate attempts by composers (or performers) to mimic or communicate certain emotions; or to put it in its most sophisticated terms, the claim that, if music does not in itself convey emotions or affects, it captures the forms of these feelings. (pp. 105–106)

What is not explained in Gardner's treatment of musical intelligence is how these core abilities actually function in the behaviors of students working with sound compositionally. He does recognize the perceptual ability of students at young ages to hear musical structure, to be able to tell if an ending to a piece is more or less appropriate or to appreciate the relationships between key structures, musical contours, phrase structures, and cadence points. In considering the growing evidence of music development as testimony to musical intelligence, Gardner also cites the work of Bamberger (1982, 1991) and her explanation of a students' ability to focus on the *figural* nature of the "felt" groupings of a musical fragment as opposed to the more *formal* properties of groupings that are learned from teaching and propositional knowledge.

Gardner rounds out his chapter on music intelligence by citing evidence of its existence based on criteria noted above, namely data from historical and empirical studies or various types, functional aspects of brain-damaged individuals, descriptions of exceptional people with music capabilities, and the representation of music as a symbol system.

REIMER AND MUSICAL INTELLIGENCE

Gardner's views of intelligences have not gone unchallenged or questioned. For example, some have argued that, despite the care taken by Gardner to provide careful criteria, the scientific evidence for intelligences identified is not substantial enough and that more rigorous review is necessary (Willingham, 2004). Many have wondered why only seven or eight intelligences and have openly considered other candidates for "intelligence" status. Some have argued that Gardner's isolation of these human capacities is more like abilities or talents rather than intelligences (Morgan, 1996). Other theorists, such as Sternberg (1985), take a more comprehensive view of intelligence and argue for clusters of skills under such labels as analytic, creative, and practical ability. Still others adhere to a much older view by maintaining the existence of a "g" or general factor (Carroll, 1993) rather than the breakdown of intelligences in the manner described here.

But of major importance for us in music teaching and learning is the criticism offered by many that Gardner's theory lacks the details of just how the musical intelligence core abilities work themselves out in practice by the many kinds of musicians working in our culture today. Perhaps the most important work done on addressing this matter comes from Bennett Reimer as part of his latest textbook on the philosophy of music education (Reimer, 2003).

In Chapter 7, Reimer advances his own theory of music intelligence by first endorsing the spirit behind the Gardner work but then adding substantially new claims that extend and refine.

> I will argue that Gardner's notion of musical intelligence, helpful as it has been in certain respects, is not sufficiently descriptive of the diverse ways intelligence is manifested in the domain of music. . . . The limitations of Gardner's conception, I will suggest, stem from a concept of intelligence so general as to not define precisely what constitutes it, leaving its application uncertain and confusing. (Reimer, 2003, p. 201)

Reimer reminds us that the notion of a musical intelligence is really long overdue in our literature. We often become distracted or even confused by the special usages of words like "talent, gift, prodigy, precocity, competence, accomplishment, ability, skills . . ." (p. 202) and so many more when all such terms can be considered as part of the notion of musical intelligence on a par with other more recognized intelligences such as those of linguistics and logical-mathematics. For this, Reimer is grateful to Gardner and, one would presume, other theorists who argue for multiple intelligences.

Rather than approach intelligence as a problem-solving and creative product-making enterprise, Reimer defines it as follows:

> *Intelligence consists of the ability to make increasingly acute discriminations, as related to increasingly wide connections, in contexts provided by culturally devised role expectations.* (p. 204, italics original)

Reimer takes great care in describing each aspect of this definition and helps us understand how this can relate to any aspect of human ability and particular for music. The ability to make discriminations (differentiations) in increasingly more subtle ways is a clear example of gaining a finer understanding of patterns of experience. Relating this to wider realization of connections broadens and deepens this understanding. "That capacity to perceive more precisely while at the very same time comprehending more inclusively may well be the defining quality of human intelligence" (Reimer, 2003, p. 205). In this conjoining of discrimination with broadening, the human imagination plays a critical role in the process of meaning-making. Also important here is Reimer's strong belief that the ability to make acute discriminations and make connections exists in all of us to some extend and that the range of abilities in this regard is quite varied from one to another and is subject to continual development. This has enormous implications for music teaching, using strategies for engaging the learning in opportunities to develop depth and breath.

The second major part of Reimer's definition is the influence of culture and the notion of culturally determined roles. The cultural piece is critical and acts as kind of a backdrop for the application of intelligent behavior. "Without a culture to provide guidelines within which order may occur out of an infinite number of possible discriminations and connections, thinking and doing could only be chaotic" (p. 208). On this point, Reimer and Gardner are in agreement. The existence of a variety of roles in a culture is only briefly mentioned or accounted for in Gardner's accounting, but plays a major part of Reimer's theory. In the final pages of his .chapter, Reimer introduces a number of roles that musicians play in our culture, including composition. This attempt to demonstrate the variety of applications of musical intelligence across the spectrum of work in music is absent from Gardner's chapter and is fundamental to Reimer's.

> Musical intelligence as I conceive it is the level of one's ability to experience music as meaningful, informed by sensitive discernments and broad understandings, in each particular musical role engagement in which one becomes involved. The flexibility, breath, inclusiveness, and role specificity of this concept allows musical intelligence to be regarded as being based on the reality of how people actually experience music as a meaningful cultural artifact, capable of being assessed in ways authentic to its complex nature, related to different musical roles one can play, and amenable to improvement through systematic, experience-focused education. (pp. 213–214)

There is much more to Reimer's vision of music intelligence than is related up to this point, but I will save other dimensions of his theory until later as I develop a case for the way both Gardner's more general view and the more specific one by Reimer align to form a close partner to my descriptive model of creative thinking in music.

Connecting a Model of Creative Thinking to Composition Intelligence

I will now present my own claims about the relationships between what I believe to be a compositional intelligence and a model of creative thinking in music. In so doing I hope to make a case for the importance of engaging student music composition intelligence as a way to enhance creativeness and, ultimately, their ever growing, sophisticated understanding of music as art.

INTELLIGENCE AND CREATIVITY

Much has been written in the past on the relationship between these two large constructs. In terms of quantitative evidence drawn from correlation studies the general finding has been that the two capacities co-vary in a positive direction but that the relationship is often not a significant one (Batey & Furnham, 2006). One concern in questioning these older studies is that the measures used to assess both creativity and intelligence from that time is suspect. Often creativity was measured by a test like the *Torrance Tests of Creative Thinking,* a paper and pencil tool that examines written and figural responses. Standard IQ scores on measures that are based on a single-score approach for linguistic and logic-mathematic content represented intelligence. In more recent times, scholars have suggested that the two constructs share much more than has been realized in the past, although creativity is more likely to be realized when products are evaluated by knowledgeable others in a social context (O'Hara & Sternberg, 1999).

Gardner endorses this latter view in a recent lecture given at Harvard that summarizes the first twenty-five years of work on his multiple intelligence theory (Gardner, 2010, January 26). In the final minutes of his talk, a question was asked about the relationship between his multiple intelligence work and creativity. His response is transcribed below:

> Along with Mihaly Csikszentmihalyi, who is a very distinguished scholar, I do not think of creativity as something simply in the head. Whereas I do think of intelligence as pretty much in the head—it's a set of computers. Creativity is always an interaction in an individual with his or her abilities, a domain of study such as music . . . , and a group of judges who decide what is good or not good. You cannot know how creative a person is even if we could look inside the brain and see all intelligences because you must know what society they live in, what domains in which they work, and what privileges they are afforded such as what schools they have attended, what scholarships they have won, and where their work has been displayed. We think of creativity as a systemic system and not a property of mind/brain. That said, I will conclude with this comment. When I first started studying creativity . . . I really thought it was about your computers and how good they were. I now since have come to believe that the individual is distinguished less by how the computers are and more by their motivation. Creative people are people who like to take chances, don't mind falling flat on their face; and when they do, they pick themselves up and they try again. (Last 3 minutes of video clip)

As I will soon stress in the next section, the role of the "computer" that might represent music intelligence with its processing of musical information, as well as the enabling environment and historical context in which individuals find themselves all combine to help explain creativity.

Reimer also endorses this more intimate and systematic connection between intelligence and creativity. For Reimer, creativity is a particular kind or style of intelligent functioning and is defined by the cultural context in which it resides.

> Creativity can then be defined, using the Western construct as a basis, as the making of discriminations and connections that "transcend those traditionally made in regard to ideas, rules, patterns, relationships, or the like," and in

which those discriminations and connections bring "meaningful new ideas, forms, methods, interpretations, etc." into being, the discriminatory connections having been made with "originality, progressiveness, and imagination." (Reimer, 2003, p. 215)

Reimer distinguishes between those that might have high intelligence in a field but not much creativity and vice versa. For example, a jazz improviser may have great technique in playing an improvised solo, but the sounds are pedestrian and derivative. On the other hand, a person might have very creative approaches but lack the intelligence to make the sounds meaningful, resulting in work that is "superficial, or unaware, or perhaps, 'off the wall.' The creativity would be 'out of sync' with the intelligence needed to undergird it" (p. 215). The jazz improviser might create improvisations that were very unusual, but lacking in the depth or subtlety that would allow the creative work to have credibility.

REFINING THE NOTION OF MUSICAL CREATIVITY IN STUDENTS

For many years I have maintained that "creative thinking" is really a term that has its base in what most of us understand to be "creativity." "Creativity" in many ways is not a useful term because it is so misused. For example, Mom and Dad may marvel at the "creativity" of their five-year-old daughter Maria because she can "read" music. Uncle John might think Maria has "creativity" for music because she can draw perfectly proportioned quarter notes on a drawing pad. Maria's piano teacher might conclude (perhaps mistakenly) that Maria exhibits "creativity" for music because of the flawless performance of her recital piece on Sunday afternoon. Each of these achievements may be impressive and of great importance to the musical development of Maria, but *none* of them inherently has anything to do with what creativity in music really is: the engagement of the mind in the active, structured process of thinking in sound for the purpose of producing some product that is new for the creator. This is clearly a thought process and we are challenged, as educators, to better understand how the mind works in such matters—hence the term "creative thinking" (Webster, 1990). I continue to believe that creative thinking is a dynamic process of alternation between convergent and divergent thinking, moving in stages over time, enabled by certain skills (both innate and learned), and by certain conditions, all resulting in a final product.

In reviewing the many definitions of creativity for adults, nearly all have included two major elements: originality (sometimes defined as novelty) and appropriateness (sometimes viewed as value). Original or novel thinking that might be the result of divergent thought processes will not result in creative achievement without some agreement about appropriateness and value (Rothenberg & Hausman, 1976; Sternberg & Lubart, 1996).

Both originality and appropriateness are part of my conceptualization of creative thinking in music for students as well as adults. As many have suggested, what might be original to a less experienced person may be so for him or her, but not to the larger domain of music. In terms of appropriateness, products of creative thinking by less experienced people are quite capable of being judged by knowledgeable others (Hickey, 2001; Kaschub & Smith, 2009).

THE MODEL

Over the years, I have tried to maintain a model of creative thinking process that has anchored my assessment work and my conceptual writing. It is, as Leman (1999, p. 294) has suggested in Runco and Pritzker's *Encyclopedia of Creativity*, a descriptive model—useful in placing a number of ideas in context. The early model was first published in 1987 (Webster, 1987) and refined and published again in 2002 (Webster, 2002). In Figure 2.1, I show the heart of this model.

The center features movement of ideas in a path of preparation, thinking through, and verification. I make no claims as to any kind of invariant staging in the pathway and any aspect of the path can occur and recur at the will of the creator. In choosing this kind of working process, I propose a kind of reflection that is organic to creative work (Barrett, 2006). Time away from the process is, for music composition, an important part of creation (Perkins, 1981). The path is also informed by a constantly alternating pattern of divergent and convergent thinking in sound: personal brainstorming of musical ideas that are evaluated for correctness (Basadur et al., 2000).

I also claim that the process is enabled by sets of personal enabling skills that are composed of innate aptitudes, conceptual knowledge, and refined craftsmanlike skills that can be gained from knowledgeable others or through personal experience, and advanced sensibilities that relate to the overall aesthetic of the creative product.

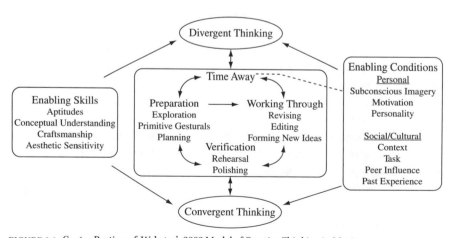

FIGURE 2.1 Center Portion of Webster's 2002 Model of Creative Thinking in Music.

Also at work are the many conditions that enable the creative process that have less to do with musical matters and more to do with both personal and social contexts. On the non-music personal side are dimensions of motivation and personality. Socially, there are factors related to where the composition is occurring, the media involved, parental and teacher support, and the role of peers. Also at stake here are personal feelings of self-efficacy and notions of identity. Social "agency" may play a role too—the ability to work independently with confidence (Wiggins, 2009).

LINKS TO COMPOSITIONAL INTELLIGENCE

At this point, it might be prudent to return to the notions unpacked above that are related to both Gardner's and Reimer's views of musical intelligence. Divergent thinking on the part of the music creator involves imaginative thought. Here the creator is exploring the many possibilities of music expression, always cataloging, sifting through, rejecting, and accepting only to change yet again. Small kernels of musical thought, which might be a melodic or rhythmic phrase, a harmony, a timbre, or even longer and more complex patterns of music, are all imagined and possibly realized on some musical instrument or for voice. These primitive "gesturals" (PGs) are all part of the exploration process that often characterizes the opening periods of creative thought. Such thinking is largely divergent in nature and relates to the core abilities that Gardner describes. The extent to which a creator is able to work with these initial ideas and then to refine them along the lines of the pathways suggested in the model may be key to his or her levels of compositional intelligence. Of course, such thinking occurs all through the creative experience as ideas are refined, then rejected, and new periods of divergence occur.

All of this is cast against convergent thinking that is more linear and more analytical. Here, the aesthetic decisions are made and the "gesturals" are turned into entities that are far from primitive. The thinking in this case is more discriminatory and driven by an emerging plan that many be conscious or subconscious. Musical material is rejected or celebrated, manipulated and fine-tuned. This kind of thinking might logically occur closer to the end of the creative process, but not always. The interplay between divergent and convergent thinking is almost magical in scope and is at the center of creative thinking and, in my view, close to what Gardner's music intelligence computer is all about.

One can also see how Reimer's notion of discrimination and connections is at work in the central core of the model. Here the creator is refining and pulling back, drawing upon both the more generative process of making discriminatory decisions and then considering a wider context. This movement is aided by greater and greater levels of personal skill in music and thus can be significantly influenced by teachers. The role of the teacher is vital in expanding the levels of musical understanding to allow for discriminatory and connective thinking.

. . . intelligence as I conceive it always exists *to some degree*. It is not something that comes into being only when some specified level of it has been attained, such that those who have demonstrated *x* amount of ability to discriminate and interconnect in some particular field of endeavor (role) are regarded as "being intelligent." In the endeavor (role), while those falling below that level is "not intelligent". Whatever level one has achieved . . . at whatever age one happens to be, is the level of one's intelligence in that role context at that point in time. (Reimer, 2003, p. 207; italics original)

We have considerable evidence from past descriptions of student compositional processes under several differing conditions in different contexts that students engage in this kind of intelligent behavior while composing. From the work on a simple and somewhat restricted music keyboard setup (Kratus, 1989) to much more freely conceived compositional settings (Barrett, 1997; Hickey, 1997; Folkestadt, 1996; Seddon, 2006; Stauffer, 2002; Younker, 2000; and many others), we find detailed and often breathtaking descriptions of the intelligent processing that both Gardner and Reimer conceptualize in their writing. I claim that this is a central core of the model of creative thinking process proposed.

In Figure 2.1, moving from the core of the model to the left box, Enabling Skills, consider how these items match with influences on music intelligence. Both Gardner and Reimer, as well as others who write conceptually about intelligence, argue for the role of genetics and certain wired aptitudes. For example, Gardner reminds us that there is considerable evidence for the "plasticity and flexibility in human growth" but that "strong genetic constraints which operate from the beginning and which guide development along some paths" (Gardner, 1983/1985, p. 32) hold enormous consequence. Edwin Gordon's work on the assessment of tonal and rhythmic imagery and his notions of sensitivity and balance (Gordon, 1965) that mark his considerable contribution to the concept of music aptitude is important as a marker for discrimination and for the basis of manipulation of pitch, time, and timbre.

The elements of conceptual understanding, craftsmanship, and aesthetic sensitivity that are suggested by the enabling skills section of the model are essential to the exercising of compositional intelligence and lead to the possibility of judging compositional products as creative.

The particular role a composer plays is to exercise the intelligence necessary to bring meaningful and completed sound structures into being as events subsequently to be shared with others. Doing so successfully requires making the exquisitely subtle and sensitive discriminations among sounds that music depends on for its existence, and connecting them in ways that both embody and expand personal/cultural meanings as only music can do. (Reimer, 2003, p. 222)

While these more advanced capabilities can be gained in many ways, they are particularly accessible through formal music education by music teachers willing and able to provide it. To increase the personal intellectual growth of students in music composition is to increase the depth of music knowledge and the likelihood for real creative achievement as judged by the culture.

Moving to the enabling conditions side of the model, both Reimer and Gardner cite the importance of culture in understanding intelligence. Cultural context allows a solid footing for understanding intelligence and assessing it adequately. "Factors such as motivation, preference, attitude, interest, ambition, learning style, and a host of additional psychological/emotional elements, implicated in myriad combinations and permutations in each individual's personality, inevitably influence the levels of intelligence . . ." (Reimer, 2003, p. 209).

The point of all of this is simply to suggest that the facets of intelligence in music as described by Gardner in a general context and by Reimer in a much more specific way, are in fact at the very core of my conceptual modeling work on creative thinking since the 1980s. What makes the products that emerge from the processes that are modeled here as worthy of a designation of "creative" in an adult context, as Gardner and others suggest, are the judgments made by experts in the field, the affordances of opportunity, and the special traits of people who are motivated to continue to take risks to innovate. In educating our youth about music through composition, we increase musical intelligence from a composition perspective and that, in turn, optimizes the possibility of creative achievement at many personal levels. The key, then, to creative achievement in music lies squarely on our ability as teachers to exercise and develop the musical intelligence that is present in all students. I believe that this is what great teachers do.

A Word of Summary

Reflection. If I were to choose one word that represents the most important goal for creating teaching environments for enhancing compositional intelligence and on to creative products, it would be this one. As students play with sound and create more and more sophisticated products, I hope that teachers will encourage reflection. What are you doing here to create what you what? Does this sound like what you want? Is this what you intended? Would you like to try something else to achieve a different effect? What is your intent for the long-term of the piece? Are you shaping the direction that you want? Would you like to try something different in your next piece? Questions of this sort are seemingly endless.

And questions of this sort that *interrogate intentionality* do several things for the learner that are consonant with my descriptive model of creative thinking and for the enhancements of musical intelligence that are in line with both Gardner and Reimer. Learning to thoughtfully reflect on creative work is perhaps the one ultimate goal for learners, and for that matter, teachers.

References

Bamberger, J. (1982). Growing up prodigies: The mid-life crisis. *New Directions for Child Development*, 17, 61–78.

Bamberger, J. (1991). *The mind behind the music ear: How children develop music intelligence*. Boston, Massachusetts: Harvard University Press.

Barrett, M. (1997). Invented notations: A view of young children's musical thinking. *Research Studies in Music Education*, 8, 2–14.

Barrett, M. (2006). "Corrective collaboration": An "eminence" study of teaching and learning in music composition. *Psychology of Music*, 34(2), 195–218. doi: 10.1177/0305735606061852.

Basadur, M., Runco, M., & Vegas, L. (2000). Understanding how creative thinking skills, attitudes and behaviors work together: A casual process model. *Journal of Creative Behavior*, 34(2), 77–100.

Batey, M., & Furnham, A. (2006). Creativity, intelligence and personality: A critical review of the scattered literature. *Genetic, Social, and General Psychology Monographs*, 132, 355–429. doi 10.3200/MONO.132.4.355–430.

Binet, A., & Simon, T. (1916). *The development of intelligence in children*. Baltimore, Maryland: Williams & Wilkins. Reprinted 1973, New York: Arno Press; 1983, Salem, NH: Ayer Company.

Carroll, J. (1993). *Human cognitive abilities: A survey of factor-analytic studies*. Cambridge, UK: Cambridge University Press.

Elpus, K. (2007). Improving music education advocacy. *Arts Education Policy Review*, 108(3), 13–18.

Folkestad, G. (1996). *Computer Based Creative Music Making*. Goteborg, Sweden: Acta Universitatis Gothoburgensis.

Fowler, C. (1990). Recognizing the role of artistic intelligences. *Music Educators Journal*, 77(1), 24–27.

Gardner, H. (1983/1985). *Frames of mind: The theory of multiple intelligences*. New York: Basic Books.

Gardner, H. (1999). *Intelligence reframed: Multiple intelligences for the 21st century*. New York: Basic Books.

Gardner, H. (2006). *Multiple intelligences: New horizons*. New York: Basic Books.

Gardner, H. (2010, January 26). Multiple intelligences: The first 25 years [Video file]. Video posted to http://www.youtube.com/watch?v=tDtZEpf_SJ4

Gordon, E. (1965). *Musical aptitude profile*. Boston, Massachusetts: Houghton Mifflin.

Guilford, J. (1967). *The nature of human intelligence*. New York: McGraw Hill.

Hickey, M. (1997). Teaching ensembles to compose and improvise. *Music Educators Journal*, 83(6), 17–21.

Hickey, M. (2001). An application of Amabile's consensual assessment technique for rating the creativity of children's musical compositions. *Journal of Research in Music Education*, 49(3), 234–244.

Kamin, L. (1995). The pioneers of IQ testing. In R. Jacoby & N. Glauberman (Eds.), *The bell curve debate: History, documents, opinions*. New York: Times Books.

Kaschub, M., and Smith, J. P. (2009). *Minds on Music: Composition for Creative and Critical Thinking*. Lanham, Maryland: R&L Education—A Division of Rowman & Littlefield Publishers, Inc.

Kaufman, A. S. (1990). *Assessing adult and adolescent intelligence.* Boston: Allyn and Bacon.

Kratus, J. (1989). A time analysis of the compositional processes used by children ages 7 to 11. *Journal of Research in Music Education,* 37(1) 5–20. doi 10.2307/3344949.

Leman, M. (1999). *Music.* In M. Runco & S. Pritzker (Eds.), *Encyclopedia of creativity.* Vol. 2, pp. 285–296. San Diego, California: Academic Press.

Morgan, H. (1996). An analysis of Gardner's theory of multiple intelligence. *Roeper Review,* 18, 263–270.

O'Hara, L. A., & Sternberg, R. J. (1999). Creativity and Intelligence. In R. Sternberg, (Ed.), *Handbook of creativity.* Cambridge, UK: Cambridge University Press.

Perkins, D. (1981). *Mind's best work.* Boston: Harvard University Press.

Reimer, B. (2003). *A philosophy of music education: Advancing the vision.* Upper Saddle River, New Jersey: Pearson Education, Inc.

Rothenberg, A., & Hausman, C. (1976). *The Creativity Question,* Durham, North Carolina: Duke University Press.

Seddon, F. A. (2006). Collaborative computer-mediated music composition in cyberspace. *British Journal of Music Education,* 23(3), 273–283. doi 10.1017/S0265051706007054.

Stauffer, S. L. (2002). Connections between the music and life experiences of composers and their compositions. *Journal of Research in Music Education,* 50(4), 301–322.

Sternberg, R. (1985). *Beyond IQ: A triarchic theory of human intelligence.* New York: Cambridge University Press.

Sternberg R., & Detterman, D. (Eds.) (1986). *What is intelligence? Contemporary viewpoints on its nature and definition.* Norwood, New Jersey: Ablex.

Sternberg, R., & Lubart, T. (1996). Investing in Creativity, *American Psychologist,* 51(7), pp. 677–688. doi 10.1207/s15327965pli0403_16.

Webster, P. (1987). Conceptual bases for creative thinking in music. In C. Peery (Ed.), *Music and child development,* pp. 158–174. New York: Springer-Verlag.

Webster, P. (1990). Creativity as creative thinking. *Music Educators Journal,* 76(9), pp. 22–28.

Webster, P. (2002). "Creative thinking in music: Advancing a model." In T. Sullivan, & L. Willingham (Eds.), *Creativity and music education,* pp. 16–33. Edmonton, Alberta: Canadian Music Educators' Association.

Wechsler, D. (1958). *The Measurement and Appraisal of Adult Intelligence* (4th ed.). Baltimore, Maryland: Williams & Witkins.

Willingham, D. (2004). Reframing the mind. *Education Next,* Summer, 19–24.

Wiggins, J. (2009). *Teaching for musical understanding* (2nd ed.). Oakland, Michigan: Center for Applied Research in Musical Understanding.

Younker, B. (2000). Thought processes and strategies of students engaged in music composition. *Research Studies in Music Education,* 24(1), 24–39.

Note

1. Several editions of this book have appeared since 1983. The 1985 paperback version was used in preparing this chapter. Other copyrights exist, including 2004 and 2011.

3 }

What Pre-Service Teachers Can Learn from Composition Research

Maud Hickey

When editors Michele Kaschub and Janice Smith first asked me to write a chapter summarizing research geared toward teaching composition to elementary and secondary students in order to inform pre-service music teacher education, I was skeptical. But as I began my investigation I was pleasantly surprised to see the amount of relatively recent and energized research in this area. This chapter presents a summary of current research that examines teaching music composition in (or related to) general school music and music performance programs. The purpose of this summary is to provide university music-teacher educators (henceforth known as MTEs) and their students with information from research, so that future school music teachers are prepared and confident to implement effective music composition activities in school music programs.

Introduction

There seems to be renewed attention toward teaching music composition in school music. The genesis for the current discourse, publications, and research activity is likely the *National Standards for Arts Education* (Consortium of National Arts Education Associations, 1994) where music composition, first explicitly listed under Standard 4, was deemed an important outcome for K–12 students. Since the publication of the *National Standards*, numerous articles and conference presentations have followed with practical ideas for music educators. However, recent regional and national polls and research studies on the status of music composition activities in classrooms routinely show that improvisation and composition are either at the bottom of priorities for K–12 music teachers, or the least implemented (Byo, 1999; Eureka Facts, 2007; Fairfield, 2010; Kirkland, 1996; Orman, 2002; Phelps, 2008; Riveire, 1997). One of the consistent reasons given for not implementing composition in K–12 programs is that music teachers feel unprepared. While some practical sources for music teachers in the classrooms appeared after the standards were published, little has been written (or researched) about how *music teacher educators* can help prepare pre-service teachers to teach their own students upon entering the teaching force.

Nearly 20 years after the publication of the *National Standards* I sense a renewed interest from researchers investigating the issues surrounding how to teach composition in schools, as evidenced by a relatively new and growing body of research. One purpose of this chapter is to organize and disseminate what is known thus far based on this growing research compilation, and another is to summarize this research for MTEs in order to help them focus their efforts in an informed way for preparing future music teachers to teach composition to K–12 students.

A Need

The need for the work compiled in this text, and specifically this chapter, is reflected in a recent survey study (Crawford, 2004) and in policy writings (Abrahams, 2000; Bell, 2003). Crawford (2004) presented a survey to pre-service music education faculty at 97 accredited NASM institutions around the United States in order to assess current perceptions of faculty regarding music composition in teacher training, as well as to examine levels of comfort and proficiency levels these faculty feel for including composition activities in teacher training. A response rate of 51 percent yielded 49 surveys to provide at least a glimpse into thoughts from music education faculty about preparing pre-service music teachers to teach composition. Her survey found that while the majority of respondents do not themselves compose, nor have been instructed on how to teach composition to their music education students, 94 percent believed that they were still capable of providing opportunities to compose music in music education coursework. Qualitative responses revealed a wide range and variety of composing activities and methodologies in the various music education programs, as well as an indication that there was little time to fit in such experiences.

Several studies point to the lack of preparation of future music teachers (Adderley, Schneider, & Kirkland, 2006; Bell, 2003; Fonder & Eckrich, 1999; Orman, 2002; Riley, 2009; Schopp, 2006), or lack of overall institutional support for such preparation (Abrahams, 2000). Riley (2009) found that with time and attention devoted to the *National Standards* in pre-service education, pre-service teachers belief in the importance of, and perceptions of their ability to implement the standards improved. However even after this preparation, responses directed specifically at composition standard 4, worded as: "I feel that it is *important* to implement Standard 4," "I am *interested* in *implementing* Standard 4," "I feel *responsible* for implementing Standard 4," and "I am *trained* to effectively implement Standard 4," had the lowest responses among the 9 Standards both before *and* after this instruction. She concludes that music teacher preparation programs must aid in preparing teachers to teach music composition in order to turn this lack of confidence around. Bell (2003) also noted in the conclusion of her study on teachers' perception of their readiness to teach the standards: "Higher education institutions and schools districts must play a stronger role in disseminating standards information" (p. 156).

Approaches to K–12 Composition: The Research

It is rather easy to find classic texts on composition by or about renowned composers (e.g., Hindemith, 1942; Rimsky-Korsakov, 1964; Schoenberg, 1988; Stravinsky, 1942/2000), traditional composition texts for higher education study (e.g., Cope, 1997), and now even texts for any music consumer to learn to compose (e.g., *Music Composition for Dummies*, Jarrett & Day, 2008; and *The Complete Idiot's Guide to Music Composition*, Miller, 2005). But these resources mostly assume individuals work as a lone composer, or in a one-on-one dyad as found in university settings for music composition students. They do not provide the practical information about how teachers in public schools might facilitate music composition where K–12 school spaces present the challenges of time, space, and numbers—that is, many children to teach in one (often small) space.

Research studies based in K–12 classrooms, or intended for informing K–12 classrooms, will help MTEs learn more about the best ways to teach and prepare their pre-service teachers to be prepared to teach music composition. These research studies are discussed below and organized around the following themes: eminence; university composition students; differing perspectives and circumstances (teacher/ student); ensemble classrooms; technology, and pre-service teacher education. After summarizing the major findings from these research studies, I provide some examples of practical resources for MTEs, and then conclude with ideas for further research.

"EMINENCE" AND THE HIGHER EDUCATION PERSPECTIVE

While it may not be very helpful to read biographies of how the great composers compose, nor to read texts devoted to rules of music composition for university composition majors, some researchers have found value in studying "eminent" composers to inform classroom composition in K–12 settings. Lapidaki (2007) makes a strong philosophical argument for music educators to strengthen their ability to teach music composition by learning about the creative processes and thoughts from twentieth and twenty-first century composers. In the cases of research in this area, an "eminent" composer is identified as a professional composer, or a composer teaching composition in a university setting.

Margaret Barrett (2006) studied a teacher-composer dyad at the tertiary level in order to identify beliefs and practices that can inform composition teaching in K–12 classroom settings. In this case study approach observing a university composer

("composer-teacher") and his student Barrett identifies 12 specific teaching strategies used by the composer-teacher:

1. extended thinking, provided possibilities;
2. referenced work to and beyond the tradition (signposting);
3. set parameters for identity as a composer;
4. provoked the student to describe and explain;
5. questioned purpose, probed intention;
6. shifted back and forth between micro and macro levels;
7. provided multiple alternatives from analysis of student work;
8. prompted the student to engage in self-analysis;
9. encouraged goal setting and task identification;
10. engaged in joint problem finding and problem solving;
11. provided reassurance;
12. gave licence to change.
    (2006, pp. 201–202).

In addition, three themes emerged that related to the composer-teacher's beliefs and practices. The first, "composer-model," highlighted the importance of the composer as a model for his/her student. The second, "enterprise," stressed the importance of the composer's support of student initiative and imagination. "Composer-voice" was the third and pointed out the importance of giving students room to find their own voice. These 12 strategies and 3 themes have implications for MTE approaches to teaching future teachers in their own composition as they can be models for the important relationships that should be formed between music teachers and their own students. One of the challenges is balancing unique composer-voice with specific strategies to compose, all while managing a classroom.

In a similar case study, Barrett and Gromko (2007) observed a dyad of a composer-teacher and a graduate student in a university setting. They point out two key teaching and learning strategies found in the interactions of the dyad: problem finding (which includes procedural and conceptual problems); and, problem solving. Though not as explicit as the list of specific strategies identified in Barrett (2006), the kinds of procedural and conceptual problem finding align with the 12 strategies identified above. In both the Barrett (2006) and the Barrett and Gromko (2007) work, the importance of viewing the dyad approach as a creative collaboration between teacher and student was emphasized.

Two other studies looked at "eminent composers" by comparing the processes and products of expert composers with novice composers. Kennedy (1999) compared the compositional processes of a high school student and a collegiate composer while Younker and Smith (1996) examined the nature of compositional thought processes in an adult expert composer, an adult novice composer (a practicing music educator), an expert high school composer, and a novice high school composer when each was undertaking a melodic composition task. They found similarities and differences that might help highlight areas for pre-service teachers to be aware of when teaching composing.

Through semi-structured interviews, observation, and document analysis, Kennedy's case study (1999) noted the similarities between the high school student and collegiate composer in that they both began with an exploratory phase, both noted the significance of inspiration, and both realized the importance of manipulating materials. Younker and Smith (1996) utilized a "talk-aloud" methodology and then verbal protocol analysis to devise an overall model of the composing process. Like Kennedy (1999), they found that the "expert" composers began with an exploration phase at the start of their composing and worked in a gestalt manner but that the novice composers did not. The novice composers began with a more note-to-note, atomistic approach. Kennedy found that the younger composer needed less time to finish, and that her composition was less mature, complex, and individualistic than the expert composer.

The findings from Younker and Smith (1996) and Kennedy (1999) resonate with an earlier and similar study by Colley, Banton, Down, and Pither (1992) that compared three college level ("novice") composers to an expert composer. Colley et al. (1992) found that the expert's large knowledge base and access to a larger set of procedures and tools in composing allowed him to composer in a more "gestalt" manner, while the novices tended to approach the task in a more systematic way.

UNIVERSITY COMPOSITION STUDENTS

A few studies examine collegiate music composition students as a way to help MTEs begin to understand more about teaching pre-service teachers. Carter (2008) examined the personal identities and identity formation of four undergraduate music composition majors through a case study analysis and narrative lens. Carter found, like studies mentioned previously here, that the identity of the young composers is very important, influenced not only by their self-identification as a composer, but also by the society around them. An implicit yet important finding for pre-service music education is the significance of identity formation of "composer" in student composers and the role of positive environments to facilitate this formation. All four composers denied any direct influence from their K–12 music education, but "indicated that creative musical opportunities in their elementary and secondary musical programs might have facilitated their compositional development" (Carter, 2008, p. 274).

Lupton and Bruce (2010) compared models of composition teaching in the literature to their analyses of two composition courses ("Jazz Composition" and "Sound Composition") for non-composition music majors in a university setting. Their phenomenographic study presents a teaching model based on the literature, and then a learning model, based on case studies of two composition students in a University courses. The two models revealed similar hierarchical models that stressed a combination of "art" (personal voice and creativity) within the tools and craft needed to compose. The four themes that emerged from the compositional teaching model were "learning from the *masters; mastery of techniques; exploring ideas and developing voice,*" (p. 4) whereas from the "learning" model were craft, process, and art (composing to express oneself). Lupton and Bruce found subtle differences between the types of composing (sound composition and jazz composition), but mostly discovered that "Both models include knowledge and skills in relation to compositional techniques and both include the creative process that seems essential in developing the composers' identity and self expression" (p. 15). Similar to Carter's findings, the development of composer "voice" (or identity in Carter's case) was found to be essential. Lupton and Bruce (2010) urge that when creating a composition course in the university setting that both the teaching and learning models be utilized. They provided specific suggestions for assessment in the developing voice/creativity process that might prove useful for MTEs. They are:

- submission of work-in-progress for formative feedback;
- reflective portfolio where students document their personal learning journey through developing their compositions, including the meaning they make from the process; and the way they have expressed themselves through their compositions;
- exegesis explaining the context of the work; and
- summative performance of compositions (live or recorded).
  (Lupton & Bruce, 2010, p. 17).

The studies cited thus far examine the perspectives or styles of university composers or university composition students in order to inform K–12 music composition teaching. The studies that follow look directly into K–12 classrooms and offer research perspectives from both teachers and students in these settings. First I will share those studies that focus on the teacher, followed by those that provide the students' perception.

DIFFERENT PERSPECTIVES IN K–12 CLASSROOMS

The Teacher

Gould (2006) and Bolden (2009) study music composition teaching through the observations of, and thoughts from, teachers. Gould observed teacher Carol Matthews as she worked with a group of children ages 5–7 and a second group of children ages 8–10. Gould found that Matthews used music composition as part of everyday experiences and lessons, a "provocation" in the Reggio Emilia context. Matthew's view of the composition process is very improvisational, "unrestricted by pre-existing curricular standards or traditional norms of musical quality" (Gould, 2006, p. 203). For Matthews, the composition/music experience is about "making informed, mindful musical decisions in response to lived musical problems in the material process of composing" (p. 203). Gould stressed that this mindful approach to music and music composition should be a part of every pre-service music teacher's instruction.

Bolden (2009) offers the perspective of a teacher who teaches secondary music students in an urban setting. Jesse, the teacher, taught two large classes of students who did not enroll in the traditional band, or choral ensembles. The students worked at MIDI keyboard/computer stations, alone, or in groups of two or three, using the software GarageBand®. Bolden's data include observation field notes, interviews with Jesse and his principal, and recordings of in-class dialogues with Jesse. Four themes evolved from the analysis: "authentic assignments," "theory with practice," "diagnose and fix," and "involving." All of the themes point to a student-centered approach. Jesse would allow problems to emerge and then work with students to find solutions, use the opportunity to teach about a theoretical concept, or connect to the students' musical worlds. Similar to the findings in the Gould (2006) study, Bolden found that effective composition teaching should be approached with the student's prompt and need considered first. Composing becomes a means for students to express their individuality and identity, and teachers must be flexible in the teaching moment to facilitate this.

Ruthmann's study (2008) focused on the lived experiences of a teacher, Mary, and her students throughout a 10-week exploratory general music class that took place in a music technology lab. The students were working on creating a movie soundtrack using music sequencing software on a computer workstation and MIDI synthesizer. This particular study focuses on the resonance and tensions between Mary and one particular student, Ellen (a pseudonym). Emotional tensions arose when Mary's intent and Ellen's approach did not align. Ruthmann points to the wish for freedom and voice often displayed by children in the composing process, and how teacher directions might conflict with this. Ruthmann warns "Teachers run the risk of eliminating all creative choice on the part of students if parameters for composing are so strict that these become more of a theoretical or scientific puzzle to solve as opposed to a creative composing endeavor" (2008, p. 55).

Dogani (2004) sought to understand the perspectives of primary teachers as they taught music composition to children. Six teachers, from a variety of urban schools in England, were observed utilizing a case study methodology. In addition to interviews and observations, Dogani asked the teachers to reflect on a tape of their teaching in comparison to a "control tape" in order to highlight and identify important facets of their own teaching. The results showed that teachers approached composition in a controlled fashion, and admitted they lacked the confidence to really use composition as a creative tool for their students' music making. Their role was strictly teacher-centered. This seemed to be in direct contrast to the teacher approaches highlighted in Gould (2006) and Bolden (2009)—perhaps because of the lack of confidence and music training background in the teachers from Dogani's work.

Younker (2006) provides a view of composition pedagogy and interaction in the classroom from the view of a 5th-grade music teacher, Laura. Specifically, Younker sought to examine the role that critical thinking and reflection plays for Laura while teaching music composition. Laura not only found the reflective process useful for her role as a teacher of music composition, but also found herself reflecting "*with the students as she encouraged and prompted them to identify and solve problems, and to think and act like composers*" (Younker, 2006, p. 163).

Perhaps the most unique "teacher perspective" comes from a composer herself, who reflects, in an auto-ethnographic style, on her experience teaching composition to children in an elementary program. The purpose of Bosch's study was to detail and discuss some of the problems of teaching music composition to children in a school classroom setting, and how these problems are addressed by existing methods and resources as well as her own method (Bosch, 2008). The experience of teaching composition, and especially to children in school, was her first and Bosch details the lessons learned in this experience through the eyes of her professional composer self. She outlines ways in which teachers can facilitate composition in a classroom, emphasizing that anyone can compose. Her definition of the composer or improviser—"a musical creator is someone who listens very carefully for what the next note will be" (p. 22)—makes the case that composing is an important music education activity and that listening is the most important part of compositional or improvisational process.

Composition in Groups

It is likely that for many K–12 teachers, their only chance to compose with students is in large groups. Kaschub (1997) presents a process of generating and then refining a group-conceived composition with six 6th-grade general music classes, and a large high school choir. She used a professional composer as a guide, and documents the trials and errors and lessons learned from this process over time. She describes herself as the facilitator, and at times, "translator" for the composer, communicating his ideas and words to the students. Issues that evolved from the process included communication between composer and students, consensus building, compromise, and notation. As a result of the study, Kaschub felt confident enough to take on the challenge of group composition without guidance in the future.

Like Kaschub, Miller also situated her study within the context of a typical music teacher's workday, which in Miller's case, involved movement between schools, teaching several groups of children ranging from kindergarten to grade 5 who only receive music lessons one time per week (Miller, 2004). Utilizing a "naturalistic action research" design, Miller, as teacher-researcher, engaged in year-long cycling between action, reflection, and collaboration with two non-music teacher colleagues. Miller found that composing with active and large classes of elementary music students was not only possible, but beneficial as well. "Composition actually allows the students to work at their own level of understanding more than other more traditional music class activities" (Miller, 2004, p. 67). Both Miller's (2004) and Kaschub's (1997) studies provide practical strategies for MTEs and pre-service teachers to consider.

MacDonald and Miell, along with other colleagues, have done extensive research on the effect of friendship and other social factors on the quality of music compositions and collaboration (MacDonald & Miell, 2000; MacDonald, Miell & Mitchell, 2002; MacDonald, Miell & Morgan, 2000; Miell & MacDonald, 2000). All of these studies found that friendship pairing had a positive impact on the quality of children's final compositions, except in the case of older children (MacDonald et al., 2002). Transactive (collaborative) dialogue seemed to be greater between friends and therefore is thought to positively impact the quality of their compositional efforts.

In the MacDonald et al. (2002) study, the researchers modified the task given in previous studies by making it more structured, and only studied female pairs to eliminate a gender bias possible from the previous studies. They attributed the lack of transactive dialogue among older children in this study to the fact that the task was structured, asserting that perhaps it "required less negotiation between the children regarding instrumentation and musical organization" (MacDonald et al., 2002, p. 158). The results from all of this work suggest that " . . . allowing children to work together in pairs based on supportive relationships would indeed be helpful—particular for children who lack experience" (Miell & MacDonald, 2000, p. 366). They also felt that the open-ended tasks were more conducive to collaborative learning (MacDonald et al., 2002). These implications should impact music composition methodology in the preparation of pre-service music teachers.

Two studies utilized theoretical models to analyze the dynamics of group student composition tasks (Burnard & Younker, 2008; Fautley, 2005). Burnard and Younker (2008) utilized Engeström's Activity Theory (AT) as an analytical tool for understanding student group composing and arranging in two different settings. Using the AT theory, they analyzed the types and direction (e.g., "horizontal" or "vertical") of composing that were used among small groups of 5th grade children, either in an open-ended composing task, or a more structured arranging task. They found that the "tool" or instruments chosen as well as knowledge and background of the participants had the most direct effect on the style of compositional approaches. The "confident" tool users tended to take over the activities through task-directed talk (in the open composition) or task-directed action (in the arranging task). Understanding the dynamics of group interaction can be helpful for teachers when assigning groups to work on composition activities in order to assure the most favorable and rich interaction among all of the participants.

Fautley (2005) developed a model of the group composing process based on distributed cognition theory and then tested it by observing children composing in an open-ended group composition task. His results confirmed the model—that is "all aspects of the composing process were taking place at the group level" (p. 54). Fautley recommended that because learning in a group is distributed, a group approach to music composition might be optimal as a first step toward more advanced and solo music composition accomplishments. Fautley also viewed his model as useful for teachers in order to target appropriate formative assessment strategies, and as a potential sequential composition outline.

From the Child's Perspective

What do children think about while composing? Given little teacher direction or structure, what freedoms and constraints play into children's choices for music composition? How do age, task structure, experience, and musical background affect children's compositional choices from their perspective? In this section the presented research examines composition from the child's perspective, through their own words and music, as well as reflections and observations by others.

The purpose of the Burnard and Younker (2002, 2004) studies was to uncover common composing strategies among children. They drew from data banks of previous research on children composing in different ages and task conditions and in different learning situations and across different countries. Their analyses of multiple data sources (e.g., verbal responses, verbal reports, interviews, observations, the musical products) found three distinct "pathways" to composing: Linear, Recursive, and Regulated. While these styles were different, the researchers found that the absence of any formal instruction did not seem to affect the composers' ability to think both divergently and convergently (Burnard & Younker, 2002, 2004). Perhaps the most important outcome of this research for pre-service or young teachers is that "Teachers need to perceive creativity in ways that resonate with students' approaches to composing" (2004, p. 71).

In a non-interventionist approach to the study of six 6th-grade children composing over one school year, Stauffer (2002) found that while the composers were very different, she discovered connections between their compositional approaches and their life and musical experiences. Four themes emerged as having the most direct influence/connection on the young composers' processes: instrument influences; familiar melodies; media, school, and home references; and ensemble influence. Each student's experience in these areas directly affected their compositional choices and processes in composing.

Kennedy (2002) observed four high school students as they were presented with two compositional tasks: one was to set a short poem for voice and an acoustic instrument, and the other was to complete a composition of their choice using an electronic computer workstation. She found listening was a key component for all four composers, both as a way to contextualize their work and as inspiration for ideas. Kennedy also noted that all four composers began with exploration or improvisation and also tried to avoid written notation (they preferred the computer task over the acoustic task). As a result of her study, Kennedy constructed a model and compared it to previous models of the composition experience, which will be discussed further below.

Younker (2000) was looking for patterns of thoughts and strategies within and across three different age groups of composers: 8, 11, and 14 years old. Younker collected verbal data through "think-aloud" procedures while the children were composing an open-ended task on a computer, and she also gathered data from semi- and open-structured interviews with these children. Younker noted the following recursive activities from all of the participants: exploring, recording, listening, evaluating, and editing. These activities occurred for different lengths of time and in different sequences, and were related to the students' confidence in their work as opposed to their age level. As in the Stauffer study, Younker found that most of the children used previously known material within their compositions. And like other researchers, Younker found more variability than similarities of the composers, especially those *within* the same age groups.

Major and Cottle (2010) utilized a case-study approach to determine how teachers might effectively support children's thinking *about* composing, and the relationship between teachers' questioning approaches and children's dialogic responses. Eight "mixed-gender" pairs of 6- and 7-year-old children composed together over four weeks while engaging in a structured composing task. Because they were paired to collaborate on a problem composition, it was not surprising that much of their work centered on problem-solving through talk rather than exploration. The research highlighted the importance of the adult in questioning the children in order to help them think critically about and reflect on their composition process. Children learned about the process along the way because of this active adult "scaffolding" their thinking. "When adults ask questions which require recall or remembering, pupil responses tend to be exploratory or descriptive but when adults ask open-ended questions and when they knowingly encourage evaluative, problem-solving and reflective responses, then these higher-thinking responses are demonstrated in children's dialogue" (Major & Cottle, 2010, p. 298).

Smith (2008) examined the type of task structure on the musicality of, and task preference for, 9- and 10-year-old children's recorder compositions. She found that musicality was highest when the task was most structured (children selected a poem and created a song with the instructions of using the poem for their composition and that the composition be something that people could sing). But Smith found that children's preferences were varied, with about half of the children preferring a more open-ended task, and the other half preferring the closed task.

These recent studies of teachers in K–12 classrooms as well as the children who are composing point to similar themes: the importance of child-centered approaches with adult scaffolding; the effect of task structure and tool on the outcome of a composition task; and the variability of children's approaches to composition— aligning with the importance of voice in composer identity from the studies of professional composers or composition students. The next set of studies comes from views of composition in the ensemble classroom and composition utilizing technology; it concludes with studies that are specific to pre-service education.

ENSEMBLE CLASSROOMS

Research on composition in ensemble classrooms is sparse, perhaps for the reason that the primary goal is not to compose in an ensemble, but to perform. However, in a recent survey designed to understand New York State band directors' attitudes toward, and implementation of, composition and improvisation, Schopp (2006) found that there is positive support for teaching composition and improvisation by band directors, but few of them actually implement these activities. Time and fear (by both teachers and their students) were the most cited reasons for not composing in ensembles. Schopp suggests that concerted efforts in pre-service education may be able to change this, and also points out the necessity of collegiate band programs to offer models of ensemble composition and improvisation activities.

Aware of the lack of teacher preparation materials for future music ensemble teachers, Koops sought to develop and field-test a music composition curriculum for middle school bands and then assess whether it was adequate for "overcoming the obstacles of teacher-training, resources, time and large group composition" (2009, p. 96). In a preliminary survey of eight middle school band directors Koops found, as did Schopp (2006), that all of the band directors believed that composition should be included in performance music education. In this action research study, Koops created a curriculum for middle school band, and then field-tested the curriculum himself and with five other band directors. He encouraged the other directors to adapt his lessons as needed, and then, at the conclusion of the study, reflected with them in a focus group, to learn from their experiences. Koops' efforts were successful and showed evidence that teaching composition in ensemble contexts is possible. Kaschub (1997), described above, also indicates the positive experience for an ensemble in a composition project.

Two studies explored the efficacy and impact of music composition activities during a band rehearsal but outside of the rehearsal itself (Dammers, 2007; Randles, 2006). Using a pre-test/post-test design, Randles (2006) explored the relationship between composition experiences in a high school instrumental ensemble and student self-efficacy. Members of a high school band ($N = 77$) were given time to compose music on a computer (using GarageBand® or Finale) during their band rehearsals over a period of 12 weeks. Students had one to three opportunities for this composition experience; 20 members of the band did not compose. While Randles examined the relationship between self-efficacy (using a researcher-devised "Self Esteem of Musical Ability" (SEMA) scale) and several other factors, he found the strongest relationship was between students' SEMA scores and their music composition experiences. A stepwise multiple regression indicated that composition experiences were the strongest predictors of music self-efficacy. Randles found a way to allow performance students to experience music composition, without the interruption of an ensemble rehearsal, by allowing a small group of students to take turns at composition stations over time. The directors of the ensemble did not notice the interruptions, making it a potential viable alternative for integrating composition into an ensemble experience.

Dammers (2007) had students compose during a band rehearsal using a composition prompt to construct a melody that mirrored aspects of the music that was being rehearsed in the band. As in the Randles study (2006), the participants composed during the band rehearsal, using a simple notation program, at computer stations away from the band. A panel of judges rated the compositions for creativity, craftsmanship, and conceptual understanding. Conceptual understanding was defined as the "appearance of aspects of the model piece [composition they were performing in band] in the students' compositions" (Dammers, 2007, p. 17) and was examined for the purposes of implementing an aspect of comprehensive musicianship in the band rehearsal. Dammers found only a moderate correlation between a student's playing ability and the creativity and craftsmanship ratings of their compositions, but low correlation between conceptual understanding scores and the compositions. He surmises that the reason for a low connection between the compositions and the concepts learned in the band rehearsal was that such transfer needs to be made more explicit and more often in the course of a rehearsal.

Stringham (2010) studied the perception of students who were given opportunities to compose and improvise in a high school band. He also looked at the relationship between composition achievement and music aptitude (among other factors). As in the Dammer's study (2007), Stringham asked students to compose music based on an arrangement they were learning in their band using an established sequence of musical and improvisation method. "Composition achievement" was assessed by mean judge ratings on a task in which the students were to notate a bass line and melody to *Amazing Grace*. Stringham found that music aptitude (as determined by the *Advanced Measures of Music Audiation*, Gordon, 1989) was a weak predictor of composition achievement. Qualitative data revealed that students found the sequence and exercises in composition helpful. Stringham concluded that composing and improvising in a high school band is possible.

TECHNOLOGY

Bosch (2008), from her perspective as a composer thinking about teaching composition to children, presents a negative critique of the use of technology in helping children to compose. She criticizes software like GarageBand® as just too easy—not allowing the child to hear the music or notes before stitching them together. "I am glad for technology to help my students to notate their pieces, to play their pieces and also to share their pieces over the Internet. But I do not want technology to help me, or my students, to compose" (Bosch, 2008, p. 93). While not specifically looking at the effect of technology on music composition, many studies (e.g., Bolden, 2009; Dammers, 2007; Randles, 2006; Ruthmann, 2008; Stauffer, 2002; and Younker, 2000) utilize technology as the tool for the composing process that they are studying. There is a growing increase in the use of technology as a composition tool and in research that has looked at not only its efficacy as an instructional tool, but also its providing for rich possibilities for group work and collaboration.

The purposes of Nilsson and Folkestad's study were to describe the processes and products of children's computer-based music composition and to gain a greater understanding of what composition means to children (2005). The authors observed nine children, ages 6–8 years, over a two-year period as they composed using a MIDI keyboard and computer-sequencing program. They collected stages of the composing process in digital files, participant observation and interviews. Nilsson and Folkestad found five variations of creative music making, oscillating between the synthesizer, the music, or playing in the foreground or background of their activities. They found that the different kinds of task instructions presented "invitations to play" and effected one or more of the variations of composing to come to the foreground.

A recent group of studies examines explicitly how technology-based composition can foster collaborative learning. Hewitt (2008) focuses on collaborative learning of computer-based approaches to composition, specifically the uses of "transactive" and "non-transactive" communication in 16 children ages 10 and 11. Transactive talk is that which is collaborative, and non-transactive dialogue indicates lack of collaboration between working partners. The children were paired to work together on a melody composition task using computer software developed by Hewitt. Hewitt video-recorded the pairs working together and transcribed the verbal interchanges to analyze the types of dialogue. Results showed that dialogue varied between pairs and within pairs as children took on different roles during the composition task, but that transactive dialogue was a "fairly substantial part of the total pupil talk during the study" (Hewitt, 2008, p. 23), pointing to positive working collaboration among the pairs of children. In contrast to studies by MacDonald and colleagues (MacDonald & Miell, 2000; MacDonald, Miell & Mitchell, 2002; MacDonald, Miell & Morgan, 2000; Miell & MacDonald, 2000), however, Hewitt found no significant influence based on musical expertise, friendship pairs, or nature of transactive communication. Hewitt cautions the reader to not make the leap that transactive communication is better because of the music task, nor that working in pairs is better for creativity.

Gall and Breeze (2008) found that the use of eJay software in a music-learning environment helped to foster collaboration among students, but also proposed that the teacher is central to mediating this process. The longitudinal study that observed teachers in classrooms with children composing on computers utilized an iterative process that consisted of initial exploration, pilot design, the pilot itself, and then reflection using the video data by teachers and researchers. The 10- and 11-year-old students were asked to work in pairs on a compositional task that was set by a form. Findings from the data showed that the children enjoyed the task and felt that they were being creative, and that overall the computer software was conducive to collaborative learning.

Reynolds provides two studies examining the use of computer tools in music composition activities for children (2003, 2005). Reynolds (2003) observed eight children, ages 9- to 12-years, over the span of 10 weeks as they composed music in a computer rich classroom, and concluded, essentially, that all children can compose and that providing the computer as the vehicle to do such allows them to explore their creativity in powerful ways. His 2005 study observed seven 10- to 12-year-old children over a period of 20 weeks to see how they used and made decisions with software as they composed. He used the Swanwick and Tillman developmental model (1986) as a scaffold for studying the participants' choices. When Reynolds discovers that the computer compositions do not align necessarily with the age-appropriate sequence in the Swanwick and Tillman model, he asserts that "the computer, as a scaffold, has allowed the child to display a stage of potential development" (2005, p. 242).

Online tools for mentoring music composition students have the potential to provide valuable experience and learning for pre-service music teachers. Sam Reese has been a leader in championing and studying the potential for online composition mentoring (Reese, 1999, 2000a, 2000b; Reese & Hickey, 1999). Bolton (2007) presents a recent qualitative study that sought to examine the effect of an online composition mentoring module on the skills, knowledge and interest of three teacher education students. He found, as did the Reese studies, that an online mentoring initiative had a positive effect on the three pre-service teachers, and he lauds this kind experience as a way for MTEs to help prepare future educators in teaching music education.

Specific to Pre-Service Education

Crawford's survey (2004) of music education faculty and Riley's survey (2009) of the perceptions of pre-service teachers on implementing composition in music teaching reveal stark but hopeful realities of the state of music teacher education. MTEs and pre-service teachers indicate the desire to include composition in their teaching and learning, but struggle with how to do so. Crawford found that those faculty who perceived there to be a higher level of flexibility in their programs for changing coursework to include compositional training also believed they were proficient in providing compositional training (p. 91). There was no relationship between compositional proficiency or activity to institution size, number of music education faculty, nor faculty perception of their own composition preparation. The need for flexibility in implementing compositional training at the university level is obvious, and here Crawford's results point to a direct correlation between that flexibility and competence in providing training. Riley (2009) shares ideas for lesson planning that integrate music composition directly into methods courses.

Hewitt (2002) compared a group of collegiate pre-service "generalist" teachers (no formal music training) to a group of pre-service "specialist" teachers while working in group compositions tasks. The group of "generalists" did not have any prior formal musical training but were likely to be teaching music to young children in school, and the group of "specialists" consisted of applied music majors pursuing secondary education. Besides the obvious differences in technical acuity, Hewitt highlighted other concerns of teachers who may someday teach music composition to young children. Managing a performance, evaluating compositions, and utilizing standard notation were the prominent concerns of the generalist teachers. Hewitt also found that generalist teachers were unable to gather ideas as quickly, and move into a development stage of composing, as the specialists could. Hewitt pointed out that many of these issues relate to confidence in music ability. While Hewitt's study was not concerned with the specialists' confidence or ability to teach music composition (the study took place in Scotland where likely these students had composition experiences in their secondary education), it offers that specialists who *do not* have composition experience need practice and experience in order to develop confidence in doing so.

Summaries/Themes from the Research

Perhaps the most relevant and consistent finding among the studies in this review is the importance of the development and recognition of students' individual voices in music composition (Barrett, 2006; Bolden, 2009; Burnard & Younker, 2002; Carter, 2008; Gould, 2006; Lupton & Bruce, 2010). This celebration of individuality points to the need for composition to be about facilitating expression in music, rather than offering any direct "how-to." This may come as a relief to MTEs and even their pre-service teachers, knowing that the rules do not matter as much as developing an atmosphere of facilitation and collaboration. Children's approaches to composing are as individual as each child, and these approaches are influenced in multiple ways. Different students prefer different tasks, and a student-centered approach is most appropriate. "The major themes that arise from this comparative analysis across multiple data banks concern an emphasis upon individual differences that celebrate a related diversity of composing styles" (Burnard & Younker, 2002, p. 257). This also means that MTEs should guide pre-service teachers in designing tasks according to students' needs, and then cultivate a disposition that can tolerate ambiguity in facilitating them.

That there are differences between expert and novice composers is probably obvious, but what is known about these differences might prove useful for MTEs and future music teachers. While experts tend to begin in exploration and take a gestalt approach, novices, without guidance, tend to approach composition atomistically and step-by-step (Barrett, 2006; Colley et. al. 1992; Hewitt, 2002; Kennedy, 1996; Younker & Smith, 1996). However, later studies show somewhat of a conflict with this finding. Specifically, Kennedy (2002) and Younker (2000) indicate that young composers do begin in an exploratory manner. It may be that the task itself supports or deters an exploratory start (Stauffer, 2002). Understanding that expert composers often begin composing in an exploration phase might guide approaches to composing for pre-service educators and eventually their students.

In addition, and also quite obvious, expert composers have previous knowledge and skills, tools, and techniques that aid them in composing (Burnard & Younker, 2008; Colley et al., 1992; Lupton & Bruce, 2010). These "tools" can only be developed by composing, and therefore, in order to develop as composers themselves, pre-service teachers should have many opportunities to compose in their pre-service education. There is then a need for creative and flexible ways to fit this into pre-service teachers' already full requirements.

Researchers found that both expert and novice composers move through stages (Barrett, 2006; Burnard & Younker, 2002, 2004; Kennedy, 1999, 2002), and that reflection helps children move along through stages (Major & Cottle, 2010). The kinds of tools one uses and the tasks that are set up clearly affect the composition processes and outcomes (Burnard & Younker, 2008; Nilsson & Folkestad, 2005; Ruthmann, 2008; Smith, 2008; Stauffer, 2002). Awareness of stages and development in the composition process, the influence of tools and task, and the use of reflection to document these would seem to be a crucial skill for pre-service teachers to develop. " . . . through adopting a pedagogy of composing that begins with the inclusive practice of seeking and understanding their students' musical intentions, teachers may be more successful at supporting their students' development as composers" (Ruthmann, 2008, p. 56).

Confidence seems to play a key role in successful composition experiences for student and adult composers (Hewitt, 2002; Younker, 2000; Younker & Smith, 1996). A teacher who can model composition (Barrett, 2006; Hewitt, 2002), give choices in the process, and even act as a co-creator (Barrett & Gromko, 2007; Dogani, 2004) will help develop confidence in her students. Once confidence can be attained, then self-efficacy may follow (Randles, 2006). Reflection in the process of teaching and composing may work to strengthen knowledge and confidence as teachers learn (Dogani, 2004; Younker, 2000). Perhaps MTEs can scaffold the modeling and reflection process for pre-service teachers, not only by composing themselves, but also by working with university composition professors to provide models for collaboration (Carter, 2008; Kaschub, 1997). Working with University composers in the pre-service classrooms may also help pre-service teachers see models of collaboration in action that they can eventually take into their own classrooms and communities.

"Listening emerged as an aural tutor of form, theory, and harmony" (Kennedy (2002, p. 103). A broad variety and many listening opportunities emerged as a theme for successful composition among several studies (Bosch, 2008; Kennedy, 2002; Smith, 2008; Stauffer, 2002; Younker, 2000). As Bosch noted, "Perhaps composing is not as much about the creation of masterpieces as it is about listening" (2008, p. iii). The development of pedagogically sound listening lessons is likely a routine characteristic of pre-service teachers' education. Why not link composition exercises right into these lessons? This would potentially save time for MTEs and provide the natural fit that listening and composition embrace.

Several researchers provide models of the composing process of children in classrooms (Burnard & Younker, 2004, 2008; Fautley, 2007; Kennedy, 2002; Stauffer, 2002; Younker & Smith, 1996). It might prove fruitful for MTEs, with their pre-service teachers, to examine, compare, and contrast these models in order to be more aware of the possibilities that may arise in classrooms of children.

Technology provides a powerful tool for facilitating creative composition in classrooms (Reynolds, 2003, 2005), through online communication (Bolton, 2007; Reese, 1999, 2000a, 2000b; Reese & Hickey, 1999) and has shown to support collaborative learning (Gall & Breeze, 2008; Hewitt, 2008). Though the focus of their studies was on composing in the ensemble, it is interesting to note that both Dammers (2007) and Randles (2006) both utilized music technology to facilitate the composition process. Teacher preparation in music technology should certainly include opportunities for composing and learning about software that can provide composing activities for children. Online composition mentoring and partnerships could provide ideal opportunities for pre-service teachers to mentor composition students.

Collaboration and "friendship" pairing appears from some studies to heighten the quality of children's compositions (MacDonald & Miell, 2000; MacDonald, Miell & Mitchell, 2002; MacDonald, Miell & Morgan, 2000; Miell & MacDonald, 2000). Others supported collaboration and group composing as well (Burnard & Younker, 2008; Fautley, 2005; Gall & Breeze, 2008; Hewitt, 2008). This student-centered approach permeates throughout as an important theme for teachers.

The ability to improvise as a teacher and be flexible in the moment, allowing student ideas to emerge and move through the classroom, is very important for successful composition teaching (Bolden, 2009; Gould, 2006; Ruthmann, 2008). "Just as there is no one right way to compose, there is no one right way to teach or evaluate compositions. Instead, both the teacher and the composer must approach composition as a problem-solving exercise" (Younker, 2003, p. 237). This disposition is crucial for pre-service teacher development as a teacher of music composition.

Resources for MTEs and Pre-Service Music Teachers

There are a handful of practical books for teaching composition in the classroom, although most of these are published outside of the United States and thus may be difficult to obtain. These include: *Composing in the Classroom* by David Bramhall (1989), *Learning to Compose*, by John Howard (1990), *Composing Matters* by Patrick Allen (2002), and *Sounds in Space, Sounds in Time: Projects in Listening, Improvising and Composing* by Richard Vella (2003). *Minds on Music: composition for Creative and Critical Thinking* (2009) by Michele Kaschub and Janice Smith is the first thorough and practical book to help teachers manage music composition in PreK–12 classrooms that is published in the United States.

Two additional books that are less about how to teach composition and more about philosophical ideas and results from working with children are *Why and How to Teach Music Composition: A New Horizon for Music Education*, edited by Hickey (2003), and *Children Composing 4–14*, by Joanne Glover (2000).

Challenged to pick a list of the "best" journal articles for pre-service teachers to read in preparation for music composition, I would recommend the studies by Kaschub (1997); Bolden (2009); Miller (2004) and Ruthmann (2008), in which they describe "typical" classrooms and their honest attempts to bring music composition into those classrooms. These may provide helpful contextual (and practical) understandings for pre-service teachers. Mary Kennedy's 2002 work provides a wonderful literature review that summarizes studies of professional composers (which is out of the context of this paper). This information would be helpful to pre-service teachers as well. Riley (2009) provides ways in which she has implemented music composition into her general music methods classes.

For those teaching instrumental methods and looking for ways to integrate some reading about successful composition ideas in band I recommend the work of Koops (2009), in which he provides lesson plans for use in a band or orchestra setting.

Conclusion and Suggestions for Further Research

Hopefully this summary of literature will be useful for MTEs and will stimulate them to read the studies in depth in order to help guide practices in music teacher education programs. There is still a great need for research to better inform practices of teaching music composition in K–12 classrooms. What seems to be missing are developmental studies. While all of the studies reviewed above vary from early elementary, across several grades, and into high school and university education, there are no attempts to understand developmental abilities or trajectories.

It may also be useful to have more quantitative studies helping MTEs and pre-service teachers understand the benefits of music composition. Randles (2006) offers a glimpse of this as he found a positive correlation between self-efficacy and composition experiences, but it may prove useful to find other empirical evidence of the potential positive effects of music composition.

It is clear however, from all of the research on music composition with children thus far, that children *can* compose and enjoy doing so. There does not seem to be a consistent formula for "how-to," and in fact many teachers have learned that a student-centered and emergent approach to the process of teaching composition is the most satisfying. Learning to allow students' unique voices and identities to emerge seems to be the most important element, and MTEs can scaffold this by modeling composition activities in their courses. It is now time for MTEs to provide the composing experiences required to develop future music teachers' confidence to get out and "just do it!"

References

Abrahams, F. (2000). National Standards for music education and college preservice music teacher education: A new balance. *Arts Education Policy Review, 102*(1), 27–31.

Adderley, C., Schneider, C., & Kirkland, N. (2006). Elementary music teacher preparation in U.S. Colleges and Universities relative to the National Standards—Goals

2000. *Visions of Research in Music Education*, 7. Retrieved from http://www-usr. rider.edu/~vrme/.

Allen, P. (2002). *Composing matters*. Heinemann Educational Publishers.

Barrett, M. (2006). Creative collaboration: An eminence study of teaching and learning in music composition. *Psychology of Music,* 34(2), 195–218. doi: 10.1177/0305735606061852.

Barrett, M. S., & Gromko, J. E. (2007). Provoking the muse: A case study of teaching and learning in music composition. *Psychology of Music,* 35(2), 213–230. doi: 10.1177/0305735607070305.

Bell, C. L. (2003). Beginning the dialogue: Teachers respond to the National Standards in Music. *Bulletin of the Council for Research in Music Education*, 156, 31–42.

Bolden, B. (2009). Teaching composing in secondary school: a case study analysis. *British Journal of Music Education,* 26(2), 137–152. doi: 10.1017/S0265051709 008407.

Bolton, J. M. (2007). Developing composition pedagogical knowledge: Music teacher education students as online mentors. *Australian Online Journal of Arts Education,* 3(1), 1–13.

Bosch, M. (2008). *Everyone can compose music*. Doctoral dissertation, Princeton University, Princeton, NJ.

Bramhall, D. (1989). *Composing in the classroom. Opus 1 & 2*. London: Boosey & Hawkes.

Burnard, P., & Younker, B. A. (2002). Mapping pathways: Fostering creativity in composition. *Music Education Research,* 4(2), 245–261.

Burnard, P., & Younker, B. A. (2004). Problem-solving and creativity: Insights from students' individual composing pathways. *International Journal of Music Education,* 22(1), 59–76. doi: 0.1177/0255761404042375.

Burnard, P., & Younker, B. A. (2008). Investigating children's musical interactions within the activities systems of group composing and arranging: An application of Engeström's Activity Theory. *International Journal of Educational Research,* 47, 60–74. doi: 10.1016/j.ijer.2007.11.001.

Byo, S. J. (1999). Classroom teachers' and music specialists' perceived ability to implement the National Standards for Music Education. *Journal of Research in Music Education,* 47(2), 111–123. doi: 10.2307/3345717.

Carter, B. (2008). *A qualitative examination of undergraduate music students' compositional identity*. Doctoral dissertation, Northwestern University, Evanston, IL.

Colley, A., Banton, L., Down, J., & Pither, A. (1992). An expert-novice comparison in musical composition. *Psychology of Music and Music Education,* 20, 124–137. doi: 10.1177/0305735692202003.

Consortium of National Arts Education Associations. (1994). *National standards for arts education: what every young American should know and be able to do in the arts*. Reston, VA: MENC.

Cope, D. (1997). *Techniques of the contemporary composer*. Australia: Schirmer.

Crawford, L. A. (2004). *Leadership in curricular change: A national survey of music education faculty perceptions regarding music composition in teacher training*. Master's thesis, University of the Pacific, Stockton, CA.

Dammers, R. J. (2007). *Supporting comprehensive musicianship through laptop computer-based composing problems in a middle school band rehearsal.* Doctoral dissertation, University of Illinois at Urbana-Champaign.

Dillon, T. (2003). Collaborating and creating on music technologies. *International Journal of Educational Research,* 39(8), 893–897. doi: 10.1016/j.ijer.2004.11.011.

Dogani, K. (2004). Teachers' understanding of composing in the primary classroom. *Music Education Research,* 6(3), 263–279. doi: 10.1080/1461380042000281721.

Eureka Facts. (2007). *National standards in the American music classroom preliminary report.* Rockford, MD: Eureka Facts.

Fairfield, S. M. (2010). *Creative thinking in elementary general music: A survey of teachers' perceptions and practices.* Doctoral dissertation, University of Iowa, Iowa City.

Fautley, M. (2005). A new model of the group composing process of lower secondary school students. *Music Education Research,* 7(1), 39–57. doi: 10.1080/14613800500042109.

Fonder, M., & Eckrich, D. W. (1999). A Survey on the Impact of the Voluntary National Standards on American College and University Music Teacher Education Curricula. *Bulletin of the Council for Research in Music Education,* 140, 28–40.

Ford, A. (1992). *Inventing music.* Sydney: Australian Music Centre.

Gall, M., & Breeze, N. (2008). Music and eJay: An opportunity for creative collaborations in the classroom. *International Journal of Educational Research,* 47(1), 27–40. doi:10.1016/j.ijer.2007.11.008.

Gordon, E. E. (1989). *Advanced Measures of Music Audiation.* Chicago: GIA Publications, Inc.

Gould, E. (2006). Dancing composition: pedagogy and philosophy as experience. *International Journal of Music Education,* 24(3), 197–207. doi: 10.1177/0255761406069639.

Glover, J. (2000). *Children composing 4–14.* London: Routledge.

Hewitt, A. (2002). A comparative analysis of process and product with specialist and generalist pre-service teachers involved in a group composition activity. *Music Education Research,* 4(1), 25–36.

Hewitt, A. (2008). Children's creative collaboration during a computer-based music task. *International Journal of Educational Research,* 47(1), 11–26. doi: 10.1016/j.ijer.2007.11.003.

Hickey, M. (ed.) (2003). *Why and how to teach music composition: A new horizon for music education.* Reston, VA: Rowman & Littlefield Education.

Hindemith, P. (1942). *Craft of musical composition,* Mainz, Schott.

Howard, J. (1990). *Learning to compose.* Cambridge: Cambridge University Press.

Jarrett, S., & Day, H. (2008). *Music composition for dummies.* Hoboken, NJ: Wiley Publishing.

Kaschub, M. (1997). A comparison of two composer-guided large group composition projects. *Research Studies in Music Education,* 8, 15–28. doi: 10.1177/1321103X9700800103.

Kaschub, M., & Smith, J. (2009). *Minds on music: Composition for creative and critical thinking.* Reston, VA: Rowman & Littlefield Education.

Kennedy, M. A. (1999). Where does the music come from? A comparison case-study of the compositional processes of a high school and a collegiate composer. *British Journal of Music Education,* 16(2), 157–177.

Kennedy, M. A. (2002). Listening to the music: Compositional processes of high school composers. *Journal of Research in Music Education,* 50(2), 94–110. doi: 10.2307/3345815.

Kennedy, M. A. (2004). Opening the doors to creativity: A pre-service teacher experiment. *Research Studies in Music Education,* 23(1), 32–41. doi: 10.1177/1321103X040230010301.

Kirkland, N. J. (1996). *South Carolina Schools and Goals 2000: National Standards in Music.* Doctoral dissertation, University of South Carolina.

Koops, A. P. (2009). *Incorporating music composition in middle school band rehearsals.* Doctoral dissertation, University of Southern California, Los Angeles.

Lapidaki, E. (2007). Learning from the masters of music creativity: Shaping compositional experiences in music education. *Philosophy of Music Education Review,* 15(2), 93–117.

Lupton, M., & Bruce, C. (2010). Craft, process and art: Teaching and learning music composition in higher education. *British Journal of Music Education,* 27(3), 271–287. doi: 10.1017/S0265051710000239.

MacDonald, R., & Miell, D. (2000). Creativity and music education: The impact of social variables. *International Journal of Music Education,* 36(1), 58–68. doi: 10.1177/025576140003600107.

MacDonald, R., Miell, D., & Mitchell, L. (2002). An investigation of children's musical collaborations: The effect of friendship and age. *Psychology of Music,* 30(2), 148–163. doi: 10.1177/0305735602302002.

MacDonald, R., Miell, D., & Morgan, L. (2000). Social processes and creative collaboration in children. *European Journal of Psychology of Education,* 15(4), 405–415. doi: 10.1007/bf03172984.

Major, A. E., & Cottle, M. (2010). Learning and teaching through talk: music composing in the classroom with children aged six to seven years. *British Journal of Music Education,* 27(3), 289–304. doi: 10.1017/S0265051710000240.

Miell, D., & MacDonald, R. (2000). Children's creative collaborations: The importance of friendship when working together on a musical composition. *Social Development,* 9(3), 348–369. doi: 10.1111/1467–9507.00130.

Miller, B. A. (2004). Designing compositional tasks for elementary music classrooms. *Research Studies in Music Composition,* 22, 59–71. doi: 10.1177/1321103X040220010901.

Miller, M. (2005). *The complete idiot's guide to music composition.* Alpha Publications.

Nilsson, B., & Folkestad, G. (2005). Children's practice of computer-based composition. *Music Education Research,* 7(1), 21–37. doi: 10.1080/14613800500042042.

Orman, E. K. (2002). Comparison of the National Standards for Music Education and elementary music specialists' use of class time. *Journal of Research in Music Education,* 50(2), 155–164. doi: 10.2307/3345819.

Phelps, K. B. (2008). *The status of instruction in composition in elementary general music classrooms of MENC members in the state of Maryland.* Master's thesis, University of Maryland, College Park.

Randles, C. (2006). *The relationship of compositional experiences of high school instrumentalists to music self-efficacy*. Master's Thesis, Michigan State University, East Lansing.

Reese, S. (1999). Potentials and problems of internet-based music composition mentoring. *Southeast Journal of Music Education,* 11, 1–11.

Reese, S. (2000a). Integration of on-line composition mentoring into music teacher education. *Contributions to Music Education,* 28(1), 9–26.

Reese, S. (2000b). *Effects of online mentoring on quality of feedback about student compositions.* Paper presented at the Annual Meeting of the Association for Technology in Music Instruction, Toronto, Canada.

Reese, S., & Hickey, M. (1999). Internet-based music composition and music teacher education. *Journal of Music Teacher Education,* 9(1), 25–32. doi: 10.1177/105708379900900105.

Reynolds, N. (2003). *Musical composition and creativity in an ICT-enriched learning environment: a case study*. Paper presented at the 3.1 and 3.3 working groups conference on International federation for information processing: ICT and the teacher of the future, Melbourne, Australia.

Reynolds, N. (2005). The computer as scaffold, tool and data collector: Children composing with computers. *Education and Information Technologies,* 10(3), 239–248. doi: 10.1007/s10639-005-3004-9.

Riley, P. E. (2009). Pre-service music educators' perceptions of the national standards for music education. *Visions of Research in Music Education.,* 14. Retrieved from Visions of Research in Music Education website: http://www-usr.rider.edu/~vrme/.

Riveire, J. H. (1997). *California string teachers' curricular content and attitudes regarding improvisation and the national standards*. Doctoral dissertation, University of Southern Californa.

Rimsky-Korsakov, N. (1964). *Principles of orchestration*. Dover Publications.

Ruthmann, S. A. (2008). Whose agency matters? Negotiating pedagogical and creative intent during composing experiences. *Research Studies in Music Education,* 30(1), 43–58. doi: 10.1177/1321103X08089889.

Schoenberg, A. (1988). *Fundamentals of music composition*. United Kingdom: Faber and Faber.

Schopp, S. E. (2006). *A study of the effects of National Standards for Music Education, number 3, improvisation and number 4, composition on high school band instruction in New York State*. Doctoral dissertation, Teachers College, Columbia University, New York.

Smith, J. (2008). Compositions of elementary recorder students created under various conditions of task structure. *Research Studies in Music Education,* 30(2), 159–176. doi: 10.1177/1321103X08097505.

Stauffer, S. L. (2002). Connections between the musical and life experiences of young composers and their compositions. *Journal of Research in Music Education,* 50(4), 301–322. doi: 10.2307/3345357.

Stravinsky, I. (2000). *Poetics of music in the form of six lessons* (14th printing). First published in 1942. Boston, Massachusetts: Harvard College.

Stringham, D. A. (2010). *Improvisation and composition in a high school instrumental music curriculum*. Doctoral dissertation, Eastman School of Music, Rochester, New York.

Swanwick, K., and Tillman, J. (1986) The sequence of musical development: A study of children's composition. *British Journal of Music Education,* 3(3), 305–339.

Vella, R. (2000). *Musical environments: A manual for listening, improvising, and composing.* Sydney, Australia: Currency Press.

Younker, B. A. (2000). Thought processes and strategies of students engaged in music composition. *Research Studies in Music Education,* 14(1), 24–39. doi: 10.1177/1321103X0001400103.

Younker, B. A. (2003). The nature of feedback in a community of composing. In M. Hickey (Ed.), *Why and how to teach music composition: A new horizon for music education,* pp. 233–242. Reston, VA: Rowman & Littlefield Education.

Younker, B. A. (2006). Reflective practice through the lens of a fifth grade composition-based music class. In P. Burnard & S. Hennessy (Eds.), *Reflective practices in arts education,* pp. 159–168. Springer Netherlands.

Younker, B. A., & Smith, W. H. (1996). Comparing and modeling musical thought processes of expert and novice composers. *Bulletin of the Council for Research in Music Education,* 128, 25–36.

4 }

The Compositional Turn in Music Education: From Closed Forms to Open Texts
Randall Everett Allsup

It is usually unwise to predict the future. Writing about technology is equally imprudent, as the enthusiasm surrounding today's innovations will surely be met with eye-rolling incredulity in only a few short years. With this caveat in mind, and with some generosity from my reader, I will attempt in this chapter to peer into the future of music education—to conceptualize a new human relationship to music and aesthetic need, one that is interwoven among complex relationships of self-interest, communication, multiple technological modalities, and translocal contexts. I will argue that music education lingers on the edge of a significant rupture in practice and pedagogy, a turn from a closed-form concept of musical performance and score interpretation that reached its logical conclusion in the praxial pedagogy of Elliott (1995) to a reconfigured practice of composing, where creating, playing, and sharing exists within and across open discursive fields. It is the intention of this chapter to examine and articulate the texture of this turn.

As a methodological device, I will refer to the "prophets" of the past and present, particularly those well-known composers that represented the sensibility of their day, and today's Internet composer-musicians whose efforts and effects portend a shift in social and musical relationships. Prophecy, after all, is the realm of the artist more than the theorist (Attali, 1985). It is the artist, on the exterior of custom and institutional knowledge, who outlines the contours of her age, intuiting those changes that future writers will articulate in ruminations like the one I now submit. Moreover, many of today's musical prophets can be found hiding in plain sight, outside conservatories and schools of music, communicating in vivo through media and social networking sites, in bars and in basement studios.

Prophets like the rock group Atomic Tom, the unstoppable band whose famously stolen instruments led to an Internet sensation.[1] "Fortunately," they tell viewers on YouTube (5,000,000 hits and counting), "we know how to improvise." Turning a case of bad luck into fame, the four musicians are captured performing live on a Manhattan-bound subway—all on individual iPhones. The drummer taps beats on his, the guitarists strum, pick, and pluck at theirs, and the lead vocalist uses an iPhone microphone app to record and be heard. Self-consciously hip, deservedly self-satisfied, and having lots of fun in the process, their creativity and dexterity ask us to consider the porous nature of contemporary artistic domains, what counts as expertise and mastery in these settings, as well as the manner of transfer from one modality to another.

Or, there is the open-source artist known as Kutiman, who mines YouTube for video content that he splices into a mashed-up collage of repeated loops and citations.[2] Kutiman appears to have a democratic fondness for amateurs of all capacities, creating an interwoven text of musical offerings, strands of which only approximate consistent pitch and even tone, provoking questions of genre specificity, authorship, intention, talent, and the mythology of origins. Then there are the two random college friends, Jake and Kurt, who—with a million followers watching—musically out-duel each other on increasingly strange and hilarious instruments.[3] Starting with an ordinary recorder, then the glockenspiel, moving to a "crockenspiel" (a child's five-note bell set shaped like an alligator), old game boy consoles, a zither, an ocarina, Jake and Kurt, like Kutiman, visually and musically invent and recompose stunning arrangements of classical and popular tunes. Imagine Lady Gaga's "Bad Romance" on squeaky toys. Their movement between musical styles and instruments, computer dexterity, sense of humor, and dance and fashion savvy make our ordinary conceptions of musicianship seem limited and limiting.

If these composing-musicians are prophets of their day, just what are they trying to communicate? How do we interpret their message? Most obviously, they are exhibiting a kind multimodal fluency that goes beyond a commonsense notion of interdisciplinarity, embracing the fullest range of expressive space available to them: exploring digital and physical geographies through sonic and visual arenas; producing, exchanging, and consuming shared efforts and artifacts, acoustic and digital; playing knowingly through gesture and fashion, flattening, extending, and confusing identities. They are composing more than music; they are composing selves through sound and text. A new definition of composition has emerged, I argue, decoupled from its tradition sense: "composing," as distinct from "composition," becomes an unfinished, discursively productive, self-interested and self-creating event in which fluency in transcontextual multimodalities facilitates communication and independence within self and in relationship with others.

In this chapter, I intend to flesh out this definition through theory and example, and to locate its emergence within the broader aesthetic movement that took place over the late twentieth century. In the next section, I will contrast this new conception of composing with its traditional sense, where "composition" is seen as a mono-directional process whose telos aims at a closed musical work with internally consistent laws. From there I will look at the pedagogical implications of an education in closed forms, as compared to teaching and learning through open texts, suggesting that the familiar notion of musicianship inhered in the latter must yield to new ways of participating in music, ways that are consistent with my definition of "composing." The chapter will conclude with a bold (and probably foolish) forecast for what music education might look like in the twenty-first century.

The Pedagogical Logic of the Closed Form

What you are, you are by accident of birth; what I am, I am by myself. There are and will be a thousand princes; there is only one Beethoven.

—Ludwig van Beethoven

I would like to thank all the people and artists involved in this project. I had a great time searching for you, working with you.

—Kutiman

I contrast this turn from closed forms to open texts with the quotes above. There is the great composer Beethoven, a prophet of his own time, whose self-declared genius makes a prince look common. Then there is Kutiman, whose pseudonym is an effort to hide his compositional handprint, thanking others for opening their sources to him. Indeed, this comparison could hardly do worse than begin with Beethoven and the Romantic ethos that spawned the contemporary music conservatory and its commonsense notions around the purpose of art, where it is encountered, and how and to whom it is taught. Many theorists (Detels, 1999; Goehr, 1994; Nettl, 1995; Small, 1997) have noted the way institutional boundaries have hardened around what counts as music (the masterpiece), the audience it is intended for (the cultured, the knowledgeable), and how it is interpreted (utter fidelity to its creator).

At the top of this pyramid remains the Beethoven-like composer, the genius. It is important to emphasize that it is in the composer's interest to secure and tighten the relationships between his work, from the executant who translates his work through performance sound to the audience who is expected to understand and appreciate his inventions (Stravinsky, [1942] 2003; Copland, 1963). Throughout much of the twentieth century, many of North America's great universities had as a "resident conservator," the greatest composer they could hire, usually a European émigré from the Second World War. Many of these composers and their apologists acted as public music educators. Knowing that their efforts at conservation were threatened by democratic taste and a general aversion to difficulty, they lectured audiences with brilliant polemics against American popular culture and popular taste, while scolding performers to demonstrate their highest understanding of the European tradition to which they were bequeathed (Adorno, [1934] 2002; Babbitt, 1958; Hindemith, 1952; Schoenberg, 2010). It is not incidental to note that the conservative character of most American conservatories and university music education programs, with their current emphasis on classical music and strong performance practice, is a direct result of this trans-European legacy.

Sealing in an art form has certain obvious advantages. Innovative knowledge gets quickly codified, procedural know-how apprenticed and passed on, technologies are protected from large-scale change, practice-specific meanings become inhered through repetition and obedience, and mastery is easily recognized and celebrated. These ongoing efforts to secure these relationships have resulted in a social contract between the adherents of a given tradition and the laws of its practice, what Elliott (1995) came to call praxis.

For Stravinsky ([1942] 2003), another prophet of his day, this social contract secures its pedagogical structure, demanding a deep bond of submission on behalf of its initiates. He writes, "The secret of perfection lies above all in [the student/performer's] consciousness of the law imposed upon him by the work he is performing. And here we are back at the great principle of submission that we have so often invoked in the course of our lessons. This submission demands a flexibility that itself requires, along with technical mastery, a sense of tradition and, commanding the whole, an aristocratic culture that is not merely a question of acquired learning" ([1942] 2003, 127). In a pedagogy of closed forms, "a person's performance of a given composition is a robust representation of his or her level of musical understanding of that work and the musical practice of which it is a piece" (Elliott, 1995, p. 59). This performed understanding or this sense of performative speculation, "clearly depends on some fluency of manipulative ability and on an awareness of certain shared conventions of expressiveness" (Swanwick, 1988, p. 72).

Stravinsky is right that all art involves some kind of flexibility between the signified and the signifier, but pay close attention in the excerpts above to the exercise and preservation of these codes of signification and the technical mastery required to represent an understanding of them. What counts as success in a tradition of closed forms are 1) the degree to which the composer can exercise his will through the codes of his tradition; and 2) the degree to which the performer can accurately represent the will of the composer by demonstrating mastery of its traditional codes. Formal music education, that is Western music education of the nineteenth and twentieth century, has been preoccupied with the training of the musically intelligent performer—"readers" or "decoders" of the canonic works of an elite cadres of creators. For Elliott, "To make and listen for music intelligently requires musicianship. Developing musicianship is essentially a matter of induction; students must enter and become part of the musical practices (or music cultures) they intend to learn . . . The musicianship underlying any practice of music making and listening has its roots in specific communities of practitioners who share and advance a specific tradition of musical thinking. Musical practices swirl around the efforts of practitioners who originate, maintain, and refine established ways and means of musicing as well as cherished musical histories, legends, and lore" (Elliott, 1995, p. 67). Elliott suggests that to take part in a tradition or specific cultural practice is not only to learn to master its internal laws and maintain its specified norms, but to absorb and advance its ideology, an act of robust submission.

The problem with the internalization of a given culture's histories, legends, and lore is that induction often takes place through commonsense practice, and so we often confuse the obvious with the real. I would like to take aim at the universal applicability of this self-evident notion of musicianship, the central concept around which Elliott's praxial pedagogy is based, knowing that for most musicians and music teachers, "good musicianship" is just another way of saying "good music education." Who could possibly have anything to say against musicianship, one might wonder? I argue that while the value of musicianship will remain important for certain kinds of musical experiences—those musical experiences that come through interacting in closed musical forms—its absolute value as the normative end of music education will become increasingly less useful as today's composer-musicians find the hard categories around traditional practices irrelevant to their needs or too cumbersome to master. And, because the very concept of musicianship is implicated in the great mono-directional chain of composer-object-performer-audience, with its conservative texture woven into the educational and cultural institutions that grew out of and now support this chain, its commonsense nature or doxa has effectively blinded us to new visions of music-making, creating, sharing, and learning—intertextual relationships that circulate independent of a sovereign originator and independent of a bounded cultural center or tradition. Nor, as in the case of Atomic Tom and other composing-musicians like them, is a long apprenticeship in these forms worth the time it takes to master them. Other modalities are available, easier to learn, and constantly emerging.

By moving now to articulate a turn in the field of aesthetic thought that breaks with a notion of closed forms for what French poststructural theorists like Barthes (1977) call the "Text," I move to a plural concept of multimodal musical literacy, one that captures the spirit of composing as defined earlier. In the following section, Barthes's term "work" stands for the system of closed forms that I have just described and the idea of musicianship as the exercise of its logic.

The Aesthetic Turn from Closed Forms to Open Texts

In fact, we cannot observe the creative phenomenon independently of the form in which it is made manifest.

　　—Igor Stravinsky

The theory of the text can coincide only with a practice of writing

　　—Roland Barthes

To capture the sensibility of an age, or to locate change in artistic direction, Barthes and Stravinsky both suggest looking at a culture's artistic practices, at the ways in which its prophets find expression through the codes (Beethoven/Stravinsky) or the modalities (Atomic Tom/Kutiman) available to them. "By its fruit we judge the tree," wrote Stravinsky ([1942] 2003), "Judge the tree by its fruit then, and do not meddle with its roots. Function justifies an organ, no matter how strange the organ may appear in the eyes of those who are not accustomed to see it functioning" (p. 49). This quote captures both the impending crisis of the closed form as felt by the artist in the mid-twentieth century and the reactionary defense needed for those difficult works that were becoming increasingly distasteful to popular audiences (think polytonality, abstract expressionism, and hard bop). These classic metaphors of tree, fruit, organ, and root reveal qualities or characteristics of what Barthes in the 1970's critiqued as the "work."

According to Barthes (1977) in his classic essay, "From Work to Text," the work is constituted by hierarchy, location, and the categorical divisions of genre, form, and labor. Its fruits are the outgrowth of historical effort, rooted in the practices of great or classical traditions like European orchestral music or American jazz. It is no coincidence that Stravinsky looked to the metaphor of a tree to defend the aesthetic sensibility that Barthes would later call the work. In the modernist imagination, the tree captures at a glance idealized associations like endurance, deep-rooted history, and the inevitability of progress (Deleuze & Guattari, 1983; Lesko, 2001). After careful harvesting and dissection, the fruits of its artistic and pedagogical practices can be scientifically justified and advanced, and thus applied universally. According to Elliott, "all music students (including all general music students) ought to be viewed and taught the same basic way: as reflective music practitioners engaged in the kind of cognitive apprenticeship we call music education." (1995, p. 74)

To illustrate this manner of music education, Elliott writes about his experiences learning jazz as a young trombonist. "I recall my teacher setting me the musical problem (or challenge) of performing a slow jazz ballad. This ballad required a very smooth, legato style. With a few carefully chosen words about breath support and articulation (formal knowledge), and a brief model of legato playing (practical concept), my teacher coached me toward performing the ballad musically—that is, in relation to the criteria and traditions of the jazz practice (the musical whole) of which the selected ballad was a part" (1995, p. 61). Though unexceptional to most readers, a more complete narrative of the pedagogy of closed forms is hardly possible. In this rendering, the teacher is poised as an expert whose responsibility is to make plain the functions of a finished form; the initiate is positioned as a deficit learner who needs to demonstrate the proper decoding of a representative work before moving on to more difficult challenges; the object under investigation is utterly knowable; the representative work is sealed within a larger whole; and the functioning of this education takes place through induction and apprenticeship.

The solidarity of this guild system, if it ever was universal, began to break down in the latter twentieth-century, mutating from a closed concept of discrete practices capable of a precise and predictable pedagogy to an open methodological "field" of relative and unstable frames of reference (Barthes, 1977). Anticipating in prophetic fashion the sampling culture of 1990s hip-hop and contemporary mash-up artists like Kutiman and others, Barthes outlined a new aesthetic theory in which diversity-affirming webs of relationships replaced the self-contained forms that traditional composers like Stravinsky sought to control, and performance educators like Elliott sought to replicate. For Barthes, the text exists at the moment of production; it is an unfinished field in which a plurality of signifiers (meanings, enunciations, touches, and discourses) interacts above and below the level of propositional knowledge. The text does not displace explicit codes or propositional knowledge—it cannot—but the relative value of an explicit code, (say) a perfectly tuned octave or properly demonstrated legato tonguing, is determined within and through its relationship to other signifiers/discourses within the larger field in which it is being composed. For example, for a composing-musician like Kutiman, the ideological sanctity of perfect intonation [that is, an explicit or commonsense law of musical practice] often gives way to a democratic (albeit less popular) discourse around amateurism when he purposefully samples musicians who do not or cannot play in tune, thereby challenging ideological notions of talent and purity of sound that exist at the explicit level of signification.

Who would possibly argue for out-of-tune octaves or misinterpreted trombone articulations? The question is fair, but misdirected. It is by attending to those meanings or discourses that are embedded at the level of the self-evident that we can expose and thus possibly correct the uneven power relationships that lie hidden in norm-governed cultural practices where internal and external laws are perpetuated by the very fact of their neutrality or normalcy. We all recognize that in the Western conservatory mindset, it is more than unorthodox to work with an out-of-tune octave, it is absolutely forbidden. The prohibitions that circulate around closed concepts like intonation, articulation, time, and notation are so strict that obedience or submission to their laws governs nearly every aspect of music-making. Taken to its logical conclusion, these laws place more importance on the right results of sonic structure than on the right results of human need. As this chapter concerns music education broadly, one outcome of the ideology of closed forms has been a legacy of fear and musical bullying by directors and cultural care-takers who place abstract musical percepts and concepts like musicianship and "being musical" above abstract human values and concepts like care and justice.

At its most obvious, Barthes's concept of text is a challenge to the supreme place that the elements of music hold in the Western art imagination. The video "text" by Atomic Tom referred to earlier is, in point of fact, a "performance event," not a "work," and not a "bounded cultural phenomenon." Certainly it is one in which the norm-governed musical elements of pitch, rhythm, duration, dynamics, and texture do contribute to the make up of the text, but they are only assigned relative meaning, interacting as they must within a discursive field of multiple modalities that include, but are not limited to, gesture, location, self-expression, and aesthetic need. To evaluate this group's "musicianship" is entirely beside the point. In fact, the praxial criteria for the exhibition of good musicianship places an a priori limit around a musical event by dissecting the event into the mere sum of its functioning parts, rather than conceiving the event as something larger and potentially more interesting. To read the music video of Atomic Tom as an unbounded irreducible text is to appreciate the complexity of the human need that drove the event into production.

"The Text is plural" writes Barthes, "the Text is not a coexistence of meanings, but a passage . . . The plural of the Text depends, that is, not on the ambiguity of its context but on what might be called the stereographic plurality of its weave of signifiers." Its substance may "come from codes which are known but their combination is unique" (1977, p. 159). The work depends upon grammar, but the text "is woven entirely with citations, references, echoes, cultural languages (what language is not?) . . ." (1977, p. 160). Today's mash-up aesthetic, for example, exerts the democratic right to "sample" whatever musical language it finds useful, even if its citation is only a faint echo of the original. Given this premise, it is fair to ask—what homage or respect does an author deserve? What if anything does a bluegrass band owe to its tradition when (hypothetically) it decides to borrow from the lexicon of jazz harmony and the affect and attitude of 1970s glam rock? What if such a group finds inspiration in the tangled roots of several traditions, and not one?

New metaphors have emerged that suggest a dramatic change has taken place in the terms upon which the social contract between composer, performer, and audience is now drawn. For Gould (2005), we might enter a tradition from the perspective of a nomad, which gives the traveler the advantages of new eyes and new ears. The nomadic journey for Gould is a purposeful act of decentering commonsense knowledge, as the pleasure of constant relocation and shifting perspectives serves to dissolve the myth of primal origins and final resting places. In contrast to Stravinsky, Lather (1993, p. 680) compares "the tree as the modernist model of knowledge with the rhizome (systems with underground stems and aerial roots, whose fruits are tubers and bulbs) as the model for postmodern knowledge." "Rhizomatics," Lather writes, "are about the move from hierarchies to networks and the complexity of problematics where any concept, when pulled, is recognized as 'connected to a mass of tangled ideas, uprooted, as it were, from the epistemological field' (quoting Pefanis, 1991, p. 680). Both writers offer a theory of knowledge that does not depend upon a single root source, whether that source is the original composer, the tradition he wrote in, his notated score, or the codified unwritten practices that are defined and advanced by its practitioner-educators. There is never only one way to know a piece of music, never only one way to interpret it, perform it, use it, or cite it. The social contract upon which the praxial philosophy of music education was built has now been turned on its head, with the curiosity-seeker in charge, not the teacher, not the author-composer.

In traditional encounters with a closed form, Barthes writes that "the author is reputed the Father and the owner of his work: literary science therefore teaches respect for the manuscript and the author's declared intentions" (1977, p. 160) while society asserts the work's legality through copyright law and through soft power institutions like conservatories and schools of music. "As for the Text," asserts Barthes, "it reads without the inscription of the Father." He continues, "the metaphor of the text is that of the network; if the Text extends itself, it is as a result of combinatory systematic" (1977, p. 161). Here Barthes makes his most notorious claim, the idea for which he is most famous: the death of the author. "It is not that the Author may not 'come back' in the Text, in his text, but he does so as a 'guest' . . . If he is a novelist, he is inscribed in the novel like one of his characters, figured in the carpet; no longer privileged [or] paternal" (1977, p. 161).

In the case of music and music education, this notion of the death of the author needn't be simply that the composer has completely gone away and the tradition in which he wrote has vanished. Rather, the curiosity-seeker can approach any kind of music and read the codes left behind as an open text or interpretive event, which means that acquaintance with a composer's intentions and the tradition in which he wrote will be useful only to the degree that the composer has something of interest to communicate to the reader. This communication may be profound and require years of traditional study (as mentioned earlier, the concept of musicianship will not and should not disappear) or the communication may be a mere flirtation, a passing attraction. Returning to the question posed earlier: what homage or respect does an author deserve?

What if anything does a band, bluegrass or otherwise, owe to its hereditary source? I might answer these questions as Barthes would. The composer and his tradition, as a guest in his own work, is owed hospitality—depending of course on the behavior of the guest and the appreciation he shows his host.

Several important questions have been raised. What would a pedagogy of music look like that placed the interests of the curiosity-seeker before the expectations and expertise of the teacher? What would it mean to make tradition a guest in our classrooms, and not a bully? What happens to formal music education when it is unsealed from propositional knowledge, demonstrative know-how, and musical wholes? The next section will wrestle with an alternative model to musicianship and praxial pedagogy, one that looks expansively at learner capacity and the human interest to compose and share.

From Musicianship to Multimodal Musical Literacies

Without developing some competency in the procedural knowings that lie at the core of musical practices and musical works, and a first hand knowledge of the circumstances in which these knowings apply, a listener's perspectives on and relationships with music will remain moot in the most essential regard.

  —David Elliott

How would we teach if we assumed all youth were literate?

  —Lalitha Vasudevan

This final section begins with the assumption that all learners are curiosity-seekers; and that all learners come equipped with diverse capacities and appetites.

I continue with the claim that the act of composing is embedded in all aspects of our productive lives, most visibly in the lives of the young people all around us. Writes Vasudevan (2010), "Right now, in parks, renovated warehouses, front steps, playgrounds, friends' basements, and cafés all around the world, young people are seeking and creating spaces to be. Within these contexts, they are engaging in a range of multimodal literary practices: accessing and participating in a variety of digitally mediated spaces, creating and disseminating representations of self, communicating with multiple audiences, and acquiring and producing informational texts" (p. 88). This aspect of text-making, or composing, comes by way of "the reconfiguration of the representational and communicational resources of image, action, sound, and so on in new multimodal ensembles" (Jewitt, 2008, p. 241). From this perspective, "a multimodal approach allows educators and researchers to attend to a wider range of resources and practices involved in composing, which are especially visible in digital composing" (Vasudevan, 2010, p. 91). In consequence, "new relationships between production and dissemination are made possible across a range of media and technologies, *remaking the conditions and functions of authorship and audience* (Jewitt, 2008, p. 243, italics added).

What can we learn from literacy specialists like Vasudevan and Jewitt about the changing nature of communication, youth culture, and education? Why are these language specialists attracted to the idea of composing, more than traditional views of literacy like English reading and writing? What is their purpose in unsealing language literacy from a closed notion of composition into one that is captured in the gerund composing? I propose that the turn that took place in the disciplinary field of language literacy over the last thirty years hints to a new framework for thinking about music education in the twenty-first century.

Like the static notion of musicianship, early ideas of language literacy were seen "as an autonomous neutral set of skills or competencies that people acquire through schooling and can deploy universally" (Jewitt, 2008). To be a literate member of society, a student was taught to read and write, and school was the place where the forms and functions of English language was taught, just as the band room or private lesson studio was the place to learn to read and play music. Although the student was likely to speak English at home, and to listen to and watch all kinds of music outside of school or the studio, learning the forms and functions of these disciplines assumed that the student arrived at these lessons as a blank slate.

The problem with this view of literacy, musical or otherwise, is that without considering broader or more nonconventional capacities, "deficit theories blamed the students and their families for poor performance in school" (Hull & Schutz, 2001, p. 578). About the same time that Barthes was writing about the aesthetic turn from work to text, Basso (1974) introduced the term "writing event" as a way to capture the multi-dimensional and intertextual fields within which a communicative act occurs. This epistemological shift refused to differentiate between the functions and forms of speech and writing, collapsing them into a larger intertwined field or "text." Today, "the interdependence of modes in communicating meaning is amplified by a semiotic landscape that is characterized increasingly by practices of social mediation and artifacts of cultural affiliation" (Vasudevan, 2010, p. 92). The aim of today's multimodal literacy movement is to capitalize on the considerable capacities that students bring to an everyday writing event or communicative act by amplifying fluency across methodological fields.

A musical pedagogy of open texts is one that places composing at the center of all activities. It assumes that all students come to an educational encounter equipped with multiple literacies, and that they wish to employ the largest range of modalities available to them to communicate with others and to create self-reflective musical events. The music pedagogy I am describing is a dramatic turn from the educational practices of the last two hundred years, as embodied in Stravinsky's famous book *Poetics of Music* and reaching its logical conclusion in Elliott's *Music Matters*. The following comparative chart is an attempt to highlight this disruption.

While the aesthetic turn from closed forms to open texts is a historical rupture, I believe its contrasting pedagogies can coexist in ways that are not inherently

Pedagogy of Closed Forms	Pedagogy of Open Texts
end is musicianship	end is multimodal literacy
primary objective: performing works	primary objective: writing texts
learner seen as: performer	learner seen as: hyphenated composer-performers
music conceived as: bound, essential, reducible	music conceived as: transcontextual, hybrid, and irreducible
structured by demonstrative codes	interwoven with multiple modalities (including explicit codes)
non-transferable skills	all skills are transferable
student seen as deficit learner	student seen as equipped with multiple capacities
governed by laws and codes	governed by imagination and need
experienced through: the representational work	experienced through: unbounded events
aims at proper interpretation	aims at communication with audience
musical ends shape educational means	human ends shape educational means
uses copy-written materials	uses open-source materials (copy-lefting)
distinguished practitioners	anonymous players
tradition is master	tradition is guest
student as apprentice	teacher as guide
teacher is master	student is host
lengthy apprenticeships	exigent needs
diversity-adverse, diversity-phobic	diversity-affirming
norm-governed	self-governed
expert-driven	curiosity-driven
virtuosity is ideal	amateurism is aim
taught the same way to all	taught differently to each
primary metaphors: trees, roots, fruits, organs	primary metaphors: rhizomes, networks, fields, webs
philosophical orientation: praxialism, multiculturalism	philosophical orientation: democratic multiculturalism, feminism, cosmopolitanism, critical theory

disruptive. As long as there are cherished art forms that need preserving, then the kind of praxial pedagogy that Elliott endorses will have a place in conservatories and schools of music around the world. Indeed, we might look to the burgeoning field of museum education to learn additional ways of making the music and art of past eras come alive (Hubard, 2007). Yet whether a pedagogy of open texts is a disruption or not depends on a perceptional shift that is subtle, but profound. There is quite a difference, for example, between teaching young people jazz and teaching young people jazz so that they can do something with jazz. In the former conception, the point of learning is in service of the preservation and extension of a well-loved art form. In the latter conception, the point of learning is to equip the student with tools for a journey that is her own to compose and not her teacher's, or her teacher's teacher.

Nor does a pedagogy of open texts prohibit an educator from teaching the explicit codes of a traditional art form. It simply asks the music educator to negotiate with the students their terms of induction and apprenticeship, potentially equalizing the power relationships and hierarchical imbalances between stakeholders. This perceptional shift will make teaching different for each learner as the educator, seeing each student as endowed with creative potential and multiple capacities, crafts learning around the students' needs rather than the educator's expertise alone or the canonic laws of the favored tradition. What if tradition were just a guest in the study of jazz, classical, or bluegrass music? I dare say that some students would enjoy a lengthy acquaintance, and others would not. Nor are the pedagogies of closed forms and open texts mutually exclusive from the student's point of view: a student may opt to linger in one domain, and then switch to the other, depending upon the individual needs.

A prediction about the future of music education that I promised at the beginning of this chapter: in coming generations, fewer music students will come to educational settings for long apprenticeships in closed art forms. What this has to say for the classical arts and their survival is not necessarily the concern of this chapter.

Like everyone else, I have historical forms that I cherish and would be heartbroken to see fade away. Students, I predict, will want to learn the various crafts and sounds of music for composing. Not to make "compositions" in the Beethoven-sense, with pen, manuscript, and piano. They will do this, as Vasudevan is already suggesting, in cafés and classrooms, and on subway platforms and neighborhood stoops. They will move from acoustic guitars to iPhones (or whatever emerges as the latest musical platform) and back. They will mix bluegrass with jazz harmonies, and will count as compositional sources the discourses that circulate around fashion, politics, and the body. They will compose as self-formative individuals, linked in relationship to others, growing and evolving across physical time and real and virtual geographies. Composing, I predict, will become increasingly unfinished, a process of sharing and linking, and looping and quoting, all within fluid layers of meaning that evolve and mutate as contexts change.

This will require new dexterity from music educators, as we switch from an education in performance and the closed-form interpretation of a "work" to educating through facilitation with a new generation of hyphenated composing-performers. We will need to expand our own teaching-performing modalities. Teaching will be more difficult than ever. We may need to keep one foot planted in the traditions of the past as we step boldly into the musical worlds our students are composing. The teacher as guest will replace the master/apprentice model that is at the heart of a pedagogy of closed forms. Traditions and authors will be guests, too. All the better. As the prophets of our new age suggest, there will be plenty of room for everyone.

References

Adorno, T. ([1934] 2002). The dialectical composer. In *Essays on Music*. Edited by Richard Leppert. Trans. S. H. Gillespie. Berkeley & Los Angeles: University of California Press.

Attali, J. ([1977] 1985). *Noise: The political economy of music*. Trans. B. Massumi. Minneapolis: University of Minnesota Press.

Babbitt, M. (1958). Who Cares If You Listen? *High Fidelity*, 8(2), 38–40, 126–27.

Basso, K. (1974). The ethnography of writing. In R. Bauman & J. Sherzer (Eds.), *Explorations in the Ethnography of Speaking* (pp. 425–32). Cambridge, UK: Cambridge University Press.

Copland, A. (1963). *Copland on Music*. New York: W. W. Norton & Company Inc.

Barthes, R. (1977). *Image, music, text*. Trans. S. Heath. New York: Hill and Wang.

Deleuze, G. and Guattari, F. (1983). *On the line*. Trans. J. Johnston. New York: Semiotext(e).

Detels, C. (1999). *Soft Boundaries: Re-Visioning the Arts and Aesthetics in American Education*. Westport, CT: Bergin and Garvey.

Elliott, D. (1995). *Music matters: a new philosophy of music education*. New York: Oxford University Press.

Goehr, L. (1994). *The imaginary museum of musical works*. New York: Oxford University Press.

Gould, E. (2005). Nomadic Turns: Epistemology, experience and women university band directors. *Philosophy of Music Education Review*, 13(2), 147–64.

Hindemith, P. (1952). *A Composer's World: Horizons and Limits*. Cambridge: Harvard University Press.

Hubard, O. (2007). Productive information: Contextual knowledge in art museum education. *Art Education*, 60(4), 17–23.

Hull, G. and Schutz, K. (2001). Literacy and learning out of school: a review of theory and research. *Review of Education Research*, 71(4), 575–611.

Jewitt, C. (2008). Multimodality and literacy in school classrooms. *Review of Research in Education*, 32, 241–67.

Lather, P. (1993). Fertile obsession: validity after poststructuralism. *The Sociological Quarterly*, 34(4), 673–93.

Lesko, N. (2001). *Act your age! A cultural construction of adolescence*. London: Routledge Falmer.

Nettl, B. (1995). *Heartland Excursions: Ethnomusicological Reflections on Schools of Music (Music in American Life)*. Champaign-Urbana: University of Illinois Press.

Pefanis, J. (1991). *Heterology and the postmodern: Bataille, Baudrillard, and Lyotard*. Durham, N.C.: Duke University Press. Quoted in Lather, P. 1993. Fertile obsession: Validity after poststructuralism. *The Sociological Quarterly*, 34(4), 673–93.

Schoenburg, A. (2010). *Style and Idea: Selected Writings*. Trans. L. Black. Berkeley & Los Angeles: University of California Press.

Small, C. (1997). *Musicking: The meanings of performance and listening*. Hanover, NH: Wesleyan University Press.

Stravinsky, I. ([1942] 2003). *Poetics of music*. Cambridge: Harvard University Press.

Swanwick, K. (1988). *Music, mind, and education*. London: Routledge.

Vasudevan, L. (2010). Re-imagining pedagogies for multimodal selves. *National Society for the Study of Education*, 110(1), 88–108.

Notes

1. "Atomic Tom- Take Me Out (Live on NYC Subway)," YouTube video, 4:33, posted by "AtomicTomVEVO," October 18, 2010, http://www.youtube.com/watch?v=19KBAcJ53ak.

2. "Kutiman-Thru-you-03-I'm New," YouTube video, 6:22, posted by "kutiman," March 7, 2009, http://www.youtube.com/watch?v=EsBfj6khrG4.

3. "Baby . . . on RECORDER?!?!" YouTube video, 1:47, posted by KurtHugo-Schneider, March 23, 2010, http://www.youtube.com/watch?v=sBF-_WMY8HU

Model Practices in Teaching Composition

SECTION } III

Model Practices in Teaching Composition

Teachers new to teaching composition benefit from examining models of successful practice. The challenge in preparing teachers to facilitate composition is in finding those models—and in finding them across a wide range of school-based settings. Since composition in PreK–12 is a relatively new focus for music education, experienced practitioners who can serve as models or mentors may be difficult to locate. The chapters of this section provide descriptions of successful teaching and learning practices situated within general music, choral music, instrumental music, and a specialized composition program. The ideas found in these chapters are applicable to students of diverse ages, abilities, and experience levels.

Sandra Stauffer interrogates how music teachers can prepare to engage children in the creation of original compositions. She describes the importance of forming a personal stance toward musical creation by examining four topics: children, creativity and creative thinking in music, the self as teacher and creator, and the place of creativity in education. She argues that the roots of an effective pedagogy are found in the particular kinds of problems teachers identify and in the decisions teachers make that are related to planning, implementing, and monitoring of creative music making experiences for children.

Teachers need to carefully consider how scaffolding is used within the process of teaching children to compose. Jackie Wiggins and Michael Medvinsky warn that too much teacher support can easily become intervention in or even encroachment on children's creative work. Throughout their chapter, the authors suggest ways to foster and enable learner success without inappropriately asserting influence. The approach they advocate positions the learners' ideas at the core of the process and allows those ideas to flourish. The suggestions that close the chapter guide teachers toward actions that allow students to find a sense of ownership, personal meaning, and artistic success.

Since some young composers will excel beyond their classmates as composers, Daniel Deutsch discusses ways of working with more advanced and gifted young composers. Citing examples from his own teaching, Deutsch vividly depicts his work with talented students and how he encourages them to take risks and provide feedback to each other. He also describes how to help students find the time and space in their busy lives to compose. Finally he discusses how to connect young composers to the larger world of composition by participating in recitals, festivals, and competitions.

Alexander Koops offers ideas for teaching composition in instrumental ensembles. He considers the problems involved in finding sufficient time, getting experience with composition pedagogy, using music notation, and the issues inherent in composing with large groups. Next he offers ideas for incorporating composition activities in instrumental methods classes. The chapter concludes with general guidelines for including composition in instrumental ensembles.

Katherine Strand notes that choral methods and literature classes are ideal opportunities for studying a wide variety of exercises suitable for engaging students with composing in choral ensembles. She begins by outlining a rationale for composing in choral settings that balances performance and creation. The effectiveness of the exercises is made evident as she uses a larger work created by one of her music education students to illustrate the process of guiding students from highly supported to more autonomous compositional work.

In the final chapter of this section Alice Hammel uses the five domains of teaching and learning as delineated in her 2011 book, *Teaching Music to Students with Special Needs: A Label-Free Approach* to discuss modifying instruction for children with special learning needs. In addition to the five domains, Hammel employs four teaching approaches to examine the suggestions found in the others chapters in this section in order to provide guidance for teachers working with children with special needs within the framework of composition lessons and activities. Finally, she provides a model for constructing case studies of children that pre-service teachers could use to further their understanding of the various learning processes experienced by the wide range of students likely to be found in school music programs.

5 }

Preparing to Engage Children
in Musical Creating

Sandra L. Stauffer

This chapter addresses one facet of the tremendously complex matter of music teacher education. Specifically, how can music teachers be prepared to engage children in creating music? Teacher preparation of any sort is complicated by the beliefs, values, and experiences of pre-service and in-service teachers and by the beliefs, values, and experiences of the teacher educators who work with them. These complex dynamics interweave with considerations of who and where the learners are, historical and evolving conceptions of what the content is (music, in this case), ideas about why and how it should be taught, and a complex web of social, cultural, political, and educational contexts. Given this rather knotty set of conditions, teaching and learning are anything but predictable. There are no easy answers to the questions that arise in music teacher education in general, or to the more specific question of how to prepare teachers to engage children in creating music. Even if there were "answers," the shifting conditions described above would likely make them only marginally relevant in some contexts and out-of-date in others before this book leaves the publisher's press. This chapter aims, then, not at "what to do" but rather at "ways to think" about teaching and learning that can inform opportunities for engaging children in musical creating.

So, before we begin, let's review.[1] The key words of the chapter title—*preparing, engage, children, creating*—point to the some of the key assumptions underpinning the chapter content. *Preparing* music teachers is typically considered the mission of undergraduate music education programs, post-bachelor's degree certification courses, or masters-plus-certification degrees. One of the myths haunting the educational imaginary is that at the end of these programs the individuals enrolled in them are "prepared" to teach. Neither 120 credits hours of course work, nor one semester of student teaching, nor thirty-six weeks of graduate work imbedded in the schools, nor any other combination of classroom and field experiences can adequately prepare anyone for a career that may last thirty years or more. Simply put, things change. The fluidity of social, political, musical, and educational contexts precludes an endpoint to preparation. Further, as individual educators mature and acquire musical, teaching, and life experience, *their* views of teaching, learning, music, children, and creating shift. Teachers are always becoming who they are. Learning to teach is a life-long experience—a continuous process that begins tacitly in the experiences of childhood and youth, unfolds in teacher preparation classes, grows in graduate and professional development experiences, and matures with experience. *Preparing* never ends.

Engage signals a perspective about the nature of the student-teacher relationship and the role of the teacher that is grounded in a Deweyan conception of education. John Dewey, one of the most prolific education philosophers of the twentieth century, believed that schools should be genuine forms of active community life in which teachers and students work together in continuously unfolding and interactive experiences relevant to the interests of the child, the contexts of the community, and the public good (Dewey, 1902/1990, 1943/1990). From this perspective, crucial responsibilities of the teacher include crafting an environment and facilitating experiences that engage children not only in genuine and meaningful doing but also in thought and reflection that links personal knowledge and social experience. Dewey's thinking about education evolved throughout the first half of the twentieth century, and some of his ideas continue to raise questions that challenge educators. For example, who and what "teaches" in educational environments? What experiences are educative? Whose ideas have merit? Who has agency? Is the teacher a leader or a learner or both? These questions remain apropos for educators at any level, and they are particularly relevant to ethical matters that underpin creating in music. For example, if music composition is "taught," then whose musical ideas count? What gets called a "composition" and who decides? Who has agency and who is doing the musical creating? What kinds of experiences in creating music are authentically educative, who decides, and how do we know? Rather than answer these unanswerable questions, this chapter rests on ideas derived from thinking about them. Four of these ideas are: children are creative; learning occurs in meaningful and authentic *engagement* with music; learning occurs in the interactions of children with children and children with teachers; and, one of the most crucial responsibilities of music educators is to create an environment for creating.

This chapter also focuses specifically on preparing to engage *children*—people from birth to about twelve years of age—in musical creating, and in their rich musical lives. Teacher preparation typically foregrounds schools as the places of learning, directs attention to the characteristics of learners and strategies for teaching in different levels of schooling (e.g., preschool, elementary school, middle school, high school), and focuses on certification of adults who work with learners in these particular places. But the lives of children are not confined to the place of school, and the community of "music educators" includes more people than those who have state-endorsed certificates to teach. Children live the experience of learning and musicking in multiple ways and multiple contexts, and they often do so on their own, without adults around. And, music educators (writ large) engage with children not only in schools, but also in studios, community centers, civic and religious ensembles, camps. This chapter moves toward a broader conception of teacher preparation—one that is not about "elementary school," the place-bound language of teacher education (Stauffer, 2009a), but rather a conception of teacher preparation that is about *children* wherever they are and about the preparation of those who interact with them in music, whomever they might be.

The word *creating* rather than composing is also crucial to the thinking in this chapter. For some readers, and even for parents and other community members who are stakeholders in the education of children, "composing" may be associated with the effort of a single (usually adult) person working alone to "write" music that will be performed by someone else for someone else at a public event usually called a concert. But musical creating is considerably more broad and diverse than this rather limited view, and conflating "composition" with "creativity" in music is profoundly misleading (Barrett, 2003). Perspectives of musical creating vary by culture, context, genre, style, person, and more. While children can and do "compose," they are musically creative in multiple ways; engaging in "composing" is only one way in which children demonstrate their creative capabilities. Being conscious of the multiple dimensions of children's creative abilities and the multiple ways in which children create in and through music may be crucial to nurturing the very specific act of composing.

Finally, you—the readers—are diverse too. You may be a faculty member at a liberal arts college in a rural town who is responsible for the preparation of both future music educators and future classroom teachers, a university faculty member in an urban environment who teaches music methods classes for undergraduate and graduate music majors and pedagogy classes for performers, a practicing teacher or graduate student seeking insights about creating with children, a performer or conductor curious about creativity, a studio teacher with children who are inventing their own music, or an undergraduate student wondering about this particular dimension of your future career. Your contexts, experiences, and motivations for reading this chapter vary widely. My aim is to provide points of departure for thinking about practice that can be considered through the multiple lenses of particular music learning contexts.

Research in teacher education is vast; the literature on music teacher education is substantial. Likewise, research on creativity is vast; the literature on creativity in music is substantial. But research at the intersection of these literatures—how to prepare teachers to engage children in musical creating—is quite scarce. The good news is that these studies, though few in number, demonstrate or at the very least imply that teacher education experiences in all their diverse forms[2] *can* make a difference in how music educators think about, facilitate, and engage in creative music-making with students (e.g., Kennedy, 2004; Miller, 2004, 2012; Odena & Welch, 2007, 2009; Randles, 2009). Further, findings of studies drawn from the more extensive literatures mentioned above provide additional information from which recommendations for preparation and practice can be inferred.

The remainder of this chapter, then, is comprised of two sections relative to preparing to engage children in musical creating: developing a personal stance, and constructing an effective pedagogy. The first section posits questions aimed at developing principles on which to build practice. Questions focus on uncovering beliefs and developing thinking about four topics: children and creativity, creativity and creative thinking music, self as teacher and creator, and the place of creativity in education. The second section invites thinking about the pedagogy of creating in music, including but not limited to composing. Pedagogy is a matter of decision-making and problem-solving, and the second section focuses on particular kinds of problems and decisions relative to planning, implementing, monitoring, and responding to creative music-making experiences for and with children. The two sections of the chapter are meant to inform each other, blending theory with action.

Throughout both sections, the text in boxes provides suggestions for reading, discussion, observation, practice, and reflection. These suggestions are drawn from a variety of resources. Readers will certainly have more ideas, and new resources and ideas will (and should) replace these as new knowledge emerges in research and practice. Dewey held that education for children occurs in genuine, meaningful doing *and* in thoughtful reflection that links knowledge and experience. This principle applies to teacher education as well. To restate the fundamental aim of the chapter, the text box suggestions do not aim at "how to teach" answers, but rather at "ways to think" about teaching and learning that can inform the daily problem-solving inherent in pedagogical decisions and musical engagements with children. If preparing to teach is a lifelong (or at least career-long) experience, then "how to think" is as important as "what to do."

Developing a Stance

Beliefs, values, and actions are closely related. For example, if you *believe* that eating certain foods leads to a longer and healthier life, and if you *value* longevity and health, then your eating *actions* probably reflect those beliefs and values. Furthermore, the intensity of your beliefs and values about food and health likely has something to do with the intensity of your commitment to your preferred dietary practices. Likewise, the act of teaching is informed by beliefs and values that may range from implicit unarticulated assumptions derived from experiences as a learner as well as social and cultural norms, to consciously and critically considered principles derived from dialogue, study, and individual reflection. Whether tacit or explicit, strongly held or taken-for-granted, one's beliefs about children, creating, the self, music, and education inform teaching practice.

This section raises questions aimed at examining beliefs about children as musical and creative learners, creativity and creative thinking in music, self as teacher and creator, and the place of creativity in education. These four areas of questioning are similar to Schwab's curricular commonplaces: subject matter, student, teacher, and milieu (1983). Visiting or revisiting what one believes (and why) is a crucial part of the career-long processes of becoming a teacher in general and preparing to engage children in musical creating in particular.

WHAT DO YOU BELIEVE ABOUT CREATIVITY?

When you use the word "creativity," what do you mean? How do you know whether someone or something is creative? Where do innovative ideas come from? How do creative people do what they do? These questions and others have fueled the writing of philosophers and researchers who have studied creativity from the nineteenth century to the present (Becker, 1995). Since 1950, scholars in Western cultures have generally focused on the creative process or product, characteristics of creative people, or environments that seem conducive to creativity. Their research questions and their definitions of creativity reflect one or more of these trajectories. For example, process questions and definitions have to with how the creativity unfolds, including whether there are steps or stages in the creative process and what those might be. Product questions have to do with the qualities of what is created. Why are some products or ideas considered creative but not others? How do we know? Person-related definitions and questions have to do with identifying characteristics of people who are creative, sometimes in order to predict who might be creative in the future. Questions regarding place have to with the context or environment in which creativity occurs. For example, why does (or did) creativity seem to flourish in some times and places but not others?

Given the complexities and possibilities outlined above, the definition of creativity may seem as elusive as the phenomenon. Still, considering how creativity is defined may be crucial, for in addition to the work of researchers, "creativity" has entered the lingo of politicians, policy makers, and the popular press, with the implication that creativity is something we should enact in order to achieve certain ends. For example, Florida (2002) argues that "human creativity is the ultimate economic resource" and that we are living in a "creative age" driven by "creativity as the fundamental source" of both economic growth and social change (p. xiii, xxix). In education, the writers of documents for the Partnership for 21st Century Skills have designated the ability to "think creatively," "work creatively with others," and "implement innovations" as skills "essential to prepare students for the future" (P12 Framework Definitions, p. 3–4). Conversely, other writers caution that the word "creativity" has become so popularized that it has become meaningless, "for it is applied like sparkling paint to book titles, do-it-yourself projects, or performance groups" (Lowenfeld & Brittain, 1987, p. 74). Writing specifically to music educators, Webster (1990) notes that "creativity" has been used in so many contexts to refer to so many things that the word has lost its power and meaning. He suggests that "creative thinking" may be a more apt term, for it indicates both an ability in the domain of music and the potential for nurturing that ability in educational contexts.

So what is creative thinking in music? According to Webster (2002), creative thinking in music is "the engagement of the mind in the active, structured process of thinking in sound for the purpose of producing some product that is new for the creator" (p. 26). Webster (2002) asserts that the potential for creative thinking exists in all kinds of musical engagements, including performing, improvising, composing, and even listening and analyzing. Based on extensive study of various models and theories of creativity, Webster has advanced a comprehensive model of creative thinking in music that includes not only these potential means of engaging in musical creative thinking, but also a creative process model, key creative thinking skills, and a set of conditions that can enable creativity in music. Webster's model and definition of creative thinking in music are important considerations in preparing to engage children in creating music for two reasons. First, his definition points to *thinking in sound* as the core ability of musically creative thinking. Second, his model points to a conception of musical creative thinking that is broader and more comprehensive than composing alone. Indeed, Webster states that creative thinking in music "occurs at various levels, from the spontaneous songs of the very young child to the products of the greatest minds in music" (2002, p. 27). (See Chapter 2 for Webster's model.)

While Webster's model extends creative thinking beyond the confines of composing, it is important to recognize that the model is thoroughly rooted in Western music practices as well as Western science and thinking, and that these are not the only human conceptions of creativity. In Scandinavia, for example, creativity is "understood as an attitude toward life, a way to come to grips with the problems of existence" (Smith & Carlsson, 2006, p. 202). In a study of 211 people from 28 linguistic-cultural groups in Arab Africa and sub-Saharan Africa, researchers found abundant and diverse historic, traditional, and contemporary examples of creativity and creative practices, but only the Arabic language included a word for creativity (Mpofu et al., 2006). Diverse ideas about creativity in the arts exist as well. In Japan, cultivating an inner sense of richness during arts learning is more valued than the creation of new objects (Matsunobu, 2011). In the Community Music movement in the United Kingdom, music "events" draw people together in a "creative approach to musicking practice" in which freedom of expression and invention are emphasized rather than products (Higgins & Campbell, 2010, p. 5, 17). Informal music-making practices, which include a great deal of musical creativity, have been well documented among popular musicians (Green, 2002) and among the tune-bending practices of folk music communities (Kruse, 2012; Waldron & Veblen, 2009). "Composing" is generally not the word associated with musical creating in these any of contexts. Caution is warranted, then, when considering any definition of creativity or musical creative thinking, for it is inevitably tied to social, cultural, and historical perspective and practice.

What do you believe about musical creativity or creative thinking in music? What counts? Why do you think so? Whether in garage bands (e.g., Campbell, 1995) or with GarageBand® (e.g., Randles, 2010), musical creating and musical creative thinking seem to be limitless in possibilities. Observing, learning from, and thinking about these diverse musical practices can lead to new and enriched ideas for engaging children in musical creating (Jaffurs, 2004).

Projects

- Research definitions of creativity by checking reference materials such as the *Encyclopedia of Creativity* or by reading the writings of historical and contemporary creativity researchers such as J. Paul Guilford, E. Paul Torrance, Teresa Amabile, Mihalyi Csikszentmihalyi, Howard Gardner, and Robert Sternberg. Consider how their definitions and models of creativity focus on or account for person, product, process, and place, and how they have changed over time.
- Write your own definition or description of musical creativity or musical creative thinking. Consider ways in which people are creative in music. Have you ever labeled something or someone as musically creative? What was it? Why did you think it was/is creative?
- Interview someone you consider to be creative in music or in some other domain.

RELATED READINGS

- In "Creative Thinking in Music," Hickey and Webster (2001) provide an updated discussion of Webster's 1990 definition and description.
- Lucy Green (2008) challenges music educators to think differently about musical creativity and provides a pedagogical model in *Music, Informal Learning and the School: A New Classroom Pedagogy*.

WHAT DO YOU BELIEVE ABOUT CHILDREN?

Are children creative? Whether your answer is "yes" or "no," why do you think so? What evidence do you have? One of the crucial theoretical arguments in creativity research (particularly in psychology) has to do whether creativity exists at all among children. Some contemporary creativity theorists define creativity relative to culture-transforming products of adults (e.g., Csikszentmihalyi, 1996). From this perspective, children may be inventive but not really creative since they rarely (if ever) transform culture. These theorists suggest that what we call "creative" in children derives from adults' romanticized views of children's specific actions and childhood in general (Sawyer et al., 2003). Other theorists argue that adult conceptions of creativity are not the most appropriate lens for viewing the inventiveness of children. Instead, children's creative acts should be viewed relative to the child doing the creating and to the ways in which what is created is original and useful for that child (Runco & Charles, 1997). This latter view has some merit from a musical point of view. Ethnomusicologists have identified the music-making of children as related to but distinct from adult music-making and therefore creative in ways particular to childhood and children's cultures (Blacking, 1967/1995; Campbell, 2010).

So, what does the musical creativity of childhood sound like? Put another way, what counts as creative thinking in music among children? Researchers have looked to children's music-making for clues and evidence. In early childhood, spontaneous music-making, particularly spontaneous singing, appears to be one indication of children's creative capacities in music. The content of children's spontaneous chanting and singing includes not only variants, transformations, and fragments of familiar songs, chants, and sounds found in their sociocultural contexts, but also includes musical material that appears to be completely original (Mang, 2005, Morehead & Pond, 1978; Tarnowski & Leclerc, 1994; Whiteman, 2009; Young, 2002). While it can be argued that children's spontaneous songs are simply experimentation with the sounds, musics, and languages of their cultures, or that what they do only *seems* inventive because their developing cognitive capacities make it more likely for them to work in fragments than in wholes, Young (2003) cautions against characterizing children's music-making as "exploratory" or "experimental" low-level random activity (p. 56). Close observations of young children indicate that they use spontaneous singing and chanting to communicate with each other, to comment to themselves and others on what they are doing, or simply to do what children do—play (Sundin, 1998; St. John, 2006; Whiteman, 2009). As Pond (1981) notes, children's spontaneous improvisations, whether with their voices or with instruments and objects in their environments, "are acts of making; they are not nor are they meant to be about anything—they simply exist as things that have been made; and the pleasures is in the making" (p. 11).

In the middle and later years of childhood, children continue to create music on their own in both informal settings as well as in formal music learning contexts. In Ghana and The Gambia, for example, children learn and reinvent complex songs, dances, and hand-clapping games (Dzansi, 2004; Koops, 2010), much the same as children engage in musical exchanges on Australian and U. S. playgrounds (Harwood, 1993; Marsh, 1995). In these contexts, distinctions between making (as in performing) and creating music are blurred, as are the lines between teacher and learner, for children themselves serve in both roles. Further, whether creating with their voices and bodies or the instruments they learn to play as they mature, or the acoustic and digital media available to them, children appropriate, reject, adapt, and transform musical gestures gleaned from their social and cultural worlds *and* continue to invent and transform their own sonic and musical gestures (Campbell, 2007; Stauffer, 2002; Thompson, 2007; Webster, 2007). Likewise, any quick tour through YouTube reveals innumerable ways in which young people, including children in the middle and late stages of childhood, reinterpret, remix, mash-up and invent music in their own ways and for their own purposes. Burnard (2007) suggests this complex and interconnected cultural and social sources of and settings for children's music-making to the superculture of children's musical creativity.

One of the crucial differences between formal and informal contexts in the musical superculture of children's creativity may be the role of adults. Children learn directly and indirectly from adult role models, whether family members, teachers, media icons, or musical "stars." While adults are present in most or all of the contexts of children's lives, adults may have a direct and even intentional impact on children's musical creating in formal learning contexts such as schools and music studios, and that impact is worth further consideration. The role of adults and pedagogical thinking of adults relative to children's musical creativity is the topic of the second half of this chapter. For now, consider again the question that opened this section: Are children creative? What you believe may make a difference as you prepare to engage children in musical creating.

Projects

- Are children creative? Why do you think so (or not)? How do you know? Describe ways in which you've seen or heard children being creative, either in music or in other ways.
- Obtain permission to watch a child or a group of children at play, or observe a child or children in your own family. Look for examples of spontaneous music-making, such as singing, rhythmic moving, chanting, using found sounds, or playing instruments. What seems to be made-up or invented? What seems connected to family, media, society, culture?
- Obtain permission to interview an older child about his or her music-making. Campbell (2010) provides a sample protocol and sample interview questions in the appendices of *Songs in Their Heads: Music and Its Meaning in Children's Lives.*

RELATED READINGS

- Campbell's *Songs in Their Heads* (2010) includes multiple examples of individual children and groups of children making music and creating music.
- Published case studies, descriptive studies, and pedagogical articles provide examples of children engaged in making and creating music in various settings, including at home (e.g., Barrett, 2009, 2011), in preschool environments (e.g., Barrett, 2001; St. John, 2006; Young, 2002), in piano lessons (e.g., Miller, 2012), in general music classes (e.g., Beegle, 2010; Bolden, 2009; Miller, 2004; Wiggins, 1994), and with technology (e.g., Bolton, 2008; Mellor, 2007; Nilsson & Folkestad, 2005; Stauffer, 2001a).
- McCord (2004) provides a rare glimpse of creating music with children with learning disabilities.

WHAT DO YOU BELIEVE ABOUT YOURSELF?

Do you consider yourself creative? In what ways, or how? Does your definition of creativity apply to yourself? Are the ideas you have about the creativity of others, including the creativity of children, related to your own creativity? Your conceptions of yourself and your abilities may have a great deal to do with the ways in which you engage with children who are creating music and the ways in which you choose to facilitate or respond to children's creative musical expressions. While teachers cite space, time, and resources as potential barriers to engaging children in musical creating, music researchers have found that pre-service and in-service teachers' uncertainties about their own musical and creative capacities, their questions about how to facilitate creative musical activities, and their varied definitions of creativity appear to be related to what they choose to do (or what they report they do) with children and creative music-making (Blom, 2003; Bucura & Weissburg, 2011; Clennon, 2009; Odena & Welsh, 2007, 2009; Strand, 2006). Teachers who have more experience creating than their peers are likely to do more creating with students or to engage students more frequently in creative musical experiences (Odena & Welsh, 2007). In other words, teachers' conceptions of themselves as creative people—what you believe about yourself—impacts what teachers do.

Adult thinking about creativity, including musical creativity, is linked to past and present experiences. Teachers derive ideas about musical creativity from their own music-making, from teacher preparation courses, and from their teaching experiences both in school and outside of school (Odena & Welch, 2007, 2009). Further, similar to the learning of children, both formal and informal experiences contribute to adult conceptions of creativity. For example, an informal conversation with or an observation of a colleague who is adept at facilitating children's creativity may be as informative as a week-long seminar on the topic. Similarly, childhood memories of teacher-learner interactions may have as much to do with teaching practice as an undergraduate course. Still, teachers who have experienced improvisation and other musical creating in the teacher preparation coursework tend to enact these kinds of engagements in their practices (Koutsoupidou, 2005). And, while individuals who have more music knowledge and experience tend to be more comfortable engaging in musical creating than those who have less knowledge and experience (Clennon, 2009; Kennedy, 2004), those who have *diverse* music-making experiences, including informal music-making, tend to view musical creativity more broadly than their peers (Odena & Welsh, 2009). On the other hand, experience can also constrain conceptions of musical creativity when individuals want to "get it right," conform to an artificial model or standard, or insist that music theory knowledge precede creative musical engagements (Kennedy, 2004; Stauffer, 2001b). One of the potential values of informal experiences in life and even in teacher preparation may be that they are more open-ended and even playful, allowing adults to lighten up and explore ideas that may become catalysts to creative thinking or (for teachers) to changes in practice (Koops & Taggart, 2010).

The creativity of adults, particularly teachers, is important to children because teachers provide role models for creative thinking, and what teachers think about creativity in general as well as their own creative capacities is projected in their pedagogy (Csikszentmihalyi, Rathunde, & Whalen, 1993; Hogg, 1994; Randles, 2009). Sternberg & Williams (1996) suggest that "the most powerful way to develop creativity in your students is to be a role model. Children develop creativity not when you tell them to, but when you show them." Teachers who are excited about the subject matter, who continue to nurture and invest in their own knowledge and abilities (in this case, their own musical and creative experiences), and who effectively communicate their interest, excitement, and curiosity appear to be memorable to students as well as effective in arousing students' curiosity and promoting their intrinsic motivation to create (Csikszentmihalyi, Rathunde, & Whalen, 1993; Odena & Welsh, 2007). While adults, particularly teachers, may feel constrained by impersonal curricular mandates and educational policies that stifle individuality, attending to one's own creative impulse and need for renewal in any number of ways can make a difference not only in personal perspective but also in how music educators think about, facilitate, and engage in creative music-making with students (Jaffurs, 2004; Odena & Welsh, 2009; Randles, 2009).

Projects

- Inventory your personal creativity, or write your own creativity autobiography. Do you consider yourself a creative person? Why or why not? What kinds of activities do you engage in or what kinds of things do you do that *you* consider creative. How does it feel to create? Have you had any high points or low points? What contributed to those?
- Nurture your own creativity in some way. Choose a project that might be as small as doing an ordinary activity in a different way (e.g., grocery shopping at your favorite supermarket but going through the aisles in the opposite direction than you usually do, or driving to school via a different route) or something more involved that interests you. Your project does not have to be in music. Keep track of your experience. What did you see, hear, feel, notice? Share your experience and observations with a colleague.

RELATED READINGS

- In the final chapter of *Explaining Creativity: The Science of Human Innovation* (2006), Keith Sawyer provides a list of ways to practice creativity, as well as suggested readings and some cautions about creativity myths.
- E. Paul Torrance, one of the founders of the gifted and talented education movement in the 1960s, wrote a 30-page monograph entitled "Creativity: What Research Says to the Teacher" (1963). Although it is an older source, the suggestions and observations derived from Torrance's research remain interesting for contemporary readers. Compare Torrance's suggestions for teachers to those of Sternberg and Williams (1996).
- The articles by Jaffurs and Randles cited in the section above provide interesting examples of music educators extending their own creativity.

WHAT DO YOU BELIEVE ABOUT CREATIVITY AND EDUCATION?

As noted earlier, the word "creativity" appears not only in the discourse of researchers and educators, but also in that of politicians, policy makers, and the popular press, with the implication that creativity is something to be enacted in order to achieve certain ends, including educational ones. This is nothing new. In 1967, in the lead article of the first issue of the *Journal of Creative Behavior*, J.P. Guilford, one of the key figures in the history of creativity research, wrote that "creativity is the key to education in its fullest sense, and to the solution of mankind's most serious problems" (p. 13). He was not alone. Other creativity researchers and educators of Guilford's era, most notably E. Paul Torrance, developed and popularized educational creativity programs targeted specifically at identifying and educating children who, as adults, could help the United States compete in and win the space race as well as solve other perceived economic, scientific, and social problems. Prior to the 1960s, Graham Wallas, an economist and member of the London (England) County Council and Education Committee, wrote a book entitled *The Art of Thought* (1926) in which he claimed that young people who had a well-developed "art of thinking," could help humankind avoid disasters such as war and solve problems brought about by the less-than-positive consequences of the Industrial Revolution. In other words, better thinking—creative thinking—could help solve social problems.

Decades later, the inclusion of creativity or creative thinking in education as a means of solving social problems remains a popular notion. In 1999, the British National Advisory Committee on Creative and Cultural Education described creative and cultural education as a crucial investment in human capital. They defined creative education as "forms of education that develop young people's capacities for original ideas and actions" and cultural education as "forms of education that enable them to engage positively with the growing complexity and diversity of social values and ways of life" (Robinson, et al, 1999, p. 5). In online talks, public lectures, and books, Ken Robinson, chair of the committee and Professor at the University of Warwick, notes that "creativity now is as important in education as literacy, and we should treat it with the same status" (Robinson, n.d.). In 2002, the U.S. Partnership for 21st Century Skills released its first white paper, identifying "creativity and intellectual curiosity" as one of the key learning skills (p. 9). Other contemporary writers describe creativity as part of the "knowledge economy" in the marketplace of social, political, and economic ideas in contemporary societies and therefore crucial in education (Peters, Marginson, & Murphy, 2009).

Two important (and potentially competing) shifts in the history of thinking about creativity in education are worth noting. First, moves toward including creative thinking in education in the 1960s were aimed primarily at so-called talented and gifted children who, it was thought, could be identified through testing and given enriched instruction that would enable them to perform at high levels and develop into leaders and innovators in any number of domains and disciplines. Today, creative thinking tends to be viewed as a capacity or potential of every child and more broadly conceived, though specialized programs or differentiated instruction for students with extraordinary abilities still exist. Second, descriptions of creativity as part of the "knowledge economy" point to a potentially troubling commodification of creativity and objectification of creative thinking as something that can be measured, traded upon, and even bought and sold in a power politics of organizations, corporations, and nations where the individual and her abilities and initiatives may become lost or beside the point. Inasmuch as power and politics have also to do with access and equity, which continue to be problematic in education as well as in other facets of contemporary societies, discourses that commodify or objectify creativity and creative thinking or that relegate creativity and creative thinking to the privilege of some at the expense of others must be actively challenged.

The view in this chapter is that creativity is a mindset, a way of being. Creative thinking involves curiosity, questioning, wondering, exploration, problem-finding, problem-solving, and even making errors. Arts education researchers suggest that educational practices that acknowledge and respect children's thinking, allow children to ask questions and to construct or co-construct knowledge in interactions with peers and adults, and foster children's sense of agency in the learning process can support their creative capacities and empower them as creative thinkers (Connery, John-Steiner, & Marjonvic-Shane, 2010). Such an approach—one that views engagement in music as empowering, expressive, and meaningful for children in their own right—may be consistent with historical and contemporary ideas about the potential of educational experiences to foster individual and collective creative thinking and, potentially, transform societies and cultures for the better.

Projects

- Search for commentary about education and creativity in the popular press and media. What messages are communicated about the value of creativity or creative thinking? To whom or for whom? What assumptions about creativity, education, politics, or the marketplace underpin these discourses?
- Examine contemporary and/or historical curriculum documents in music and in other disciplines for statements about creativity or creative thinking. Consider both what is said and what is not said. How restrictive or open-ended are the statements you find? How is creativity defined or described? What do the documents imply about the creativity of children? Of adults? About the value of creativity or creative thinking?

RELATED READINGS

- Robinson's revised edition of *Out of Our Minds: Learning to be Creative* (2011) provides one perspective about the ways in which thinking about education and creativity intersect (or not) in the twenty-first century.
- The authors of *Vygotsky and Creativity: A Cultural-Historical Approach to Play, Meaning Making, and the Arts* (Connery, John-Steiner, and Marjonovic-Shane, 2010) provide multiple examples of ways in which educators can facility children's creative thinking.

Constructing a Pedagogy

The second section of this chapter invites thinking about the pedagogy of creating in music. Pedagogy, the topic of this section, is linked to beliefs or guiding principles, the topic of the previous section. The pedagogical practices of someone who believes that creative thinking in music occurs in multiple ways, that children are creative in their own right, that creative thinking continues to evolve in adult life, and that educational environments can support creative thinking in music are likely to be different from the pedagogical practices of those who hold different points of view. Beliefs and practices are connected.

Like many other practices, pedagogy requires creative thinking. It involves not only advance planning, but also constant decision-making and adjustment as teachers engage with children and their complex, evolving social and musical worlds. This section focuses on four broad categories of pedagogical thinking relative to preparing to engage children in musical creating: freedoms and constraints involved in decisions about creative thinking experiences and tasks included in education contexts; considerations regarding the social conditions of musical creating; supporting and responding to children's musical creative thinking in progress; and the multiple roles of adults in children's creative music-making.

FREEDOMS AND CONSTRAINTS IN PEDAGOGICAL DECISIONS ABOUT MUSICAL CREATIVE THINKING

One of the paradoxes in the creativity literature and even in definitions of creativity has to do with freedom and constraint. For example, product-oriented definitions of creativity often include both the implied freedom of novelty and the implied constraint of usefulness. Process-oriented definitions of creativity focus on both the divergent thinking needed to arrive at new ideas and the convergent thinking used to verify them. Person-oriented definitions describe creative individuals as having "a great deal of curiosity and openness on one hand, and an almost obsessive perseverance on the other" (Csikszentmihalyi, 1996, p. 326). Place-oriented definitions suggest that transformations of a domain are "creative" only to the extent that others in the field recognize them as so, either in the moment or further along in history. From any of these perspectives, creativity or creative thinking is a matter of both freedom *and* constraint.

Pedagogy at its best is creative thinking about teaching and learning in action, and several paradoxes related to freedom and constraint lie at the heart of pedagogical thinking in music. The nature and value of experience is one of these paradoxes. For example, researchers who study the lives and works of novelists and poets note that personal experiences, particularly the observations and feelings associated with experience, are often the capital for literary creativity (Johnson, 2006; Moran, 2010). Other scholars articulate the commonsense notion that we are unlikely to create in any meaningful way a domain in which we lack experience (e.g., Csikszentmihalyi, 1996). At the very least, creative thinking begins with what we already know and feel, tacitly or implicitly, based on our experiences. On the other hand, experience can become associated with tunnel vision, entrenched thinking, or the psychological problem of functional fixedness,[3] in which familiarity with an object or a way to solve a problem inhibits the ability to see alternatives, overcome what one already knows, or be playful with ideas (Finke, Ward, & Smith, 1992; Sternberg, 2003; Weisberg, 1988).

A crucial question for educators, then, is what kinds of experiences support the development of creative thinking in music? Here music educators must confront one of their own historical functional fixedness problems. In curriculum documents and teaching texts, the word "create" frequently appears with "compose," "improvise," or "arrange," implying that musical creativity occurs in tasks and lessons having to do with these specific kinds of musical engagements. But this view constrains pedagogical thinking in that it valorizes certain traditions and is antithetical to the notion that creative thinking can permeate all kinds of musical engagements in all kinds of musical cultures, including the cultures of children. Further, it points toward musical creating as an *event*-centered practice (as in the making of a piece to be created, rehearsed, and performed) rather than a continuously lived and living *person*-centered experience available to everyone in all kinds of musical interactions. Pedagogical practices in which teachers promote creative thinking and encourage playfulness with musical ideas while singing, playing, and listening are as vital to musical creative thinking as lessons focused specifically on composing, improvising, or other creative engagements. Questioning practices that encourage curiosity, exploration, and wonder during performing and listening as well as during improvising and composing aim toward creative thinking as a disposition to be nurtured in every musical activity *as well as* an ability related to the invention of new musical gestures and pieces. A "both-and" pedagogical perspective that views all musical activity as an opportunity for creative thinking *and* that includes specific music creating projects may be crucial for learners on the younger end of the educational spectrum.

Another pedagogical paradox has to do with the freedom and constraints imbedded or implied in activities aimed specifically at musical creativity, including composing and improvising. To what extent should tasks be opened or closed? What kinds of parameters, if any, should be provided in creative projects? How do children perceive freedoms and constraints, and how does this impact their creative thinking? Researchers who have studied children as they compose and improvise have found that different children respond to the same tasks in varied ways, depending on their learning styles, backgrounds and experiences, and self-concepts as musical creators (Beegle, 2010; Burnard, 1995; Stauffer, 2003). While children's individual preferences for freedom and constraint vary (Bucura & Weissburg, 2011; Smith, 2008), they tend to respond more positively and to create in more musical ways when tasks or projects are authentically musical rather than theoretical, when they can experiment with sounds as they create rather than working without sound (as in notating without hearing), when they have opportunities to generate their own ideas, and when they perceive opportunities to create as relevant and meaningful (Barrett, 2003; Beegle, 2010; Kaschub, 1999; Wiggins, 2002).

What does this mean for pedagogy? Burnard (1995) suggests that teachers differentiate between "instructional" tasks for learning information or techniques and "composition" tasks in which children have creative and expressive agency. Instructional tasks tend to be more constrained and are often designed to provide children with experience using new tools or techniques, much like an exploratory experience or an etude. While these types of tasks are useful in that they provide children with a growing fund of knowledge and information, instructional tasks typically are different from compositional tasks in terms of creative agency, musical intention, and sense of purpose. For example, creating an eight-measure piece that uses different dynamics is an instructional task; creating a piece of music that would be good for putting a baby to sleep or feeling calm is a compositional task. The instructional task results in an etude using dynamics that children would be unlikely to create on their own outside of the instructional environment and that they would probably not identify as their own music. However, creating calming music is something children *may* do on their own apart from the educational environment, and the result may be something children refer to as their own song or music. Both tasks provide an opportunity to learn about dynamics, particularly when the compositional task includes opportunities for children to talk about their music with an adult or more knowledgeable peer who can help them label what they have created. The implication here is that both instructional and compositional tasks, as defined by Burnard, can be useful, as long as educators are conscious about what is learned and the extent to which the experience engages creative thinking and develops children's identities and agency as musical creators.

Finally, evidence from studies of children as composers suggests that time, tools, and techniques are interactive in their musical creative thinking processes (Stauffer, 2001a, 2009b). For example, when presented with a new sound source or medium, children frequently need time to find out how it works and what it sounds like before shifting into a creating experience. As children become familiar with tools and techniques *and* as they have time, including repeated opportunities, to create with them, they become more fluid, adept, and confident as musical creators. While music educators are appropriately concerned about amount of instructional time, children can and do engage in musical creative thinking and grow in their abilities to invent their own musical worlds even within the limited time frames in school and studio lesson settings (Miller, 2004, 2012). A pedagogical attitude that accepts all music experiences as opportunities to develop creative thinking as well as an awareness that children are musically creative outside of school contexts can reshape notions of time restrictions. Time invested in musical creative thinking is well worth the effort. Simply put, children get better at composing by composing (Kaschub, 1999; Kennedy, 2004; Stauffer, 2002); they get better at creative thinking in music through experiences that involve creative thinking in, through, and with music. A pedagogy that supports and nurtures creative thinking in multiple ways *within* learning environments may ultimately enhance the creative musical engagements of children where they happen the most—in their daily lives.

Projects

- Brainstorm lists of questions you might ask, as a leader or teacher, that open opportunities for musical creative thinking when children are singing, playing instruments, or listening to music. Consider how your questions might cultivate a disposition for musical creative thinking.
- Explore published sources and curriculum guides for materials, lessons, or activities related to engaging children in creating music. What freedoms and constraints are articulated or implied in the materials you find? To what degree do children have agency? How musically authentic are the suggested tasks?
- In a methods class or with a group, experiment with creating music using different media to accomplish the same musical purposes. For example, create a piece of music for walking through your neighborhood at night. Use only voice and body sounds. Then make a second piece (and separate) piece using only a recorder. Then make a third piece using only a software program such as Morton Subotnick's *Making Music*. Consider how time, tools, and techniques interact and impact your pieces. What are the constraints in this set of tasks? What does your musical experience and life experience contribute to the music you create? Did you experience any functional fixedness? If you chose to listen to peers' pieces in between each task, how did listening to others influence your own ideas?

RELATED READINGS

- Several authors have written about freedom and constraints and/or different kinds of task structures in creative music experiences for children, including Barrett (2003), Bucura & Weissberg (2011), Kaschub and Smith (2009, see Chapter 3), Smith (2008), and Wiggins (2002).
- Blair (2006, 2007, 2009) and Dunn (1997, 2006) provide examples of ways in which a disposition of creative thinking might be encouraged through listening experiences and listening maps.

SOCIAL CONDITIONS OF MUSICAL CREATING

One of the enduring questions in creativity research in general has to do with the balance of social context and individual psychological processes (Sawyer, et al., 2003). Like the pedagogical paradoxes of the previous section, the individual and social are not oppositional binaries; they coexist. Whatever children create (and even when and how they create) has some connection to their social worlds, and at least to some extent, children rely on others to provide support (directly or indirectly) for their creative engagements. In fact, some of the leading creativity theorists argue that creativity is "an emergent property of the group, field, or society, rather than a property of individuals" (see Sawyer, et al, 2003, pp. 227).

While children may invent music on their own and with others in all kinds of contexts, this section focuses specifically on pedagogical questions and decisions music educators make when they work primarily with children in school or other group settings. Some concerns are immediate and (on the surface) practical: When creating music, will children work on their own or in groups? In groups of their own choice or groups arranged by the teacher? In same-gender groups or mixed-gender groups? What size should the groups be? Other pedagogical decisions require thinking about longer-term concerns: Should the groups stay together for several projects or regroup? When and how should individuals or groups working apart from each other share their work? Other concerns have to do with the dynamics of individual voices and ideas within group composition experiences. Are all children's voices heard and ideas expressed in group creating situations or do some children dominate? What happens to different working styles or ways of expressing musical ideas when children work in groups?

Fortunately, the music education literature includes numerous examples of children creating music in pairs (e.g., Macdonald, Miell, & Mitchell, 2002), in small groups (e.g., Beegle, 2010; Burland & Davidson, 2001; Wiggins, 1994), and in whole class projects or within the context of large groups (e.g., Koutsoupidou & Hargreaves, 2009; Miller, 2004), as well as examples of children creating music on their own (e.g., Miller, 2012; Smith, 2008; Stauffer, 2001, 2002). Although not all of these studies occurred in school contexts, the results of these investigations as well as the experiences of music educators and the informal observations of parents and other adults indicate that children are successful creators of music both on their own *and* in groups. Further, some children may benefit from exchanges with peers or with older collaborators when engaged in group musical creating (Macdonald, Miell, & Mitchell, 2002; Wiggins, 2000). These observations are consistent with Vygotsky's theory that children co-construct knowledge through socially situated action (Moran & John-Steiner, 2003).

The music education literature is rather silent, however, on questions having to do with how to arrange groups for small-group creating experiences. The cooperative learning research in general education suggests that group sizes ranging from two to several can be effective (Slavin, 2011), but little is known about the effects of group size in relationship to the ages and stages of musical development or group creative experiences in music. We also know little about whether different group sizes are more or less effective for different kinds of musical tasks, or about the relationship between group size and learning style of the individual. The general education literature *does* suggest that children's ability to work effectively in groups cannot be assumed, and that children who give elaborate explanations in group contexts learn more than their peers (Slavin, 2011). For now, music educators must rely on pedagogical literature (e.g., Kaplan & Stauffer, 1994; Kassner, 2002; Kaschub & Smith, 2009), thoughtful observation, questioning, and prompts that encourage all students to talk, and commonsense considerations of class or ensemble dynamics when children work in groups.

Gender and friendships are also important social considerations when children create music together, and here the music education literature provides more information. In a study of eleven-year-olds creating music in groups of six, the researchers arranged children in groups both randomly and by different combinations of friendship and gender (Burland & Davidson, 2001). They found that although the music children produced was not affected by the type of social grouping, their social interaction and enjoyment of the composition tasks was affected; children in single-gender groups of friends enjoyed the tasks more. In a different study, a researcher found boys' motivation to compose was lower than girls' motivation at the beginning of the investigation (Leung, 2008). By the end of the study, however, the boys' self-efficacy scores had increased. The results of these studies do *not* mean that children should create music in only single-gender groups of friends or that boys' motivation to compose is lower than that of girls. Initial hesitation to create should not be mistaken for resistance to creating, and enjoyment of tasks, while important, is not the only consideration in learning experiences. Rather, these studies point to gender and friendship as social considerations in children's music creating experiences specifically and in music pedagogy in general.

While gender may *seem* an immediate and practical concern ("Should children work in same-gender or mixed-gender groups?"), gender is a social construction that is a crucial component of children's developing identities. Children glean information about gender and identity and learn about gender roles, including ideas about gender and music, through their social interactions with family and friends, in the community, in the media, and in school. Gender discourses (e.g., girls are nice and boys are strong; all children have a mother and a father) are powerful and pervasive. By ages eight to ten, children are well aware of gendered musical practices, and may talk about music, including their own compositions, in gendered ways (Charles, 2004). The same research also shows that teachers have gendered music ideologies, use gendered language about music, and even have gendered expectations about the music boys and girls should create. In as much as teachers are key social players in the formative years of childhood, thoughtful consideration of the ways in which language and action communicate gendered messages to children about themselves and about the music they create must be a crucial concern for developing pedagogy and practices.

Group creating experiences fit well with the time constraints of music education in schools and in other settings where music educators work with children in groups. Children are individuals with their own creative impulses, however, and they do have idiosyncratic working styles as well as distinctive and individual compositional identities and voices (Miller, 2012; Stauffer, 2002, 2003). Group creating experiences assume an overlap of the sociocultural and personal musical experiences of children, and that children are able to negotiate a shared space and find meaning together given their differences. While that may be the case, it is also likely that some cultural and social norms, some kinds of music gestures, and some ways of thinking will prevail over others within group creating experiences. Children as young as fourth grade are aware of and able to articulate the differences in their own experience when creating music individually and in groups, and as with freedoms and constraints, children have preferences for individual and group tasks (Bucura & Weissburg, 2011). For all of these reasons, music educators' pedagogical decision-making should include consideration of the balance of individual and group creative musical thinking opportunities.

Projects

- In a methods class or study group, compose a piece of music on your own. Make notes or write a reflection about your ideas, your process, and your satisfaction with your work. Then, compose a piece with a colleague or in a small group, and make similar notes or write a reflection. On your own, compare your experiences in these two different social conditions, then talk about your observations with others.
- Observe children on the playground or an athletic field, in a classroom, or in a music setting. Notice their interactions—their work or play in groups or on their own. How do they interact? Who controls the group dynamics? If a teacher or another adult is present, how does that person organize, manage, or monitor groups? If possible, focus on one group working or playing together. Where do their ideas come from and how do they exchange them? What roles do they assume on their own? Who is included and how do they include each other and their ideas? Who is excluded or silent?
- Think about the ways in which gender and music are associated in your experience. Do you associate different kinds of music, certain instruments, or particular musical roles with gender? Do you see evidence of such associations in your social and musical experiences? What is the impact or message of these associations? Then consider the ways in which your own talk, actions, and thinking about music reflect ideas about gender when interacting with children. If possible, record yourself working with a group of children or teaching several individual lessons. Does your tone of voice, inflection, or type of language change (questions, directives, information, requests) depending on the gender of the child? Do you encourage or allow different kinds of choices depending on gender? Do you call more often on students of one gender than another? What gendered expectations do you have (if any) about what instruments the children will play, what their music would sound like, their ability to work together (if in groups), or the nature of their social interactions?

RELATED READINGS

- Wiggins (2003) describes how children compose in elementary classroom groups and how individuals function within those groups in "A Frame for Understanding Children's Compositional Processes." Stauffer (2003) discusses individual children's work in "Identity and Voice in Young Composers."

- In *Minds on Music: composition for Creative and Critical Thinking*, Kaschub and Smith (2009) discuss features of both individual and group composition, and provide suggestions for classroom composing as well as lesson suggestions.
- Kassner (2002) provides information about cooperative learning and grouping students in music contexts.
- Bergonzi (2009) asks critical questions of all music educators about music education practices and gender in "Sexual Orientation and Music: Continuing a Tradition."

SUPPORTING CHILDREN'S CREATIVE PROCESSES

In addition to the matters of freedom and constraint, task and time, and social and individual opportunities articulated above, pedagogy also involves knowing what to do once plans are implemented and children are actively engaged in creating. As suggested earlier, if creative thinking in music is a disposition that can be nurtured in every possible musical engagement, then strategies such as questioning and problem posing can be used in-the-moment to prompt creative thinking throughout all music experiences. However, when children are engaged specifically in inventing their own music, additional strategies that sustain the environment for creating and attend to the different stages and phases of children's creative processes can be useful.

The general creativity literature suggests that creative thinking begins with both generating and exploring ideas (Finke, Ward, & Smith, 1992). In the music education literature, creative thinking is often described as beginning with exploration or experimentation (Kratus, 1989, 1994; Webster, 1990, 2002). Musical exploration in action may look and sound like play, trial-and-error, stopping and starting, or simply messing around with sounds and gestures. And, although exploration frequently appears to have something to do with finding an initial musical gesture or starting place, part of children's experimentation may also have to do with finding a timbre or group of timbres they prefer (Beegle, 2010; Stauffer, 2002). Some researchers suggest that children's early explorations (when working in groups) include conversation in which they define a musical problem for themselves or redefine a musical problem posed by the teacher (Burnard & Younker, 2004; DeLorenzo, 1989; Wiggins, 1994). Taken together, these data suggest that allowing time for the sometimes chaotic and noisy business of exploration, as well as demonstrating curiosity about children's sonic experimentation are pedagogical strategies that support creative thinking in music.

As children move past initial stages of exploring into what some researchers describe as development of their musical ideas (Beegle, 2010; Kratus, 1989; Wiggins, 1994), adults in the environment must continue to find ways to support them while allowing children's creative impulses to remain their own. This can be a tricky pedagogical business, for research grounded in social psychology suggests that creativity is fueled by internal motivation and constrained by external pressures, including the perception of surveillance, the need to feel competent, or concern with what others think (Amabile, 1996; Hickey, 1997). While different writers have demonstrated the ways in which extrinsic motivators, such as rewards and competition, can dampen creativity and even, in the some circumstances, discourage preteen and teenage children from continuing to engage in particular domains or activities (Amabile, 1996; Csikszentmihalyi, 1996; Csikszentmihalyi, Rathunde, & Whalen, 1993; Hickey, 1997), other researchers suggest that, like freedoms and constraints, different children respond in different ways to external motivators and social conditions such as rewards, competition, and even ordinary feedback (Hennessey, 2003).

Feedback is one of the most subtle and pervasive social conditions of educational environments; teachers are responsible for monitoring progress individual and group progress, and particularly at younger ages, children may be eager to share their work. Seemingly innocuous verbal feedback comments that teachers intend as encouragement (e.g., "good job") may have the effect of halting creativity in progress when children, particularly young children, perceive the remark as a signal that they are "done" or have satisfied the task and/or the teacher. Conversely, feedback, commentary, or questions that provide information *to* children or request information *from* them tend to feed intrinsic motivation and fuel creative thinking momentum (Amabile, 1996; Bledsoe & Boyajian, 2011; Bucura & Weissburg, 2011). Questions or requests such as "How did you work that out" or "Explain what this part is about" demonstrate interest in the children's ideas and invite them to articulate their own thinking and intentions. What children say or do in response may propel intrinsic motivation and the propensity to continue as well as cue adults about information needed in the present or kinds of instructional or creative projects to plan for the future. Similar kinds of feedback questions and commentary (e.g., "Where did this idea come from" or "How will these two ideas connect?") as well as "wonderments"[4] or provocations (e.g., "I wonder what's going to happen next" or "What's going to make a good ending?") can also be helpful in keeping the creative process going, stimulating further interest, or solving the pedagogical problem of staying on task when individuals or groups feel stuck or "finish" before their peers.

One of the challenges for those preparing to engage children in musical creating has to do with their varying ages and stages of development among them. Music educators in elementary schools may work with students in early, middle, and late stages of childhood. How a five-year-old child thinks and learns is quite different, in some respects, than how a twelve-year-old student thinks and learns. Part of pedagogical expertise involves knowing how to adjust tasks and feedback to support children's creative musical thinking given differences in their individual and group abilities, learning styles, experiences, and stages of cognitive, emotional, and social development. This is particularly important when considering revision in creative work, including whether and how children revise and what teachers can do to support the process of revision. Webster (2012) defines revision as "active consideration of new material in the face of old with the idea of improving a final product," and emphasizes that helping young composers learn how to revise their music is crucial to children's learning and a critical responsibility of teacher. Balancing student agency and instructional goals may be one of the most challenging pedagogical puzzles educators face. It may be helpful to consider the different meanings of the word "revision" and how they play out in the creative thinking of children at different stages of development.

For example, Webster (2012) provides an excellent description of a sixth-grade boy, Carson, who composes music both in school and at home on his own. Carson responds positively to suggestions from teachers in school and in a lesson-like environment outside of school, particularly when the teachers are sensitive to his intentions and ask him questions that help both Carson and the adults know what he wants to accomplish. As a result of their interactions, Carson makes revisions that improve his music both in his own estimation and that of the adults in Webster's account. In Carson's story, revision occurs to single pieces in progress over multiple sessions, and, based on Carson's case and his own extensive research, Webster provides teachers with excellent pedagogical suggestions for composition in general and revision in particular.

In contrast to revision of a single piece of music over multiple sessions, younger children have different revision strategies. In a different case study, Meg, a third-grade student, revises her musical ideas not by continuing to work on the same piece over time, but rather by making a new (and separate) piece using the same idea in each session several weeks in a row (Stauffer, 2001a). This is an important developmental distinction that appears to align with a developmental shift in children's creative thinking in music and music cognition that occurs somewhere between ages 7 and 9 (e.g., Brophy, 2002, 2005; Kiehn, 2003; Younker, 2000). Similar to researcher observations, anecdotal information from art and classroom teachers suggests that while young children may develop an idea in progress within a single session, they revise their ideas (and improve in fluency and facility) over time *not* by returning to and revising single drawings or stories over several sessions, but rather by making new drawings or stories using the same or similar ideas. This developmental difference may be linked to children's perception of time, including past and future. Young children's attention is to the immediate; what they finish one day is "done," and they are ready to start anew. Older children are more ready and more able to think forward and backward in time and, as a result, appear to be more likely to continue working on and revising ideas in a single piece over multiple sessions. Taken together, the implication for pedagogy is that a "both-and" perspective is also useful when considering how to support children's development and revision of ideas: both opportunities to revise ideas and pieces over time *and repeated opportunities to create* different pieces that use the same ideas, tools, or techniques support children's musical creative thinking.

Repeated opportunities to create music may also be valuable developmentally and pedagogically in another way. Throughout the creative literature, writers refer to instances of an idea occurring during time away from actual work on a creative task—a phenomenon similar to what Wallas described as incubation and illumination in his 1926 *The Art of Thought*. Like adults, children need think time, both in the midst of creating and during time away from creating. Children's tendency to "play around" during moments when teachers believe they should be on task may be means of working through or "incubating" an idea. When work on a single project extends over multiple sessions, encouraging children to think about their work until they return can promote incubation. Creative thinking does not necessarily occur on demand or pop up conveniently in the middle of a lesson. Educators should be aware that children's best ideas and most productive creative thinking may occur *not* when they are in the classroom, but when they are on their own and when they feel most like creating.

Finally, creative pedagogical thinking should also be directed toward two opportunities that occur at the end of the creative process or the conclusion of a creative thinking project in music: the opportunity to present or perform what has been created, and the opportunity to reflect and assess. Children deserve and should be permitted opportunities to share through performance or demonstration music they have created in both informal ways and in formal settings. Anything less subverts the value and ownership children feel in their own work and diminishes intrinsic motivation to create by emphasizing their ability to recreate the music of others over their ability to create and share their own music. Sharing their work is not necessarily part of assessment, however, assessment is part of educational environments and cannot be ignored. While teachers may feel nervous about assessing children's creative work, assessment in the form of both rubrics and reflection, particularly when collaborative with children instead of leveraged against them, are part of learning. (Assessment is covered in detail elsewhere in this book.) By providing children with opportunities to share their creative work *and* to reflect on their musical creative experiences, educators provide them opportunities to develop habits of curiosity, courage, and openness associated with a creative disposition in music.

Projects

- Consider how intrinsic and extrinsic motivators have impacted your own creative work or thinking. When you created something (in music or otherwise), why did you do it? For personal enjoyment? To fulfill an assignment? For yourself or someone else? For a social purpose or an event? How did different creative experiences and different kinds of motivators feel, or how did you respond?
- Develop a list of questions, prompts, and provocations or wonderments that can be used to support children's intrinsic motivation and fuel or maintain the moment of their creative processes. Consider the ways in which the questions and statements on your list invite children to extend their own thinking. In observations of children with others or in your own work with children, note

how children respond to intrinsic and extrinsic motivators, including feedback statements.

- Observe children in the process of creating their own music, and, if possible, watch children of different ages or developmental levels. Make notes about the ways in which children work—their questions, their processes, their thinking, how they use time, how they generate ideas, and so on. Look for similarities and differences between younger and older children.
- Observe children in an art education setting. What happens when one child or group of children "finish" before others? Consider the question from both child and teacher perspectives.

RELATED READINGS

- In an essay that encourages teachers to embrace their own agency, Webster (2012) provides numerous suggestions for developing a pedagogy of composition that is respectful of students' intentions while also encouraging revision and development of their ideas. See also his 2003 essay on revision.
- Kaschub and Smith (2009) provide numerous suggestions for prompting and extending creative thinking in progress in *Minds on Music: composition for Creative and Critical Thinking.*

THE MULTIPLE ROLES OF ADULTS

"Everything depends on the *quality* of experience which is had," Dewey wrote in *Education and Experience* (1938, p. 27). Dewey believed for experiences to be educative, educators were responsible for attending to multiple matters: the capacities of the students; the extent to which experiences were interesting and relevant to students and their worlds; the interactions of students with each other, the teacher, and the community; the ways in which an experience aroused in the learner a quest for more information and the production of new ideas; and the potential for the learning and ideas derived from one experience to become the grounds for the next. Certainly, Dewey's challenge to educators of his time continues to ring true. To act upon his challenge in a pedagogy that supports children's creative thinking in music requires of music educators the capacity to confront personal and systemic constraints, the courage to take risks, and a good deal of commitment.

Like creative thinking in music, creative thinking in pedagogy is bound by freedom and constraints. Discourses that advocate for creative thinking compete with (often louder) criticisms of schools as environments that somehow manage to extinguish children's creativity. While educators may be intrinsically motivated to enact a pedagogy that supports creative thinking, they also cope with discourses that criticize them (usually as a faceless group) for failing to enact impersonalized and restrictive curricula to meet a mandated measurable standard. In addition to feeling caught between competing challenges and constraints of current and historical social and political ideologies, educators may feel personal constraints related to their own conceptions of creativity and creative thinking in music, the creative capacities of children, and their own pedagogical and creative abilities. Enacting a pedagogy that supports children's creative thinking can be challenging in multiple ways.

Overcoming personal, professional, and political constraints and moving toward a pedagogical practice that nurtures children's creative musical abilities requires the courage to take risks and to cultivate one's own curiosity, wonder, and interest in creating. Transforming pedagogy may also require the courage to shift or redefine the relationship of teacher and student as one that is more collaborative than didactic, and to redefine the relationship between the content of the curriculum and those for whom it is intended. After all, teachers do not teach subjects (music). Rather, "they assist *children* in their attempts to learn by becoming familiar with and addressing the unique needs of their students," including their need to create music, and by creating environments that facilitate meaning making that occurs in and through creating (Marjanovic-Shane, Connery, John-Steiner, 2010, p. 223).

Children have no need of adults to be creative; they are musically playful and inventive on their own. The commitment adults can make to children—what adults can do in schools and elsewhere—is to enact pedagogies that develop communities of creative musical practice, that extend children's musical capacities, and that nurture and support creative thinking as a disposition—a fundamental part of human life. Children deserve nothing less.

Projects

- Consider the ways in which your own thinking about creative thinking in music may be constrained, either as teacher or student or musician, and then consider ways in which you can challenge yourself to move past those constraints.
- Contribute to the literature cited throughout this book by developing a project that supports children's musical creative thinking, documenting what you do, and writing about it for others.

References

Amabile, T. (1996). *Creativity in context: Update to* The social psychology creativity. Boulder, CO: Westview Press.

Barrett, M. (2001). Constructing a view of children's meaning-making as notators: A case-study of a five-year-old's descriptions and explanations of invented notations. *Research Studies in Music Education*, 16, 33–45.

Barrett, M. (2003). Freedoms and constraints: Constructing musical worlds through the dialogue of composition. In M. Hickey (Ed.), *Why and how to teach music composition: A new horizon for music education* (pp. 3–27). Reston, VA: Music Educators National Conference.

Barrett, M. (2009). Sounding lives in and through music: A narrative inquiry of the "everyday" musical engagement of a young child. *Journal of Early Childhood Research*, 7, 115–134.

Barrett, M. (2011). Musical narratives: A study of a young child's identity work in and through music making. *Psychology of Music*, 39, 403–423.

Becker, M. (1995). Nineteenth-century foundations of creativity research. *Creativity Research Journal*, 8, 612–617.

Beegle, A. (2010). A classroom-based study of small-group planned improvisation with fifth-grade children. *Journal of Research in Music Education*, 58, 219–239.

Bergonzi, L. (2009). Sexual orientation and music education: Continuing a tradition. *Music Educators Journal*, 96 (2), 21–25.

Blacking, J. (1967/1995). *Venda children's songs*. Chicago: University of Chicago Press.

Blair, D. V. (2006). Look what I heard! Music listening and student-created musical maps. (Doctoral dissertation). Retrieved from ProQuest Dissertation and Theses. (Accession Order No. AAT 3401840)

Blair, D. V. (2007). Musical maps as narrative inquiry. *International Journal of Education and the Arts*, 8 (15). Retrieved at http://www.ijea.org/v8n15/.

Blair, D. V. (2009). Learner agency: To understand and to be understood. *British Journal of Music Education*, 26, 173–187.

Blom, D. (2003). Engaging students with a contemporary music-minimalism-through-composing activities: Teachers' approaches, strategies and roles. *International Journal of Music Education*, 40, 81–99.

Bolden, B. (2009). Body parts, the water cycle, plants, and dolphins: Adventures in primary-grade whole-class composing. *General Music Today*, 22 (3), 8–13.

Bolton, J. (2008). Technologically mediated composition learning: Josh's story. *British Journal of Music Education*, 25, 41–55.

Bledsoe, R., & Boyajian, H. (2011). Teacher feedback and its effects on student creativity. Unpublished manuscript. Arizona State University.

Brophy, T. S. (2002). The melodic improvisations of children aged 6–12: A developmental perspective. *Music Education Research*, 4 (1), 73–92.

Brophy, T. S. (2005). A longitudinal study of selected characteristics of children's melodic improvisations. *Journal of Research in Music Education*, 53, 120–133.

Bucura, E., & Weissberg, J. (2011, February). *Children's Musical Empowerment and Composition Task Design*. Paper presented at the Desert Skies Symposium on Research in Music Education, University of Arizona, Tucson, Arizona.

Burland, K., & Davidson, J. W. (2001). Investigating social processes in group music composition. *Research Studies in Music Education*, 16, 46–56.

Burnard, P. (1995). Task design and experience in composition. *Research Studies in Music Education*, 5, 32–46.

Burnard, P. (2007). The individual and social worlds of children's musical creativity. In L. Bresler (Ed.), *International Handbook of Research in Arts Education, Part I* (pp. 353–374). Dordrecht, The Netherlands: Springer.

Burnard, P., & Younker, B. A. (2004). Problem-solving and creativity: Insights from students' individual composing pathways. *International Journal of Music Education*, 22, 59–76.

Campbell, P. S. (1995). Of garage bands and song-getting: The musical development of young rock musicians. *Research Studies in Music Education*, 4, 12–20.

Campbell, P. S. (2007). Musical meaning in children's cultures. In L. Bresler (Ed.), *International Handbook of Research in Arts Education, Part I* (pp. 881–894). Dordrecht, The Netherlands: Springer.

Campbell, P. S. (2010). *Songs in their heads: Music and its meaning in the lives of children.* (2nd ed.). New York: Oxford University Press.

Charles, B. (2004). Boys' and girls' constructions of gender through musical composition in the primary school. *British Journal of Music Education*, 21, 265–277.

Clennon, O. D. (2009). Facilitating musical composition as 'contract learning' in the classroom: The development and application of a teaching resource for primary school teachers in the UK. *International Journal of Music Education*, 27, 300–313.

Connery, M. C., John-Steiner, V. P., & Marjanovic-Shane, A. (2010). *Vygotsky and creativity: A cultural-historical approach to play, meaning making, and the arts.* New York: Peter Lang.

Csikszentmihalyi, M. (1996). *Creativity: Flow and the psychology of discovery and invention.* New York: Harper Collins.

Csikszentmihalyi, M., Rathunde, K., & Whalen, S. (1993). *Talented teenagers: The roots of success and failure.* Cambridge: Cambridge University Press.

Cutietta, R. A. (2001). *Raising musical kids: A guide for parents.* New York: Oxford University Press.

DeLorenzo, L. C. (1989). A field study of sixth-grade students' creative music problem-solving processes. *Journal of Research in Music Education*, 37, 188–200.

Dewey, J. (1902/1990). *The child and curriculum.* Chicago: University of Chicago Press.

Dewey, J. (1938). *Education and experience.* New York: Collier Books.

Dewey. J. (1943/1990). *The school and society.* Chicago: University of Chicago Press.

Dunn, R. E. (1997). Creative thinking and music listening. *Research Studies in Music Education*, 8, 42–55.

Dunn, R. E. (2006). Teaching for lifelong, intuitive listening. *Arts Education Policy Review*, 107 (3), 33–38.

Dzansi, M. (2004). Playground music pedagogy of Ghanaian children. *Research Studies in Music Education*, 22, 83–92.

Finke, R. A., Ward, T. B., & Smith, S. M. (1992). Creative cognition: Theory, research, and applications. Cambridge, MA: The MIT Press.

Florida, R. (2002). *The rise of the creative class.* New York, New York: Basic Books.

Green, L. (2002). *How popular musicians learn: A way ahead for music education.* Aldershot, England: Ashgate.

Green, L. (2008). *Music, informal learning and the school: A new classroom pedagogy.* Aldershot, England: Ashgate.

Guilford, J. P. (1967). Creativity: Yesterday, today, and tomorrow. *Journal of Creative Behavior*, 1, 3–14.

Harwood, E. (1993). Content and context in children's playground songs. *Update: Applications of Research in Music Education*, 12, 4–8.

Hennessey, B. A. (2003). Is the social psychology of creativity really social? Moving beyond a focus on the individual. In P.B. Paulus (Ed.), *Group creativity: Innovation through collaboration* (pp. 181–201). Oxford: Oxford University Press.

Hickey, M. (1997). The computer as a tool in creative music making. *Research Studies in Music Education*, 8, 56–70.

Hickey, M., & Webster, P. (2001). Creative thinking in music. *Music Educators Journal*, 88(1), 19–23.

Higgins, L., & Campbell, P. S. (2010). *Free to be musical: Group improvisation in music.* Lanham, MD: Rowman & Littlefield, in partnership with MENC: The National Association for Music Education.

Hogg, N. (1994). Strategies to facilitate student composing: A focus on music as an empowering agent. *Research Studies in Music Education*, 2, 15–24.

Jaffurs, S. E. (2004). The impact of informal music learning practices in the classroom, or how I learned how to teach from a garage band. *International Journal of Music Education*, 22, 189–200.

Johnson, P. (2006). *Creators: From Chaucer and Dürer to Picasso and Disney.* New York: HarperCollins.

Kaplan, P., & Stauffer, S. L. (1994). *Cooperative learning in music.* Reston, VA: Music Educators National Conference.

Kaschub, M. E. (1999). Sixth-grade students' descriptions of their individual and collaborative music composition processes and products initiated from promoted and unprompted task structures. Ph.D. Dissertation, Northwestern University. *Dissertation Abstracts International*, 60(06), 1955A.

Kaschub, M., & Smith, J. (2009). *Minds on music: Composition for creative and critical thinking.* New York: Rowman & Littlefield. Published in partnership with MENC: The National Association for Music Education.

Kassner, K. (2002). Cooperative learning revisited: A way to address the standards. *Music Educators Journal*, 88 (4), 17–23.

Kennedy, M. A. (2004). Opening the doors to creativity: A pre-service teacher experiment. *Research Studies in Music Education*, 23, 32–41.

Kiehn, M. T. (2003). Development of music creativity among elementary school students. *Journal of Research in Music Education*, 51, 278–288.

Koops, L. H. (2010). "Deñuy jangal seen bopp" (They teach themselves): Children's music learning in The Gambia. *Journal of Research in Music Education*, 58, 20–36.

Koops, L. H., & Taggart, C. C. (2010). Learning through play: Extending an early childhood music education approach to undergraduate and graduate music education. *Journal of Music Teacher Education*, 20(2), 56–66.

Koutsoupidou, T. (2005). Improvisation in the English primary classroom: Teachers' perceptions and practices. *Music Education Research*, 7, 363–381.

Koutsoupidou, T., & Hargreaves, D. J. (2009). An experimental study of the effects of improvisation on the development of children's creative thinking in music. *Psychology of Music*, 37, 251–278.

Kratus, J. (1989). A time analysis of the compositional processes used by children ages 7 to 11. *Journal of Research in Music Education*, 37, 5–20.

Kratus, J. (1994). Relationships among children's music audiation and their compositional process and products. *Journal of Research in Music Education*, 42, 115–131.

Kruse, N. B. (2012). "Sheer spine": Evoking past and present in the southern highlands. In M. S. Barrett, and S. L. Stauffer (Eds.), *Narrative soundings: An anthology of narrative inquiry in music education* (pp. 79–94). Dordrecht, The Netherlands: Springer.

Leung, B. W. (2008). Factors affecting the motivation of Hong Kong primary school students in composing music. *International Journal of Music Education*, 26, 47–62.

Lowenfeld, V., & Brittain, W. L. (1987). *Creative and mental growth* (8th ed.). Upper Saddle River, NJ: Prentice Hall.

Macdonald, R. A. R., Miell, D., & Mitchell, L. (2002). An investigation of children's musical collaborations: The effect of friendship and age. *Psychology of Music*, 30, 148–163.

Mang, E. (2005). The referent of children's early songs. *Music Education Research*, 7, 3–20.

Marjanovic-Shane, A., Connery, M. C., & John-Steiner, V. (2010). A cultural-historical approach to creative education. In M. C. Connery, V. P. John-Steiner, & A. Marjanovic-Shane (Eds.), *Vygotsky and creativity: A cultural-historical approach to play, meaning making, and the arts* (pp. 215–232). New York: Peter Lang.

Marsh, K. (1995). Children's singing games: Composition in the playground? *Research Studies in Music Education*, 4, 2–11.

Matsunobu, K. (2011). Creativity of formulaic learning: Pedagogy of imitation and repetition. In J. Sefton-Green, P. Thomson, K. Jones, & L. Bresler (Eds.), *The Routledge international handbook of creative learning* (pp. 45–53). Abingdon: Routledge.

McCord, K. A. (2004). Moving beyond "That's all I can do": Encouraging musical creativity in children with learning disabilities. *Bulletin of the Council for Research in Music Education*, 159, 23–32.

Mellor, L. (2007). Computer-based composition in the primary school: An investigation of children's "creative" responses using the CD Rom *Dance eJay*. *Musicae Scientae*, 20, 61–88.

Miller, B. A. (2004). Designing compositional tasks for elementary music classrooms. *Research Studies in Music Education*, 22, 59–71.

Miller, B. (2012). Student composition in a private studio setting: Comparing students' and parents' perceptions with teacher assumptions. In M. S. Barrett, and S. L. Stauffer (Eds.), *Narrative soundings: An anthology of narrative inquiry in music education* (p. 305–327). Dordrecht, The Netherlands: Springer.

Moran, S. (2010). Commitment and creativity: Transforming experience into art. In M. C. Connery, V. P. John-Steiner, & A. Marjanovic-Shane (Eds.), *Vygotsky and creativity: A cultural-historical approach to play, meaning making, and the arts* (pp. 141–160). New York: Peter Lang.

Moorhead, G. E., & Pond, D. (1978). *Music of young children: Pillsbury Foundation Studies*. Santa Barbara, CA: Pillsbury Foundation for Advancement of Music Education.

Mpofu, E., Myambo, K., Mogaji, A. A., Mashego, T.-A., & Kheleefa, O. H. (2006). African perspectives on creativity. In J. C. Kaufman & R.J. Sternberg, Eds., *The International Handbook of Creativity* (pp. 456–489). New York: Cambridge University Press.

Nilsson, B., & Folkestad, G. (2005). Children's practice of computer-based composition. *Music Education Research*, 7, 21–37.

Odena, O., & Welch, G. F. (2007). The influence of teachers' backgrounds on their perceptions of musical creativity: A qualitative study with secondary school music teachers. *Research Studies in Music Education*, 28, 71–81.

Odena, O., & Welch, G. (2009). A generative model of teachers' thinking on musical creativity. *Psychology of Music*, 37, 416–442.

Partnership for 21st Century Skills. (n.d.) P12 Framework Definitions. Retrieved from http://www.p21.org/, August, 2011.

Partnership for 21st Century Skills. (2002). *Learning in the 21st Century*. Washington, D.C.: Partnership for 21st Century Skills. http://www.p21.org/

Pond, D. (1981). A composer's study of young children's innate musicality. *Bulletin of the Council for Research in Music Education*, 68, 1–12.

Peters, M. A., Marginson, S., & Murphy, P. (2009). *Creativity and the global knowledge economy*. New York: Peter Lang.

Pritzker, S. R., & Runco, M. A., Eds. (1999). *Encyclopedia of Creativity*. San Diego, CA: Academic Press.

Randles, C. (2009). "That's my piece, that's my signature, and it means more . . .": Creative identity and the ensemble teacher/arranger. *Research Studies in Music Education*, 31, 52–68.

Randles, C. (2010). The relationship of compositional experiences of high school instrumentalists to music self-concept. *Bulletin of the Council for Research in Music Education*, 184, 9–20.

Robinson, K. (n.d.) http://www.ted.com/talks/ken_robinson_says_schools_kill_creativity.html

Robinson, K. (2011). *Out of our minds: Learning to be creative*. Revised edition. West Sussex, United Kingdom: Capstone Publishing Ltd.

Robinson, K., et al. (1999). *All Our Futures: Creativity, Culture, and Education*. Report of the National Advisory Committee on Creative and Cultural Education, United Kingdom. Retrieved from: http://www.google.com/url?sa=t&rct=j&q=&esrc=s&source=web&cd=1&ved=0CE4QFjAA&url=http%3A%2F%2Fsirkenrobinson.com%2Fskr%2Fpdf%2Fallourfutures.pdf&ei=G73TT67fDoGs8QSGi7zSAw&usg=AFQjCNF7dlIlqUliofnNP88EmUds4pp0Fw&sig2=hLTFrXaiU4207xeMJC9l0Q

Runco, M. A., & Charles, R. E. (1997). Developmental trends in creative potential and creative performance. In M. A. Runco, Ed., *The Creativity Research Handbook*, Vol. 1 (pp. 115–152). Cresskill, NJ: Hampton Press.

Sawyer, R. K. (2006). *Explaining creativity: The science of human innovation*. New York: Oxford University Press.

Sawyer, R. K., John-Steiner, V., Moran, S., Sternberg, R. J., Nakamura, J., & Csikszentmihalyi, M. (2003). *Creativity and development*. New York: Oxford University Press.

Schwab, J. (1983). The practical 4: Something for curriculum professors to do. *Curriculum Inquiry*, 8 (1), 5–23.

Slavin, R. E. (2011). Instruction based on cooperative learning. In R. E. Mayer & P. A. Alexander (Eds.), *Handbook of research on learning and instruction*. New York: Routledge.

Smith, J. (2008). Compositions of elementary recorder students under various conditions of task structure. *Research Studies in Music Education*, 30, 159–176.

Smith, G. J. W., & Carlsson, I. (2006). Creativity under the Northern Lights: Perspectives from Scandinavia. In J. C. Kaufman & R. J. Sternberg, Eds., *The International Handbook of Creativity* (pp. 202–234). New York: Cambridge University Press.

St. John, P. A. (2006). Finding and making meaning: Young children as musical collaborators. *Psychology of Music*, 34, 238–261.

Stauffer, S. L. (2001a). Composing with computers: Meg makes music. *Bulletin of the Council for Research in Music Education*, 150, 1–20.

Stauffer, S. L. (2001b). Pre-service and in-service teachers' perceptions of children and adolescents as composers. In Y. Minami & M. Shinzanoh, (Eds.), *Proceedings of the third Asia-Pacific symposium on music education research & international symposium on Üragoei and gender*, Volume 1 (pp. 159–164). Nagoya, Japan: Aichi Arts Center.

Stauffer, S. L. (2002). Connections between the musical and life experiences of young composers and their compositions. *Journal of Research in Music Education*, 50, 301–322.

Stauffer, S. L. (2003). Identity and voice in young composers. In M. Hickey (Ed.), *Why and how to teach music composition: A new horizon for music education* (pp. 91–111). Reston, VA: Music Educators National Conference.

Stauffer, S. L. (2009a). Placing curriculum in music education. In T. A. Regelski & J. T. Gates (Eds.), *Music education for changing times: Guiding visions for practice* (pp. 175–186). Dordrecht, The Netherlands: Springer.

Stauffer, S. L. (2009b). When children create music using technology. *The Orff Echo*, 42 (1), 30–33.

Sternberg, R. J. (2003). The development of creativity as a decision-making process. In R.K. Sawyer; V. John-Steiner; S. Moran; R. J. Sternberg; J. Nakamura; & M. Csikszentmihalyi, *Creativity and development* (pp. 91–138). New York: Oxford University Press.

Sternberg, R. J. & Williams, W. M. (1996). "Teaching for creativity: Two dozen tips." Retrieved: http://www.cdl.org/resource-library/articles/teaching_creativity.php.

Strand, K. (2006). Survey of Indiana music teachers on using composition in the classroom. *Journal of Research in Music Education*, 54, 154–167.

Sundin, B. (1998). Musical creativity in the first six years: A research project in retrospect. In B. Sundin, G.E. McPherson, & G. Folkestad (Eds.), *Children Composing* (pp. 35–56). Malmö, Sweden: Malmö Academy of Music, Lund University.

Tarnowski, S. M. & Leclerc, J. (1994). Musical play of preschoolers and teacher-child interaction. *Update: Applications of Research in Music Education*, 13 (1), 9–16.

Thompson, C. M. (2007). The arts and children's culture. In L. Bresler (Ed.), *International Handbook of Research in Arts Education, Part I* (pp. 859–863). Dordrecht, The Netherlands: Springer.

Torrance, E. P. (1963). *Creativity: What research says to the teacher*. Washington, DC: National Education Association.

Trilling, B., & Fadel, C. (2009). *21st century skills: Learning for life in our times*. San Francisco, CA: Jossey-Bass.

Waldron, J., & Veblen, K. (2009). Learning in a Celtic community: An exploration of informal music learning and adult amateur musicians. *Bulletin of the Council for Research in Music Education*, 180, 59–74.

Wallas, G. (1926). *The art of thought*. London: Johnathan Cape.

Webster, P. R. (1990). Creativity as creative thinking. *Music Educators Journal*, 76(9), 22–28.

Webster, P. (2002). Creative thinking in music: Advancing a model. In T. Sullivan, & L. Willingham (Eds.), *Creativity and music education* (pp. 16–33). Edmonton, Alberta: Canadian Music Educators' Association.

Webster, P. (2003). What do you mean, "Make my music different?" Encouraging revision and extension in children's music composition. In M. Hickey, (Ed). *Why and how to teach music composition: A new horizon for music education*. Reston VA: MENC: The National Association for Music Education.

Webster, P. (2007). Computer-based technology and music teaching and learning: 2000–2005. In L. Bresler (Ed.), *The International Handbook of Research in Arts Education* (1311–1328). Dordrecht, The Netherlands: Springer.

Webster, P. (2012). Towards pedagogies of revision: Guiding a student's music composition. In O. Odena (Ed.), *Musical creativity: Insights from music education research* (pp. 93–112). Surrey, England: Ashgate.

Weisberg, R. W. (1988). Problem solving and creativity. In R. J. Sternberg (Ed.), *The nature of creativity* (pp. 148–176). Cambridge: Cambridge University Press.

Wiggins, J. H. (1994). Children's strategies for solving composition problems with peers. *Journal of Research in Music Education*, 42, 232–252.

Wiggins, J. (2000). The nature of shared musical understanding and its role in empowering independent music learning. *Bulletin of the Council for Research in Music Education*, 143, 65–90.

Wiggins, J. (2002). Creative process as meaningful musical thinking. In T. Sullivan & L. Willingham (Eds.), *Creativity and music education* (pp. 78–88). Edmonton, Canada: Canadian Music Educators' Association National Office.

Wiggins, J. (2003). A frame for understanding children's compositional processes. In M. Hickey, Ed., *Why and How to Teach Music Composition: A New Horizon for Music Education* (pp. 141–165).

Whiteman, P. (2009). Type, function, and musical features of preschool children's spontaneous songs. In M. R. Campbell & L. Thompson (Eds.), *Research Perspectives: Thought and Practice in Music Education* (pp. 37–62). Charlotte, North Carolina: Information Age Publishing.

Young, S. (2002). Young children's spontaneous vocalizations in free-play: Observations of two- to three-year-olds in a day-care setting. *Bulletin of the Council for Research in Music Education*, 152, 43–53.

Young, S. (2003). Time-space structuring in spontaneous play on educational percussion instruments among three- and four-year-olds. *British Journal of Music Education*, 20, 45–59.

Younker, B. A. (2000). Thought processes and strategies of students engaged in music composition. *Research Studies in Music Education*, 14, 24–39.

Notes

1. This is a paraphrase of the opening sentence of *Raising Musical Kids: A Guide for Parents* (Cutietta, 2001): "Let's stop and review before we go any further." Cutietta's intent was to draw attention to the message in the title of his book, as mine is here to draw attention to the message in the chapter title. Thanks, Rob, for permission to borrow the idea.

2. Teacher education is conceived broadly here and may include experiences that range from engaging pre-service and practicing teachers in composition to action research projects to reflection on personal musical experiences and teaching practices.

3. Functional fixedness, or a mental block in using an object in a new way, was first described in 1945 by gestalt psychologist Karl Duncker, who asked subjects to attach a candle to a wall, given only the candle, a book of matches, and a box of thumbtacks. How would you solve this problem?

4. A word borrowed from Evan Tobias via the community of music education scholars at Northwestern University.

Scaffolding Student Composers
Jackie Wiggins with Michael Medvinsky

Five ten-year-olds sat together on the floor creating a ternary piece for classroom xylophones and percussion. They were one of six groups in the room working on the same project. Lynn had just approached the teacher asking her to join the group because they needed help.

MRS. W: Is there anything I can do to help you finish?

LYNN: Well, I know my part in the beginning but Suzanne needs help with the A . . .

KIM: We need you to guide us along.

LYNN: Yeah. Guide us along.

MRS. W (laughing): Guide you along? Well, do you want to play what you have so far?

Before offering assistance, the teacher needed to determine where they "needed help."

LYNN: One, two, three, go.

Lynn played an introduction on the conga drum punctuated by Kim's cowbell at the end of each phrase. Two other group members began a melody on xylophones, starting in the middle of what seemed to be the introduction.

MRS. W: Are they supposed to be playing already?

Making a momentary evaluation of the situation, she had begun to identify the problem, but sought verification from the students before helping them find a solution.

LYNN (to the metallophone players): You're not doing it right.

MRS. W (trying to get a sense of the plan): Does Lynn go first?

LYNN: Yeah. Me and Kim start.

MRS. W (to the xylophone players): Are you supposed to play with them though?

LYNN: No, it's Sheila's fault. She's not doing it right. We are supposed to
   play ours two times first.
SUZANNE: No, you do it three times.
LYNN: O.K.
MRS. W: Play it the way it's going to be.

They played the introduction followed by the A theme.

LYNN: And that's it. That's all we have.

They had not needed "guidance" after all, only reassurance that they were on
the right track, and a better understanding of what still needed to be done.

MRS. W: Well, that's a beautiful A section! Sheila, you haven't played at all
   yet, right? Are you the B? (She nods.) O.K. Let her make up her part and
   then you just need your ending and you'll have the whole piece.

By the end of the class, these students had successfully completed a piece in
ABA form, with the A and B themes played on xylophones and the introduction and coda played on the conga, punctuated by cowbell. They did not seek
any further assistance from the teacher. They had needed a momentary bit of
support from the teacher but, in general, had sufficient understanding of the
problem to develop a viable solution on their own. (Excerpted from Wiggins,
2009, pp. 19–20)

What does it mean to be a teacher in a classroom where learners are composing
original music? What can we do to support their creative process and music learning? How much support is too much? When does support become intervention
or even encroachment? How can we foster and enable learner success without
inappropriately asserting influence so that learners' ideas flourish and remain at the
core of the process? Are there decisions teachers can make and actions teachers can
take that have the capacity to enable learners to compose successfully, in ways that
are personally meaningful to them?

The best answers to these questions are embedded in what makes good teaching
in any field. In all learning settings, learners need to be actively engaged in the
processes and with the concepts of the discipline they are learning. In many ways,
processes of creating within any discipline require more individual, independent
work than other ways of engaging within that discipline might. However, since
learning is an act of the individual, the best learning situations are those that engage
learners' individual, independent thinking whether or not they are involved in
creating. For example, writing a story is a much more overtly creative process than
reading a story—but reading is actually a highly personal and creative process, with
individual interpretations of the text varying greatly. One can teach reading by
helping everyone understand the 'right' interpretation—but one can also teach
reading through honoring multiple interpretations and thereby providing a much
richer, more validating, and meaningful experience for all involved. Of course,

parallels exist between this language arts scenario and processes of composing and listening to music. Describing how teachers might support student composers is not very different from describing ways teachers might support students' music listening or performing. So let us begin by considering learning processes and how teachers can best support learners' efforts in all learning situations.

Scaffolding Learning

Learning is a process of the individual. As we go through life engaging in experience, we formulate our own understanding of the world around us: its nature, how it works, what it means to us. From this perspective, learning is a highly personal process. However, from the work of sociocultural theorists (e.g., Rogoff, 1990, 2003; Vygotsky, 1978; Wenger, 1998), we know that learning is also a highly social process in that it almost always takes place in a social context. It is within this realm that the art of teaching resides. Teaching is a social process. Within this context, following Dewey (1998), learners need to take an active role, engaging and constructing their own understanding.

When we look at learning as something the learner does rather than looking at teaching as something the teacher does *to* the learner, it changes our understanding of our role as teachers. In 1966, Bruner characterized the support that teachers give learners as *scaffolding*. As researchers and teachers continued to explore this metaphor, broader and broader interpretations emerged. Although this idea is nearly fifty years old, it still may offer the best description of the work we do as teachers. Everything teachers do to support student learning can be considered scaffolding, including framing and planning the learning experience, providing appropriate groundwork to foster and enable student success in the experience, and assessing student understanding throughout the experience. Most importantly, scaffolding characterizes the teacher's role and way of being in the classroom.

Scaffolding rooted in teachers' understanding of both learning processes and musical processes might be considered *artful teacher scaffolding* (Wiggins & Espeland, 2012). Artful teacher scaffolding requires a high level of understanding of learning and teaching as well as, in arts education settings, a high level of understanding of the art form and artistic process being taught. Successful music teaching requires extensive and insightful understanding of both musical and learning processes.

As we consider multiple ways in which we might scaffold music learning, we need to keep in mind the role of *learner agency*. Bruner (1996) describes agency as a "sense that one can initiate and carry out activities on one's own," linking it to aspiration, confidence, optimism, skill, and know-how. Rogoff (1990) has helped us understand that, since learning involves venturing into the unknown or less known, risk-taking is intrinsic to the process. Taking risks places learners in a vulnerable position, which is why scholars like Noddings (2003) and Freire (2002) feel a safe, supportive environment is so essential for empowering learning. Van Manen (1991) asks teachers to become reflectively aware of their pedagogical influence, assuring that their orientation is always to what is good for the learner, that their intention is to strengthen the learner's possibility for being and becoming.[1]

The pedagogical decisions we make and pedagogical actions we take in our attempts to scaffold the learning of others must be rooted in a deep understanding of what it means to foster agency in learners. It is the learners themselves who will engage and achieve. We cannot do it for them, although we can do it *with* them. We must consider how we approach all music learning experiences to best enable all learners to function musically, think musically, and grow musically.

Scaffolding Composing

In scaffolding student composers, we must consider our actions and ways of being within the teaching process itself, but it is equally important to consider the environment in which the process will take place. The environment includes the psychological and sociological nature of the learning setting, the pedagogical nature of the lesson design, the nature of the preparatory work that precedes the creative experience, and the nature of the musical skills and knowledge the teacher brings to the situation.

SUPPORTING STUDENTS MUSICALLY

To scaffold student composers, teachers need to have the aural skills, knowledge, and experience to be able to hear, understand, and work with students' musical ideas. They need the musical knowledge and experience to be able to have a sense of possibility of where musical ideas might go, how they might be set and developed, how students might be hearing the ideas they suggest.

In a study of an extensive data set analyzed for instances of teacher scaffolding, Wiggins (2011a) identified seven ways teachers scaffolded learners musically. In these data, the teachers were scaffolding student songwriting, usually in whole-class, collaborative composing settings. Some of these data were drawn from instances when teachers were working with a small group of students who had sought assistance. In all cases in this study, teachers were involved in composing *with* students in some way. In the experiences analyzed, teachers were found:

- Helping students musically realize ideas they were able to conceive and communicate in some way, but not fully realize musically.
- Establishing a starting point from which they could travel (a suggested key or basic harmonic structure within which they could generate melodic ideas).

- Creating and playing a harmonic accompaniment that either fit with what students' melodic ideas implied or served to lead the creation of new melodic material.
- Accompanying in a way that supported student singing of the sections that were already created, as a context for the development of new material.
- Sharing information about musical conventions to help them create a song that they would accept as musically valid (in terms of the music of their experience).
- Identifying interesting melodies as they were suggested within the group— sometimes softly and timidly from the rear of the room—coaxing them forward into the collaborative discussion.
- Supporting whole group singing of the more complex ideas suggested by individuals to be sure they were accurately represented and appropriately valued in the product. (pp. 98–99)

In other kinds of classroom composing settings, teacher scaffolding looks quite different. Where students are composing without direct teacher support, teacher scaffolding is of a different nature and occurs before the composing begins, when students request assistance, and when final products are shared (a time when teacher comments may scaffold future work). To compose on their own, students need to be working on their own—away from teacher intervention with time to think, plan, experiment, and enact their music, bringing it to life. In the sections that follow, we will talk further about how to establish the kind of environment needed to foster this kind of work, what teachers can do in prior lessons to lay the groundwork to enable students to compose successfully, and how teachers might offer support when student composers seek their advice or help.

FOSTERING A SUPPORTIVE ENVIRONMENT

To be willing and able to engage with confidence, learners need to perceive the learning setting as supportive and non-threatening. The environment must enable and nurture learners' personal and musical agency. They need to believe that the teacher and their peers will value their ideas and suggestions. Establishing a safe, supportive, comfortable, nonjudgmental learning environment is not something that can be done on the day of a creative experience only. Creative process blossoms in classrooms where learners are accustomed to expressing ideas about music and having those ideas valued and validated. You need to begin by engaging students in performing and listening experiences in which you seek their ideas. Once such an environment is established, creating music will seem like just one more activity that happens in the midst.

Further, it is important to understand the role of peers in the learning of individuals. Learning is a social process, a collaborative process. Music learning experiences should be structured to build on this quality and enable learners to benefit from peer mentoring, coaching, thinking, ideas, processes, approaches, reactions, and so forth (see Wiggins, 1999/2000, 2009). Making space for these kinds of interactions to occur means planning for them to occur. It also requires teachers to think about what will be happening in the learning setting from the perspective of the learners and not from the perspective of the teacher. What will learners be doing? How will they be engaged? At what points will they have opportunity to interact without the teacher's monitoring or intervention?

FOSTERING INVENTION AND ARTICULATION OF MUSICAL IDEAS

Composing involves thinking in music, inventing music, generating and articulating musical ideas. Young children invent music and sing to themselves or move in ways that reflect it all the time (Bjørkvold, 1989; Campbell, 2010; Davies, 1992; Young, 1995, 2002). Generating and articulating musical ideas is a central part of their lives. As children grow within the constraints of school and society, they may learn to feel less and less comfortable engaging in this kind of free musical invention and improvisation. It therefore becomes important for these kinds of experiences to be a regular part of music learning from the very earliest experiences. Young music learners can easily improvise to create particular moods, settings, feelings, conversations, introductions, interludes, codas—whatever fits the moment. When expressing through music has been an integral part of learners' prior experience, composing is a logical next step. Conceiving original music ideas become second nature.

It also is important to understand that even young, novice composers have an idea of what they want to "say" musically before they play or sing it—much the same way we have an idea of what we want to say before we speak. We may not know the exact words we will say when we speak, but we know the general idea— and we know if we have misspoken. The same is true of young composers and improvisers articulating musical ideas. Researchers who have looked at what learners actually do when asked to compose or improvise on instruments have amassed considerable evidence that youngsters are (as children often express it) "looking for their music" on the instrument. They have a sense of what they want it to sound like and "look for it" by playing until they "find it." Then they tend to repeat it almost incessantly until they "know it," as they say, because playing it repeatedly is how they keep it alive until it is internalized and can be replicated at any time.

RESPECTING AND HONORING LEARNER VOICE

Composing is a process of personal expression, regardless of whether the creator is an expert or a novice. Part of nurturing and honoring learner agency is enabling and honoring learner voice. For novice composers, creating original music is an opportunity for them to say something that is important to them. When learners seem to be resistant to teacher suggestions, that resistance often is rooted in the ownership they feel for their process and product. Scaffolding young composers requires understanding that the music belongs to the learners (see Wiggins, 2011a). The teacher's role is to share expertise as learners perceive it is needed, not to use expertise to invade their space and process uninvited. Scaffold respectfully—respectful of learners' musical ideas and visions of the work in progress. Learners will eagerly and happily seek assistance when they need it (as in the situation in the opening vignette). When they intentionally seek help, they will give the teacher their undivided attention. It is worthwhile to wait for those moments.

MEETING LEARNERS WHERE THEY ARE

Compositional experiences in which learners engage require them to use understandings and skills they currently possess. Determining the sophistication and nature of learners' understanding and skill level means connecting with them, knowing them. When teachers work with learners they do not know well, they will need to engage them in a series of experiences designed to help them understand where they are in their musical experience and understanding. Once they have worked with learners over a longer period of time, they may be able to deduce this understanding more informally.

However, it is essential to recognize that the largest, richest source of prior experience is the learners' musical experience outside of school. Considering the broader musical landscape in which most music learners reside, it would behoove us to consider and take seriously the musical experience that learners bring into learning settings. When music learners are given the opportunity to create music without constraints of style or genre, they often choose to compose in the style most familiar to them, often filled with characteristics commonly found in pop music. This music is the soundtrack of their everyday lives, pervasive in all their most personal experiences. Older students rely on music as a metaphor to help them understand feelings and situations they cannot articulate.

Teachers need to take the time to talk with learners about the music they know and value in order to be able to meet them where they are and enable their success and growth. In a supportive learning environment, students value the understanding the teacher brings to the learning process, but teachers also must value the understandings that learners bring, learned through peer collaboration and their own prior experiences both in and out of school. The teacher becomes a mentor/learner and the student becomes a learner/mentor. Valuing the music students bring into the classroom supports them as musicians and musical thinkers. Engaging students in conversations about their music and musical thinking fosters mutual respect. Ask them why they connect so deeply with a piece of music or what made them choose a particular piece to share. Ask how is it meaningful to them. Especially for upper elementary through secondary students, their choices will be reflective and personal.

The harmonic progressions that are the foundation for popular music may differ from the structures of more traditional music. The teacher's understanding of the sonority and modality of the music of learners' experience is a key component in scaffolding their compositional process. Being aware of and versed in this area will enable a teacher to support the process of realizing the sounds that are in the ears of the composers. Understanding the genre and styles of the music with which learners identify enables the scaffolding process to be transparent and embedded within the affective qualities of their composition and process.

LAYING GROUNDWORK THROUGH PRIOR EXPERIENCE

An important part of scaffolding learner's capacity to compose is the set of experiences in which they engage before the composing experience. The best way to ensure that novice composers will know how to proceed and succeed is to engage them in prior experiences that enable them to develop the understandings and skills necessary to complete the compositional task. In addition to being valuable experiences in themselves, well-designed prior experiences can *lay groundwork* for the composing process (Wiggins, 2009). Consider the opening vignette. Before these students were asked to compose a piece in ABA form, they had performed and listened to bi-thematic music with an awareness of the nature of the thematic material and the formal structure of the works. They also had analyzed the form of several ternary works. The composing experience would not have been the proper place to introduce the idea of bi-thematic music or ternary form. To be able to conceive of original material, learners need to have a solid understanding of the framework and possibilities *before* they are asked to engage in the process.

Once learners engage in composing regularly in the learning setting, what they learn in one experience scaffolds their ability to work in the next. On the most simplistic levels, they may learn that they work well with or do not work well with certain peers, for whatever reasons. Given the option of choosing their co-collaborators, they will tend to gravitate toward peers with whom they have had successful experiences in the past. Both socially and musically, each experience enables subsequent experiences to flow more smoothly. It can be important to keep this in mind if the initial experiences have been less than smooth. Experience generally produces better, more complex, and more efficient work. Students develop their own ways of working, personally and with their peers, as they might through engaging in any experience repeatedly. Even though the compositional problems will increase in complexity as they become more knowledgeable and proficient, their experience in the process enables them to work more expediently: to understand their choices and possibilities, to become better able to know which ideas will work well and what they might do with them, to become smarter assessors of their own work, to provide better responses to peers, and so on.

In addition, learners' experience hearing the work of peers often raises the level of all the work produced. Teachers who are inexperienced in composing with students often do not realize that time spent sharing the products of students' creative efforts can be some of the most important teaching moments. It is important to allot sufficient time for sharing at the end of a project. Sharing times are moments of celebration of student ideas and accomplishments, but they also are rich opportunities for assessing what students have understood and the depth and nature of that understanding. Sharing is also a fertile opportunity for students to learn from one another. After spending extended, productive time wrestling with a musical problem and with issues they may have encountered in their work, students are most curious about their peers' solutions to the larger problem that was posed and about how their peers may have addressed the same issues they faced in solving it. Sharing provides learners insight into multiple ways of solving problems, providing both models and food for thought the next time they are asked to compose.

Students who compose together in a classroom develop shared ideas and traditions that teachers will see surface in the work of multiple groups of students across the school year. Students borrow and adapt ideas they have heard in peers' work, transforming them for their own purposes, much the same way that professional composers learn from the work of peers and those who came before. Of course, students in music learning settings also draw on musical ideas they have studied in the works of professional composers and learned through non-school music experience—but it is important not to discount the importance of how much they learn from their peers as well. It all contributes to a constant spiral of improvement in their capacity to represent in sound the ideas they seek to express.

FRAMING COMPOSITIONAL PROBLEMS TO FOSTER SUCCESS

To know how to frame compositional problems that will foster learner success, it is essential to have some understanding of the nature of compositional process. Researchers who have studied learners' compositional processes in learning settings describe the process as holistic and contextual (see Wiggins, 2006).

From a contextual perspective, there is evidence, even in the work of novices, that learners enter the process with a general, preconceived vision of how the final product should sound (Wiggins, 2006). Often, these preconceived visions are similar across the peer group, even before there has been any musical or verbal communication. These common visions of what the work will be can be rooted in the nature of the problem (e.g., if they are asked to compose music that fits a particular mood or feeling), but are also rooted in the music of their common experience, which is one reason it is so important for the teacher to know something about that music. The vision will be influenced by learners' prior experiences in the music learning setting (including music they may have heard, performed, or created together in the past), but it is much more heavily influenced by the music that learners' engage with in their non-school experiences.

So learners enter a collaborative composing experience with a certain amount of shared vision of what the final product will be. Then, within this vision, they begin to generate and experiment with thematic material, judging it initially in terms of its appropriateness to the larger vision. They may reject one another's ideas with comments like, "No, that isn't right" or "No, it doesn't sound like that." The prevalence of comments like this in the initial stages of young composers' work is part of what leads researchers to suggest that they enter the situation with preconceived ideas. If there were no preconceived ideas, how would they determine whether an idea was a good one?[2]

From a holistic perspective, we have learned through experience that it is easier for novice composers to conceive and develop musical ideas if the parameters of the compositional problem deal with the more holistic—the more metadimensional—qualities of the work. Wiggins (2009) suggests that what we have traditionally called the *elements of music* that undergird most music curricular planning might better be broadened to include some of the more metadimensional qualities of music that also are essential to understanding music. Wiggins proposes that we consider reframing the standard elements of Western music (e.g., pitch, rhythm, timbre, dynamics) as *dimensions* of a musical work and broader, more encompassing qualities (e.g., form, texture, architecture, affective qualities, simultaneity, sense of ensemble, historical or historical context, personal context) as *metadimensions of music.*

In general, framing compositional problems from the perspective of broader, metadimensional qualities provides a viable context within which composers can generate musical ideas. Learners conceiving of and articulating musical material are thinking and operating in the context of the music of their culture. If they are enculturated into Western music, they will invent material that uses Western scales, rhythms, meters, and so on. Sometimes well-meaning teachers will try to "simplify" a compositional problem for learners by restricting the pitches or rhythms they can use. Such a practice seriously stifles young composers who think in Western music. If, for example, Western-born learners are restricted to the pitches of a pentatonic scale (a common practice for using classroom xylophones with removable bars), they often ask the teacher if they can have the missing bars in order to be able to play their tune (the tune they have in their heads and are "looking for" on the instrument).

Understanding the contextual and holistic nature of composing process informs the way we need to design compositional problems for learners. The easiest way to frame a compositional problem is to use a metadimensional quality as a point of entry (or "doorway in") (Wiggins, 2009). First, problems should be framed with only one point of entry. To ask students to compose a piece that is in a particular form, with a particular texture, that suggests a particular mood, and moves in a particular meter would cripple the students' capacity for success. The compositional problem has to foster, not stymie, creative thinking. Think of the problem as a frame within which the students will think and create. Think of it as a blank canvas that has shape, but not much more. That kind of problem is easy to "fill in"—much easier to work within than if the musical material itself is constrained. As students enter and work within the broader contexts, they will need to make decisions about and operate within all the other dimensions and metadimensions of music, even though you have not specified that they need to. Such is the nature of dimensions (or elements) and metadimensions; all music contains them all.[3]

A lesson might be designed using *form* as a point of entry (a form learners have studied and understand well). As they work, learners will fill the formal framework with their own musical material. An *affective quality* could be a point of entry (compose scary music or a lullaby or celebratory music or background music for a scene in a children's book) or perhaps *texture* (compose a tune with a background or a conversation between two characters) or *architecture* (compose a work that slowly builds in intensity to a climax and then suddenly cuts off to silence). Notice how easy it would be to generate ideas to fill the spaces in these contexts—so much easier than it would be to compose a melody using only sol-mi-la and a particular rhythm pattern. Filling broader parameters with one's own ideas is much easier than working in a situation where the nature of those ideas has been specified and/or restricted. Even the least experienced musicians can fill a space with sounds that generate a particular mood or shape or intent—much more easily than they could if they needed to be concerned about which pitches they needed to play when.

PROVIDING TIME AND SPACE

All this important work takes time. The level and complexity of musical thinking that we are talking about here and the construction of those ideas into a musical work takes time. It also takes personal space—time and space away from others—time to think. Musical thinking is not quiet—not for the novice. It manifests itself as singing to oneself, vocables, "doodling"[4] on instruments, tapping, wiggling, humming, and so on. Twenty-five students composing together generate a lot of sound. Children can learn what is necessary sound and what is not, but teachers also have to be prepared for the fact that this process is not a silent one.

In other settings, Wiggins (1999/2000; Wiggins & Espeland, 2012) has shared descriptions of a teacher she observed scaffolding the composing a class song with a group of seven-year-olds. For more than ten minutes, at the start of a class session, the teacher stood over on the side of the classroom, interacting quietly with children who approached her with ideas, trying some out softly on her keyboard. At the same time, all over the room, children were singing the lyrics to themselves, trying all different permutations of different melodies, singing in long extended think-alouds. From her own quiet musing, the teacher offered some quiet musical suggestions on the keyboard, without calling attention to what she was doing, that the children took up as a frame for their independent work. After the ten minutes, she invited them to share their ideas. Because the children had had sufficient time and personal space to conceive and work out their personal ideas, many contributed melodies in clear, confident voices and the collaborative song was completed in about fifteen minutes.

From researcher field notes describing this experience, a found poem[5] emerged that encapsulates the themes reflective of what was happening:

> The room percolates with ideas
> In an *en masse*, simultaneous think-aloud.
>
> Space for thinking
>   Intentional time and space . . .
> Subtle suggestions
>   That support and frame invention
> More time . . .
>   (She is thinking and experimenting too).
>
> Almost everyone in the room is singing or speaking
> So many ideas coming at once.
>
> Creating space for learners to
>   think in sound
>   experiment
>   evaluate
>   vary
>   adapt
>   and transform their ideas
> Until they are ready to share them
>   In a safe, comfortable environment
>   That welcomes and nurtures their ideas.

Students' Experience with Artful Teacher Scaffolding

The students in Mr. Medvinsky's sixth-grade music classes were engaged in a unit on "change" songs: songs designed to promote social change to make the world a better place. After studying and analyzing "change" songs from a range of historical periods written in a range of styles, the students were invited to work together as a class to compose their own "change" song. Once completed, the students in all classes would have an opportunity to hear the work of their peers in other classes. Let's look in on a class whose members were collaborating to compose a song called, "Yes We Can," inspired by the theme of Barack Obama's presidential campaign.

Erika said, "Mr. M, I know how this part goes," and then, as illustrated in Figure 6.1 (on the next page) sang the part.

Students often talk about knowing "how a song goes" when it hasn't been composed yet. Comments like these inspire researchers to conclude that young

FIGURE 6.1 Erika's vocal model for "Yes We Can".

composers conceive of musical ideas before articulating them, in the same way as a person speaking knows what he or she wants to say before speaking.

The class really liked Erika's idea and began singing the melody with her. Mr. M found the melody on the piano, in the key of Bb major, and began playing the melody line along with the class as they sang. After a few times through this part of the song, he added a tonic chord to support the melody.

"Mr. M, I like the way the piano feels with the words," said Skyler. Others agreed, so Mr. M responded, "Great. How do you think the next chord should sound?"

Even though the melody was only partially completed, they had begun to think about chords to support it. Their hearing of the melody was harmonically contextual. They may not have known which specific chords would work, but they knew which chords sounded right and wrong (in relation to their conception of how the song should sound). Their understanding of chord relationships was rooted in their life experience with Western music, further informed by their work during prior classroom experiences analyzing and working with tonic, dominant, and subdominant chords (which they called "home," "away," and "resting" chords.[6]) They could hear the horizontal movement from the beginning of the phrase through to the end. They may not have known what to call the chords they could hear, but they had the sound they wanted in their ears even though they had only just created the melody.

Skyler suggested, "We need a lower sounding chord next."

"Okay," said Mr. M. "Let's try it from the top. One, two, ready, go." The class sang the melody from the beginning as Mr. M accompanied the first phrase with a I (Bb) chord and the second phrase with a vi (g) chord. The students stopped singing and immediately began talking to each other about the sound of the new chord with their melody.

"Mr. M, can we try that again?" asked Wendy.

"Sure," said Mr. M: "One, two, ready, go." The class sang the melody again while Mr. M accompanied.

Skyler contributed, "I like it, but I think since we are singing the same thing twice, we need to have the same chord twice. Can we try that?"

"Sure. One, two, ready, go." The class sang the melody again, this time with Mr. M playing the tonic chord to accompany both phrases. The students stopped singing and again began talking to one another about the sound of the chords with their melody.

FIGURE 6.2 Harmonization adopted for "Yes We Can".

Skyler commented, "That doesn't sound right. Me and Jamie were talking about deepening the sound of the piano, but keeping the same chord. Can you do that?"

"Let's try it," said Mr. M, and then explained that as they sang the first two measures, he would keep the same chord in the right hand of the piano but move the bass note to a lower pitch. Together they experimented a few times until the students heard what they wanted. They all agreed that the second phrase should be accompanied by a Bb chord with a G in the bass, as shown in Figure 6.2.

The class continued to work on the accompaniment, fleshing it out with additional instruments, eventually deciding to move the bass notes to a bass guitar.

As the process continued, decision after decision was made, one being that they chose to have one verse of the chorus sung in Spanish. Ultimately, the students named the song, "Yes We Can (*Si Su Puede*)."

When the project was finished, Mr. Medvinsky commented, "As a collective 6th grade, every class was very connected to and loved their own 'change' song, but everyone thought 'Yes We Can (*Si Su Puede*)' was the coolest."

In this instance of artful teacher scaffolding, note the importance of the teacher's own musicianship and the ease with which he was able to enable the students to realize the sounds in their ears. Also note the ways in which the students asserted musical leadership and were the primary decision-makers, supported by the teacher's musicianship.

During the next class session, Mr. Medvinsky engaged the composers of "Yes We Can (*Si Su Puede*)" in a conversation about their perceptions about how he had supported their writing of the song. He was curious about their awareness of the nature of his scaffolding processes. An excerpt from that conversation appears below. The students did most of the talking, with only an occasional prompt or question from their teacher.

You are kind of like a guide . . . but not a leader. *We* are the leaders.

You never say anything to us unless we ask you. You help us get it right but, if we are doing it all by ourselves, you don't jump in.

Instead of asking *you*, you tell us to ask *each other*.

You help us, but you don't do it for us.

When you suggest something, you give *us* the option of what to do with it.

When I come to you with my songs, I already have the notes in my head, but they don't always fit. You help me figure out what goes where.

We can write our songs, but we need your help to figure out the background. We don't need someone to write the song for us.

You help us make it sound like a real song.

Without you, we wouldn't have our music.

You make sure we're on track but you don't tell us where we're supposed to go. You don't say, "Well, this has to go there." You say, "Well, you might want to put that in there, but it's your song, so you need to think of it yourself. I'm just giving you suggestions." The suggestions you give us are good. Sometimes we just wouldn't have thought of them.

Your assistance gives us the empowerment to find our own answers.

Yes, a sixth-grade student actually contributed, "Your assistance gives us the empowerment to find our own answers." After living this experience and then reading the transcript of the conversation, Mr. Medvinsky commented: "I couldn't write better scripts for the discussions that happen in the music room. When you treat students like musicians and design room for them to personally express, they begin to understand the big picture of what it means to see life through music."

We invite you to listen to "Yes We Can (*Si Su Puede*)" at http://www.oakland.edu/carmu/links

You are a guide, but not a leader.
We are the leaders.

You tell us to ask *each other*
Instead of asking *you*.

You help us
But you don't do it for us.

You make sure we're on track,
But you don't tell us where we're supposed to go.

Your assistance gives us the empowerment to find our own answers.

For learners to succeed, learning environments must nurture and support learner agency and voice. For music learners to succeed, music learning environments must *artfully* nurture and support learners' *personal* agency and *musical* agency by providing opportunity for each learner to become a musical decision maker and, as Barone (1993) would describe it, a poet of his or her own musical destiny.

When music belongs to learners, they make personal choices to pursue music learning because music learning becomes a goal that is personally meaningful to them.

The process becomes self-motivational, exciting, and rewarding for all involved. Scaffolding such a process in a way that enables and allows student ownership to flourish is an art born of sensitivity, respect, musicianship, and experience. Artful scaffolding enables students to create their own musical narratives, narratives that may become powerfully meaningful in their lives. When the process becomes a deeply embedded part of the culture of the learning situation, learners begin to see themselves as creators and interpreters of music, and begin to see musical process as an integral part of their private lives. For some, it becomes one of their primary means of personal expression.

> *You* are a guide. *We* are the leaders.
> You help us, but you don't do it for us.
>
> You make sure we're on track
> But you don't tell us where we're supposed to go.
>
> *You give us the empowerment to find our own answers.*

References

Barone, T. E. (1993). Breaking the mold: The new American student as strong poet. *Theory into Practice, 32*(4), 236–243. http://www.jstor.org/stable/1476372.

Bruner, J. S. (1966). *Toward a theory of instruction.* Cambridge, MA: Harvard University Press.

Bruner, J. S. (1996). *The culture of education.* Cambridge, MA: Harvard University Press.

Bjørkvold, J. (1989). *The muse within* (W. H. Halverson, Trans.). New York: Harper Collins.

Campbell, P. S. (2010). *Songs in their heads: Music and its meaning in children's lives* (2nd ed.). New York: Oxford University Press. (Originally published 1998).

Davies, C. (1992). Listen to my song: A study of songs invented by children aged 5 to 7 years. *British Journal of Music Education, 9*(1), 19–48.

Dewey, J. (1998). *Experience and education.* West Lafayette, IN: Kappa Delta Pi. (Originally published in 1938).

Freire, P. (2002). *Pedagogy of the oppressed.* New York: Continuum. (Originally published in 1970).

Noddings, N. (2003). *Caring: A feminine approach to ethics and moral education* (2nd ed.). Los Angeles: University of California Press. (Originally published 1984).

Rogoff, B. (1990). *Apprenticeship in thinking.* New York: Oxford University Press.

Rogoff, B. (2003). *The cultural nature of human development.* New York: Oxford University Press.

van Manen, M. (1991). *The tact of teaching: The meaning of pedagogical thoughtfulness.* New York: SUNY Press.

Vygotsky, L. S. (1978). *Mind in society: The development of higher psychological processes.* M. Cole, V. John-Steiner, S. Scribner, & E. Souberman (Eds.). Cambridge, MA: Harvard University Press.

Wenger, E. (1998). *Communities of practice: Learning, meaning, and identity*. New York: Cambridge University Press.

Wiggins, J. H. (1999/2000). The nature of shared musical understanding and its role in empowering independent musical thinking, *Bulletin of the Council for Research in Music Education*, 143, 65–90.

Wiggins, J. (2006). Compositional process in music. In L. Bresler (Ed.) *International handbook of research in arts education* (pp. 451–467). Amsterdam: Springer.

Wiggins, J. (2009). *Teaching for musical understanding* (2nd ed.). Rochester, Michigan: Center for Applied Research in Musical Understanding (CARMU).

Wiggins, J. (2011a). When the music is theirs: Scaffolding young songwriters. In M. Barrett (Ed). *A cultural psychology for music education*, pp. 83–113. London: Oxford University Press.

Wiggins, J. (2011b). Vulnerability and agency in being and becoming a musician. *Music Education Research*, 13(4), 355–367. doi: 10.1080/14613808.2011.632153

Wiggins, J., & Espeland, M. (2012). Creating in music learning contexts. In G. McPherson & G. Welch (Eds.), *Oxford handbook of music education*. New York: Oxford University Press.

Young, S. (1995). Listening to the music of early childhood. *British Journal of Music Education*, 12, 51–58.

Young, S. (2002). Young children's spontaneous vocalizations in free play. *Bulletin of the Council for Research in Music Education*, 152, 4.

Notes

1. This perspective is fleshed out further in Wiggins (2009, 2011a, 2011b) and Wiggins & Espeland (2012).

2. For a more detailed explanation of researchers' perspectives on novices' compositional processes, see Wiggins, 2006).

3. This is written from a Western perspective. If it were culturally appropriate to conceive of dimensions and metadimensions of a non-Western music, some dimensions would likely be different. But the principle would be the same—that the dimensions and metadimensions were identified specifically because they are present in all music of that culture.

4. "Doodling" is in quotes here because the kind of work often described in the literature as doodling is generally, in actuality, a very intentional process of searching on the instrument for sounds already conceived.

5. Merriam-Webster's defines a found poem as "a poem consisting of words found in a nonpoetic context."

6. This is an idea suggested by Wiggins (2009) that she learned from David Walker in 1970.

7 }

Teaching Gifted Learners in Composition
Daniel Deutsch

"Composition is like a miracle," an eleven-year-old composer told me. "You make something out of nothing. You reach into your imagination and bring it into reality." When students express emotions, ideas, and images in their own compositions, they add new dimensions of meaning to their musical experience and bring their musical dreams to life. If we identify children who have strong creative potential and musical passion at an early age, we can provide them with individualized instruction and guidance that help them soar to great musical heights.

This chapter draws on my more than two decades of experience administering and teaching a music composition program for talented fifth and sixth graders in the five elementary schools of a public school district. The chapter provides guidance for organizing, auditioning, selecting, teaching, and facilitating a program for young composers, including exceptionally gifted students. The emphasis is on how to provide instruction tailored to each student's individual needs within a learning environment that encourages creative exploration.

Because talented young composers need experiences that transcend the school walls, the chapter also discusses how students can benefit from higher-level programs where they interact with gifted peers and professional composers, such as the New York State School Music Association (NYSSMA) Young Composer Program, which I helped to establish in 1998.

Although this chapter focuses on a composition program per se, the teaching strategies may be easily transferred to any educational setting in which the teacher interacts with a small group of students, such as instrumental or vocal lesson groups.

Overview of the Three Village Central School District Student Composition Program

The Three Village Central School District is located in Stony Brook, New York. Every year, approximately eighty fifth and sixth graders in the district's five elementary schools study composition in weekly small-group pullout lessons during school hours. Most lesson groups consist of four students, and lessons last for thirty minutes. The students learn to compose and notate their original music, and they publish their pieces in an annual publication titled *A Collection of Pieces by Young Composers*, which is a printed collection of the compositions completed in the given academic year. The young composers perform their pieces at an annual Young Composers Festival in June, which features more than three hours of original music by students. At the festival, each child receives a copy of the composition publication. The books are also used in music education departments at several colleges to illustrate benchmarks in student composition.

Each year, some of the more advanced students are invited to perform their works at regional and state concerts, such as those sponsored by the Long Island Composers Alliance and NYSSMA. Alumni of the Three Village program have received many awards, including the BMI Student Composer Award and the ASCAP Morton Gould Young Composer Award, and at competitions sponsored by NAfME: The National Association for Music Education. However, the emphasis of the program is not on the seeking of awards or prizes. Instead the goal is to provide a large number of students with individualized instruction that helps them to express themselves musically in unique, authentic compositional voices.

Identification, Recruitment, and Selection of Students

Because the program can accommodate only approximately eighty students, I try to select the students who will benefit most—because they are passionate about music and have the greatest creative potential. The list of possible students is narrowed down considerably by a requirement that candidates have had at least one year of instrumental study. The first step in identification is consultation with the school instrumental and general music teachers, who make specific recommendations based on their perceptions of the students' achievement, potential, work ethic, and creativity. I visit each fifth-grade classroom, describe the program to the students, and interview every interested student one by one. In the interview, I try to ascertain each child's love of music and potential for creativity. Specific musical diagnostics include having the child 1) echo a sung major triad and 2) vocally improvise the completion of a short melodic phrase. The phrase completion is often a reliable indicator of future success in composition, but not always. Sometimes, for example, an extraordinarily gifted student is too consumed by competing ideas to respond spontaneously. Each candidate's ability to read music notation and sight-sing a two-measure phrase is also tested. The criteria are interpreted holistically, not in isolation. Some of the best composers are poor note readers, or too shy to sing a phrase, or feel their musical talent to be a burden as well as a blessing.

When I have completed the list of accepted students, I discuss them with their classroom teachers to see if there are other factors I should be aware of. The students who are finally selected range from slightly above average to exceptionally gifted. I send the parents a letter informing them about the program, and the parents complete a form granting their permission for their children to participate in this pullout program.

The Creative Learning Environment

The composition class setting must be a place of mutual support, trust, and optimism. It must also be an environment that encourages experimentation, risk-taking, and inventiveness. The small-group lesson is an effective setting for teaching composition because it enables intensive individual coaching as well as cooperative learning, peer interaction, and group projects. Most students enjoy sharing their ideas with classmates and often make ingenious suggestions to one another.

The great gift of composition is musical freedom, and with freedom comes risk. It is imperative that the learning environment be accepting, tolerant, nurturing, and supportive. This is true for every educational subject, but especially so for composition. Because the first stage of composition is exploratory improvisation, it is crucial that students learn how to take risks and accept their own mistakes and those of their classmates. The creative process is full of errors, wrong turns, and dead ends. If students fear ridicule for their errors, they will never develop as composers. The errors are a vital part of the creative trajectory. In fact, many composers have found some of their best ideas by accident.

The teacher should model openness to risk by improvising often in front of the students, pushing out of the comfort zone to areas where mistakes happen. As the students witness the teacher's joy of experimentation and happy embrace of error, their willingness to experiment without fear almost always grows. It is useful to show students sketches by Beethoven and other prominent composers to illustrate how even the greatest geniuses could lurch and stumble.

Most students sense without being told that the composition classroom flourishes only in an atmosphere of trust and acceptance. The teacher's respect and support of the students are contagious and generate an atmosphere of tolerance among the students. Music may be the art form that is most intimately tied to our emotions. Because students are encouraged to express their heartfelt ideas and emotions in their compositions, they need the assurance that they will not be mocked. They are sharing not only combinations of notes and rhythms, but also the inner truth of their lives. When students are assured of an open and caring environment, they are able to make more profound artistic statements, to plumb deeper dimensions of expression. It helps to make their compositions more compelling. The empathetic exchange of creative works of affective power is one of the highest forms of communication in our schools.

In order to create an atmosphere of risk-taking, experimentation, and inventiveness, teachers may have to let go of preconceived notions of how a normative classroom should run. As Susan Engel writes, "Parents and teachers are ever eager to find ways to get the child to 'settle down' and 'learn.' Whether we do it implicitly or explicitly, we aim to remove the passionate, unruly, and playful elements in our efforts to civilize, socialize, educate, and investigate the child. Yet we know that these same 'wild' elements often drive the acquisition of the cognitive process that make the child seem more socialized and rational" (Engel, 2005).

This is especially true in a field such as music composition. The creative process is often unruly, and some of the most creative students are not conventionally "well-behaved" (Hickey & Webster, 2001). Some students need to move around the room as they think; others need to work at their instrument. Many will be singing to themselves as they construct their ideas in the classroom. At times, successful composition workshop settings may have a chaotic element. One of the challenges for the teacher is to maintain an atmosphere that combines playful invention and purposeful perseverance. Many teachers are trained to create ordered lesson plans that have specific objectives and predictable outcomes. The composition class should follow the leads of student interest and encourage unpredictable results.

Fifth and sixth graders have matured to the point where they can clearly distinguish between play and seriousness, between fantasy and reality, but they are closer than adults are to that magical time in their past when the distinctions were blurred. Some lucky artists are able to keep that sense of play alive throughout their careers: Shakespeare, Haydn, Calder, Dizzy Gillespie, Miró, to name a few. A composition teacher can use many techniques to encourage students to maintain that creative spirit of playfulness. One effective activity is structured small-group improvisation based on narratives, such as myths, folk tales, or student-created stories. The students create a storyboard of scenes and create musical elements that tell the story in sound. The narrative structure provides a formal arc for the piece, and the characters provide masks that help the students avoid self-consciousness.

In the process, the teacher encourages the students to explore extended techniques on their instruments; to listen and respond spontaneously and meaningfully to their classmates; to evoke mood, atmosphere, continuity, and surprise; and to create an overarching shape to their work. Allowing humor and sometimes even a bit of silliness facilitates the process.

Other stimuli for creativity include optical and auditory illusions, brainteasers, thought experiments, philosophical discussions, and an exposure to a wide variety of audio and video of music in a range of styles and genres. One example is a mini-lesson on graphic notation in the style of R. Murray Shafer, in which the students create and perform music based on abstract images that they and I invent. An age-appropriate philosophical discussion may focus on a quotation such as "There are some who know all of the notes, and then there are some who know the music."

THE FIRST LESSON IN COMPOSITION

In the first lesson, I welcome the students to an exciting new dimension of music-making (Deutsch, 2009). "We all enjoy playing music written by other composers, but now we get to make up our own music, with our own ideas, feelings, and emotions," I say. "There is no limit but your own imagination." The students are reassured to learn that every child who has tried to compose in the program has been successful, and that there are solutions to all compositional problems. I tell them that the class is a place where they are free to be themselves and will not be criticized or treated with anger or disrespect.

A former student, who is now pursuing a doctoral degree in composition, remembers the first lesson many years later: "One thing that sticks with me until today is that on the first day of the program, there was no talk about rules or technique. The focus was on creativity, not correctness. Since that day, both with teachers and by myself, I learned the rules and techniques associated with multiple approaches to writing music, but I never lost sight of that initial creative impulse" (Fisher-Lochhead, 2011).

The Three Village program is based on an emergent curriculum. Instruction is geared to the highly individualized knowledge, aptitudes, interests, and needs of each student. Most students have a natural tunefulness, a basic aural comprehension of simple tonality and rhythm that I try to extend organically. Rather than proceeding from a set of theory rules, I attempt to enter and expand each child's unique musical world by teaching concepts that emerge directly from the student's creative work. Children can ride bicycles without knowing the laws of gyroscopic inertia; they can make up stories without learning a list of grammatical rules. So, too, children can compose before they learn many theoretical concepts. Indeed, focusing on theory first can stifle creativity, and lead to exercise-like compositions with little affective meaning.

We begin with emotion, meaning, and idea. "Name an emotion and I will make up part of a piece based on it," I tell the students at their first lesson. "Happy, excited, sad, angry," they usually say at first, sometimes adding words like "eerie," " surprising," or even "jealous." I improvise brief piano pieces based on their ideas, modeling spontaneous improvisation and a willingness to accept the errors that occur. We discuss the specific musical factors that create the emotions described, with the students taking the lead in the conversation. The topics range from the basic contrasts of minor and major, slow and fast, loud and soft, to higher order concepts such as expectation and unpredictability. Students enjoy the deeper philosophical questions: "Why are sudden loud sounds scary?" or "Would people in a distant culture know that our minor song is sad?"

In addition, at the first lesson, the students select sets of three or four random notes and we create short pieces based on them. The purpose is to show them any pitch collection can be used to generate attractive melodies, that the transformation of motive is more important than the actual pitch content. This is another confidence builder because the students realize they are not compelled to pick the "best notes" in order to succeed in composition.

"Now it's *your* turn!" I say. "Go home and fool around on your instrument and come up with something that shows us *your* emotion, feeling, or idea. I want to hear *you* in the music. Don't worry if it is good or not good. We can fix anything you don't like about it. You may come up with a whole piece, or just a phrase, or maybe just a few notes. You don't have to write it down; just play it or sing it for us. Try not to worry. Have fun with it!"

The appeal to emotion and idea rather than theoretical concepts is the least restrictive assignment. It encourages students to rise to their highest possible levels at the outset, and it leads the children to be emotionally attached to their musical ideas. There is a kernel of truth to their music, an element of authentic aesthetic expression. In some cases, such as with a perfectionist student, the personal attachment to the musical idea may be a stumbling block, but those are relatively rare cases that will be discussed later in the chapter.

In response to the wide-open stimulus, students return to class with a broad spectrum of musical beginnings. In the first week some students create entire pieces, or large sections, often of breathtaking musical complexity. At the most advanced end of the spectrum are examples that contain chromatic harmony that the students have absorbed from their private instrumental lessons. Others contain symmetrical atonal structures intuited from exceptional mathematical ability. In the middle of the spectrum are the majority of students, who compose a phrase or two in a "normal" tonal language. At the other end of the spectrum are students who have come up with a few notes that they like, or the students who have no idea at all how to proceed.

The nonrestrictive assignment enables advanced students to skip several levels and avoid the frustration of working on boring material. It also enables them to express and begin to develop their own individual authentic musical "voices," and to create musical ideas to which they are emotionally attached.

A majority of students' initial ideas are conventional examples of simple tonality and predictable meter, because they like to "color within the lines." However, the open assignment also allows for music of vivid character and colorful idiosyncrasy: a witty pause; an intriguing paraphrase or permutation; intricate symmetries and transformations; an infectious rhythm that remains surprising after repeated hearings; a boisterous, heroic, or tender spirit; a melodic phrase with precisely detailed articulations and dynamics; perfectly placed "wrong notes"; imaginative shifts of texture and register.

Even an experienced teacher may be shocked and humbled by the rich creativity and originality of these examples. A simple restrictive theory-based assignment would not encourage these creative tendrils to grow; in fact, it could inhibit or even crush them. The excerpt in Figure 7.1 shows an example of how the open assignment allows a student to skip levels. The eleven-year-old composer, who had no formal theory training, combined his love of Chopin and Philip Glass to create compelling chromatic harmony in the opening of this piece, which went on to win a regional composition prize.

FIGURE 7.1 Example of chromatic harmony created in an open-assignment project.

The Pedagogical Approach

In response to the wide array of the students' ideas, which range from simplistic to extraordinarily creative, the Hippocratic thought arises: First, do no harm. The teacher's challenge is to help all of the students to grow as composers even though they have different abilities, backgrounds, experiences, tastes, enthusiasms, and needs. Students require different types and amounts of scaffolding; they require different kinds of coaching. Some need very close sequential support, while others need to be left on their own to incubate their ideas for an extended period. Theoretically, two different students could show the teacher the same opening melody, and the appropriate response to each would be quite different, based on the students' individual profiles, thresholds, and compositional intentions. Anyone trying to teach eighty diverse students to progress in composition should use a flexible, eclectic, and pragmatic approach.

As in all project-based education, the teaching must correspond and synchronize with the students' own creative ideas. Because the curriculum is shaped by the students' interests and passions, the children's youthful enthusiasm and energy are unleashed in the compositional work. When the instruction is based on their own music, they feel its relevance and usefulness: it does not feel like a school lesson that is imposed by the teacher's authority. For example, rather than begin with a formal lesson on melodic contour, the teacher can call attention to the shape of the student's own melody. Does it flow, or feel stuck, or "is the creature inside going on an interesting journey"?

Later on, analytic examples of classic melodies can be useful, but focusing on the student's melody makes the learning immediate, meaningful, and memorable. Similarly, one can teach elements of tonality, harmony, rhythm, and form as they emerge from the context of the student work. Some sessions include formalized mini-lessons on subjects such as acoustics, notation, mathematics and music, and topics in theory, but even these are usually timed to coincide with issues that arise in the students' work.

At the second lesson, the students play or sing their first phrases. Despite the great variety among the students and their music, and therefore among their educational needs, there are recurring issues and challenges that arise in almost every group. The most common challenges include: 1) music that is disorganized, with abrupt shifts, or unrelated ideas strung together; 2) music that is overly repetitious; 3) students who are unsure of how to begin or develop their ideas; 4) music that is too conventional; 5) music that is difficult to understand; and 6) special issues concerning exceptionally gifted students.

HELPING THE STUDENT WHOSE MUSIC IS DISORGANIZED

Figure 7.2 shows the first violin melody that Sarah plays.

I encourage the students to comment positively, but specifically, on their classmate's music: "Tell us something you like about Sarah's idea." The students comment supportively that it sounds "happy" and "lively." I ask, "Sarah, is this exactly what you want, or is it a first try at something else?" She responds that she knows it is not quite right, but that she does not know how to fix it. A classmate says, "It sounds good, but it goes off-topic."

I introduce the concept of unity and variety, pointing out how most music we like is consistent enough to have integrity, but varied enough to keep our interest. I improvise a silly story that changes topic every sentence, and the children enjoy the humor and get the idea. I emphasize the positive: "Sarah, you have enough ideas for three whole pieces! Let's pick your favorite one and save the others."

The first phrase is her favorite. I demonstrate how phrases can be repeated at different pitch levels, introducing the concept of melodic sequence. Sarah

FIGURE 7.2 Example of disorganized violin melody.

FIGURE 7.3 Evolution of violin melody through process of close scaffolding.

experiments and decides that measure 3 should repeat measure 1 one step lower, and cadence on a whole note D in measure 4. A classmate points out, "It sounds great, but too over, like it's the ending." What other notes could the phrase end on? The students sing different versions. Sarah moves from the D to an F-sharp. "Remember, Sarah, you can agree now and change your mind later," I point out. "It has to be the way *you* like it."

What next? Sarah suggests using the same rhythmic figure again. "If you repeat the same rhythm too many times, it might not be as interesting," I say. "Try using just half of it." I demonstrate several possibilities. The symmetries *make sense* to Sarah. She comes back the following week with the melody shown in Figure 7.3, and goes on to complete her first composition with ease in the subsequent weeks.

Although I supported Sarah with close scaffolding, the help was not based on coercion or criticism, but rather on a compassionate, collaborative attempt to discover the composer's intent and to help her realize the import and consequences of her own musical ideas. When making suggestions, the teacher should try to avoid being too emotionally attached to any specific suggestion, so that the student can make free choices without fear of disappointing the teacher.

HELPING THE STUDENT WHOSE MUSIC IS OVERLY REPETITIVE

Here, in Figure 7.4, is Brendan's first piano melody:

I react with this comment: "It's fun to explore a scale with chords, isn't it, Brendan? It climbs up and up like an escalator." We all sing it together, first on neutral syllables and then with solfège. "It sounds like a really good exercise or warm up," I say. We discuss the differences between exercises and "songs," returning to the concept of unity and variety, but now with an emphasis on variety. "Do you want to keep it like this, or do you want to make it more like a song, Brendan?" "More like a song." "OK, but let's keep this version as your first exercise."

FIGURE 7.4 Example of musical idea that is overly repetitive.

FIGURE 7.5 Musical idea evolves and expands after peer interaction.

Then I pose this question to the whole group: "How can Brendan make this more like a song?" The students answer, "He can change direction." "He can change the rhythm." I sing the first two measures and invite each student to improvise singing the next two measures. In this situation, it is usually easier for students other than the composer to respond, because they have some distance from the original idea. After hearing his classmates' ideas, Brendan improvises his own, borrowing a classmate's rhythm, but with his own pitches, as shown in Figure 7.5:

Brendan's cadence on the tonic pitch shows a healthy sense of tonal closure, but it comes too early in the piece, closing off the melodic and implicit harmonic motion. Many young composers inadvertently create antecedent phrases as their opening melodies. "You have created a beautiful answer. Now let's make a question that goes before it," I suggest. This is an important lesson that shows the children that compositions are not necessarily created in order, "from left to right." It also increases their optimism, because their initial idea doubles, almost magically; and since they are told that the idea can probably recur later in the piece, their four measures have grown to sixteen.

In cases like Sarah's and Brendan's, after a couple of nudges forward by the teacher and classmates, the students usually "get it," and progress based on their own musical intuition. I show them how their ideas look on paper, but encourage them to continue extensions without having the students notate them, because too often students write notes without "hearing" them, disrupting the musical flow. I often transcribe the students' ideas, but always keep photocopies, because many young composers—including highly responsible children—lose their written work at some time during the school year.

HELPING THE STUDENT WHO DOES NOT KNOW HOW TO BEGIN

In order to preserve the greatest degree of individual creativity, an effective strategy is to gradually narrow the choices. I ask the student: "What kind of feeling or mood do you want to try? Can you hear a little tune that sounds like that?" Another tactic is to try a thought experiment: "Everyone close your eyes. Imagine that you are sitting comfortably in the concert audience. Your music teacher is about to perform your composition. In your imagination, listen to how it sounds." Typically, approximately a quarter of the students will "hear" something they can use.

If that thought experiment does not trigger an idea, the next level is to offer pairs of choices: "Would you like to try something fast or slow, happy or sad, major or minor, jazzy or classical?" To break the ice, the following sequence of transformations works well: The student 1) plays a chosen scale, ascending; 2) plays the scale again, choosing contrasting dynamics for the pitches; 3) adds contrasting articulations; 4) has the option of repeating pitches; 5) has the option of skipping pitches and changing direction in the scale; 6) has the option of changing the rhythm. In this way, the student is led through an exploratory process without the possibility of creative error. Usually, something "clicks," and the student finds an aurally satisfying idea.

In the very rare case in which this does not work, the teacher can demonstrate simple arpeggiations of tonic, dominant, and subdominants, and thereby help the student to build a pattern using the triads, together with passing tones and neighbor tones, that makes sense to the child. Unfortunately, this "last resort" tactic is the one with which many composition teachers begin. In any event, as soon as possible, the student and classmates should sing the ideas to ensure their musical meaningfulness.

HELPING THE STUDENTS TO "GROW" THEIR PIECES

Students realize the essential question as they move forward is, "What sounds good next?" Some are able to extend their ideas with ease, playing or singing the continuations each week. If students present extended ideas, I record them so that I can think about them in depth without making the students play them repeatedly.

Other students need more support. For those who have trouble "hearing" the next phrase, it is often effective to have them listen while the teacher or classmates sing or play the existing music, and to encourage them to imagine the continuation. If this aural technique does not succeed, the teacher can make technical suggestions, such as retaining a motivic rhythm while transforming pitch. The teacher can demonstrate a series of solutions to the musical problem, while stressing that the young composer "owns" the work and should decide the outcome. Specific suggestions should always offer a variety of approaches, so that the student remains empowered as a creator.

A former student, now a successful adult composer and arranger, recalls that when he was stuck, the teacher was able "to guide my compositions forward, while at the same time helping me maintain my voice as a composer. He would provide several solutions to how a piece might progress, then break down the ways I could realize the one I chose. I use a version of this method to this day" (Orton, 2011).

As the students move forward linearly, they gradually begin to rise above the musical terrain and see their pieces more synoptically. The idea of form emerges naturally, as they realize the need for "a new part." They usually introduce formal contrast on their own, and the teacher can validate and explain the devices that the students have used: harmonic contrast, textural change, modal alteration, registral shifts, and so forth. Most young composers have an affinity for binary, rounded binary, and ternary forms based on their listening and playing experience. As they mature, the teacher can introduce more advanced topics, such as canon technique and additional formal structures.

When addressing issues like proportions, unity-variety, tension-release, and the dynamism and trajectory of a composition, the teacher can use non-technical intuitive language, phrasing suggestions in the form of questions or comments: "Doesn't this want to stay here a bit?" "It moves, but it knows when to stop," "You can stretch that point out more, if you want to," "Do you mean for it to change suddenly here?" "When should it change?" (Smith, 2007).

To help all the students move forward steadily, the teacher should save time at the end of each lesson for the students to verbalize their goals for the coming week. The teacher may have suggested a task or pathway for the students during the lesson, but that is no guarantee that they understand or remember how to proceed. As the students articulate their next steps, the teacher can clarify areas of confusion and help to instill confidence. It is essential that the students feel optimistic about their way forward. Before they leave the room, ask, "Who is feeling hopeful about their piece this week?" If a student responds hesitantly, or not at all, the teacher can probe to discover the problem and facilitate a solution. The teacher's empathetic encouragement and high expectation of progress are essential factors in the students' success, perhaps more influential than any of the specific teaching.

HELPING THE STUDENTS WHOSE MUSIC IS TOO CONVENTIONAL

Just as it is natural for children to pass through schematic and conformist stages in the visual arts, it is normal and healthy for them to create music that is predictable and conventional. Many students get great satisfaction from creating something "normal." It sounds real and official to them, and it keeps them safe from criticism or ridicule as being "different." In addition to being a natural part of child development, this predilection is reinforced by simple songs they sing in music classes, exercises in their instrumental lesson books, and simplified arrangements they play in their school ensembles.

By creating symmetrical phrases with melodies and harmonies that "make sense" and achieve tonal closure, students are demonstrating mastery of the most basic level of tonal composition. However, even within the framework of simple, conventional musical language, the teacher can encourage the student to create music of greater interest. One method is to appeal to physical movement and emotion. If the students' favorite sport is soccer, ask them to musically convey the feeling of scoring a goal. Particularly with girls, suggest that they dance impromptu at home and sing the sound track that should go with their dance. In both cases, the linkage with physical activity and emotion can energize and add interest to the music, without challenging the simple language the students are using.

Another way to move them away from predictability is to have a discussion about expectations and surprise: "You have done a great job landing right on the note we expect! What would happen if you were to surprise us, instead?"; "What if you hit a wrong note on purpose?"

More developed students are ready for a direct challenge. After studying different conventional scales, the students can create their own "synthetic" scales and compose in them. They can also learn contemporary techniques to transform their pitch material.

One way to expand all students' musical vocabulary is to play a wide variety of music for them: Stravinsky, Miles Davis, William Bolcom, Mahler, Josquin, James Brown, Copland, Tuvan throat singing—of course, the list is endless. Students incorporate the new sounds into their own styles in accordance with their developmental readiness and individual taste. As students mature, the teacher can encourage their aesthetic development with more detailed analysis of stylistically diverse compositions.

More advanced students also benefit from exercises that limit compositional freedom in order to develop specific technical skills (Wilson, 2001). I advocate beginning with the natural tunefulness of young composers in order to develop their own intuitive musical "voices." However, for them to progress to advanced levels, they need to learn to think analytically and discover how "to push notes around" (Deemer, 2009).

HELPING THE EXCEPTIONALLY GIFTED STUDENTS

The exceptionally gifted student presents a complex set of opportunities and challenges for the composition teacher. Although gifted students come in many varieties, they often share common traits (Clark, 1992). Some of the positive attributes are dazzling: extraordinary comprehension and attentiveness; accelerated thought processes; the ability to extrapolate exponentially; and highly advanced musical skill. It is exciting for a teacher to be understood before even finishing a sentence, or to see a fifth grader grasp group theoretic concepts that college music majors struggle with. On the other hand, the positive attributes are dialectically linked to possible problems: boredom with conventional curriculum, sometimes disguised as laziness; problems with interpersonal relationships; and perfectionism or burnout.

The teacher of gifted students may have to challenge his or her own preconceptions. Curriculum cannot move in a straight line, or at a steady pace, but should often accelerate parabolically. The students may know more than the teacher in several subject areas. The students may think more quickly than the teacher, or have more raw musical talent. Yet, if the teacher accepts this joyfully, and works confidently to unleash the potential of the children, he or she can win the children's respect and mentor them successfully. The teacher has to resist the inclination to compensate by asserting authority as a defensive counterbalance to the students' astonishing abilities.

In striking contrast to Sarah and Brendan, discussed above, who needed closely attentive scaffolding to get started on their compositions, many gifted children need a prolonged period of independent experimentation and incubation. Paul, a fifth-grader who had been able to perform pieces like Beethoven's Sonata "Pathétique" when he was eight years old, invented the piano theme shown in Figure 7.6, and began to improvise on it:

At first, Paul said that he would just like to improvise on the ideas, and not decide on one set version. In my opinion, this was because he felt it was an overwhelming task to make the hundreds of required little choices all at once. I told him that he should have fun with the improvisation for as long as he wished, but also suggested that after a lot of experimentation, it is often rewarding to create a version as a finished composition. He agreed that he would like to try that.

For many weeks, he played the gradually developing version of the piece, constantly revising and extending it in both directions, sometimes writing down sections in shorthand notation (noteheads without stems) to remember them better. I transcribed some of his improvisations, so that he could learn the proper notation, and I recorded him at each lesson and photocopied his sketches, in order to reflect on his progress. My initial feedback consisted of comments like, "Wow! It really seems to be coming together. Do you want some suggestions, or just to keep rolling with it?" He reassured me that it was going fine and that he just needed to keep "fooling around" with it. Each week I asked him how specific he wanted my advice to be, and we agreed that I would get more specific when he was ready.

Even though I knew there were many aspects he could improve, I felt that more specific intervention at the time would probably impede his progress. Occasionally I would make a suggestion like "Don't forget to let the left hand have the melody sometimes," and demonstrate. One week, his harmony seemed to imply a harmonic sequence that he did not quite understand, so I taught him and his classmates the concept of a diatonic circle of fifths progression. The entire piece was firmly in the key of G minor, and I suggested that he could achieve more large scale harmonic interest by modulating at some point, but that he should not worry about it now because it would be easy to move to another key and return to the tonic after he sketched out all of his ideas.

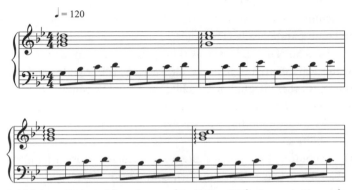

FIGURE 7.6 Initial thematic material serving as a departure point for improvisation and exploration.

Finally, after about three months, Paul announced that he had come to the end of the piece. His sketch was six pages of tiny noteheads, about four minutes of music, with many of the rhythms notated accurately. Paul's classmates, also profoundly talented, responded with applause and cries of "bravo" and "encore."

At that point, Paul was ready to hear my detailed feedback. I pointed out certain left-hand parts that were silent, or underdeveloped. "Is that on purpose, or did you not get around to it yet?" I asked. I demonstrated ways to vary the left-hand texture. I suggested that his right thumb could add inner voices to some melodic passages to enrich the texture. I demonstrated, and he eagerly offered to create the revisions by himself.

The biggest point, which I had previously hinted at, was that the entire piece was in G minor, and that it might be effective to modulate to a secondary key and then return to G minor. I showed him how his circle of fifths harmonic sequence section could be "bent" to point to C minor, much to his delight. He composed the C minor section and the return to G minor during the following week.

I helped Paul to correct his manuscript, and once the piece was lying on the page, it became easier to discuss revision. Paul sensed correctly that some of the proportions could be altered slightly—that he had improvised a bit too long in some sections. The discourse shifted between technical music terms (e.g., specific pitches, intervals, harmonies) and metaphorical concepts (e.g., flow, arrival, pacing).

I believe that my specific comments were helpful to Paul, but that the most important teaching role I played was that of a supportive, caring listener who allowed him time to incubate his ideas. Without the teacher's consistent receptivity and optimistic encouragement, he would probably not have completed it. Reflecting on the experience, Paul said, "Before, I thought that on one side there were pieces by people like Beethoven, and on the other side there was impromptu playing. Now I realize that in the middle are my own compositions."

Because their standards for achievement are so high, some gifted students are inhibited by perfectionism. Keeping the atmosphere of the classroom positive and supportive mitigates the problem, but often the students are their own worst critics. Although the thrust of the Three Village approach is to encourage students to embrace musical ideas with strong affective attachment, in the case of the perfectionist, it is often helpful to do the opposite—to help the students detach from the music emotionally, at least temporarily.

Sometimes it is comically simple, as in the following example. Jane, a talented fifth grader, had just finished her first piece, an excellent piano composition. She came into class with a sheet of music manuscript containing the beginning of her second piece, announcing, "I won't play this in front of you guys, because it's really bad. I hate it!" I said, "Jane, just write Mary on the top of the sheet." She wrote "Mary" on her page, sat down at the piano, and cheerfully played her music. Of course, she was not fooled, but even that slight distancing overcame her fear.

A stronger version of this kind of displacement is often effective. When students are overly critical of their music, I suggest that they pretend that a friend had written it: "Is that how you would talk to a friend about his or her music? Wouldn't you make helpful suggestions instead? Wouldn't you try to help find ways to fix it?" Many students find this beneficial. Also useful are cognitive strategies, such as comparing the perfectionist's negative opinion to the positive opinion of teacher and classmates and highlighting the successes of the student.

Carl is a talented sixth grader who had had a very successful year as a fifth-grade composer. He had great difficulty finding a starting idea for a new piano piece. To nudge him out of his rut, I suggested that he create his own scale, and demonstrated several unusual scales. He did not like that idea and said he would like to write in a minor key. I encouraged him to improvise some minor ideas and demonstrated some simple melodies. The next week I agreed that he could experiment with his ideas in an adjacent room. When he returned, he told me that he had not liked anything he played, and I asked him to show me just a few of the notes. I demonstrated how his minor arpeggiations could become part of an attractive melody. He agreed to work with the idea that week.

After extending the music for two weeks, Carl decided to scrap it and start on something else, but he had no idea where to begin. To detach him and make it less personal, I showed him all of the diatonic modes and improvised brief modal ideas. He liked the sound of the Phrygian mode and wrote down an effective opening passage. However, the same cycle recurred. After two weeks of work, he discarded it. I spoke with his classroom teacher, string lesson teacher, and mother, to get a broader perspective and to be sure that he was not suffering from depression. My tentative conclusion was that the problem was perfectionism and not depression. Carl assured me that he enjoyed the composition program and did not want to quit.

After he was about to reject his *third* idea, I said: "Carl, let's do an experiment. Let's finish this one. It may turn out that we made a mistake. It may not end up the way you want, but let's wait to see. We can always admit later that we were wrong. And you don't have to 100 percent approve of every idea you put in the piece. Use anything that you 70 percent approve—maybe even just 65 percent." Carl smiled and agreed. Although he needed close support, he persevered successfully to a happy outcome.

Another common problem for exceptionally gifted students, but not limited to them, is the difficulty of balancing competing demands and stresses in their lives. Some of my students go to school seven days a week, with weekends taken up by pre-college music programs, math enrichment classes, and ethnic language and culture programs. Many take weekly private music lessons on two instruments. Some of their parents expect them to do several hours of daily homework and extra math drills. The children compete in spelling bees and competitions in science, math, and music. Some extraordinarily gifted students may even be flying to other cities to perform recitals or concertos!

An important task for the teacher is to help the students to find strategies for coping with the competing demands and to create breathing room for composition in their lives. Sympathetic and frank discussion about pressures, priorities, and time management increases the children's self-understanding and coping skills. If students stressfully worry that they do not have enough time to work on their compositions, the teacher can suggest that they add just six or seven minutes for composition into their instrumental practice time, or offer to give them extra class time before the start of the school day, or during recess when the weather is inclement. In many cases, time spent improvising and composing appears to reduce the students' stress, according to reports from students, parents, and teachers.

The teacher has to know when to push and when to hold back. For example, I might say: "Hey guys, there are two opposite kinds of mistakes I don't want to make. On the one hand, I don't want to nag and pressure you too much and make you stress out. But on the other hand, I want to make sure I encourage you enough that you know I believe in your ability to do this. Which mistake am I making?" Sometimes students give direct answers to this question, leading to fruitful troubleshooting, but more often, the question leads them to recalibrate their own sense of responsibility and commitment with greater maturity.

Other school personnel may not always realize how much support the extremely gifted need, because the students' achievements and accolades are so dazzling. In fact, these students require the consistent, understanding empathy of adults whom they trust throughout their school careers. By working side by side with exceptionally gifted students, teachers can gain insights that they can share with administrators and other teachers, in order to help them better understand the substance and context of the complicated worlds these special students inhabit.

If one teaches eighty composers, chances are high that at least a few will reach extraordinary levels of achievement. The teacher has a responsibility to help their families find programs and resources that will enable these wunderkinds to grow and thrive.

Notation and Publication

All fifth graders in the Three Village program are ready to learn standard music notation. I discourage them from notating their ideas too early in the compositional process, because the act of writing can impede the creative musical flow. When students write too soon, they often get lost among the dots and lose track of the authentic musical idea. (A few students, however, are able to notate as they create, just like advanced composers.) While they create, the students often sketch their ideas with graphic or schematic notation as an aide-mémoire.

As phrases emerge with clarity, I teach the composers to notate conventionally. The instruction is two-pronged. I teach a mini-lesson on the origin of clefs and notation, and distribute teacher-created handouts titled "Music Writing Tips." A small number of students retain most or all of the information included: clefs, key and time signatures, stem placement, beaming rules, rhythm dots, flags, accidentals, dynamics, and articulation. This specific instruction is complemented by a more holistic approach that succeeds with a larger number of students. By transcribing their initial ideas, I show them how their music looks when notated properly. Most students grasp the correspondence between image and sound and are able to extrapolate successfully. Notation skills are also reinforced by melodic dictation games.

The fifth graders learn to notate by hand with pencil and paper before moving on to notation software in sixth grade. In rare cases, when music by a fifth grader contains many dense chords, ledger lines, or other complexities, we resort to notation software, because the writing task would be inappropriate. Beginning with hand-written notation presents several advantages. Students learn to notate correctly, because the computer is not there to format everything automatically. The experience of gaining musical literacy is good preparation for further studies in music theory and composition. The act of writing each note, dynamic, and articulation connects the composer to his or her work with a strong sense of authorship and ownership.

Even when Three Village students move on to notation software in sixth grade, they use it only after most, or all, of the composing has taken place. Composing *within* the software often leads students to click on notes without "hearing" them meaningfully, reducing the authentic intentionality of the music. It also often leads to overly repetitious music due to the ease of cutting, pasting, and repeating. The software may encourage "sedimentary" texture, in which the parts or voices are layered upon each other, rather than interacting with living responsiveness. The immediate feedback of the software playback is valuable, but is deceptive in areas like orchestration. Of course, when used appropriately, the software has tremendous advantages: ease of revision, extraction of parts, portability, and clarity.

The publication of the annual *Collection of Pieces by Young Composers* every year provides strong motivation for the students to persist in the sometimes tedious task of notation. After performing at the Young Composers Festival in June, the students eagerly line up to receive their copies of the book, which includes more than 150 pages of compositions with student-created artwork on the cover. The students enjoy the opportunity to study pieces that impressed them during the concert, and pieces by other students often inspire and influence them positively. The publication fosters a sense of community among the young composers. Many students and their families treasure the books for years.

Public Performance

Although the fifth and sixth graders perform some of their pieces in various venues throughout the school year, such as recitals, school plays, and talent shows, the culminating event of the year is the annual Young Composers Festival. From their very first lessons, the students look forward to the goal of public performance with varying combinations of hope, excitement, and trepidation. Completing the arc of creation from original conception to public performance is a tremendously affirming process for the young musicians.

The open-ended assignment that initiated the compositional process results in a concert of kaleidoscopic variety. One of the most common reactions by first-time attendees is surprise at the diversity of style and genre, as well as the high quality of the music. One after another, students take the stage, as soloists (sometimes with piano accompaniment by the teacher) or as members of small ensembles. The compositions might include a Clementi-like piano sonatina movement; an avant-garde string quartet based on the myth of Perseus and Andromeda; an art song about dreams; a blues composition for a jazz quintet; a fiddle tune with a rock beat; or a Chopin-inspired waltz. An arbitrary sequence of titles from the most recent concert illustrates the range of student ideas and emotions: *Simply Cool, Skipping in the Meadow, Unique, Walking Through Your Dreams, A Journey of Wishes*, and *Mysterious Loss*.

The students demonstrate their strong sense of community by enthusiastically responding to each performance, applauding and cheering for each other supportively. Because the music emerges from each student's unique point of view, the emotional impact is striking. The compositions reveal the character of the composers—sometimes confirming the personality that parents and friends know, but occasionally surprising everyone with unexpected traits. In a letter to the board of education defending the program from a possible budget cut, one parent wrote that "we, the parents, have learned more about our children through their work" in composition.

Connecting to a Bigger World

A number of advanced students benefit from experiences that transcend the school walls, such as regional, state, and national programs where they can interact with gifted peers and professional composers. Every year about a dozen Three Village students are invited to present their compositions at the Long Island Composers Alliance "Music by and for Students" Concert at Hofstra University, a program founded more than three decades ago by professional composers Marga Richter and Herbert A. Deutsch (no relation to the author).

Many Three Village students also submit their compositions to the New York State School Music Association (NYSSMA) composition evaluation program (www.nyssma.org/composition). In a typical year, NYSSMA receives more than 100 pieces written for traditional instruments and/or voice and more than 60 electronic compositions submitted by students (K–11) from across the state. Professional composers and composition teachers respond to each composition with detailed supportive written evaluations, highlighting the strengths of the composition and making suggestions for future growth. Not only the students, but also their teachers gain insight when reading the evaluations, which are narrative in format, without quantitative scores. It is important for advanced students to hear an evaluative point of view distinct from that of their teacher.

Although the focus of the NYSSMA program is on feedback and encouragement, a panel of adjudicators selects the most outstanding compositions for performance at the annual All-State Winter Conference. At the conference, the NYSSMA Young Composers participate in composition coaching workshops with professional composers and attend a seminar with the NYSSMA Composer-in-Residence, who is a distinguished artist. The list of NYSSMA Composers-in-Residence has included such fine composers as William Bolcom, Joseph Schwantner, and Joan Tower.

One past participant, who is now doing graduate work in composition and piano at Juilliard, remembers: "As composers we're naturally isolated, and to hear all of the wonderfully talented composers from the state opened me up to new and creative possibilities. The reactions and opinions of the distinguished Composers-in-Residence have stayed with me and influenced my compositional growth. It was also wonderful to be introduced to their music and have the opportunity to delve into their creative thought processes. I consider myself a lucky guy to have been included in this exploratory and inspiring atmosphere" (Deutsch, 2008).

The Impact of the Program

All of the participants in the Three Village program demonstrate some degree of mastery in composition, ranging from basic to exceptional. The students' progress is not limited to acquiring compositional skills per se. Parents, other music teachers, and the students themselves notice growth in several areas, including musical literacy, expressiveness, intonation, stage presence, and self-confidence.

After the Young Composers Festival in June, the students reflect on their experience via written answers to these questions: "What was it like to compose your own music? Did it change the way you feel about music or your instrument?" The student responses coalesce around a cluster of themes: freedom, choice, and power; expression and emotion; technical knowledge; instrumental functionality; and perspectives on composition.

The most common statement in feedback sheets (I have more than 1,200 at this point) is "Composing is fun!" This simple response is a result of our playful "unschool-like" constructivist approach and emergent curriculum. Coupled with the fun, however, is the frequent mention that composing is "hard work." Many students express greater appreciation for the work of other composers, now that they "realize that all of these composers worked hard to create these pieces and make them beautiful," as one student put it. They appreciate the intentionality of music more intensely. One student wrote, "Now, I always think: What did the composer mean by that?"

Students appreciate the freedom entailed in the process. "It was like creating a game with rules and flexibilities," said a fifth grader. "It felt good to make my own music, because it was my choice to make music that I like," wrote another. Another young composer said, "I felt I could create anything: the sound of rain, the roar of a tiger, the squawk of a bird. Composing brought out my imagination and made me more creative."

Students also appreciate the emotional outlet. "To compose my own music is bringing all my emotions through my instrument," said a sixth grader. Another sixth grader reported, "Composition was my anger management for the year!" The experience increases the students' attachment to their instruments. "Now I feel I am part of the instrument. I feel I can be friends with my piano," said a sixth grader. Another said, " Composing music allowed me to explore the limits of my instrument."

Many alumni of the program are now adults involved in professional composition and other areas of the music world. Asked to reflect on their experience in the program and its impact, they say they felt encouraged by the open atmosphere and non-judgmental mentoring, and value the emphasis placed on collaboration, which they rely on as adults. They appreciate being exposed to a multiplicity of great music in different genres and styles, and feel they benefited from learning theory and composition skills at an early age. Finally, the program improved their problem-solving skills and helped them gain confidence, especially from opportunities to present and discuss their compositions at conferences, where they met other talented peers and professional composers.

Even alumni who are in professions other than music feel the impact of the program. A Harvard plant biologist says that composition "provides a nice framework for approaching a pattern by decomposing it into its basic pieces, and then trying to rebuild it," that is relevant to his work. A clinical psychology researcher, who studies music and the brain, talks about the effect on her problem-solving skills. "I still use skills I learned from composition in my research. Some of it is obvious: I sometimes compose musical stimuli to use in an experiment, and the theory knowledge helps me understand and create different experimental paradigms. Some of it is less obvious: one thing composition taught me was that when I was stuck, there was no 'powering through' in a composition. I had to go back several bars and come up with a new melodic/harmonic plan or motif to make it work. And I feel it's often that way with research. If something's not working, it's not working for a reason. Perhaps my logic or hypotheses about the underlying mechanism is flawed, and so I need to go back a few steps and think about how to get from point A to point B in order to study or understand a particular phenomenon."

Conclusion

The Three Village student composition program provides a free and open environment in which a large number of young composers receive instruction shaped directly by their own attitudes, aptitudes, and interests. As a result, they are encouraged to develop unique compositional "voices" and express themselves authentically in their original music. All of the participants travel the creative trajectory that leads from composition to performance, so that their mastery and skills are publicly affirmed. Because the approach allows them to rise quickly to their individually appropriate levels, many gifted students demonstrate exceptional progress, and several have followed their passion all the way to careers in composition. All of the participants, at all levels of ability, emerge with a greater appreciation of music, because the program invites them into the inner world of music and deepens their musical understanding.

References

Clark, B. (1992). *Growing Up Gifted: Developing the Potential of Children at Home and at School*, Fourth Edition. New York: Merrill.

Deemer, R. (2009). Composing 101 for Music Teachers. Presentation at New York State School Music Association Winter Conference (December 3, 2009).

Deutsch, D. (2008). Celebrating 10 Years of Composition. *School Music News*, 72(2).

Deutsch, D. (2009). Mentoring Young Composers: The small-group, individualized approach. *Kansas Music Review*, 27–32.

Engel, S. (2005). *Real Kids: Creating Meaning in Everyday Life*. Cambridge, MA: Harvard University Press.

Fisher-Lochhead, C. (2011). Personal communication.

Hickey, M., and Webster, P. (2001). Creative Thinking in Music. *Music Educators Journal*, 88(1), 19–23.

Orton, M. (2011). Personal communication.

Smith, J. P. (2007). It's a matter of principles: Encouraging extension and revision in young composers. Paper presented at the Conference on Music Learning and Teaching Center for Applied Research in Musical Understanding (CARMU). Oakland University: Rochester, MI.

Wilson, D. (2001). Guidelines for Coaching Student Composers. *Music Educators Journal*, 88(1), 28–33.

8 }

Facilitating Composition in Instrumental Settings
Alexander P. Koops

Introduction

This chapter aims to give suggestions for how to prepare pre-service music teachers to teach music composition in instrumental ensembles. The chapter begins with a rationale for including composition in instrumental ensemble activities in public schools and then considers the problems of time, training, music notation, and large group composition. Then it offers suggestions for incorporating composition lessons in music education methods classes, followed by ideas for including composition activities in percussion, woodwinds, brass, and strings techniques classes. The chapter concludes with general guidelines for including composition in instrumental ensembles.

Rationale: Why Music Composition in Instrumental Music Classes?

Music composition is listed within the National Standards for Arts Education and is encouraged by leaders in the field of music education for many reasons, particularly in that it allows students to express themselves in a personal way that is very different from performing or listening to music. Reimer (2003) emphasizes composition as equally important to other areas of music such as performance, improvisation, and analysis. Elliott (1995) and Barrett (2006) stress that the benefits of composition include developing musicianship skills, listening skills, an understanding of contemporary music, and an understanding of music theory. They believe composition provides both the training for the beginning composer and an outlet for all music students' creativity.

Instrumental music ensembles represent a large part of the current public school music student population, but unfortunately, many of these instrumental programs do not include composition primarily because of lack of time (often due to performance pressure), resources, and professional training (Koops, 2009). The idea of trying to compose with thirty or more people simultaneously can be daunting. Additionally, students are usually limited in their notation skills, and notation, when used, tends to significantly limit students' creativity (Wiggins, 2001). All of these problems can be addressed and overcome in most instrumental music programs.

While composition is sometimes viewed as an activity only for particularly gifted people, the opposite idea needs to be nurtured: composition should be an integral part of every person's study of music, particularly to become a well-rounded person and musician. Music composition very effectively teaches students form, theory, harmony, and creativity. Children love composing music. It is a natural instinct for all human beings: we all have a need to express ourselves with our own unique ideas and we all are born with an innate ability to express ourselves through music, just as a toddler naturally responds to music with dance. Nurturing creativity enables wholeness in the present and in the future of student's lives. The best leaders and thinkers in the world have keen intelligence, but also active creative thought. Einstein's breakthroughs in science came because he thought creatively with visual pictures in multiple dimensions, whereas most other scientists were stuck thinking on flat paper the way things had always been thought. The key was Einstein's creativity, not his IQ (Isaacson, 2008). "A dog that wags its tail learned to do so when he was young" (Etsako, Nigerian proverb). Instilling a love of creativity and nurturing it in children helps them the rest of their lives in any occupation, activity, and contribution to society.

The Problems: Time, Training, Notation, and Large Group Composition

TIME

Most instrumental instructors focus primarily on performances and create their yearly schedule around these performances. They claim to never have enough rehearsals, except for after the final concerts—a time period that has its own set of problems. And of course, good concerts mean good programs, which in turn draw strong administrative and local support. So however could something else fit into the curriculum and schedule?

Composition contributes to the development of better musicians. Time spent in composition is an investment into their skills as well as the music program. Students who compose become increasingly aware of how music works. Teachers may program a few easier pieces at the beginning of the year to allow for a more flexible rehearsal schedule where composition can be included without pressure of falling behind in concert preparations, but once students have gained compositional skills of their own, the need for easier literature will diminish. Students will have a stronger understanding of music and will be able to perform at a higher level.

Another solution to the time crunch is to give some concerts a new focus. This is, after all, an educational enterprise, and so the focus must be on learning. A simple but unnecessary solution is to reduce the number of performances to allow for more student composition. Better yet, though, is to hold composer concerts, perhaps "An Evening with Composers" featuring a local professional composer along with some pieces composed by the programs own students. A collaborative composition completed with input from the entire ensemble can also be a special programming feature. Students are motivated by interactions with a local composer, in person in their own classrooms. Teachers should look for opportunities to commission composers and/or have them as guests in their classroom and ensemble rehearsals and performances. Composers are typically enthused by working with students in rehearsals and some are even willing to be guest conductors for concerts, particularly of their own music.

Finally, while composing can take a fair amount of time, composing activities do not have to take an entire class period, let alone a three-week unit. Short composition lessons can take as little as fifteen minutes and still produce some really exciting and unique music. And then of course, teachers can use the time at the end of the school year (that dead time after the final concert) to incorporate composition. Instead of showing videos, collecting music, and offering study halls, composing can provide a refreshing and exciting way to end the year!

PROFESSIONAL TRAINING

Music instructors need to know composition themselves and practice it, if they are going to incorporate it in their teaching. One of the problems current teachers face is the lack of professional training in applied composition as well as in teaching composition. Undergraduate students should enroll in individual composition lessons and deliberately develop composing skills while enrolled in their music programs. Active teachers should attend conferences and listen to colleagues' ideas on incorporating composition into their programs. Both music education students and teachers should challenge themselves to create a piece of new music for their own ensemble to conduct or perform in. Students and teachers should work with colleagues, professional composers, friends, and their own students to develop and refine their ideas. There are also many excellent printed resources available such as Russo's (1988) *Composing Music: A New Approach*, Hickey's (2003) *Why and How to Teach Music Composition*, or Hickey's (1997) article, "Teaching Ensembles to Compose and Improvise."

MUSIC NOTATION

Music notation is usually regarded as a key component in the composition process, but students often struggle in their attempts to write down music, and many teachers view the problems of notation as a deterrent to including composing in their curriculum. The problems with writing down musical notes should not stop teachers from including composition assignments. Rather, teachers can work on composition without notation; or if they include it, they can use graphic notation, or appropriately limited traditional notation. Students can also compose with free computer software programs such as Noteflight or MuseScore, or programs such as Logic, Finale, and Sibelius, which help with notation, or they can skip the notation altogether and just work with sounds, live performances, and recordings (including using programs like GarageBand®).

For younger students who have not developed advanced notation skills, it is easy to avoid traditional notation and still compose fun pieces that show form, harmony, and melody. Students may need to represent the music visually with pictures or words that describe the sounds or use graphic notation. Some students may want to get their ideas written down with traditional notation, and then the teacher should help. Local university students may help transcribe music as well, either during a school visit or from a recording made during a rehearsal.

Regarding the place of notation in composition assignments, Wiggin's *Teaching for Musical Understanding* (2001) emphasizes that teachers should not always ask students to write down or notate their work because even when non-standard notation is used, the act of writing it down can limit creativity. She advises teachers to consider whether the assignment truly reflects the concept or principle the students are supposed to focus on and if it contains requirements that detract from that focus. She suggests that teachers decide to include or not include traditional or graphic notation when they work on music composition, depending on the focus of the composition lesson. Whichever is the case, teachers should make sure their composition exercise is not simply a notation exercise! Learning to notate music is an important skill, but must not be equated with composing.

LARGE GROUP COMPOSITION

While composing is usually considered an activity best completed by an individual, it can in fact be accomplished with a large group. Teachers must consider whether to work on composition assignments with a large group (full instrumental ensemble), small group (chamber ensemble), or individuals. Often the constraints of classroom space and time do not allow for students to work as individuals or even as small groups.

For schools with computer labs or access to laptops or iPads, individual students can compose with free music composition and notation programs such as Musescore and Noteflight, or many other programs such as GarageBand®, Logic, Sibelius, and Finale. It may also be possible to set up a few computer stations with noise-canceling headphones in the back of an ensemble rehearsal room. One advantage of using computer programs is the immediate playback capabilities. If extra classrooms or practice rooms are available, students can certainly work on composition individually or in small groups. The advantage here is that students can hear what their live performance sounds and feels like, and immediately try out ideas on their own instruments.

In many ensemble situations, the teacher can best approach composing by simply working as a large group altogether in one room. Collaborating on a composition with a group of people is a very viable, educational, and productive activity. Group composition offers a chance for everyone to learn from each other. As students interact and experiment with various compositional ideas, the teacher can facilitate a respectful atmosphere of listening and voting on various ideas. An enthusiastic atmosphere of creativity can be encouraged and nurtured when respect and trust are established. At the end of each session, students can be given individual homework, or simply encouraged to compose individually if they feel inspired to pursue more on their own. Students will grow in their understanding of composing and develop the tools to pursue it more on their own if they are drawn to it. Additionally they will have gained a tremendous measure of musical growth and knowledge.

Instrumental Music Methods Classes

One of the easiest places to add training in composing and teaching composing for pre-service music teachers is the undergraduate music methods class. Most schools have some sort of class that covers how to teach instrumental music in schools and this section gives specific exercises that can be completed in that type of class.

SOUNDSCAPES

As an introduction to composing music, teachers should have dialogue with their students about the definition of music. Ideas of noise, chaos, melody, silence, organization, and meaning can all be part of a healthy discussion of the definition of music. Matthew and Edward Schoendorf (personal communication, April 24, 2011) offer: "Music is sound and silence, organized through time and designed to convey an aesthetic experience to the listener." This definition may be used either as a starting point, or as a comparison after some discussion and debate has taken place, and should conclude with a definition of what composing is.

Music composition may begin with simple soundscapes, that is, organizing interesting sounds. Creating a soundscape provides a non-technical way to compose while classmates are at the same technical ability, and no traditional notation is required. It also builds on the idea of music being organized sound, designed to convey an aesthetic experience to the listener, and it is easy and fun to do as a group project. For example, students could produce sounds such as blowing on an instrument mouthpiece, singing through their instruments, tapping a music stand with a pencil, bowing on the bridge, or clicking instrument keys, and then organize them into a soundscape. The meaning or aesthetic element may simply be their enjoyment of finding a unique sound, or it may be purposefully finding sounds to match an emotion such as "happy" or "sad." In addition to feelings, students can be drawn into the composing experience by trying to portray images in sound, such as a rainstorm, or a beautiful, calm beach, or an exploding volcano. Students love to produce new sounds, from silly sounds to more serious ones; everything from armpit noises to weird vocables and clicking (Koops, 2009). Additionally, recording and playing back their music is a vital part of the composing process, and students love to hear their own recordings. Finally, soundscapes are a great way to start because there are no notation limits or requirements. Figure 8.1 is an example of a soundscape composition.

Some students may feel that soundscapes and other exercises are not really music. The more teachers can tie composing activities into actual repertoire, by connecting it to what the ensemble is currently working on, can sight-read, or can listen to on a recording, the more the lesson will have an impact and inspire additional creativity. Professional repertoire that has been recorded and is commercially available that could connect with the soundscape lesson as well as other lessons includes Michael Daugherty's "Sing Sing: J. Edgar Hoover" or Joseph Schwantner's "And the mountains rising nowhere." These pieces help show exploratory sounds used creatively by professional composers for strings, winds, and percussion. There is also appropriate repertoire that middle school and high school bands and orchestras can rehearse and perform, as shown in Figure 8.2, so students understand that soundscapes really do fit into the real musical world.

A. Exploratory

Instrumental key clicks or "col legno" on stringed instruments
Blow wind through instrument or percussion/strings say "Shhhhhhh"
Make noises with mouthpiece only or strings bow over the bridge
Play long tone on lowest possible note. Crescendo and decrescendo on cue
Play highest, loudest, shortest possible note on cue from conductor

B. Rainstorm

Blow air like wind
Add clicking keys or "col legno" representing pattering rain
Stomp feet and snap
Hit stands with pencil, add random thunder and lightning from bass drum or any instrument
(Reverse) Stomp feet and snap
Add clicking keys or "col legno" to represent pattering rain
Blow air like wind

FIGURE 8.1 Suggestions for soundscapes focusing on performance techniques and themes.

Band:

Blackshaw, Jody	*Whirlwind* (Grade 1)
Bukvich, Daniel	*Dinosaurs* (Grade 2)
Broege, Timothy	*The Headless Horseman* (Grade 2) (Soundscape in introduction)
Shapiro, Alex	*Paper Cut* (Grade 2.5)
Colgrass, Michael	*Old Churches* (Grade 3)
Pennington, John	*Apollo* (Grade 4)
Whitacre, Eric	*Cloudburst* (Grade 4.5)
Duffy, Thomas	*Crystals* (Grade 4/5)
Husa, Karel	*Music for Prague 1968* (Grade 6)

Orchestra:

Easy to moderate difficulty

Brown, Earle	*Modules 1 and 2*
Rands, Bernard	*Agenda*
Meyer, Richard	*Le Divin Enfant*
Meyer, Richard	*Ear-igami*
Adler, Samuel	*A little Bit Of . . . Space . . . Time*
Yamada, Keiko	*Amadare* (Aleatoric)
Balmages, Brian	*Creatures* (Aleatoric)
Cummings, Walter	*Water Reflections* (Soundscape)
Reznicow, Joshua	*Avian Dance* (Soundscape)

Moderate to difficult

Meyer, Richard	*Rosin Eating Zombies from Outer Space*
Schafer, R. Murray	*Statement in Blue*
Erb, Donald	*Bakersfield Pieces*
Hovhaness, Alan	*Floating Worlds*

FIGURE 8.2 Repertoire list featuring aleatoric or soundscape elements.

COMPOSING WARM-UPS

Warm-ups are an essential component of all instrumental ensemble rehearsals and provide an excellent opportunity for developing composers. There is no pressure of performance or time length, and composition assignments can be connected to tie in directly with repertoire currently being studied. Both the teacher and the students can compose warm-ups individually and collaboratively, offering the unique situation of inspiring each other creatively and non-competitively.

There are many ways to incorporate composing warm-ups. Having students compose rhythmic sight-reading exercises is one of the easiest ways to begin. All instrumental ensembles at all age levels should be regularly required to compose rhythm exercises which can then be used alone or in combination for rhythmic sight-reading and training of the whole ensemble. For example, with an elementary grade band or orchestra, teachers can require each student to submit an interesting two-measure rhythm and then put all the rhythms onto one sheet to use for daily rhythm drills, an example of which is shown in Figure 8.3.

FIGURE 8.3 Rhythm compositions with interpretive markings.

Other ways to incorporate composing in warm-ups may be more specific to band or orchestra. In a string ensemble, teachers can easily incorporate students' composing exercises to work on bowing technique or finger placement. Students and teachers could compose a warm-up using a scale, but assign different bowings or articulations to the scale and vary the rhythm and dynamics, with an instruction to create an exercise that is either uplifting and energetic, or depressing and melancholy. By changing only one aspect of the scale at a time (i.e., the articulation, the rhythm, or the dynamics), students will not be overwhelmed, and by getting students to think of emotions, they move past the level of simply completing a notation exercise.

In a band, warm-ups are necessary to physically warm up the instruments so they can be tuned, in addition to helping focus students' attention and develop technique. Teachers may have students compose lip slurs and long-tone exercises to help with flexibility and endurance on brass instruments. Other effective warm-up exercises can use trill exercises, or short melodic developments (riffs, or motifs) that could help with facility in crossing over the break on clarinets.

Finally, having students write a warm-up may simply be a notation assignment or a technical exercise, but it is possible to turn it into a fun composition assignment with expression and emotion. As a professional illustration, Ravel's *Bolero* demonstrates this well. For a school composition project, to encourage emotion and creativity, students can be assigned to write a happy rhythm and a sad rhythm, making sure to include dynamics and articulation. With older students, exercises could be made longer or repeated and varied with dynamics, tempo, and phrasing. Composition assignments could also be connected to musical challenges in repertoire being studied. Teachers can ask students to play their favorite note, their worst note, highest note, lowest note, as fast as possible, as slow as possible, a short melody, or non-pitched sound as yet another fun way to dive into composing. Teachers can make large cards that are labeled with these descriptions and ask student conductors to lead the warm-up by holding up the cards and organizing soundscapes. Figure 8.4 shows an example of a long-tones warm-up composition.

VARIATIONS

Variation assignments enable students to begin or continue developing composition from basic to advanced levels. They start with someone else's material and make creative changes, allowing an easy way to engage all students in composition regardless of their technical expertise. Teachers can introduce this topic by playing a recording of some variations or performing a piece in their own repertoire that uses variations. Many famous compositions use variations that are appropriate and

Purpose: to work on long tones with crescendos on low and high notes, while holding pitch steady and centered.

Students play long tones on cue simply picking random high and low notes and switching notes at will. Strive for the best possible tones. This will create cluster chords. Another option is to have the students play notes from a specific chord, but in any range, high and low, and work on tuning that chord. More complex variations include adding in dynamic changes involving subito forte, subito piano, crescendo and decrescendo and timbre changes such as woodwinds and brass. These can be pre-assigned or simply improvised by the conductor and communicated in the moment visually. Swells, zaps, and sforzandos all add depth and creativity. Students can also take turns conducting these improvised long tone exercises.

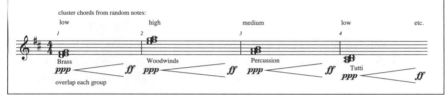

FIGURE 8.4 Sample long-tones warm-up composition.

accessible for students to listen to. Orchestral examples include Elgar's *Enigma Variations* and Mahler's *Symphony 1, Mvt. 3*, which uses the tune "Frère Jacques," but with a minor tonality. Mozart's set of variations on "Twinkle, Twinkle Little Star" (*12 Variationen über "Ah vous dirais-je, Maman"*) for piano is fun for students to listen to because they all know the tune. Richard Meyer's string orchestra piece, *Ludwig's Tango*, takes Beethoven's *Symphony V* and transforms it into a tango. John Barnes Chance's *Variations on a Korean Folksong* presents the song "Arirang" as a theme and variations. Figure 8.5 shows a sample activity for composition using a variation technique, and Figure 8.6 is an example of a composition using variation technique.

SETTING A POEM TO MUSIC

Poetry has inspired many composers over the years. Students can simply take the rhythm of the words and let that become the rhythm of a composition. Students can write rhythmic compositions and then have the option to add melody later. The melody can be limited to three notes, or the first five notes of a scale, to avoid students just picking any random notes. Establishing limits helps students focus their creativity instead of being overwhelmed by options.

Poetry provides many approaches to composing. Using rhythmic poetry, such as iambic pentameter (Shakespeare's favorite) one option can be to speak the words and identify a standard beat or rhythmic feeling. Then students can identify the

Compose a set of variations on a given theme. Consider a famous theme, such *Mary Had a Little Lamb, Ode to Joy, Twinkle, Twinkle Little Star,* or *Frère Jacques,* or make up an original theme. Consider compiling all the variations from a class into a large unified composition.

Keep it simple by having students compose for solo instruments and not include harmony or multiple instruments. Teach young students how they can simply change a little rhythm here or there, or add a note here and there and it becomes a variation. Students can do this by ear and not worry about notation, if notation will be too difficult.

Optionally, for students who have notation skills, have them write down the melody line of *Frère Jacques* for their instrument (key of B flat works well for winds and percussion, and key of D works well for strings) and then compose at least one or more variations. For young students, concentrate on small simple changes in the pitch or rhythm. For more advanced students include harmony parts at will. Suggest labeling each variation with an emotion, such as melancholy, exuberant, or angry. Consider changing time signatures and mixing major and minor or modal tonalities. Either before or after composing, listen to Mahler's variations on this tune in his *Symphony 1*, movement 3 and discuss the creative elements of the variations (minor mode; interesting choice of instruments starting with timpani and string bass; use of ostinato in timpani; etc.)

FIGURE 8.5 Exercise for composing a variation.

strong and weak (long/short or stressed) syllables and speak the words with an emphasis on the syllabic accents. Additionally, teachers can have students pat or clap the rhythm while they speak the words in order to feel and understand the connection of the syllables to the musical rhythm. Next, students can imitate the rhythm on their instruments by thinking of actually saying the words, but letting those words come out of their instruments. Finally, students can improvise pitches to go along with the rhythms. Limiting the pitches to two or three notes helps to keep the compositions from getting too chaotic. Once the rhythm and pitch are established, either aurally or with notation, students can add more dynamics and consider assigning different instruments or solos. As an example, the Vermont MIDI Project http://www.vtmidi.org/ uses the short saying "See a pin, pick it up, all the day you'll have good luck," which allows students to decode the rhythm of the words by identifying the syllables as the basis for their composition.

Alternately, poetry may be written in free verse, or other text-based sources can used to begin or inspire composition. Composer Steve Reich actually took recorded words from live interviews and imitated them as literally as he could with the sounds of a viola (female voice) and cello (male voice) to create the melodic content for his Grammy-Award-winning composition *Different Trains*, for string quartet and tape.

Variations on Frère Jacques

Arr. Kristen Zehnder

FIGURE 8.6 Student composition exploring variation. *Variations on Frere Jacques*, Kristen Zehnder, composer. Used by permission.

Poetry can also elicit certain feelings and sounds, and teachers may choose to avoid dealing with any decoding of the rhythm of the words and instead concentrate on feelings and imagery. For example, the poem "Paul Revere's Ride," by Henry Wadsworth Longfellow, has many natural sounds that are easy to imitate, such as the sound of a horse running, the cock crowing, a farmer's dog barking, a flock bleating, and birds twittering. A composition can try to capture the sounds and feelings of the poem. Alternately, a narrator can be used to read the poem while accompanied by a musical interpretation. A microphone and amplifier can help the narrator be heard over the sound of the ensemble.

CONCLUSION

Music educators can teach with the mind of a composer by sharing composition techniques with students that help them understand the music they are performing.

In addition, music educators can give students ideas of how to compose on their own and the experience of doing such. Teachers should be encouraged to have a holistic approach to music education that emphasizes creativity, and therefore naturally includes composing as an integral part of their curriculum. With this method, music programs will produce more effective performers in addition to well-rounded members of the human race.

Instrumental Techniques Classes

In this section, a variety of composition ideas will be suggested for percussion woodwinds, brass, and strings techniques classes. One or more specific composition assignments will be offered for each area, but each idea can also work for a full band or orchestra or any chamber ensemble. The strategies give examples of various composition assignments in a broad range of settings rather than projects specifically limited to a particular instrument family. Additionally, teachers could use these strategies to create their own original compositions for their public school music students in large or small ensembles, including string quartets, woodwind quintets, percussion ensembles, brass quartets, and flute choir. Teachers could also have students in the ensembles compose for themselves.

Instrumental techniques classes are a perfect place to incorporate composition, as well as improvisation, because they offer students practical hands-on experiences. Students can compose music at the level appropriate for the members of the class and in the correct instrumentation. Actually, college techniques classes are often at a level similar to a middle school instrumental ensemble, and so composing assignments can be kept in the college students' portfolios for student teaching and future teaching in elementary, middle, and high school. College students will gain understanding of important technical issues when composing for brass, woodwinds, and strings because they have to actually play the arrangements and compositions they write. Each instrument family has its own special issues including range, endurance, intonation, and key. Finally, students can incorporate composition assignments such as the examples listed earlier in this chapter as part of their applied instrumental lessons as they work with their applied instrument instructors.

PERCUSSION TECHNIQUES CLASS

The easiest techniques class to start with is percussion. Students can begin by writing a rhythmic composition, though including melody for the keyboard instruments should also be required. After basic sticking technique has been developed on snare drum or timpani, composition assignments involving snare drum, bass drum, and cymbals can be written. Next, timpani can be added, and then finally keyboards and any auxiliary instruments like cabasa, claves, congas, triangles, and tambourines.

Students write down a variety of food names and translate them into rhythms by converting the syllables into a pattern of weak and strong beats. After speaking the words in a designated rhythmic pattern, students add bass drum on beats one and three, triangle on beats two and four, and snare drum on the rhythm of the words:

Snare Drum: Blueberry Muffins; Ham Pineapple Pizza (optional: repeat!)

FIGURE 8.7 Sample percussion composition.

Students would do well to have an end-of-the-semester project involving a composition performance class period in which each student writes a percussion ensemble piece and performs it with the class. A sample percussion composition is shown in Figure 8.7.

WOODWIND TECHNIQUES CLASS

In a woodwind techniques class, composing can focus on melody writing combined with the development of technical proficiencies. For example, one of the significant challenges to overcome on clarinet is crossing the break, so a practical composition assignment could be to compose a short eight-measure melody that crosses the break at least eight times, and which actually can be quite fun to play. Creating some parts of the composition that have huge leaps from low to high, over the break, gives a nice contrast to parts that simply cross the break in half or whole steps. Melody writing can begin with graphic notation by having students draw the melodic curves of a famous melody like "Ode to Joy." Then they can try to create a new melody with a similar shape.

Students can be encouraged to stay in one key and develop the ideas of question and answer phrases. Limits such as using only the first five notes of a scale can help (note the five notes of Beethoven's "Ode to Joy"). A simple introduction of the concept of tension and repose would be appropriate here, in that students can write a four-bar melody ending on anything but the tonic (tension), and a second four-bar melody that ends on the tonic. This practice provides opportunity to teach rhythmic unity within a composition by keeping the rhythms of phrase one and two very similar, if not identical. Improvising on question and answer phrases can give an introduction to the composing assignment. Solo melodies should be completed for each woodwind instrument, showing appropriate range and special colors where possible, such as flutes flutter-tonguing.

BRASS TECHNIQUES CLASS

Brass techniques students can compose for trumpet, horn, trombone, euphonium, and tuba. The most common brass chamber ensembles include brass quintets and quartets, and the best keys in which to compose are flat keys because most brass instruments are pitched in B flat and F (Trumpet in B flat, Horn in F, trombone in B flat, Tuba in B flat). Teachers can consider assigning some composition exercises that use lip slurs, long tones, and articulation exercises in various keys as warm-ups (as mentioned in the previous section on composing warm-ups). While composing for brass players, novice composers should keep in mind that sustained notes in the upper register are very taxing and will significantly wear out young players' lips. Also, composers should note that any notes with combinations of valves, especially one and three, or one, two, and three, might have significant intonation issues. Writing for horn is especially tricky because some players naturally have a higher range while others have a naturally lower range. Good players are usually comfortable in the entire range, but in composing for young performers it is important to include optional parts or parts in octaves when the range goes high or low.

One fun composition activity involves composing and developing a short motif, the most famous example being Beethoven's motif from *Symphony V*. To develop ideas for the original motif, students can think of a movie character who has striking or notable qualities or characteristics, and then try to compose a short motif that matches. Such qualities may be noble, heroic, fast, thoughtful, funny, serious, optimistic, or pessimistic. A motif typically is just a few notes long and usually not more than a measure.

Another tool for developing a motif is to use a short name or word to create the pitch content and then manipulate the rhythm, dynamics, and tempo to give character. For example, Frank Ticheli wrote "Postcard" in memory of H. Robert Reynolds' mother, Ethel, and for the second theme, Ticheli used the letters of the name for the pitches in the theme. Transforming the name Ethel into musical notation results in the following sequence of pitches: "E" equals E natural; followed by "T" interpreted as "Te" (flat "Ti") from solfège, equaling B flat; "H" equals B natural in the German system; "E" the second time equals E flat, just for contrast; and finally, "L" becomes La from solfège, which is A natural. Ticheli explains that he "composed this brief "postcard" as a musical reflection of her character—vibrant, whimsical, succinct" (Ticheli, 1998). So once he established the motif with the name Ethel, then he manipulated and developed it to reflect a vibrant, whimsical, and succinct character. Another famous example comes from Johann Sebastian Bach, who put his name into music: "B" in German equals "B flat;" "A" and "C" are as written; "H" in German equals "B natural," as illustrated in Figure 8.8.

FIGURE 8.8 Bach motif.

Once the pitch content is derived from the letters, then the exact octaves, rhythm, dynamics, articulations, and tempo can be added to try to emphasize a certain character. The motif can then be developed through literal repetition, sequential repetition at different pitch levels, rhythmic transformation, imitation in other voices, combinations with other voices, partial modification of pitches, inversion, retrograde, augmentation, and diminution.

STRING TECHNIQUES CLASS

In string techniques class, students need to show proficiency in all the bowing articulations such as spicatto, detaché, martelé, ponticello, and sul tasto. Composition assignments should include clear use of the bowing and pizzicato articulations that students have studied, and should be limited to the keys of C, D, or G, though with advanced students, any key should work. The chaconne was a popular form during the seventeenth and eighteenth centuries, and it provides a particular compositional challenge perfect for including various string articulations (as well as various articulations on all instruments). Composers begin with a simple ground bass and then compose variations over it. The "Chaconne" by Vitali for violin and orchestra is quite popular and uses the simple set of descending pitches, G-F-E flat-D as the chaconne theme. Many other examples abound, the most famous probably being Pachelbel's *Canon in D*. William Hofeldt has written a beautiful "Chaconne" for high school orchestra. Henry Purcell has a nice "Chaconne" that has been arranged by Nelhýbel for string orchestra at the medium-easy level. Teachers can introduce composition ideas such as the chaconne by either performing a piece of repertoire that demonstrates the compositional technique, or at a minimum listen to a recording of a piece that demonstrates the technique. A sample assignment could begin with the bass line of Pachelbel's *Canon*, or the chaconne theme of Buxtehude from *Ciacona in E Minor*, BuxWV 160, and proceed to engage students in writing out a variation above the chaconne theme.

General Guidelines: Composing with Instrumental Ensembles

This chapter has covered many specific suggestions for teaching composition. In conclusion, some general recommendations follow, including an emphasis on musicality, listening back, and a nurturing environment. Composing should ideally start with an idea of an emotion or character or story rather than be an exercise such as "start and end on C and use eighth notes, quarter notes and half notes." The latter tends to result in a non-musical notation exercise. Teachers should keep in mind that composing can be done without using any traditional notation. Whenever possible, teachers should emphasize the communication of emotions and character through the composition, rather then emphasizing correct notation or other technical issues. For example, if a student performs something that he has written down with traditional notation, and the notation does not match up with the live performance, the performance should not change. Rather, the teacher should help the student change the notation to match the performance. Teachers should emphasize that notation is only a tool for communicating one's musical ideas.

An important component of composing is listening back to a composition and revising it. Teachers and students should always attempt to get a live performance and record it. Composing involves imagining the sounds and purposefully organizing them. Real music happens when the sounds are actually heard in real life; music is not the written notation on a piece of paper.

The Setting

A COMPOSITION ATMOSPHERE

Teachers should be encouraged to think creatively and experiment with new ideas in music teaching and composing. Collaboration between music teachers and other teachers should be nurtured, as deeper learning for students will result. For example, music teachers could collaborate with art teachers and use artwork to inspire a composition, like Mussorgsky did when he viewed paintings at the Hartmann exhibition 1874, in St. Petersburg, Russia. This led to Mussorgsky's composition *Pictures at an Exhibition*. Music teachers could require students to compose music for specific occasions, like a fanfare for the new superintendent, or a short cheering tune for the marching band, or a creative chorale for the school orchestra based on a melodic or harmonic section of a famous orchestral masterwork.

Instructors need to present models of composition. An appealing composition on the radio, or a bizarre sound that could fit in a current composition idea, should be shared with the class. Teachers can share how the form of current performance pieces demonstrates forms being composed by students, such as a rondo form from a classical symphony. A teacher may explain how Haydn develops a mono-thematic movement but still follows the sonata principle of tonic-dominant. In large ensemble rehearsals, students should be encouraged to gather scores to as many of the pieces as they can, and always be looking at them with the eyes of a composer—thinking about why the composer chose to write the music the way he or she did. A teacher should approach their performing ensembles as if he or she were the composer, explaining how compositions are put together and why composers chose certain timbres, forms, or harmonies. Building on the idea of teaching like a composer, an exhilarating event is to have a guest composer visit and coach an ensemble as well as help individual students on compositions. Commissioning a local composer to write something for one's ensemble and then having him work on teaching some composition lessons to students encourages young composers, offering growth for the ensemble director as well.

A TRUST ATMOSPHERE

Apart from the skills required to compose music, students also need a nurturing environment with an established level of discipline, mutual respect, and trust so that compositional ideas will not be laughed at or dismissed in a demeaning way. To be

Create a short composition lesson for a beginning string ensemble or band. Describe the objectives of the composition lesson and procedures. Consider whether it will be a group or individual composition project. If individual projects are included, create a rubric to assess the students' compositions. If possible, teach the lesson to a local ensemble. Objectives might include things such as: identifying and composing with major, minor, and diminished chords; developing an understanding of ABA form through soundscapes; composing riff's or motives; learning serial composition techniques.

FIGURE 8.9 Composition lesson for a beginning instrumental ensemble.

sure, some sounds are natural to laugh at, such as armpit noises, but jokes aside, students should be encouraged to try interesting, creative sounds and compositions without fear of rejection or disrespect. Figure 8.9 suggests an activity of creating a composition assignment for a beginning instrumental ensemble.

Conclusion

Composing in ensembles is a rewarding experience that can be a part of all instrumental ensemble programs. Issues of time, training, notation, and large ensemble group composition can all be addressed without missing out on the technical development of students, and actually improving their overarching musical skills. Incorporating composition in instrumental ensembles does not have to simply be a non-musical notation exercise, but can actually be an inspiring collaboration resulting in meaningful music.

References

Barrett, M. (2006). "Creative collaboration": An "eminence" study of teaching and learning in music composition. *Psychology of Music*, 34(2), 195–218. doi: 10.1177/0305735606061852.

Elliott, D. (1995). *Music matters*. New York: Oxford University Press.

Hickey, M. (1997). Teaching ensembles to compose and improvise. Music Educators Journal, 83(6), 17–21. doi:10.2307/3399019.

Hickey, M. (Ed.). (2003). *Why and how to teach music composition: A new horizon for music education*. Reston, VA: MENC.

Isaacson, W. (2008). *Einstein: His Life and Universe*. New York: Simon & Schuster.

Koops, A. (2009). Incorporating music composition in middle school band rehearsals. ProQuest Dissertations. DMA. University of Southern California.

Koops, A. P. (2009). Incorporating music composition in middle school band rehearsals. (Doctoral dissertation). Retrieved from ProQuest Dissertations and Theses. (Accession Order No. AAT 3389504)

Reimer, B. (2003). *A philosophy of music education advancing the vision* (3rd ed.). Upper Saddle River, NJ: Prentice Hall.

Russo, W. (1988). *Composing music: A new approach*. Chicago: University of Chicago Press.

Ticheli, F. (1998). *Postcard*. Retrieved April 12, 2011. http://www.manhattanbeachmusic .com/html/postcard.html

Wiggins, J. H. (2001). Teach*ing for musical understanding*. Boston: McGraw-Hill.

9 }

Guiding Composition in Choral Settings
Katherine Strand

Introduction

I believe it is important to ground considerations about how to prepare future choral music educators to incorporate composition in their classrooms within the larger picture of choral music in education. While it is valuable to frame choral classroom learning with national and state music standards, simply stating *that* a choral student should learn to compose does not explain to young teachers *why* a choral student should learn to compose. Looking more broadly at the purpose of choral education, the ultimate goal of choral classes could be stated as preparing young singers to lead rich, vigorous, and fulfilling musical lives. These three adjectives summarize lifelong learning goals: to be rich means to be abounding in resources or to have great value or worth; to be vigorous means to be strong, active, robust, energetic, powerful in action or effect and growing well; and to be fulfilled means to carry out, to bring into actuality, to satisfy.

Future choral music educators, even those who have never considered composing, can imagine the importance of composition in light of long-term musical learning goals. Teacher-educators have an uphill battle convincing future teachers of this value, for it seems almost ludicrous to stuff rehearsal schedules with more content when each rehearsal is already full to the brim with learning repertoire, sight-reading, vocal skill-building, and preparation for performance. However, composing can add immeasurably to choral programs (Schmid, 1997). Students can explore the richness of the composer's mind by examining scores to learn why a composer made specific choices that convey an expressive intent (Kaschub, 1997). They can become more powerful musicians by discovering new skills and by deriving enjoyment from creating as well as performing. Further, they can feel the satisfaction that comes only from taking a choral work from initial creation to live performance. Teaching composition in the choral classroom can add dimension and depth to the lives of young musicians while providing motivation, enjoyment, personal ownership, and even good repertoire for a young teacher's choral curriculum.

In this chapter, I will provide practical ideas and exercises that a college instructor can incorporate into a choral methods or literature class. Music education students should practice them in choral methods classes and use them in their future classrooms. I will first describe a rationale for incorporating composition in the choral classroom. Next, I will explore various aspects of the composing process and provide exercises to help students develop skill sets that are useful for larger composing projects. Finally, I will describe ideas to work with known melodies and to set new texts to music, and provide an example of a larger work composed by a music education student in my classroom.

Why Teach Composition in the Choral Classroom?

There are practical, pedagogical, and artistic reasons to include composition in the choral curriculum. Practically speaking, choral music is expensive. One new octavo for a thirty-voice choir can cost between $45 and $60 for voice parts alone; recorded tracks or additional instruments add another $20. A concert of fifteen choral works with only five new selections can cost $300 or more. Add to that the cost of accompanists, additional choral music for competitions and festivals, and performance costs (such as hiring the janitor for concert nights, traveling, advertising, etc.), and a choral budget can skyrocket. In an age when programs are being cut and budgets slashed, many choral directors need to reduce costs to make ends meet. In comparison, compositions by choral students cost only the paper to make copies and possibly the software to assist with creating and notating student work. When a teacher considers the pride that students feel when their works are performed in concert and the family members and friends that students will invite to hear their compositions, the expense pays for itself in dividends.

Published music tends to be limited in variability in terms of voicing, range, and technical difficulty. However, a choral director is faced with a new set of individual and ensemble needs each year. Sometimes choir directors teach boys with unchanged voices who are such good musicians that they make the top choirs, or work with freshmen women who want to sing in an unusual genre for which published music cannot be found. One year a choral director might have young singers who are great readers but need material with smaller ranges; the same choir the following year may have slower learners who have huge vocal ranges. There are a thousand unique situations that published music cannot address or, if it can, the purchases made for one year may never serve the real needs of the choral program again. In comparison, choral ensemble participants can create and arrange music to fit the individual skills and numbers of each unique ensemble. Given the challenge to compose for themselves, choral students will write music that fits their unique needs. Further, students will develop a sense of community by working for the good of their ensemble while they develop their creative musical skills.

There are unique performance opportunities for which published choral scores are not appropriate. I received a call once from a local community business member who was about to open a fast food restaurant franchise and wanted the choir to sing at the grand opening (it was a small town, so this was a momentous occasion). He wanted to hear historical versions of this fast food chain's jingles as a way to celebrate the entry of his business into the community. After a great deal of searching, I discovered that there were no published arrangements of older fast-food theme songs (it would probably not be legal to make money from these tunes). So, I asked my choir to create a specialized choral arrangement of the jingles. My students gained valuable composing experience while providing a unique service to our community.

There are also pedagogical benefits to composing with students. In order to build choral programs, it is important to teach musical skills, as well as choral and vocal technique, in a cohesive, sequential, and comprehensive manner. However, even graded lists of published literature offered by organizations such as the American Choral Directors Association may not address the specific pedagogical needs of the students. The members of any one choir may have wildly varying kinds of musical skill and training. Composing with the choir and teaching choral students to compose can help a teacher to address individual learning needs. Composing projects can be geared toward musical learning about texture, tonality, meter or form, notation-reading, or even aspects of vocal technique or choral blend. Composing can also encourage students to practice ear-training skills that might not otherwise interest them. For example, students can develop exercises to help each other learn intervals, scales, and rhythmic patterns. Or, they can challenge each other with the new sight-reading exercises.

Finally, there are artistic reasons for composing with your choir. To be perfectly honest, I fear that there are more poorly-constructed choral works in print than well-constructed works. I define a poorly constructed work in these ways:

- Octavos that use period-specific rhythmic, melodic, and harmonic gestures which become quickly dated (songs from the late 1960s come to mind);
- Octavos that use texts appropriate for young children but melodic lines and harmonies that are inaccessible to young singers;
- Octavos that are simplistic and clichéd, without harmonic or melodic interest (students may love the first read-through but quickly lose interest).

Beyond these distinctions, individual taste can lead a teacher to either like or dislike a score. Although poorly constructed octavos are often purchased for practical reasons such as "that first fall concert," choral teachers may spend a tremendous amount of money on these works that become quickly outdated and boring, provide very little material for vocal or choral technique, and are never used again.

It is not difficult to construct a choral work that will be aesthetically gratifying for both teacher and students. Exercises can build students' composing skills, which will bear fruit in full-length choral works. High-quality octavos can provide models to show students how to create a melody that expresses a text beautifully or how to add vocal and instrumental accompaniments.

There are a number of state and national organizations that are now adding composition contests to their state conventions. Winning compositions are sometimes performed by invited ensembles or, in some cases, added to an Honors Choir repertoire list. When a student wins a competition, public performance such as this can provide wonderful publicity for a whole choral program. Future choral teachers must remember that they will not only teach a new generation of choral singers; they will prepare future generations of choral composers. There is absolutely no reason to wait for that training to begin.

Including Composition in the Choral Curriculum

A teacher can add composition to the choral curriculum in a number of ways. For example, composing projects can be given as once-a-month homework assignments on the final Friday of each month. Students can bring their assignments to class on a Monday morning for small-group reading sessions and feedback, or post them on Internet sites for teacher feedback. Composing projects can also be incorporated into rehearsals. For example, the teacher can ask students to invent a warm-up to practice a specific skill or to develop an exercise to help the choir rehearse a difficult passage within a score.

Composing projects are useful after concerts and before holiday breaks, what I call "December and May" projects. A teacher can work with the class to create one piece in December and follow this with small-group composition projects in May. These small-group compositions can be tested and revised before the end of the semester and then taught to a new choir for the first fall concert the following year.

As a mentoring project, students in higher-level choirs can compose for students in younger choirs. If a director is fortunate enough to work with both the high school and middle school programs, bringing in a guest composer from the high school can be a useful recruiting tool for the feeder program. Such compositions can be added as spotlight pieces for concerts throughout the school year, or a teacher can hold a spring concert of student compositions to celebrate a year's worth of creative achievements.

Helping Learners Develop Choral Composing Skills

In an age of standardized testing, when single-answer immediate-response is drilled into students' minds, they may not have many opportunities to develop divergent thinking skills (the ability to imagine multiple answers for a single problem). Sadly, they have been trained from kindergarten to think that there is only one right answer. This means that students will need practice to develop their divergent thinking skills, just as they need to practice vocal exercises to develop their vocal technique.

Students learn to compose through observing models in addition to individual and group exploration. A choral teacher who wants to help students compose must be willing to compose. This does not mean that a teacher must be an expert composer; rather, the teacher should demonstrate the process of divergent thinking to students by composing with them in the classroom. An additional benefit to teacher modeling is that students can learn that composition, like singing, is an ability that should be continually cultivated but is never completely mastered.

Group composing exercises provide students with "support groups" to try out their ideas. Some students are not comfortable sharing ideas with a whole choir but are willing to share ideas with a small group. More importantly, working in groups allows students to test each other's musical ideas. In this way, small groups are superior even to technology for, although technology is a useful device for notating and playing multiple musical lines, it cannot truly reproduce the quality of a young singer's voice or the sound of sung text.

Composing, like all creative activity, requires some form of inspiration. Ideas and inspirations for new creations can be derived from the analysis of choral works. The teacher can challenge students to explain "why would the composer make this choice?" during rehearsal of any choral score. Some conductors will keep a paper on the wall to capture musical ideas that choir members think are particularly effective, which can then be used as the students compose. For example, the vocal score for Monteverdi's "Lasciate Mi Morire" (from the opera "Ariana," first performed in 1608)[1] can be "mined" for the descending melodic pattern, the walking bass, and the octave leaps in the melody, all of which beautifully convey despair, weeping, and woe.

The Composing Process: Rehearsing Individual Parts of the Process

Choral students should develop a number of skills that are useful in the composition process.[2] In brief, these skills involve the ability to generate musical ideas, to put ideas together to develop texture and form, to revise and choose from among ideas to express an aesthetic intention, and to codify a musical composition. Practice with each set of skills can help students to become comfortable and more sophisticated in their thinking as composers.

One of the first skills students need to develop is the ability to generate many possible answers to "solve" a musical problem. This habit of mind can be aided by practicing simple and short exercises that allow for exploration and improvisation. During such exercises, a teacher should provide an environment where students feel safe practicing their divergent thinking skills.

One such exercise is to have students form a singing circle.[3] Singing circles have been in popular culture in America and Europe for more than two decades as activities that stimulate creativity and develop community (an Internet search will reveal hundreds of singing circle websites) but are underutilized in music education. To create a singing circle, students should stand in a circle, either intermixed or in sections. The teacher, on the inside of the circle, can invent a bass-line pattern for a short chord progression, for example, I-IV-ii-V-I.

An example of a simple bass line derived from chord progression is shown in Figure 9.1.

FIGURE 9.1 Simple bass line derived from a chord progression.

Students should practice the pattern in unison. Next, a quarter of the choir will sing this pattern as an ostinato. The teacher can then invent complimentary patterns for the other three parts.

An example of additional vocal lines in shown in Figure 9.2.

FIGURE 9.2 Development of additional vocal lines.

Once all of the singers are involved the 4-part ostinato, the teacher should stand inside the circle and model how to improvise a melody (it is really much easier than it sounds). Students then take turns stepping inside the circle to improvise for 2-4 cycles of the ostinato. It is important to explain to the students that there are no incorrect improvisations in exploratory singing in this exercise—clapping, clicking, singing on non-chord tones and in dissonance, all are acceptable.

An exercise like the one described above accomplishes a variety of objectives. It allows for exploration and idea generation, for students to give each other ideas, for a group to develop a class "musical language," and for the teacher to develop a safe environment for creativity in the choral classroom. Students quickly take ownership over exercises like these. I often found high school students in the schoolyard, practicing improvisations and even inventing their own ostinati, after practicing this "game" only once.

A second exercise will allow students to practice generating musical ideas for texts. The teacher should begin with a simple four-line verse of a public domain poem such as "Rain" from Robert Louis Stevenson's *Child's Garden of Verses*[4]:

> The rain is falling all around,
> It falls on field and tree,
> It rains on the umbrellas here,
> And on the ships at sea.

The teacher can split students into small groups, giving directions like: "There are many, many poems that are inherently 'musical.' If you read this poem to yourself several times, you will find a melody forming itself in your mind. I will give you five minutes to develop a melody for this poem, rehearse your new melody, and be prepared to sing this one verse for the rest of the class." Small group performances will result in several different songs with both similarities and differences. The students can then discuss the ways that each group's composition enhanced or expressed some aspect of the poetic text. If the students enjoy this exercise, they can notate one or more of the melodies, which can later be used to develop a choral work.

A third exercise will help students consider the purpose of a musical hook. The teacher should challenge students (working in groups) to create musical hook (or jingle) to sell a product (my favorite products are dog food, auto tires, and baby lotion), or to create a hook for a pop song. The hook is a musical phrase that makes a longer work memorable.[5] For example, the pop song "Don't You Forget about Me" by Simple Minds uses a hook at the start of the chorus (also the song title) with a simple melodic idea that makes the whole song memorable. The song "Mickey" written by Nicky Chinn and Mike Chapman has a chant-like hook that is so memorable that it is difficult to remember the rest of the song: "Oh Mickey, you're so fine, you're so fine you blow my mind, hey Mickey, hey Mickey." Choral works also have hooks. For example, "You Are the New Day," written for the band Airwaves and arranged by Philip Lawson for the Kings' Singers, makes wonderful use of a melodic line on the lyrics "you are the new day" throughout the song.

Students should begin to write a musical hook by writing a single line of text that they find evocative and interesting. To sell baby lotion, for example, a line of text might be "so soft and so smooth." The teacher should remind students that spoken sounds can convey the emotional qualities desired. In this case, the "so" and "sm" create an onomatopoetic effect for warmth and the "hmmm" a person would emit while snuggling in warm blankets. Edgar Allan Poe's poems "The Bells" and "The Raven" are examples of masterful settings of onomatopoetic poetry. Once a suitable text is found, the teacher should lead the students to imagine desired rhythmic qualities for the line of text—overall speed, appropriate durations of syllables, word stress—and set the text to rhythm. Finally, students should add a melodic line that supports the text and selected rhythm. Pitch can add to the overall mood (through choice of tonality), tension or a sense of finality (through movement away from or return to tonic), and emotion (through choice of intervals for the melodic line). The newly created "hooks" can be shared for class enjoyment, evaluated for effectiveness, and kept for development into longer choral works.

While students have had several opportunities to generate musical ideas, they should learn to revise and develop musical ideas and to evaluate their ideas based upon expressive intent. Young composers do not always know that revision is a possibility and, as a result, may consider a musical idea finished when it is in its infancy. They may also be unaware of the ways that a melodic line can be developed, even though they have probably been singing works that develop melodies since their elementary choir years.

In order to practice revising musical ideas, the teacher should ask students to find the basic harmonic structure of a song that has a simple two-phrase antecedent-consequent structure, for example, "Mary Had a Little Lamb." Students should next invent a new ending for the song that will add to or change an artistic intent, for example, to increase tension. The teacher can prompt this exercise by discussing ways to increase tension by delaying the return to tonic (as in the end of the Brahms "How Lovely Is Thy Dwelling Place"), by adding more antecedent phrases (as in the melody of Carl Orff's "Oh Fortuna"). In performing their revised "Mary Had a Little Lamb" melodies and discussing the expressive results, students will learn that there are many possible ways to alter a musical idea and that any musical idea may be revised for expressive purposes.

Another exercise to help students learn how to develop a musical idea also utilizes known melodies and texts. A familiar tune such as "Simple Gifts" is rich with developmental possibilities:

> 'Tis a gift to be simple, 'tis a gift to be free,
> 'tis a gift to come down where we ought to be,
> and when we find ourselves in the place just right
> t'will be in the valley of love and delight
> when true simplicity is gained,
> to bow and to bend we shan't be ashamed
> to turn, turn will be our delight,
> for in turning, turning, we come 'round right.

Or, consider a poem such as John Keats' "This Living Hand":

> This living hand, now warm and capable
> Of earnest grasping, would, if it were cold
> And in the icy silence of the tomb,
> So haunt thy days and chill thy dreaming nights
> That thou wouldst wish thine own heart dry of blood
> So in my veins red life might stream again,
> And thou be conscience-calmed, see here it is
> I hold it towards you.

The teacher and students should first brainstorm on the ways that a musical motive, or short idea, may be developed (for example, by passing the motive between voices, putting the motive in canon or stretto, or using the motive as a cantus firmus, altering the phrase through retrograde or inversion, altering single tones or words, or extending syllables or consonants for effect as in James Erb's choral version of "Shenandoah"). The teacher should lead students to select a short phrase of the song/poem as a motive and test each of the possibilities. For homework, the students should select a different phrase and sketch out three different ways to develop their new motive. As a warm-up the next day, the teacher should ask the choir to try out one or more of the students' homework assignments. In such an exploratory exercise, it is not necessary, or even desirable, for each idea to sound wonderful. Rather, trying out both successful and unsuccessful ideas will allow young composers to hear the difference between ideas that work and ideas that do not work, all within a safe environment. An example of this exercise is shown in Figure 9.3.[6]

FIGURE 9.3 Ideas for a development section of *Simple Gifts*.

Aleatoric music can also provide fertile ground for students who are learning to develop musical ideas. Eric Whitaker's "Cloudburst" has an aleatoric section that asks singers to improvise by repeating words at random. A similar project can be developed through the use of a short silent movie as an inspiration. The teacher should ask students to observe a short movie of, for example, a moonrise. Brainstorming on descriptive or evocative words for the moonrise, the students should develop a text for their aleatoric work. Text can be repeated randomly or can be layered, tossed from section to section, performed on pitch or unpitched speech, broken apart, or repeated. Students should then decide upon a general shape for their aleatoric work (for example, they may chose to build, to devolve, to tell a sound-story, or to set a mood) and a timeline. The students should explore freely over several trials to find the most engaging expressive performance options. Once created, the aleatoric composition can be inserted into a known choral work (there are countless scores that are about the moon in publication or available for free download at the Choral Domain Public Library[7]) or can be paired with the "moon" choral work in concert.

A composer must be able to hear vertically (sounds in combination) in order to put musical ideas together in various textures and to imagine musical ideas horizontally (sounds over time) to create a musical form. One exercise to help students to develop vertical imagination involves teaching basic music theory (this exercise makes a terrific vocal warm-up as well). The teacher should ask students to voice the tonic note in a I chord and then to select any note in the chord (so that the entire chord is voiced). Next, students should voice the tonic note of a IV chord and then voice that chord, and repeat the process for a V chord. On another day, the teacher should sing or play a simple folk song and ask the choir to find and voice (and name) the tonic note of the chord that fits each phrase of the melody. Singing/playing the melody once again, the choir should fully voice the selected chords. On a third day, the students should select a voice part to sing the melody, further developing a choral accompaniment by choosing whether to sing the text in homophony with the melodic line (as in hymnody) or to accompany the melody with "oohs" or a countermelody.

Notating is a challenge for both students and teachers, simply because it is always fairly time-consuming. Fortunately, notation software such as Sibelius or Finale will help to reduce the time needed to notate musical ideas by hand. Newer software, such as AudioScore or Sibelius 6 will even notate sung melodies through a microphone input. There are also online notation programs such as Noteflight[8] that allow students to notate and hear their scores (this is particularly useful for students who may not be able to purchase expensive notation software for a home computer).

Longer Projects

Longer choral projects can include challenging students to arrange a known melody or to set new text to music.[9] Each will be discussed briefly, with exercises described to help students work through a longer composing process. There are three easily accessible ways to arrange a known song: by adding an accompaniment, by manipulating the song through development and revision, and by arranging the song through repetition and contrast.

To add accompaniment to a known song, the teacher should select a folk song[10] to arrange. Students should first learn to sing the song in unison and then decide upon a chord progression for the song, considering chords outlined by the melody. Chords chosen for an arrangement need not be the most obvious choices—even a simple change of chord from IV to ii can add musical interest. Students should next learn to play the chords on keyboard in accompaniment to the melodic line. Published choral and vocal arrangements of folk songs should be examined as models to find new ways to voice the chords underneath the melody (composers such as Brahms, Copland, and Rorem have arranged folk songs with wonderful piano accompaniments). Students can, finally, practice arpeggiating the chords, shifting chords between right and left hands, echoing phrases, and adding "riffs" in order to revise their original accompaniment.

On another day, the teacher should ask students to follow a similar procedure in order to compose a vocal accompaniment to the folk song. Beginning with chords in homophonic texture, students should explore ways to voice the chords under the melody (the teacher can remind students that the soprano does not always have to sing the melody. This is best done by introducing alternative models like shape note singing). Once the accompaniment has been developed, the teacher should lead the students to explore additional possibilities for each voice: creating appoggiaturas, incorporating silence, shaping motives, and adding ornaments. Different styles can be explored, including do-wop, hymnody, and Gregorian chant. Finally, students should invent countermelodies that can add expression or tension, alter the rhythmic patterns, or provide dialogue with the melodic line (as a fine example of chord-based melody and countermelody, the teacher can refer to the second movement of Beethoven's 7th Symphony).

Known melodies can be manipulated in ways similar to the exercises for revision and development given above. A melody can be explored for motives that can be explored and expanded. Motives can also be placed in different voices or instruments to accompany the melody, as an interlude between verses, or the students can create a true development section. The entire melody can also be altered by changing tonality or modality, changing meter, giving phrases to different voices, or by adding ornamentation.

Finally, the ideas generated by students can be arranged into a longer work. Many folk songs include an introduction (perhaps one of the motives), a simple statement of the melody, some sort of interlude or development, and a return to the melody. Hooks can serve as choruses in between verses, or bridges between verses can link the end of one melody to the beginning of the next. Musical form commonly makes use of repetition, evolution, and contrast. Students should be reminded that the arrangement should have an expressive purpose. For example, an arrangement can take a listener through a journey or tell a story that enhances the words of the song. However, musical ideas that are put together without the structure of the whole work in mind often result in a random-sounding composition.

As an exercise, the teacher should ask students to arrange an old English folk song, like "Barbara Allen," by first learning the melody, then arranging the (many) verses into choral voicing, and adding a piano accompaniment to support the vocal lines.

An example of this is shown in Figure 9.4.

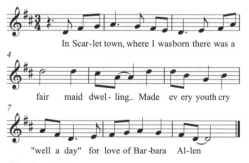

FIGURE 9.4 First verse of *Barbara Allen*.

Finally, students should practice composing their own melodies. To begin this process, the teacher should remind students that melodies can heighten the expression of a poetic text or comment on the text in unexpected ways (as an example of the latter, in a Charles Ives setting of "Shall We Gather at the River," the piano and rhythm of the words are written in such a way that they speak against the surety the text suggests). Students should first select or write a poetic text to set to music. Students should think carefully about their text before creating a melody (I suggest that they journal their reflections about the meaning of the text) by considering the mood they want to set, the sense of movement or energy they want to convey, and the sense of weight that will express the mood they wish to develop.

To help students as they begin to translate artistic intent to musical ideas, the teacher and students should review ways that a composer can establish artistic ideas: mood through tonality, pitch direction, and interval size; movement and energy through meter, rhythm, and tempo; weight through voicing, range, and tessitura. Additionally, students should consider which words in their texts would lend themselves to word painting or ornamentation (word painting is a term used to describe a melodic line that expresses a specific word, for example " . . . and the rocket's red glare" rises an octave above the preceding text in the "Star Spangled Banner"). Once a melody is created, the students can create an arrangement by adding accompaniment in voices and/or instruments, developing motives for introductions, hooks, bridges, or a true development section, and deciding upon a longer form.

I end this chapter by providing a portion of a final composition project completed by an undergraduate choral music education student in a Choral Literature class, as shown in Figure 9.5. Effie Xu chose to work with a poem by Emily Dickenson entitled "A Light Exists in Spring." Her simple but elegant setting serves as a reminder that choral music education students can compose, and enjoy the opportunity, once they build a set of skills that enables them to make informed musical choices.

A Light Exists in Spring

Lyrics by: Emily Dickinson

Music by: Effie Xu

FIGURE 9.5 *A Light Exists in Spring.* Effie Xu, composer. Used by permission.

FIGURE 9.5 (continued)

FIGURE 9.5 (continued)

References

Adderley, C. (2000). Preparation of future choral directors relative to the National Standards: Goals 2000. *The Choral Journal*, 40(10), p. 17. RILM Abstracts of Music Literature. EBSCO. Retrieved April 23, 2011. http://acda.org/publications/choral_journal

Kaschub, M. (1997). Composition in the choral rehearsal. *Music Educators Journal* 81(1), pp. 28–33. ERIC. EBSCO. April 23, 2011. doi:10.2307/3399083.

Schmid, W. (1997). National standards: Implications for choral music education. Journal of Music Teacher Education 6(2), p. 5. RILM Abstracts of Music Literature. EBSCO. Retrieved April 23, 2011. doi:10.1177/105708379700600202.

Notes

1. Also called "Lamento d'Arianna," multiple versions of this work can be found at the Choral Domain Public Library (www.cpdl.org) and elsewhere on the Internet.

2. As a reminder to the reader: choral methods students should practice the exercises provided in this section, with guidance and feedback, in addition to discussing how the exercises may be useful in the secondary school classroom.

3. Similarly, a 12-bar or 16-bar blues chord progression will provide a familiar harmonic and metric framework that will allow students to improvise, trying out new musical ideas.

4. For several possibilities, find websites like "Public Domain Poetry," found at http://www.public-domain-poetry.com/index.php. Accessed April 15, 2011.

5. There are many text and Internet sources that can provide more information about song hooks. One such source is the "Make Your Own Song" website found at: http://www.make-your-own-song.com/ http://www.make-your-own-song.com/2008/08/29/how-to-write-the-hook-of-the-song/. Accessed June 9, 2012.

6. The ideas presented here were generated by students in the Descant Choir of the Indiana University Children's Chorus, a choir of third-grade children.

7. Choral Domain Public Library has free downloadable choral scores, in which notation is provided by generous contributors. Found at http://www3.cpdl.org/wiki/index.php/Main_Page. Accessed April 20, 2011.

8. Noteflight currently has a free sign-up feature or a paid account that allows the composer to keep and manipulate scores in an online folder. Found at http://www.noteflight.com/login. Accessed April 20, 2011.

9. Michele Kaschub has written an article that outlines projects like the ones I discuss in this chapter, along with lesson plans to work with these projects over several class periods. Find her 1997 article "Composition in the Choral Rehearsal" in the *Music Educators Journal,* 84(1), pp. 28–33.

10. For American folk songs, I suggest resources such as *American Ballads and Folk Songs*, collected and compiled by John A. Lomax, Honorary Consultant in American Folk Song and Curator of the Folk Song Archives of the Library of Congress. The complete book is available as an online book with text, lyrics, and musical transcriptions. See website: http://www.traditionalmusic.co.uk/american-ballads-and-folk-songs/american-ballads-folk-songs.html. Accessed April 20, 2011. Similarly, Cecil Sharp collected and arranged English folk songs, many of which can be found online or in text.

10 }

Composition and Students with Special Needs
Alice M. Hammel

Introduction

Music educators are sometimes unsure how to include composition as part of a comprehensive music curriculum. The National Standards have solidified composition as a central part of a balanced music curriculum, and information regarding teaching composition in the music classroom is increasingly available (Kaschub & Smith, 2009). In addition, music educators are also sometimes tentative when asked to meet the needs of students with special needs in their classrooms (Hammel, 2001). Therefore, the task of teaching music composition to students with special needs may sometimes be overwhelming.

As we study the Individual Education Programs (IEP) and Section 504 Plans of our students, we often pay special attention to the current functioning levels and goals set for our students with special needs as they work in the general and special education classrooms. These current levels and goals can provide information that leads to effective adaptations and accommodations in our music classrooms and ensembles. Our knowledge of these strategies and application of this knowledge during instruction are also required by law (Hammel & Hourigan, 2011).

When adapting instruction it is important to maintain open and frequent communication with special education teachers, administrators, and staff members. By communicating with these colleagues, music educators can exponentially increase the amount and quality of techniques and information they are able to apply with specific students who have special needs. While we may only see a student a few times a week, we can share ideas with others who teach that same student, provide a more stable and similar structure and set of expectations for that student, and increase our own set of skills effective when teaching students with special needs.

A framework for delineating the specific needs of students with special needs can be met without the use of labels. An alternative paradigm is to use *The Five Domains of Teaching and Learning* (Hammel & Hourigan, 2011). These domains and their application to various classroom adaptations are discussed within this chapter. Following this introduction, *The Four Teaching Principles* (Burkett & Hammel,

2007; Hammel & Hourigan, 2011) are also utilized as a powerful accommodation and adaptation framework within the music classroom.

Later in this chapter a discussion of case studies, lesson plans, and their applications when preparing undergraduate music education students to include students with special needs is examined. The use of case studies is also important in the preparation undertaken by music educators who are currently teaching. By gathering information necessary to write an effective case study, practicing teachers can plan for inclusive teaching situations. Once this case study information has been evaluated, the act of adapting lesson plans for students with special needs is made much more meaningful.

FIVE DOMAINS FOR MUSIC TEACHING AND LEARNING

Adaptations, modifications, and accommodations that are successful in the music classroom can be applied to composition lessons and activities as well. Once we are aware of the needs and current functioning levels of our students, we can learn to apply those goals for our students as we structure composition experiences for them. These goals may be structured according to one or more of five domains. These domains are grouped as cognition, communication, physical, emotional or behavioral, and sensory needs (Hammel & Hourigan, 2011).

COGNITION

Many students with special needs struggle in the area of cognition. They require additional considerations when engaging in activities that "involve the acquisition, storage, retrieval, and use of knowledge obtained by sensory and perception systems" (Lipscomb, 1996). Cognition can be thought of as processing speed (Sousa, 2003). Students with deficits in this area often succeed when they are provided the necessary time and resources. Students who are gifted have processing speeds that can absorb knowledge with lightning speed and often require accommodations for their needs as well.

The specific needs of students who are gifted are expertly delineated in chapter 7 by Daniel Deutsch. Students who need strategies to assist them in cognitive tasks will almost assuredly benefit from these same strategies during composition activities. Students with special needs often need more time to process information. Their receptive language (input) and expressive language (output) skills can be much slower than other students in the class.

COMMUNICATION

A student with communication differences may "be developmentally delayed; English might not be his primary language; or he may have other neurological or cognitive challenges that affect processing in the brain" (Hammel & Hourigan, 2011, p. 15.). Communication difficulties can arise during any of four processes:

receptive language, expressive language, cognitive function/processing, and cultural use of language. In the communication domain, students may need multiple adaptations and modifications to insure their receptive and expressive language needs are being met. Students also sometimes struggle when language and terminology differ from that in their home community or culture. Students who need accommodations in this area often require adaptations in the mode of expression in the music composition classroom including pairing language with visual cues to assist in the understanding of concepts.

PHYSICAL

When a student has a deficit in this area, it can be difficult for her to complete a task independently. This student may be cognitively able to respond, but unable physically to demonstrate understanding or mastery. As with the area of communication, students with physical challenges often succeed when offered the choice of modality and the gift of time in the composition classroom. For example, if a child has fine motor skill challenges, using a typical keyboard as the main composition palette may be difficult. If a student has trouble with writing (because of these same challenges) he may decide that composition is "too hard" and will give up. Therefore, it is important for music teachers to provide necessary accommodations that make composition the focus, not the manipulation of equipment.

BEHAVIORAL/EMOTIONAL

IDEA (Individuals with Disabilities Education Act) has defined the area of emotional disturbance as a condition that affects students in one or more of the following ways: a) an inability to learn that cannot be explained by intellectual, sensory, or health factors; b) an inability to develop and maintain interpersonal relationships with peers or teachers; c) inappropriate types of behavior or fears in normal circumstances; d) a general pervasive mood of unhappiness or depression; and e) a tendency to develop physical symptoms related to fears associated with personal or school problems (Turnbull, Heurta, & Stowe, 2004). Students who struggle with behavioral and emotional issues can thrive in an environment that is free of sarcasm, contains specific behavioral expectations, and is filled with opportunities for expression and creativity. Composition activities can often be that successful environment for students who have behavioral and/or emotional disturbance. The opportunity to express emotions and create art that is "their own" can be a powerful motivator and part of a healing process for students who have experienced traumatic and negative events. By setting clear goals and through frequent cognitive modeling, positive behavior supports, and feedback, students with behavioral and/or emotional disturbance can become full participants in a creative classroom.

SENSORY

Sensory needs can include students who have impairments in the areas of vision and hearing. These needs also refer to students who have other sensory challenges. These challenges include hypo (too little) or hyper (too much) sensory input. These students may be overwhelmed or underwhelmed by the amount of activity and sound in an active composition environment. Adaptations to the physical environment of the classroom can be very successful for students with sensory needs. For example, some students prefer to wear headphones or ear-muffs when taking part in composition activities. The gifts of time and space as well as choices for modality reception and expression of language and other forms of communication are often successful when working with these students. By allowing students to respond orally, visually, or kinesthetically, music educators are providing a sensory environment that honors their needs.

The Four Teaching Principles Applied to Composition

Authors of other chapters in this book have provided abundant strategies that have proven effective when designing composition experiences for students. Many of these strategies may be adapted, accommodated, or modified for use when teaching students with special needs. These strategies and adaptations have been organized according to *The Four Teaching Principles* (Burkett & Hammel, 2007; Hammel & Hourigan, 2011). The *Five Domains for Teaching and Learning*, as delineated above, will also be included when appropriate within this section to refer to specific challenges students may encounter.

GENERAL RECOMMENDATIONS

Koops, chapter 8, included some very appropriate ideas that translate well when working with students who have special needs. He states: "instilling a love of creativity and nurturing it in young people can help them the rest of their lives in any occupation and activity" (Koops, Chapter 8, p. 150). This is perhaps even more important when teaching students who have learning challenges. Unfortunately, many of them are only taught basic knowledge and facts that will be used on tests, or are a part of life-skills training. The opportunity to cultivate creativity through composition may be unique within the educational programs of students with disabilities. This only increases the importance of this experience in their lives.

MODALITY

Students learn through a variety of modalities (visual, aural, and kinesthetic). Most students with special needs have one or more channels (or modalities) that are strong. It is always appropriate to continue to prepare, present, and practice objectives in all modalities (visual, kinesthetic, and aural). However, it is very important to be aware of the modality that is most successful for students who have differing learning needs. By adapting experiences through modality, music educators increase the possibility that a student with disabilities will be able to comprehend and apply knowledge to the creative composition experiences in a classroom or ensemble.

In chapter 15, Smith (p. 262) will discuss asking students to return to class with new compositional ideas. These ideas could include words, melody, or rhythm. Students with special needs often need additional time to process ideas and produce responses. The increased allocation of response time can allow the time they need to create a thoughtful and musical set of ideas. An opportunity to leave the music classroom and return with new compositional ideas can have a powerful impact on the creation process for students. Students who struggle with cognition, communication, sensory, and physical domains will benefit from these types of accommodations. This idea is also an excellent pacing adaptation as it allows students time and space to create their own art at their own pace.

Smith (p. 265) also recommended watching cell phone videos of compositions during creation and refinement. Students with special needs are sometimes very visual. By viewing the video, and having the opportunity to rehearse at home, they can gain a greater understanding of the process, the specific steps and requirements of the piece. The opportunity to engage in repeated practice of a task they will perform individually or as part of a group performance is also often very valuable. When students have difficulty in the cognition and communication domains, the opportunity to rehearse a behavior they will demonstrate in class is very valuable.

An excellent suggestion made by Wiggins (p. 115) in chapter 6 was: "When teachers work with learners they do not know well, they will need to engage them in a series of experiences designed to help them understand where they are in their musical experience and understanding." This is particularly true when working with students who have special needs. These students often have very individual, asynchronous skills and levels of understanding. Being aware of their preferred learning modalities, strengths, and areas of weakness can be particularly helpful when planning adaptations and accommodations during the compositional process. It is also good teaching practice to assess students and be aware of their strongest expressive (versus receptive) mode. Students with communication, physical, sensory, and behavioral/emotional challenges often have a strong preferred expressive modality.

In chapter 7, Deutsch discussed the importance of trial and error during the compositional process. Students with special needs often find they need more than one or two opportunities to create a product. The time they need to process is often far greater than for neuro-typical students, and this need is often not noted or fulfilled. In addition, students who are creative and are given the opportunity to learn in an active classroom are often grateful for the opportunity to learn in new modalities and with a new set of pacing expectations. Students who struggle in the areas of cognition, communication, and behavioral/emotional domains are often more successful in active classrooms with multiple opportunities to participate in process-oriented activities.

The eventual notation of compositional works was discussed by Deutsch (pp. 143–144). Students with special needs may not be able to do this in a standard format. With the use of aural, visual, and kinesthetic response modes, the possibility that their ideas will be "notated" is increased. The use of technology is welcomed and essential for students who have difficulty responding in the manner and format generally requested. By noting and adapting for this difference through modality and size, their works may be "heard" also. Students who benefit from adaptations in the areas of communication and cognition often are able to participate in creative activities with a greater degree of freedom and independence when technology is available to assist them.

The use of "support groups," (small groups) as suggested by Strand (pp. 171–173) in chapter 9, if designed heterogeneously, can be very instructive to students with special needs. If each member within each group has a specific task, students with special needs can begin to learn how to fill various roles within a group and can also benefit from contributing and receiving new compositional techniques and ideas. For example, the addition of a simple bass line derived from a chord progression can be a meaningful task within a support group. The specificity of a role within a group is also an excellent accommodation for students with behavioral/emotional challenges and for students who experience challenges in the sensory area.

The topic of rhythmic compositions was discussed by Koops (pp. 157, 160–161) in chapter 8. It may be useful to speak with the elementary or middle school music teacher to determine if a rhythm syllable system (such as *ta ti-ti*, *du du-de*, or word rhythm) was used in earlier music experiences. Using a familiar system of rhythmic manipulation as a starting place can greatly increase the initial understanding for a student with special needs.

Likewise, a melodic writing activity can be adapted by drawing on previous knowledge regarding melodic decoding and solfège. If a music educator becomes aware of the formative skill sets of her students, the sequencing of instruction and measured maturity in compositional processes can be monitored. Familiarity with melodic patterns, experience in improvisational and compositional activities, and an awareness of the melodic strategies familiar to the student (movable do, fixed do, numbers, patterning) can become powerful tools in planning instruction. Teachers who apply these strategies when teaching students who struggle with cognition often see an immediate improvement in the amount and quality of participation and understanding.

An idea from Hickey (1997) is often successful when working with students who have special needs. The SCAMPER mnemonic device (Substitute, Combine, Adapt/add, Minify/diminution or Magnify/augmentation, Put to other uses/other instruments, Eliminate, and Reverse/rearrange), as well as other mnemonics, are often extremely successful when used by students with special needs. Often, these students struggle to remember formulas and strategies. The use of a card, picture, or storyboard book to visually, aurally, or kinesthetically reinforce a process will make it possible for students with special needs, communication and cognitive domains in particular, to participate in compositional activities with a greater degree of independence.

SIZE

Koops (p. 157) stated: "Establishing limits helps students focus their creativity instead of being overwhelmed by options." These limits can include adaptations in the area of size. Students with special needs often struggle when the size of a process and the materials chosen are too large, heavy, small, light, bulky, slippery, scratchy, or tall. By adapting the size of a process, the materials chosen, and the assessment procedures utilized (all size related), they can participate in creative activities in a more significant way.

These adaptations may also include the use of flashcards for rhythmic or melodic segments, felt staves, and other manipulatives appropriate for the developmental compositional level of the students. When music educators consider size as a critical element in composition, students with special needs can learn in an environment that is more appropriate for their needs and levels of ability. Again, by providing some specific parameters, students who struggle in the behavioral/emotional domain can meet small, scaffolded goals and students with cognitive differences are able to participate in meaningful ways.

The topic of size (and modality) was addressed by Strand (pp. 175–177) in chapter 9. She discussed the advantages of students composing to meet the needs of their choir and noted that dividends included student self-worth and efficacy. Students with special needs who may not be able to participate as singing members of a choral ensemble may excel at writing or arranging choral music. Students who are unable to write with a pencil may be able to do so with software that is adapted for physical limitations. This is a very important accommodation for students with cognitive, communication, and physical limitations.

This idea also transfers to students enrolled in non-choral courses who have special needs and can contribute in a different way. Composition projects can be inherently differentiated and individualized. They can also aid in assessing the knowledge and comprehension of a student with challenges in the areas of communication and sensory behaviors. Additionally, students who are unable to notate their compositions or arrangements can dictate their music to other students. This collaborative experience can enhance the overall culture within the inclusive classroom.

The size adaptation of providing specific directions and exercises to help students learn to craft a specific compositional technique was also addressed by Strand (p. 173). Students with special needs often benefit from the opportunity to take a larger assignment and create smaller pieces. These specific exercises may be necessary for a longer period of time depending on the cognitive challenges a student may experience.

COLOR

Koops (p. 152) recommends that: "Students may need to represent the music visually with pictures or words that describe the sounds or use graphic notation." This is especially important for students with special needs, and is useful for students of all ages. The use of color can literally change the way students see music. Many students with special needs have difficulty reading black and white images. By adding color to soften the contrast and bring attention to important details, students who have sensory, attention, and processing differences can begin to learn to comprehend and manipulate materials and images used in the process of composition. Colored transparencies are often used in the inclusive classroom to assist students with this contrast.

Further accommodations in the area of color include highlighters for important passages, the use of colored chalk, pencils, puff paint, and visual representations that are as close to the original as possible. Steps within a process can also be color-coded for students to use independently in the classroom. When applying color strategies, all students may benefit from colors that designate phrases, note values, and macro form. The bars on an Orff instrument can also be color-coded to correspond with a staff line, or other sound designation for use during compositional activities.

PACING

The pace of a creative classroom can sometimes be overwhelming for students with special needs. They often find the rapidity of directions, grouping, and expectations to be much quicker than those in self-contained (or in some inclusion) classrooms. The pace of class can also be faster than they are able to process and this can cause emotional outbursts, withdrawn behaviors, and a great deal of anxiety and frustration.

The idea of choosing highly-gifted students for small group instruction was studied by Deutsch (p. 139). Choosing students with special needs for participation in small groups is also an excellent pacing adaptation. The pace of instruction and creativity can be adjusted more easily when students are occasionally able to participate in homogenous groups. This process is often effective when accompanied by heterogeneous grouping as well.

Improvised phrase completion is an excellent strategy for all students as noted by Deutsch (p. 136). This can sometimes be frustrating for students who struggle to process and express information. A teacher can experience this as a delayed response. Delayed responses can also indicate that students with special needs are wrestling with competing ideas as well. Sometimes, this extra time is imperative to success in music for students who have cognitive and communication limitations.

The compositional process can be frustrating for students who have never experienced difficulty in completing an academic or musical task. Deutsch's (p. 139) students were gifted and were practicing the experience of composition. They learned through errors and successes. Students who are intellectually and/or musically gifted may have never had to work, fail, or try again: composition may be the first time this occurs. For students who struggle daily in school, the process of composition may be another in a series of experiences that are very difficult for them and take a long time to understand. By adjusting pacing, and by allowing trial and error, all students can experience success when engaged in the creative process.

USING ALL FOUR TEACHING PRINCIPLES

A few recommendations listed in individual chapters are applicable in all four areas of adaptation. Strand (pp. 171–172) recommended that students have experience improvising over several types of chords. Students with special needs may not always be able to keep pace with a class that is improvising over more than one chord. They can often benefit from improvising over one or two chords initially and may prefer to "chime in" when the chord they are practicing is highlighted. A similar accommodation can be made when singing the bottom note in an arpeggiated chord pattern. A student can be responsible for "do" or "sol" when it occurs in the patterns while still listening and learning as she hears other students sing the other notes. These adaptations can create a more inclusive environment for students with communication and cognitive challenges.

Koops (pp. 153–154) discussed the Soundscapes Composition Activity. Students with special needs may need to compose soundscapes that are shorter in length, simpler in form, and include less variety in materials. Once parameters are set that fit the current compositional level of the student, the activity can proceed, often with great success. Students who attend music with a paraprofessional or aide may also participate with the aide, when necessary, for completion of the activity. Students with special needs may also appreciate having more time to complete their activity. It may be possible for a student to continue working on her Soundscape at home, or in her resource classroom. It may be helpful for students to have a picture schedule or social story to lead them through the activity. For some students, visuals—pictures in particular—are essential to their understanding of a task. Students may also need to touch or feel the elements to understand what is being asked. For example, holding a fluffy cotton ball may help the student to think about clouds. Drops of water may be helpful when considering rain or a rainstorm.

Manipulation of melodic and rhythmic warm-up materials was discussed by Koops (pp. 155–156). Students with special needs may be very enthusiastic about creating materials to play with their peers. Recording the sound of rhythmic or melodic patterns, or demonstrating with popsicle sticks (rhythm) or absolute pitch name or solfège icons can provide autonomy for students who are unable to notate or speak their ideas.

In addition, some students with special needs may be overwhelmed when presented with a seemingly large composition task. One suggestion is to refrain from presenting all steps or expectations for the composition project at the outset. Some students learn and perform best when the project is revealed step-by-step or in sequence. The second idea is to create a storyboard book with all steps explained visually. This book can be laminated, hole punched, and given to a student to keep during the project. By viewing and reviewing the various steps repeatedly, some students experience less frustration and anxiety, and are able to complete the project with the rest of the class.

ASSESSMENT AND STUDENTS WITH SPECIAL NEEDS

Assessing students with special needs can be difficult. Their comprehension and expression of understanding, creativity, and mastery of concepts can prove a challenge when they are asked to assess or evaluate their progress. Assessment rubrics can be adapted to fit the current compositional level of specific students with special needs. Through scaffolding, fading support, and increased expectations, teachers, students, and their families can chart progress over time. By creating a task analysis of each micro skill or step involved, all stakeholders in the process can be aware of the process, possible products, and future expectations of students with special needs.

Modeling and Role-Playing in the Collegiate Music Education Classroom

Undergraduate music education students thrive in an environment that allows them to model and role-play probable classroom situations. Acquisition of knowledge at the application, evaluation, and synthesis levels in a semi-authentic situation can be valuable. These classroom experiences coupled with field experience and practicums that include students with special needs, can increase the probability that pre-service teachers will enter the field with the competencies necessary to teach composition in the music education classroom.

Observation protocols have been designed to assist in gathering appropriate and complete information regarding students with special needs (Hammel & Hourigan, 2011). By observing students in music and general education classes undergraduate students can gain another set of skills.

CASE STUDIES

The experience of writing a case study as an undergraduate student can be the impetus for further inquiry in the area of students with special needs. Because one of the initial tasks in writing a case study is to "know the student," future interactions with special education staff and faculty will be rehearsed during this process. Furthermore, the rehearsal of these authentic teacher behaviors as undergraduate students will prepare beginning teachers as they enter a field where they will encounter many students with special needs.

Case Study Components

1. Know the student
   a. Strengths and weaknesses
   b. Severity of challenges
   c. Home support system
   d. School support system
   e. Assistive technology or personnel (including those utilized outside the school system)
   f. Previous experience in music and musical ability
2. Gather information regarding the area of challenge
   a. Etiology (type of disability, characteristics, and typical behaviors)
   b. Range of differences and impact on overall well being
   c. Services and personnel available in school system
3. Create adaptations and accommodations based on the student and learning difference(s)

   Undergraduate students often enjoy this creative assignment and are able to learn a great deal about students with specific areas of deficit or differences. Once they have researched the domain or disability, they often begin to "craft" a student for their case study. These authentic experiences mirror good teaching practice in K–12 classroom.

LESSON PLANS

Most undergraduate students write lesson plans in their methods classes. Often, these lesson plans include few, if any, adaptations, accommodations, or modifications for students with special needs. Once the students have written their case studies, a further assignment can be to have them include that student in their next lesson plan. By writing specific methods and materials adaptations to accompany a "standard" lesson plan, students can begin to practice the skill of inclusion in a meaningful way.

Lesson plans are sometimes presented as micro or full-length experiences in methods classes. Students are also sometimes able to teach in classrooms during their practicum opportunities. If accommodations for students with special needs are included in these classrooms, the actual adaptive ideas may be utilized. If not, students benefit from the ideas of their peers and from practice applying these ideas in the methods classroom.

If undergraduate students are able to engage with students with special needs in inclusive and self-contained classrooms, or to serve as a one-on-one assistant for music educators, they will be exponentially better prepared for their initial experiences as first-year teachers. Hourigan (2009) has conducted research in this area and has found that practical experience in authentic settings with students who have special needs is the most effective way to introduce and reinforce inclusive philosophies and practices among undergraduate students. These experiences, paired with the writing of case studies and adaptive lesson plans, will greatly enhance the effectiveness of beginning teachers who work with students who have special needs.

Conclusion

The experience of creating art through musical composition is of great importance to all students. Students with special needs, in particular, are sometimes given fewer opportunities to analyze, synthesize, and evaluate as part of their educational programs. While acknowledging the complex issues that arise when teaching composition to students with special needs, we are also aware that there are adaptations and accommodations available for use in reaching all students. By providing these experiences, music educators can ameliorate and intercede on behalf of students with special needs. It is a gift all students may carry for the rest of their lives.

References

Burkett, E. I., & Hammel, A. M. (2007). *On Music for Special Learners*. Reston, VA: Connect for Education.

Hammel, A. M. (2001). Special learners in elementary music classrooms: A study of essential teacher competencies. *Update—Applications of Research in Music Education*, 20(1), 9–13.

Hammel, A. M., & Hourigan, R. M. (2011). *Teaching music to students with special needs: A label-free approach*. New York: Oxford University Press.

Hickey, M. (1997). Teaching ensembles to compose and improvise. *Music Educators Journal*, 83(6) 17–21. doi 10.2307/3399019.

Hourigan, R. M. (2009). Preservice music teachers' perceptions of a fieldwork experience in a special needs classroom. *Journal of Research in Music Education*, 57(2), 152–168.

Kaschub, M., & Smith, J. (2009). *Minds on music: Composition for creative and critical thinking*. Lanham, MD: Rowan & Littlefield.

Lipscomb, S. D. (1996). The cognitive organization of musical sound. In D. A. Hodges (Ed.), *Handbook of music psychology* (pp. 133–177). San Antonio, TX: IMR Press.

Sousa, D. A. (2003). *How the gifted brain learns*. Thousand Oaks, CA: Sage Publications.

Turnbull, R., Huerta, N., & Stowe, M. (2006). *The individuals with disabilities education act as amended in 2004*.

SECTION } IV

Composition and Technology

SECTION } IV

Composition and Technology

Continuing evolutions in technology have made composition accessible to an ever-widening range of people interested in making their own music. Among the most exciting opportunities offered by technological innovations are the possibilities for distance learning, collaborative composition, and real-time interaction with professional composers. These education-enhancing options, available in any properly equipped classroom, make it possible for teachers and students access to a community of composers that may extend to a nearby school district, a university classroom, or to the other side of the globe.

With so many options available (and more to follow), the question of how to select technology that will facilitate composition is an increasingly important consideration for educators. Richard Dammers provides guidance for evaluating the use of technology to facilitate composition. He urges teachers and teacher educators to consider the learning objectives of the composition project and the students' skills and prior knowledge first. Then, they should evaluate the available space and technology hardware resources. Finally, they can select specific software platforms that best fit the needs and parameters of their students and the composition activity at hand.

Probably one of the best-known school composition programs is that of the Vermont MIDI Project (VMP). Director Sandi MacLeod writes about the lessons learned in the fifteen years of the project's existence. She addresses common problems and their solutions. These include: 1) lack of expertise in composition pedagogy, 2) lack of personal experience composing, 3) lack of time for planning, 4) lesson development and implementation, and 5) lack of access to computers. She briefly outlines the history and mission of the VMP discussing the role of technology and mentoring in the project. She then presents the mentoring guidelines of the project and examples of mentor comments. Finally, she discusses the benefits of partnering with pre-service educators and a model of how that has been done.

Bruce Carter outlines a Virtual Composer-in-Residence Program that he has facilitated for the past few years. He delineates the involvement of his collaborators, who include professional composers, classroom teachers, methods class students, and middle school band students. He provides examples of the types of composition tasks that were offered, the use of technology in the project, and what some of the limitations were. Finally, he offers conclusions on the efficacy of a virtual composer project and the possibilities for its replication.

11 }

Capitalizing on Emerging Technologies in Composition Education

Richard Dammers

Composing has been a long-neglected area in music education in the United States, due in part to the practical difficulties of composing in classes designed to teach performance skills. Advances in technology provide capabilities that lower the barriers to incorporating composition into many types of music classrooms, including performance ensembles. In order to utilize the pedagogical possibilities provided by technology, teachers need to make a series of evaluations. This process starts with considering the learning objectives of the composition project and the students' skills and prior knowledge. Then, after evaluating the available space and technology resources, teachers can select specific software platforms that best fit the needs and parameters of their students and the composition activity at hand.

Advantages of Computer Technology

Computer technology may not be optimal for every composition project, but it can provide a number of advantages. The primary advantage is that students have greater control over musical materials. Computers provide easy access to an audio realization of their compositions, allowing for many cycles of creating, listening, reflecting, and revising. This is markedly different from performance activities in which students are focused on executing a portion of piece in real time (a very convergent thought process). With composition, students are allowed to think divergently without time constraints and they are freed from the need to coordinate with other players in an ensemble.

Technology also changes the instructional dynamic of a classroom. With the incorporation of headphones, it is possible for individuals or multiple groups of students to simultaneously work on independent compositions in the same classroom, without creating cacophony. Technology also frees a teacher from "one size fits all" instruction. By carefully matching the software interfaces to the compositional task and individual students' needs, teachers can tailor a composition project to ensure individual student success. For example, a student with extensive background in classical piano might be best served by composing in a notation program with a MIDI piano controller, while a student with limited performance experience might be better served by composing in a loop-based program. Both students will be able to engage with musical materials and make musical decisions, but with different levels of scaffolding (or support provided by the computer).

While notation software and sequencers have been around for decades, dropping price points (in some cases to the point of being free) and the increasing portability of computing devices are greatly increasing the availability of computer-based composing at the students' seats in the music classroom. Through utilizing a desktop computer, laptop, tablet, iPod, or phone, it is becoming much easier for teachers and students to access composing software in class; and with the advent of cloud computing, students can continue their composing outside of the class.

These advances hold exciting pedagogical possibilities for teachers and changes are not limited to the music classroom. The same availability and democratization of access to music creation is being experienced in the broader culture. In many cases students are already creating music outside of school, and the professional world continues to place greater emphasis on creative thinking. Music educators who ignore the new possibilities for teaching composition run the risk of having a curriculum that is less relevant to society. Many teachers tend to teach as they were taught, overlooking opportunities that were not available for their teachers. It is imperative that teachers examine and professionally evaluate the possibilities of technology-based music creation, utilizing it when it serves their students and bypassing it when it does not.

Considerations for the Selection of Music Software

Before selecting which type of music software to use for composing, there are broader issues to consider. Insuring that technology serves music instruction (rather than vice versa) has been a consistent theme in the music education technology literature (Reese & Davis, 1998; Williams & Webster, 2006). This principle is especially important in technology-based music classes. Unless a course is designed as vocational education (i.e., preparing students for a job in music recording or production), the primary focus should be on musical concepts and skills and not the technology itself. While some instruction in particular software or hardware is inevitably necessary, this instruction should be limited to only what is needed to allow students to function musically in that environment. It is an easy trap to teach to the software program rather than the music, but technology is highly transitional, while musical content generally remains constant. Musical learning will remain valuable for students, while knowing how to operate outdated software programs will not.

In addition to focusing on music over technology, it is important to clarify the aims of each particular composition project. Having a clear understanding of these aims will aid in selecting the right technology environment. The following questions can help teachers clarify their technological needs when planning composition activities: what should students learn through this experience? Are there specific learning objectives intended, or is the composition task designed as a more open-ended creative experience. What particular types of musical decisions do students need to be able to make? Is there a live performance involved? Do other musicians need to be able to play the composition? How will the final composition be presented? In order to be able to select the best composing environment for their students, teachers need to clarify and reflect upon what they hope to accomplish through each composition activity.

Teachers must also examine their students' prior experiences, knowledge, and skills, both while designing the composition activity and before selecting a software environment. It is important to consider students' abilities to read standard notation, keyboard skills, prior software experience, performance backgrounds, learning styles, and overall musical development. The interfaces of music software programs vary widely, placing different levels of skill demands upon the students. Thinking of this in reverse, different pieces of software provide different levels of scaffolding or support. Considering the level of support a student needs is important when choosing among available software environments.

One of the advantages of utilizing music technology and composition activities is that students do not need to all do the same thing at the same time. It is much easier to differentiate instruction (Tomlinson, 1999) according to individual students' interests, readiness, and learning styles. This not only includes providing compositional tasks appropriate for students, but also selecting suitable software environments. For example, consider three students in a general music class. The first, a student with an extensive piano background, might be composing using a MIDI keyboard and notation software; the second, a self-taught guitarist, might be composing in a sequencer with a graphic notation interface; and the third, a non-performing student, might be exploring chord functions by composing with Band-in-a-Box. All three students are extending their musical knowledge by working in a software environment that provides enough scaffolding/support to allow them to be successful, but also provides enough freedom for the product to reflect their musical thought.

Before selecting the software/app environment to be used, the teacher should consider where the students would compose, both in terms of the physical space, and the type of computing device. Often, this factor will be determined by the availability of computing hardware at school. In many cases, music teachers choose between taking their class to the school's computing lab or using a small number of computers in the music classroom. Both are viable options, but have implications for scheduling and the type of software selection. In the shared lab option, the whole class composes at the same time, probably in a limited amount of time. Free online software may be a desirable option, since it may not be possible to purchase multiple copies of software for only a few days of usage. File storage is also a consideration. How will students retrieve and turn in their work? Cloud (or Internet-based) computing simplifies this process and may be the best route for working in a shared lab.

These issues play out differently when using an in-class station. It is more affordable to purchase software for a smaller number of computers. If students compose in the music room, file storage is less of a concern since students and the teacher will be able to access the same computer. With computers in the music classroom, the students can have access whenever the music class meets (unlike heavily scheduled shared school computer labs). The challenge in this case is the higher student-to-computer ratio, which may necessitate group work or rotating students through the composition activity over a longer time frame.

Portability and Accessibility

As software becomes more affordable and computing devices become more portable, technology-supported composition is no longer limited to the lab or music room station. As many schools move to laptops, students (with headphones) can compose in their seats in the music classroom. This trend will continue as students' phones and tablet devices become increasingly sophisticated music computer devices. (iOS devices provide a wide variety of instrument interfaces, and notation software, currently lagging, will soon be available as well.) In situations where schools provide laptops, or in the foreseeable future where students will just bring their own devices, concerns regarding scheduling and student to computer ratio are no longer an issue.

The increasing in portability of computing is particularly useful for incorporating composition into performance ensembles. While the incorporation of diverse musical activities has been shown to not be detrimental to performance levels, directors are often reluctant to give up rehearsal time for a trip to a lab or to rotate students through a computer station. With laptops or tablets at their seats, students can now compose in rehearsal when not playing or singing. Picture a director stating, "Woodwinds, please work on your melodies while the percussion and brass work on cleaning up this syncopated rhythm." Observations in one study found that students are able to complete a compositional task in rehearsal and are engaged in a musical task for a greater portion of the rehearsal than students who are asked to just sit quietly while not playing (Dammers, 2007).

The advent of cloud computing is also expanding the reach of technology-supported composition. In cloud computing, the software and user files are stored on and accessed through the Internet, greatly decreasing the importance of the computer hardware. This has practical implications for music teachers. The software, often free, no longer needs to be installed on a specific computer, which allows the software to be used anywhere in the school and allows the students to easily access their compositions, at home. This greatly expands the opportunities for both formal class-based projects and for informal, student-initiated composition.

After evaluating the pedagogical objectives, the students, and the classroom settings, music teachers have the information they need to select a software environment. Most music software is not designed for educational use. Instead, it is often designed either to print music, record music, or produce a sound file of synthesized sound and prerecorded loops. As software programs have become more powerful, the lines between these categories have become somewhat blurred. However, the basic functionalities of the programs remain and are a useful framework for teachers to examine when selecting a software environment to support composition. For this chapter, software will be examined in the following categories: notation, recording, digital audio workstations, accompaniment, and educational software.

Notational Software

Notation software provides support to student composers in several ways, as compared to projects that would be traditionally accomplished with paper and pencil. It simplifies the notation process by providing multiple modes of note entry, simplifying revision, and eliminating the need to copy individual parts by hand. It also provides an audio realization of the composition at any point in the compositional process. This ability is important, as it supports student revision throughout the composition process for students who cannot audiate their score or do not have access to a piano keyboard (and/or the keyboard skills needed to play their score). For a vast majority of students, this capability makes composing more accessible and meaningful.

Additionally, notation programs' transposition features allow younger students to write for other instruments without having to manually transpose their parts. Picture a beginning flute player who wants to write a duet for herself and a friend who plays alto saxophone. She can now do so without having to learn how transpose up a major 6th (while still in her first year of playing).

Notation software programs are best suited for composition projects which are intended to be performed by others, and for projects situated in classes based on reading standard notation (i.e., band, choir, and orchestra). Often with younger students, a primary learning objective of a composition project is to help students secure their note reading skills.

Notation software programs vary in price from free to $250. Selecting a program is balancing the cost (and resulting level of accessibility for students) with needed features. MuseScore and Noteflight.com, which are free, are most accessible options. Noteflight is cloud-based and MuseScore is a free download, which makes them easy to put in any lab (even without a budget) and students can also use them at home. After that, there is Finale and Sibelius (and Crescendo—an expanded version of Noteflight), which are more expensive. Finale and Sibelius offer several levels of their programs at increasing levels of cost. Most composition projects do not require the full set of editing features in paid versions of the software, but teachers should examine whether a particular project might require some features not always available in the free programs. This includes the ability to have a full score of instruments, real-time note entry (where the user plays in the notes via a MIDI keyboard), changing key and/or meter in mid-score, high-end sounds for playback, and the ability to save the score as a Web page. Often, it is possible to work with a combination of programs, where the students work in a free or less expensive program, and the teacher uses a high-end program. For example, in a band setting, students might use a basic program to compose a twelve-bar melody for their individual instruments, while the teacher uses a higher end program to compile and publish the melodies for everyone in the band to play.

Software for Recording

Recording software is a more recent area of development in music software. As the storage capacity of computers has increased and file compression has become more efficient, computers have become effective sound recording and editing devices. The ability to record and edit sound on a typical computer, with little to no extra equipment, has simplified and democratized sound recording. This opens new possibilities for recorded composition assignments that are fundamentally different from notation-based composing. Students can create by finding and recording sounds in their world. Using these sounds, they can modify and shape these sounds into their own expressive work. As this requires a minimum of technical training, projects of this kind provide a direct route to thinking creatively in sound, regardless of musical or technological background.

Recording software also provides new opportunities for students who are musical performers. Students can now capture their improvisations and compose directly on their instruments, as opposed to having notation software mediate their composition. The ability to multi-track recordings also allows students to create and record multi-part pieces by themselves.

The free, open-source program Audacity is a good resource for these projects. It is available for Windows, Mac, and Linux operating systems. It is a multi-track recording environment that allows users to record, cut-and-paste (not unlike word processers), as well as modify recorded sounds (and sounds imported from pre-existing recordings). Available effects include stretching, reverse, fade, reverb, change pitch (transpose), and change tempo, to name just a few. In essence, this free program can allow students to have extensive abilities to capture and modify sounds.

Many other music software programs are able to record in addition to their other capabilities, including all of the Digital Audio Workstations discussed in the next section. Of these, GarageBand® (included on all Mac computers) and its low-cost PC equivalent, Mixcraft, are particularly accessible for recording-based composition projects.

Digital Audio Workstations

Digital Audio Workstations (DAWs) allow users to work with different kind of musical information. In addition to recorded material discussed in the previous section, the user can also input MIDI data, which triggers a synthesizer on the computer. (Typically, a user selects an instrument sound and then plays in a part via a MIDI keyboard). Most DAWs also include a library of pre-recorded loops (either MIDI or digital audio), which the user can drag-and-drop into their composition. This variety of ways of interacting with sound brings added functionality for the user. For example, a student might start composing a section of their piece by dragging a looped drumbeat into their piece. Then, she might select a bass sound that seems to fit, work out a bass line, and then record that line into the bass track through a MIDI keyboard. After that, she might plug in her guitar and record a rhythm guitar track, and finally, record herself singing a vocal track. Each type of information is used: loops, MIDI data, and recorded audio.

Almost all DAWs use a track-based layout as the primary interface. In this layout, each instrument or voice (which could be looped, MIDI, or digital audio) receives its own line or track. The tracks are then stacked one above the other. By scanning vertically, the user can see how each track relates to the other. Individual tracks can be edited and manipulated in side windows. The visual representations vary depending on the type of data (MIDI or digital audio). While some programs do include aspects of standard notation, DAWs primarily rely upon piano roll and waveform representations.

Track layout and usage of graphic representations of sound allows users to begin to intuitively work with sounds (as compared to working in standard notation). This can provide an important piece of scaffolding for "non-reading" students. These interfaces also provide for a "zoom-out" view of a work, which can be useful for learning about larger scale formal structure.

Teachers should also consider that most DAWS are designed to work with popular styles of music, often dependent upon repeating patterns. While neither a positive or negative aspect, the teacher should consider the style desired in a particular composition project and then determine if the program is a good fit for the style, particularly in terms of available timbres and input structure. Often DAWs can be used, but the composition project will need to include specific parameters (i.e., guidelines for selection of instruments and use of loops), and teachers will need to provide guidance in the use of a DAW in order to address a particular concept. For example, addressing dynamics by showing how students to adjust attacks and volume in individual tracks.

There is a wide range of DAWs available ranging from free (e.g., GarageBand® for Macs, and the online Myna at www.aviary.com) to more expensive (ProTools, Logic, Digital Performer, and Ableton Live). For most composition projects, basic DAWs such as GarageBand® and Mixcraft, are more than adequate, but in technology- and production-oriented classes, the additional features of higher-end DAWs can be useful. The relatively intuitive nature of DAWs (particularly basic DAWs) can be useful in reaching students of a wide range of musical experience and skill.

Accompaniment Programs

Although intended as a practice tool for improvisers, the accompaniment program Band-in-a-Box can be a useful tool for beginning composers as well. Band-in-a-Box is designed to take a set of user-entered chords and realize the chord progression in a wide variety of styles. For beginning composers, this provides an easy way for them to explore chord progression without having to develop the ability to realize the individual notes themselves. Students can then write their own melodies in Band-in-a-Box, or they can export their progression for further work in another program. This is particularly useful for composition projects that are designed to be exploratory in nature.

Educational Software

While most music software is not designed specifically for instructional purposes, there are some programs that are specifically intended for use in music classrooms. Some of these also include compositional aspects, which are particularly useful for younger students. The Groovy Music series (Groovy Shapes, Jungle, & City) includes a simple sequencing screen, in which students place various icons that play loops designed to work together. Students can earn additional sound icons by completing lessons in other parts of Groovy. In a more open approach to composing, Morton Subotnick's Creating Music and creatingmusic.com, students are given a template upon which to draw melodic ideas. The vertical axis represents pitch, horizontal axis is duration, and color represents timbre. Both programs are useful for providing initial compositional experiences for students.

A Few Thoughts

Having examined the categories of music technology software, there are a few other factors to consider. Many of the notation programs and DAWs include the option of integrating video with the sound files in the program. This can be useful in some composition assignments, where the video is used to provide formal structure to the composition, and helps the student composer to focus on his or her expressive aims. Beyond supporting composition, this approach provides students an opportunity to examine the role of soundtracks in our multimedia world. This expanded awareness will hopefully encourage an awareness of how these soundtracks (e.g., in film, television, games, and commercials, etc.) are used to influence our decisions. Video soundtrack assignments are generally engaging for students, and help to connect our music instruction to their daily world.

Regardless of the type of compositional project, the process of revising is central to supporting student learning through composing (Webster, 2003). When composing in a technology-based environment, students will often just add to or write over musical ideas, rather than revise and rework earlier ideas (Dammers, 2007). Teachers therefore need to design composition projects with built-in peer and teacher feedback opportunities that encourage reflection and revision.

Whether providing informal feedback or making a final evaluation of student work, teachers must seek to separate out which aspects of the composition represent the students' musical thinking, and which aspects are more the result of the software environment. As a part of the process, it is helpful to have students write post-composition reflections, to encourage them to think about the compositional process. This not only deepens the students' experience, but allows for the teacher to understand the relationship between the students and the software. Reading a student's reflections along with listening to a student's composition helps teachers gain a greater understanding of how much (or little) the work represents the student's intent. Going forward, teachers can then modify the parameters of the assignments, finding the balance point where students are able to create successful works that reflect their musical thinking.

Finding the correct level of scaffolding or support is a central concern when using technology in a composition project, but it is not the only factor. It is also important to consider the appropriate level of openness or structure in an assignment to match individual students' learning styles. It is possible to correctly match a technology environment to a students' level of musical skill, but still not find success when the student flounders because he or she does not possess the executive function to work through an open compositional task. Inversely, some students may become disengaged when they find the parameters of a project too restrictive. While technology can be extremely useful in allowing students to successfully compose, it is still just a tool. The teacher's ability to understand his or her students and how to best support their learning is still the critical factor.

References

Dammers, R. (2007). *Supporting comprehensive musicianship through laptop computer-based composing problems in a middle school band rehearsal.* Unpublished Doctoral dissertation, University of Illinois.

Reese, S., and Davis, A. (1998). The systems approach to music technology. *Music Educators Journal*, 85, 24–28.

Tomlinson, C. A. (1999). *The differentiated classroom: Responding to the needs of all learners*. Alexandria, VA: Association for Supervision and Curriculum Development.

Williams, D. B., and Webster, P. R. (2006). *Experiencing music technology* (3rd ed.). Belmont, CA: Thomson Higher Education—Wadsworth.

Webster, P. R. (2003). "What do you mean, make my music different? Encouraging revision and extensions in children's music composition. In M. Hickey (Ed.), *Why and how to teach music composition: A new horizon for music education* (pp. 55–65). Reston, VA: MENC-The National Association for Music Education.

12 }

The Vermont MIDI Project: Fostering Mentorships in Multiple Environments
Sandi MacLeod

Introduction

The Vermont MIDI Project (VMP) is a collaborative community of teachers, students, pre-service educators and professional composers who focus on music composition. As of July 1, 2012, this organization will be know as Music Composition Online Mentoring Program (Music-COMP). Utilizing online communication to connect and share work, the community helps students from the beginning stages of their composition to completion. The online discussion and work samples provide models for teachers as they guide composition activities in their own classrooms. Many of the compositions are designed for live performance and are ultimately performed by the composer, by peers, or by professionals.

The lessons learned and presented in this chapter are derived from discussion, observation, and reflection from experiences of VMP participants over time. Working with an estimated seventy thousand students in grades 3–12 from diverse communities over fifteen years provides depth and breadth of insights into the composition process. Teachers in the project address challenges that are similar to challenges educators encounter today; lack of expertise in the pedagogy of composition; lack of personal composing experience; lack of time for planning and lesson development; lack of access to computers.

Since the beginning, VMP teachers and composer mentors have readily shared what they learn. The hope is that prospective music educators will take the processes and guidelines outlined and build on them to implement composition programs of their own. Composition begins with individual teachers and their students. While it may not be possible to connect with professional composers on an individual school level, using the lessons learned from VMP's connections with eighteen different composers over the last fifteen years includes that perspective into the guidelines in this chapter. VMP teachers and composer mentors firmly believe that music composition belongs in every music class.

John Kratus (2010) praises VMP as one of three worldwide programs that create new opportunities for students and move music education toward a new era. His article decries music education programs focused exclusively on performance. Kratus believes that the current paradigm lacks vision and response to the rapid cultural and social changes in the world.

> Another example of sticky music education is the Vermont MIDI Project. The project uses the internet to connect student composers in general music classes with professional composers and with collegiate music education and composition majors. The students in Vermont create MIDI files of their original music, which are sent to music majors and professional composers. The students in Vermont receive detailed appraisals of their music in its first draft and throughout the revision process. Here, younger and older musicians form a virtual community of composers, making use of technology to bring people together and promote the creativity of individuals. (p. 46)

A group of five music educators conceived the project in 1995 in response to their dilemma over how to successfully teach composition in their music classrooms as directed by the new National Standards for Arts Education (1994). Since none had received training in teaching composition during their teacher preparation programs, they sought the advice of a professional composer. During these conversations, the idea of using software and the computer to facilitate student engagement in composition was suggested. From there the next step was to take advantage of emerging technology in online communication to connect the teachers and students in their schools with the professional composer for guidance and support.

Much has been learned about composition and effective mentoring from the work of thousands of students and dozens of teachers in varied school settings since 1995. The project connects small schools with large ones; elementary, middle and high schools; schools from inside Vermont and several outside the state. Although the project began with a base of Vermont schools, the list of participating schools now includes schools in Virginia, Illinois, Indiana, New York, Connecticut, and Massachusetts. A category of Independent Study students allows participation by students who are homeschooled and students who attend schools that do not participate in the project. Current Independent Study students live in Vermont, New Hampshire, Connecticut, Massachusetts, Minnesota, and Arkansas. A new initiative will connect students and their teachers from private instrumental instruction studios as they seek to embed composition into student's experiences.

Over the many years of the project, students have discovered they have new musical voices through composition. They tell us they listen differently, play or sing differently, and think about music differently. VMP students have been selected for the Young Composer's Concerts at the Eastern Division for MENC. Students earn honors in the prestigious Morton Gould Young Composers Awards sponsored by the ASCAP Foundation. One VMP young composer was featured on National Public Radio's *From the Top* program featuring outstanding young musicians from all over the country and an occasional outstanding young composer. Some students who began composing in elementary and middle school enrolled as composition majors at Curtis Institute of Music, Ithaca College, Eastman School of Music, and Harvard University. A number of students in VMP have continued to explore composition as music education majors in college, and graduates now implement composition into their school curriculum.

VISION AND MISSION

The vision of VMP is to generate multiple opportunities for every student to compose music in all music classes and performance ensembles. The project facilitates an educational environment where students feel as much a composer as they are a performer or listener. Since the inception of VMP, the mission has been to embed composition into the curriculum. One fifth-grader said,

> Well now that I'm a composer, I do a lot more with music. I enjoy music now. I actually play French horn now in band because I enjoy composing so much and I play piano. Yeh, I like to compose and I like music. Last year when I started composing it kind of opened up like this new world to me of music. (Umpteen Productions, 2006)

Essential to the mission of VMP is professional development for teachers. Every summer a Music and Multimedia Institute brings together teachers from participating schools and others who are interested the work of VMP. The institute focuses on reflection and critique in a creative learning format while developing implementation strategies for teacher's individual school curricula. During the year, workshops and online sessions are held both to address individual needs and questions and to facilitate group sharing of successes and challenges.

Beginning in 2000, VMP added live performance opportunities to bring the composition and performance community together in a celebration of the extraordinary work of students. Since much of the work is written for acoustic instruments, a logical next step is to hear these pieces with real instruments such as woodwinds, strings, brass, percussion, piano, guitar, and voice. In addition to the twice-yearly project-organized performance events, collaborations with other organized groups such as the Vermont Symphony Orchestra, Vermont Youth Orchestra, Vermont Contemporary Music Ensemble, and others present work by competition or invitation.

THE ROLE OF TECHNOLOGY: INAUGURATION THROUGH DEVELOPMENT

The early years of VMP began when computers were uncommon in the classroom. Electronic communication was at the very early stages and the Internet was something few people used. The growth and opportunities provided by emerging technology played a crucial role in the Vermont MIDI Project in the early years as well as in the developments in subsequent years. The idea that students could compose and would share their compositions with a professional composer online attracted the attention of a grant committee and provided the initial monies for this collaboration.

As an organization, VMP harnesses technology to facilitate the organization's mission and vision; technology as tools for composition; as tools for communication; as tools for sharing and feedback on student work; to disseminate resources; to highlight the work of the project. As new technology tools are released, members of the project evaluate if they will enhance the learning and community of VMP. In the fall of 2009, members were offered Noteflight Learning Edition® accounts linking cloud computing/server based software and class management tools. Skype® video and audio conferencing became the standard tool for meetings and web conferences for support or to connect with professional composer mentors. The desktop sharing feature has been invaluable in technical support for a variety of purposes.

The first file exchanges of student work were sent between the teachers in the project through e-mail and attachments. Gradually some teachers felt confident enough to share student compositions with the professional composer mentor. This sharing took place via dial-up accounts where the interchange was strictly between adults. In 1996 when the first VMP website for discussion and posting of files was launched, the real value of mentorship became obvious. With a website open to every school in the project, but closed to the public, all teachers could view all the works by all students shared online within this safe community.

The project teachers observe the dialogue and developing work of their own students and all others sharing on the mentoring site. This open organization of the website within the community is significant and caused a major impact on the growth and development of VMP. A professional composer mentor delivered the first professional development for teachers. He shared his one main plan about how to begin and develop work with students. Soon teachers began to design their own assignments for their own classes. The success or limitations of these new lessons were observable as student work was posted to the website. Participating educators could notice that Teacher A was asking students to compose based on ABA form. Teacher B developed a lesson using question and answer techniques while Teacher C started his group with a known tune and asked students to create their own variations on this tune. This same kind of curriculum sharing that propelled the project forward in the initial years continues today.

Many teachers utilize the website with their classes for multiple examples of compositions and for practice and refinement of the techniques of reflection and critique. Teachers observe the development of compositions and follow the feedback provided by the professional mentors to their own students as well as to students in other schools. Teachers who participate regularly in online mentoring show remarkable growth in their ability to teach composition as they assimilate the skills and language demonstrated by the professional composer mentors.

The initial VMP community communicated online as they embedded composition into the curriculum. This exchange was an early example of a professional learning network (PLN). Students sharing work online for feedback by professional composers and others demonstrated the power of Web 2.0 possibilities before most educators were thinking about or identifying this current phenomenon.

Notation software has been utilized within the Vermont MIDI Project much more frequently than other types of music software for several reasons. Teachers are committed to providing opportunities for students to use and master music literacy and notational fluency. Since much of the work has been for instruments (not a computer performance), students need a way to clearly communicate their ideas. The use of standard notation allows students who want mentoring from professionals to find a common language that relates directly to their work-in-progress. When students print and display their completed compositions, they feel like they have truly become composers. Since notation software is visual, guidance from teachers is required to tune students into the aural aspects of the work. The successful students seem to be guided more by their ears than their eyes.

Fostering a Community for Mentoring

Lessons learned from the mentoring experiences of VMP can guide novice educators to develop language and attitudes to use with students when discussing student compositions. A professional composer is not the necessary ingredient in a fruitful feedback loop. The essential component is respectful and insightful conversation that guides young composers to explore possibilities and make their own decisions. This dialogue may be between teacher and student or between peers.

The term, "mentoring" often denotes one expert providing guidance for one novice. Within the Vermont MIDI Project, feedback is provided in multiple ways and by multiple groups of individuals. These include professional composer mentors, in-service educators, pre-service music education majors, and some of the young student composers. While the level of expertise is different with each group of mentors, the opportunity to review the work-in-progress and provide suggestions for the students to reach their intent or goal is key to the process.

One notion of mentoring is a one-to-one interaction between one expert or experienced individual and one student or younger person. VMP employs a cadre of up to ten professional composers at any one time, each with varied backgrounds, experiences, and interests. Student composers often receive feedback from multiple mentors rather than discussing their work with just one expert. Receiving timely feedback on student work-in-progress is also a value in VMP.

While mentoring sometimes involves others beyond the professional composers, the most influential online mentoring comes from the composer mentor cadre. The professionals have experience composing music, listening to and studying the works of other composers. All draw upon a wide range of musical influences including the popular styles many students enjoy. They capitalize on this with suggestions for listening when addressing questions that come up. Each has expertise in the elements of music and with various instruments or voice. The use of stories and metaphors enhance the feedback. Each of our professionals has experienced the struggles of getting from the initial idea to completion and may relate personal stories as well.

While the professional composer mentors take the leading role on the website, the process for most students begins in the classroom with peers listening to work by peers providing suggestions for changes or improvements. Teachers provide feedback at the classroom level and sometimes post suggestions online for their own students or others. Several collegiate music education programs mentor as part of a methods or seminar class. A few experienced middle and high school students in the program provide feedback on the website. Some are assigned the task by their teachers; others choose to give back to the project by commenting on the work of younger students. Several alumni continue to stay involved by providing mentoring as time allows.

The process of reflection and critique is the foundation of the Vermont MIDI Project. Making critique a part of the culture of the classroom enriches the creative experience for everyone. Critique should be planned, guided, and practiced. It should begin early in the composition while in development. As students critique the work of others, they develop musical vocabulary, communication skills, and a higher level of understanding of the composition process. In the classroom and online, young composers are asked to describe their piece or tell the inspiration behind the work. They learn to ask for feedback on a section of their composition about which they feel unsure. They might ask what they could do next in a piece. They have specific questions on the range or playability of instruments. Some students describe in detail all the events they plan such as the form, the role of each instrument, the tonality, or other ideas. Others provide the basic story behind their original idea.

There are students who seem to have no pre-determined plan or inspiration when they sit down at the blank sheet of the notation on the computer screen. This group is often the hardest to mentor, as one purpose of feedback is to help students reach their intention or goal. One VMP teacher remarked that asking students to describe their intent before sitting down at the computer produced a remarkable change in the results and in student engagement in the composition process. One student's intent was to develop a story about sailors finally spotting land and going ashore while another student's intent was simply to create something light and airy. A third student chose the specific form, key, and instruments before beginning. Intentions, whether specific in terms of a storyline, or general in terms of an emotion, style, or form, work well for students who previously may have simply put rhythms and pitches down before knowing the direction they wanted to take with their composition (C. Pingel, personal communication, April 28, 2011).

MENTORING GUIDELINES

Within VMP, guidelines ensure a productive and respectful interchange. There are separate guidelines for mentors, for teachers, and for students establishing the responsibilities for each group (http://www.vtmidi.org/mentorguidelines.htm). These guidelines are presented to collegiate mentors before they begin working with students in schools in the online environment. They are applicable to all who embark on mentoring young composers.

1. Think like a detective.
   a. What can I tell about the skill level of the student composer?
   b. What is their intention or goal for this composition?
2. Think like a teacher.
   a. How can I help the student achieve their goal?
   b. How can I make them feel successful?
   c. How much information can I give them at one time?
   d. How specific should I be with my comments?
3. Prepare comments like a short order cook.
   Respond with a scrumptious sandwich. The term "critique sandwich" was coined by some 5th grade students and has provided a vivid metaphor for structuring feedback.
   a. Begin with a comment or two supporting the student effort. Point out something that worked well. This gets the student's attention and makes them feel supported.
   b. Provide a rich filling to the sandwich with substantive and clear comments. Be specific. Don't overstuff or the sandwich will be hard to swallow.
   c. Add the top layer of bread for the sandwich with a word of encouragement to the student and their work.
4. Think like a composer.
   a. What changes might make this composition stronger?
   b. Point out possibilities, don't give directives.
   c. Answer questions the student might have posed.
5. Additional protocols from VMP for mentoring.
   a. Always use respectful language. Humor is acceptable, sarcasm is not. Words like "might," or "could" and phrases such as "Have you considered . . . " provide the students with the opportunity to explore possibilities.

      Example—Professional mentor to a 5th grader: "As you continue to revise your piece, you may want to change the flute part a little. Right now the flute plays the same thing 7 times in a row, which may be a little too much. What would happen if it played some different notes, but kept a similar rhythm? Maybe it could go up instead of down at the end of the phrase? Try some new ideas for the flute part, and see if you like them." (Retrieved April 15, 2011, http://vtmidi .greenriver.org/work [password protected].)

Another example—Professional mentor to a 7th grader: "One thing for you to consider as you continue, is that right now as the piece goes on, it seems to be losing some of the interesting chromatic language you were using in the beginning . . . Can you find ways of using some of the interesting chromatic language that you started the piece with in these later sections?" (Retrieved on April 15, 2011, http://vtmidi.greenriver.org/work[password protected].)

b. Use language for suggestions and an occasional score demonstration when text is too cumbersome. Do not take a student score and "fix" it for them.

c. Provide timely responses.

d. Keep the age and experience level of the student in mind.

e. Ask questions of the student when necessary for clarification.

Example—Professional mentor to 5th grader: "You wrote that you 'think we have some wrong sounding notes.' I'm curious what you mean by this. Which notes sound wrong to you? I didn't hear anything that jumped out at me as 'wrong' sounding, but would like to know which parts you're not happy with. (Retrieved on April 15, 2011, http://vtmidi.greenriver.org/work[password protected].)

Another example—Professional mentor to high school student: "I'm not clear on exactly what your question is when you say. 'What I need help and advice on is how to *get* to that point. As a listener, what do you feel would be the most fulfilling to listen to (in terms of fast, slow, loud, etc. for the next section?)" (Retrieved April 15, 2011, http://vtmidi.greenriver.org/work[password protected].)

f. "Let go" of the piece when students indicate they are finished or close to the end. You may recognize many more suggestions you could make, but you need to phrase any further suggestions carefully.

Example—9th grader to professional mentors: "Thanks to all who provided me with feedback and encouragement. I have added dynamics, more bowings (but not all) and new material to my piece. This is my final posting and hope to continue composing." (Retrieved April 15, 2011, http://vtmidi.greenriver.org/work[password protected].)

g. Be sincere. Students see through exaggerated praise.

h. If a piece is accepted for live performance, score preparation details may be more direct.

Professional mentor to 8th grader—"Redundant dynamic marking—clarinet m. 19—delete the MF. Extra metronome marking at the top of pg. 4—delete."

Expressive, or "mood" markings like "aggressively" or "relaxed" are often helpful to performers at the beginnings of sections." (Retrieved April 15, 2011, http://vtmidi.greenriver.org/work[password protected].)

LESSONS LEARNED WITHIN VMP OVER TIME

While technology enables all students to create compositions regardless of their skill level in music, care must be taken not to let the technology or software determine the outcome. VMP students, teachers, and composer mentors have been exploring the use of software for composition for many years and have developed some strategies and solutions to address issues they observe with students. Often students feel like they are not composing unless seated at the computer working on a score. While everyone works differently, teachers can support activities that lead to more successful composition projects.

1. Encourage sketching.
   Student artists and professional artists maintain a sketch pad. In music, students sometimes have the notion that composing only occurs when working at the computer. Students should be encouraged to use the idea of sketching both at the computer and away from it.

   Teachers may create ways for young composers to practice exploring concepts and techniques prior to a more open-ended composition project. Consider this a warm-up or compositional etude. (Kaschub & Smith, 2009.)
2. Listening is practicing.
   Students and teachers alike bring their notions of how to practice for instrumental performance to the task of composing. While it is essential to spend the majority of instrumental or vocal practice time actually playing or singing, composing is different. Listening to a wide variety of musical examples from classical to pop to jazz to world music brings new sounds to each individual's listening library. Listening as practice needs to be more active than passive.
3. Provide tools to work beyond the classroom.
   Technology software programs come in a wide range of prices and capabilities. When students have a composition program at school, but no software to use at home or outside the music classroom, the amount of composition most accomplish is minimal. To some students (and teachers) this is frustrating. Students need time to create, to reflect, to share it with others for feedback, and to revisit for revision.

   Today's web-based technology tools with low-cost or free programs available on the Internet are viable solutions. Encourage students to take advantage of these or provide these tools through school-wide subscriptions where student work is stored on the Web with files accessible anywhere and at anytime.

4. Embed composition activities at all grade levels and in all music classes, including performance ensembles.

One key observation is the importance of starting in elementary years and continuing to offer composition experiences as an integrated whole in the curriculum. Involvement in composition allows students to uncover self-expression and engages them in finding unique ways to solve compositional tasks. The opportunity to compose often does not occur until a student is a junior or senior in high school, which is when traditionalists feel students have enough theory background to compose. However, students at all levels can compose when guided by skillful teachers. Students in VMP tell us they learn so much about music by composing music.

One VMP high school senior confessed,

> I'm a tuba player and . . . sometimes it's a bit on the boring side, when you're playing six whole notes tied together or something like that. I guess one thing I used to do, I'd be apt to maybe fancy up the tuba part a little bit during band and play whatever I'd feel like playing, using my ear to make it sound good. I guess now that I've composed, you feel like you owe it to the composer to do what they told you to do. You realize how intentional every note is and every staccato, every tenuto, every dynamic marking. It wasn't an accident. They put it in there for a reason. (SBO Magazine, 2009)

The idea that composition activities enhance an instrumental curriculum was supported in a research study (Riley, 2006). This study provided composition experiences for an experimental group and the regular band rehearsal-based curriculum for a control group. The results support composition activities for performance ensembles for those educators worried that students will not perform as well on their instrument or in the performance ensemble.

> Given that [students] who engaged in music composition activities and students who did not engage in music composition activities both experienced gains in individual music achievement and gains in individual instrumental music performance, it seems that an approach to teaching middle school band classes that includes music performance, listening and composition is effective. In this study, students who performed, listened to and composed spent approximately one-half as much time on music performance activities as students who performed and listened to music, yet these students experienced the same improvement in individual student instrumental music performance. (Riley, 2006)

Web 2.0 tools with available software for composition provide a solution to instrumental and vocal performance ensembles where class time for group interaction and practice is important for success. Although there is research to support the benefits of taking time within the regular rehearsal schedule, another option is to utilize available Web 2.0 tools to provide students with a composition tool and occasional homework assignments to complete outside the regular rehearsal. It is important that teachers provide feedback and opportunities for sharing. Again, much of this can be done with a Web 2.0 environment. Another consideration is to use an online composition curriculum designed for flexible use such as independent study, homework, or in class exploration.

5. Teachers should compose.

It is important that teachers experience new tasks in a similar way to what they expect of their students. When teachers compose and submit their work for critique, many discover they guide students more successfully through a process that can be intimidating. One elementary band director composed a piece at the summer institute to present at the first concert for his beginning ensemble. The teacher reported that almost every rehearsal began with more than one individual asking, "Can we practice the piece you wrote for us?" The students presented a stellar performance and there was an enormous appreciation from the audience of parents, colleagues and the administrators (C. Olzenak, personal communication, November 10, 2004).

Below are excerpts from an online request from one teacher to his middle school band members who were concurrently in general music and composing within the class. The piece was completed and eventually performed by those same middle school band members.

Here's a piece I have started and is far from finished. Working on it here will give me an opportunity to emphasize some key points that I have been talking about in this class. Look at how simple the rhythms are, how much stepwise motion there is, how melodies repeat and give the ear something to hold on to, how the main theme starts and ends on "Do," how we are in the key of A, how the various notes come together to produce chords in the key of A.

This is also an opportunity for you to help me. Gwen asked me to try the tempo faster and it made a big difference. Yes, "I like it" is nice and "You're the best composer in the world" would make me feel special, but there's more to giving feedback than that. I want to know about technical elements of the piece and how changing them would make my presentation more effective. I want sentences that begin with "In measure . . . ". I want comments based on the elements we have been learning about and other thoughtful, practical and non-judgmental ideas. Think of what you might like to hear and give me help getting there. (Retrieved April 15, 2011, https://vtmidi.myhaikuclass.com/danseiden/putneyexploratorymiddleschool/cms_ßpage/view).

IMPLEMENTING MENTORING IN MULTIPLE ENVIRONMENTS

Mentoring is a powerful process for student composers. It begins with the individual student reflecting on their own work so they can ask for suggestions and sort through the suggestions they receive. Within VMP, classes who practice this classroom-level mentoring to provide and receive feedback develop a sense of camaraderie around the process of composition. It is common to hear questions such as "Chris, can the trumpet play this?" or "Sylvia, can you help me figure out which chord sounds better here?" Or "Who has an idea for a better title?" Communication of this sort reflects 21st-century learning skills and fosters a sense of collaboration and problem-solving.

The benefits of establishing a composition community can create opportunities for student works to be performed in different community locations. Gaining momentum for a composition program at the school level requires awareness and support by both school level administrative and the community. Since the majority of adults have never composed before, there seems to be a mystique about composition. Demonstrating that students have the ability to create amazing works by showcasing a wide variety of original compositions can do much to ensure composition becomes embedded into the curriculum.

Mentoring programs can be as straightforward as peer-to-peer or older students with younger students. As mentioned before, this requires modeling and repeated practice. Mentoring can begin at the local level. Cloud computing software such as Noteflight with a comment feature can be enabled by young composers to solicit and accept feedback. The comment feature, once selected as an option, is viewed by any user in the community so it is important to develop a respectful and supportive class culture for critique. Noteflight Learning Edition® and others can set up groups that provide for individual school or district level communities.

Reaching beyond the school level, two teachers could connect students in different buildings or communities to share a comment of the work of other students. Perhaps a professional composer in the community would be interested in looking at a representative sample of student work and providing feedback. One word of caution, do not overwhelm the professional with twenty sol-me-la compositions by third-graders or she may lose her enthusiasm quickly. Select two or three works from the entire class and ensure students will consider revisions if provided feedback.

PRACTICUM POSSIBILITY FOR COLLEGIATE MENTORS

Several music education collegiate programs engage in mentoring on VMP as part of three different options: during a general music education methods course, as part of an ongoing seminar for music education students, or as an elective Independent Study. These music education majors engage in an additional field experience that can be completed on campus or at home, wherever students have access to the Internet.

The collaboration with the University of Vermont music education program requires collegiate students enrolled in a general music methods course to compose themselves and to engage in VMP online mentoring with students in elementary, middle, and high school. Each collegiate mentor follows two students and responds with online feedback, from the beginning of a composition to completion. These compositions are created at the computer with the intention of having real instruments perform the work. The change in the composition over time affirms how important the feedback and other aspects of the mentoring relationship can be, and how this increases the possibilities for students throughout the grade levels to succeed at composition. (See complete conversations and works at http://www.vtmidi.org/student.htm.)

One additional benefit for the pre-service educators is that they are working alongside professional composer mentors in VMP. Learning what to say and how to say it by observing several professionals at work provides great models for future feedback. Reese (2003) describes the continuum of responses to composition from least directive to most directive by highlighting specific language used in his observations of professional composers and experienced teachers. Collegiate mentors reflect on their own and others' choice of words and observe the results in this online dialogue. They develop supporting and respectful language that encourages the student to remain in charge of their own work. Keeping in mind the purpose of developing a student's creative musical voice and helping them reach their intent is evident in the online mentoring program and all who participate at VMP.

Collegiate music education and composition programs can enhance their music training programs through online mentoring while not requiring additional travel or time away from campus. The potential for online sharing with a multiplicity of schools provides unique opportunities not always available in the immediate vicinity of the college program. In the Johnson State College seminar program, music education majors mentor VMP students for three or four semesters as part of the program. This provides the additional experience of observing students over time.

VMP is singled out as "transformative" (Reese, 2004) by observers of the work over the years. Since 1995, the project has maintained the commitment to its mission of embedding composition into the curriculum. As an early innovator in music and technology, the project not only survived, it thrived. Technology changes encourage continued transformation to harness the best new tools and provide more opportunities for students to explore composition as part of a holistic music education program.

References

Consortium of National Arts Education Associations. (1994). *National standards for arts education*. Reston, VA.

Kaschub, M., and Smith, J. P. (2009). *Minds on Music: Composition for Creative and Critical Thinking*. Lanham, MD: R&L Education—A Division of Rowman & Littlefield Publishers, Inc.

Kratus, J. (2010). Music education at the tipping point. *Music Educators Journal,* 94(2), 42–48. doi: 10.1177/ 002743210709400209.

Reese, S. (2003). Responding to student compositions. In M. Hickey (Ed.), *Why and how to teach music composition.* Reston, VA: MENC.

Reese, S. (2004). Perspectives for planning for technology integration. *TRIAD, OMEA.* February/March, pp. 33–38.

Riley, P. (2006). Including composition in middle school band: Effects on achievement, performance, and attitude. UPDATE: Applications of Research in Music Education, 25(1), 28–38. doi: 10.1177/875512330602500101.

Kuzmich, J. (2009). Creativity, teamwork and the Vermont MIDI composition project. *School Band & Orchestra.* Retrieved April 15, 2011. http://www.sbomagazine .com/7806/archives/march-2009/creativity-teamwork-and-the-vermont-midi-composition-project/.

Umpteen Productions (Producer). (2006). New perspectives in arts integration. Grant report (video production). Available from Vermont Arts Council, 136 State Street, Montpelier, VT 05633-6001.

13 }

Digital Natives and Composition in the Middle School Band: From Imagination to Music

Bruce Carter

Anyone can make the simple complicated. Creativity is making the complicated simple.

—Charles Mingus

Music educators, like Mingus, understand the complex challenges that lie ahead in any attempt to make the complicated simple. Teaching students to compose music in a manner that fosters creativity is just such a challenge. Teachers must help students explore the world of music and create their own music while guarding against tasks and activities that may overwhelm their newly emerging capacities. Simple exercises and projects can too easily snowball into complicated activities where opportunities to exercise creativity and artistry become secondary to the sheer execution of the task. Yet, with careful thought and planning, composition can present abundant opportunities for an extensive range of musical learning.

Although I am both a composer and a music teacher-educator, I had very little to share about teaching composition either in traditional one-to-one lessons or in groups when practitioners sought my advice. My own experiences teaching composition in classrooms often left me discouraged as I struggled to present instructional practices appropriate for middle school students. However, there is an ever-expanding palette of tools and resources that are both appealing to students and well-suited for educational purposes that music teachers can draw upon to overcome many of the challenges educators have faced. Indeed, we can now make many of composing's complexities simple.

Introducing the Virtual Composer-in-Residence Program

In this chapter I will share the most recent iteration of a composition program designed to support the study of composition by middle school band students. Drawing upon a community of classroom teachers, undergraduate methods students, and professional composers, the virtual composer-in-residence program (VCRP) seeks to create a multifaceted community dedicated to sustained, meaningful, composition study. Perhaps what sets this program apart from others is the focus on distant learning, or the "virtual" component of the residence and the nested learning environment created between musicians and educators at various stages of the musical experience.

The VCRP began four years ago when a middle school band teacher wrote me in frustration over the difficulties of finding a professional composer to visit and mentor her students. At that point the topic of online learning was pervasive in academic discourse, making the intersection of the composition instruction and distance learning obvious, at least in theory. During my first attempt at initiating a distance-learning curriculum for composition study, I served as the virtual composer-in-residence and began exploring the successes and difficulties of online teaching and learning. From that initial program it also became apparent that the middle school students and classroom teacher required more one-to-one advising than one composer could provide. For that reason undergraduate method students were invited to take part in the program. In this way the undergraduate students were able to learn more about the compositional and musical processes unique to middle school students.

In addition to my role as coordinator, there are four active groups in this project: professional composers, classroom teachers, undergraduates enrolled in undergraduate methods courses, and middle school instrumental students, as shown in Figure 13.1.

At the beginning of the fifteen-week program each of the group's responsibilities are briefly outlined:

Professional Composers: Principally, the role of the composer is to provide curricular suggestions, as well as general counsel to all involved. At the end of the program, composers are expected to compose a ten-minute band work that draws upon compositions created by the middle school students. This composition will be performed for the community and serve as the capstone musical experience for the program.

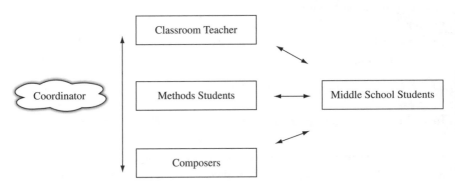

FIGURE 13.1 Five components of virtual composer-in-residence.

Classroom Teachers: Incorporate ten minutes of daily composition exercises into band rehearsals. Additionally, help students develop their online composition portfolios and utilize numerous composition applications. Lastly, oversee communication between band students, undergraduate methods students, and the professional composers. Classroom teachers also help advise and structure compositional exercises provided by the professional composers and program coordinator. Classroom teachers are not expected to have experience composing and are encouraged to learn along with their students.

Undergraduate Methods Students: Undergraduate music education students are expected to serve as mentors for the middle school band members. Students are expected to complete creative exercises provided by the professional composers to better understand potential obstacles or frustrations. After each composition exercise, the methods class will talk as a group to develop ways of meaningfully guiding band members. In this way, the methods students are both learning how to compose and how to critique and guide others.

Middle School Band Students: Middle school band students are expected to complete one composition exercise per week. Students will receive feedback on their work from various sources including their classroom teacher, undergraduate mentors, professional composer, and program coordinator. Students should remember that one essential element to composing is revision, and are encouraged to read and respond to feedback in a positive way.

Program Coordinator: The role of program coordinator is multifaceted. The primary responsibility is to create a means for all involved to interact with one another. In the past a website or blog has successfully allowed for easy communication between all involved. Before starting, the fifteen-week program of study goals and assessment criteria are discussed with professional composers, classroom teachers, and methods students. The program coordinator should monitor the blog and interactions between all groups looking for ways to replicate successes and diminish potential roadblocks.

At the beginning of this semester-long program, all of the adults involved in the project are provided with a series of readings related to teaching composition in a K–12 setting. The purpose of this initial step is three-fold. First, the readings prevent the obvious error of being ahistorical. While composition resources are limited in number, numerous readings provide meaningful instruction for both teachers and students. Second, and perhaps more importantly, the process creates a dynamic dialogue between groups, fostering a sense of community as problems and obstacles are shared. Lastly, in past years, all involved have found the readings profoundly influenced their approach to composition study.

The next step in the program is to create a blog that serves as a virtual meeting point for the professional composers, classroom teachers, undergraduate method students, and me. At this point salient issues are outlined and discussion threads established to foster a dialogue between groups. Topics are grouped and summarized to guide everyone involved. Additionally, questions are provided at the end of each grouping to stimulate online conversation.

Initial Readings to Guide the VCRP

In this section I provide a sample of the readings and guiding questions provided to stimulate discussion among the adults engaged in the VCRP program. In the first few iterations of the program I found that teachers were overwhelmed by suggested readings. Accordingly, I now only provide the implication sections of articles presented here, or excerpts from books that speak directly to the topic being discussed. The readings are grouped according to important topics in the compositional process such as challenges of: a) starting with standard notation; b) writing for transposing instruments; c) arranging; d) utilizing non-standard notation; e) technological considerations. The two topics I have chosen to incorporate in this chapter include obstacles to composition instruction in the classroom, and composition practices of eminent composers.

OBSTACLES TO COMPOSITION INSTRUCTION IN THE CLASSROOM

Most teachers have similar anxieties as they begin the program. They are encouraged to openly discuss concerns so everyone involved in the VCRP program can anticipate and stem potential difficulties. Teachers who find tasks unfamiliar or who feel uncomfortable with compositional processes are likely to avoid incorporating composition in their classrooms (Kennedy, 2002). In numerous research articles, teachers admit that taking time away from performance preparation is often a source of anxiety (Reid, 2002; Strand, 2006). To guide discussion on the blog I posted the following questions: a) how important is communication with school administrators and parents concerning VCRP?; b) how can the director advocate for a band class but then teach topics like composition that may seem extraneous to some?; c) how can students be motivated musically if performance is not the central mission of the ensemble?

Other obstacles of composition instruction often described by teachers include classroom size, overly noisy environments, and limited instructional time. Teachers may have the desire to use composition activities, but do not have the instruments, space, software, or instructional guides to do so (Kennedy, 2002). According to Berkley (2004), one main reason teachers do not incorporate composition into the classroom is that there is a lack of publications about composition pedagogy and teaching strategies. However, recent texts such as *Minds on Music: composition for Creative and Critical Thinking* (Kaschub & Smith, 2009) specifically address concerns and fears music teachers may have when incorporating composition instruction into classrooms. Guiding questions in this section include: a) how can technology help overcome difficulties expressed in group or classroom composition?; b) does a noisy environment suggest an unmanageable learning environment?; c) what is the appropriate balance between unorganized or free composition time and time dedicated to typical rehearsal strategies?

COMPOSITIONAL PRACTICES OF EMINENT COMPOSERS

A few books illuminate issues and concerns surrounding the compositional practices of eminent composers. However, the texts are often philosophical in nature or provide complex theoretical or abstract approaches to compositional practice at the college level (Adolphe, 1999; Ford, 1992; McCutchan, 1999; Piirto, 1992). In contrast, other textbooks written by eminent composers provide highly technical, prescriptive, approaches to composition study (Hindemith, 1942; Persichetti, 1961; Piston; 1987). Besides these few sources, very little is known about the teaching practices of composer-teachers (Barrett, 2006).

In recent years, researchers have begun questioning eminent composers about their uses of compositional pedagogy (Barrett & Gromko, 2001). For example, Lapidaki (2007) interviewed eminent composers to examine the ways they describe and analyze the composition process. Lapidaki had two goals for pursuing this study. The first was to obtain a better philosophical understanding of contemporary composers. She states:

> With so many researchers of music education looking at the compositional processes of students in classrooms and music technology laboratories, it would be very helpful to acknowledge and draw philosophical implications for music composition in schools from recognized composers' voices and their individual composing realities. (p. 96)

The second goal of the study was to explore how a more philosophical understanding of composers could inform the practice of composition instruction at all ages. Lapidaki states, "a music teacher needs to indeed grasp how this creative process works in a real world context in order to foster and expand the student composer's craft of composition in educational settings at all levels" (p. 94).

After examining the lifestyles and compositional practices of the eminent composers, Lapidaki cites four prevalent themes: a) the composer, the conscious, and the unconscious; b) the beginning of the compositional process; c) moving the compositional process forward; and d) the composer between tradition and innovation. Lastly, Lapidaki states that composer-teachers should strongly encourage students to write in styles and ways that differ from the composer's own compositional practices. In this way, students are pressed to find their own voices and to seek out new and original ways of expressing themselves.

Barrett (2006) provides one of the most recent and thorough research articles exploring compositional practice. Building on preliminary work, she investigates the ways composition instruction is taught, learned, and perceived within music programs. The participants in her study included an eminent composer-teacher, a composition student currently enrolled as an undergraduate major, and a composition major that had recently graduated, but also studied with the same eminent composer.

The following teaching strategies were observed during the lessons by the composer-teacher:

1. extended thinking, provided possibilities;
2. referenced work to and beyond the tradition;
3. set parameters for identity as a composer;
4. provoked the student to describe and explain;
5. questioned purpose, probed intention;
6. shifted back and forth between micro and macro levels;
7. provided multiple alternatives for analysis of student work;
8. prompted the students to engage in self-analysis;
9. encouraged goal setting and task identification;
10. engaged in joint problem finding and problem solving;
11. provided reassurance;
12. gave license to change.

For each of the teaching strategies listed above, Barrett provides detailed examples of the dialogues between the composer-teacher and student.

In addition to the teaching strategies, Barrett also notes three prevalent themes that emerged from her experiences with the three composers—composer model, enterprise, and composer voice. The theme of composer model refers to the ways the student-composers described their teacher's influence. Concerning the theme of enterprise, Barrett states: "to be enterprising includes showing initiative and imagination, and taking risks in new endeavors" (p. 211). Lastly, the theme of composer voice emerged when Barrett noticed that the student composers all credited their teacher for helping them find their own individualized style. When discussing the philosophy of his teacher, one of the student-composers remarked, "his style was not to be the grand composer-teacher and saying that the only way you can learn is by studying my works, you know the composer-teacher was allowing me to experience my own identity and my voice" (p. 211). Furthermore, the composer-teacher insisted that young composers be provided with the opportunity to explore multiple types of writing styles to find a voice they felt was their own. Barrett concluded that eminence studies have the potential to inform the teaching and learning practices of music at all levels. She states:

> Whilst the teaching of composition in school settings has few parallels structurally with the one-on-one tutoring employed in this study, the teaching strategies observed may be modified and adapted to accommodate these settings. (p. 214)

Guiding questions that accompanied this section included: a) how can details about the composition process of eminent composers affect the approach of composition study in the VCRP program?; b) could studying composition from the perspective of academic or art music composers negatively influence the VCRP program?;

c) should musical examples be given to students to serve as markers of good composition? Regarding the last question, "c": if so, provide examples and explain the choice.

Response of Collaborators

By engaging professional composers, classroom teachers, and methods students in discussion, everyone involved is able to create an egalitarian space for learning and discovery. For these collaborators (the term I use to describe everyone except the middle school students), the exchange of ideas concerns not only the topic of composition pedagogy, but also what each group's role can be when teaching the middle school students and one another. Serving as program coordinator, I provide general guidelines and expectations from all involved; specific curricular and pedagogical considerations are not prescribed.

This open format is much more time-consuming for everyone. In many ways, it would be easier for the program coordinator to provide specific instructions. Yet, by allowing the collaborators to question both the compositional process and their roles in the VCRP, they are encouraged to think more deeply and creatively.

Initially, the primary goal was to teach middle school students how to compose. However, somewhat organically, the program now teaches musicians at various stages of their musical and educative lives how to discuss and present composition lessons.

The Role of Technology

Lastly, the VCRP program relies heavily on technology to effectively communicate and create musical ideas. Rapid development of both hardware and software has substantially changed the way the collaborators have interacted over the past three years. Educators have numerous technological resources available to us now that we did not have just five years ago. Faster Internet speeds, increased access to the Internet, increased availability of computers in schools, and larger percentages of students who have computers at home make the use of online learning experiences more widely available. In this section I outline three ways technology was utilized during the virtual residency.

Numerous companies provide spaces on the Internet for free blogs such as Google (www.blogspot.com) and Yahoo (www.yahoo/blogs). Communicating with co-collaborators and middle school students through the blog was very effective during the residencies. I have begun exploring the possibility of using Facebook,

Google Plus, or similar social networking applications to provide a more direct and simpler form of communication.

The middle school students were encouraged to ask questions about their work and review comments made about all of the compositions uploaded on the site. In addition to the blog, collaborators and students were able to video-conference with one another during their classes. Services like Skype®, Elluminate, or iChat make video conferencing easy to set up and use in the classroom. After the very first video exchange, it was evident that video-conferencing would profoundly impact the experience for everyone involved. Although socially awkward at first, students and directors quickly grew comfortable with me being "in the room" and within a few days were eager to interact and share their work.

Second, educators no longer need to rely on music notation software programs that are expensive and sometimes difficult to learn. Several online notation programs with no downloading requirements are now free and easy for young students to use. In each year of the residencies I utilized Noteflight, a smartly designed program that allows individuals to create accounts and save their work. I selected Noteflight because it is easy to learn yet complex enough to allow users to write one or more multiple parts, play them back, edit them, and post them online for others to view.

At the top left-hand side of the example shown in Figure 13.2, you can see the Noteflight menu screen that allows the composer to easily touch a desired musical element and place it on the staff. Within one lesson, most students were able to use the notation system with ease. The collaborators are consistently impressed to see that students utilized the online notational system to not only write music, but also to teach themselves unfamiliar rhythms and melodies found in their band literature. In this way, students were excited to learn and utilize standard notation as a tool for expressing their ideas because of an intrinsic motivation. When investigating musical ideas through standard notation, students approached musical concepts that would encourage problem-solving and learning at their own pace. For the collaborators, this was one of the clearest examples of the composition instruction positively impacting the overall musical learning of the students.

Usually, each composition lesson consisted of one prescriptive notated musical element. The online notational software allowed students to more easily confront tasks that required traditional notation. With the software, students could:

FIGURE 13.2 Screenshot of Noteflight score.

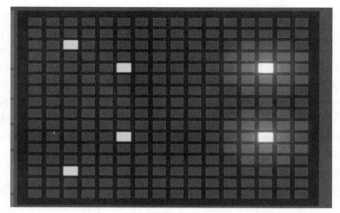

FIGURE 13.3 Screenshot of a free notation tone matrix from http://tonematrix.audiotool.com/. Retrieved June 24, 2012.

easily identify when a measure did not have the appropriate number of beats, readily transpose score and parts, and most importantly, play music back to revise their work.

Technology not only aided in communication and notation, several new programs and websites were ideal for encouraging free composition. One example of free notation is the tone matrix available at http://tonematrix.audiotool.com/. At this website, visitors can use the matrix to create musical loops. The matrix, as shown in Figure 13.3 provides a powerful visual and aural tool for teaching basic musical elements. The simple but effective website served as a wonderful way to demonstrate the interaction between harmony and rhythm.

Besides free play on the computer, students were asked to improvise on their instruments using their invented tone loop. Starting composition activities at the computer often provided students with opportunities for quick successes. To build on these accomplishments, students were encouraged to create music on the computer that could be played along with their instrument. On the whole, students did not have to be prompted; they readily adapted musical experiences gained from computer-based instruction to their band instruments.

Composition Instruction for Everyone

In the most recent iteration of the VCRP, I encouraged the classroom teachers and undergraduate method students to complete the composition assignments provided by the professional composers before the middle school students started. This served as an important step in helping the co-collaborators detect potential difficulties and prevent future frustrations for the younger students. Additionally, for many of the professional composers, this was their first experience providing lessons to younger students. The classroom teachers and methods students were able to provide an opportunity to test lessons and reshape curricular decisions.

Although each year of the VCRP program includes different groups of co-collaborators and students, many of the compositional elements are similar. For example, concepts of silence and sounds, planned and intermittent, pitched and non-pitched, functional and non-functional, are explored in sequenced and deliberate ways. Working from a palette of deliberate silence, students are encouraged to consider musical elements with technologies that focus on loops and free composition play. The primary purpose of this musical play is to focus on music creation without the troubling issue of notation.

Examples of composition exercises that were more free in nature, and were designed for students to explore various soundscapes, follow:

> Instructions: Select a piece of kite string that is almost as long as you are tall. Stand on the string with your left foot, and after wrapping the string around your index finger a few times, place your finger gently into your ear. The sound you hear when your pluck the string with your left hand should resemble a string bass. Can you make the string sound higher or lower? How? What happens if a friend touches the new "string bass" around the mid-way point? Next, using a metal coat hanger from your closet, loop the string around hanger 5-6 times, wrap the ends around your index fingers and gently place both fingers in your ears. The hanger should now be hanging around waist level in front of you. What happens when you swing the hanger and strike various elements around the room?

As described above, the composition program Noteflight provides an accessible introduction to musical notation. Students are encouraged to find ways of notating music created in free play, or in their musical loops. Exercises using non-traditional notation are often among those most difficult for many of the band musicians. At this juncture, the undergraduate methods students are able to play an important role in mentoring the middle school students. Each undergraduate student is assigned three–four young students to mentor and directly interact with over the fifteen-week program. The mentoring is always most intense when students attempt to meaningfully recreate musical ideas in traditional notation. This mentoring relationship also alleviates the stress classroom teachers feel when trying to cater to the individual needs of all the students.

Examples of composition exercises that were more prescriptive in nature included:

> Instructions: Find a friend's musical phrase that interests you. Can you think of two ways you would change the melody to make it sound like something you have written? Describe your new melody in words to someone who may never get to hear it. Notate the original melody and your new melody. Bonus Challenge: Notate your new melody in a way that looks completely different but sounds the same. How can you accomplish this?

Obviously, in the VCRP program, teacher involvement was not an issue—each band director was excited about integrating composition instruction. However, in the past, band directors have consistently stated that time "taken away" from rehearsals was a significant source of stress. Additionally, the directors each discussed their own frustrations and feelings of uncertainty when attempting to help students in a process that was open-ended and foreign. Throughout the process the teachers were encouraged to call or Skype® so we could talk through their questions and address any anxieties. This consistent dialogue was key to the virtual residency. It was evident that the teachers enjoyed talking through their learning experience in addition to sharing the stories of their students' successes.

Drawbacks of a Virtual Program

The biggest drawback described by the professional composers concerned the inability to improvise with students, in time, to just have fun making music. The inability to move from improvised, collaborative musical play into notated musical work was often described as a weakness. As the speed of the Internet increases, I hope the professional composers will be able to make music with students—online and in real time, without delay. Additionally, the professional composers often struggled with the large scope of the program. For most composers, their concept of a composition lesson is an intimate, highly individualized mentoring experience. Understanding the needs and abilities of a middle school student, both musically and socially, is typically a source of consternation in the beginning. The classroom teacher and program coordinator can help the learning curve become less steep for the composers.

Conclusions

The opportunity to work with a composer and witness the perspective and process of a professional musician can be meaningful for numerous reasons. Students have the opportunity to interact with a musician without fear of consequences imposed by a grading system, freeing them to express themselves musically. Students might ask the composer questions not only about the creation of music itself, but of career and educational trajectories (Tsisserev, 1997). Additionally, experiences working with living composers who help students to realize their creative music-making and improvisation may bridge the gap between prior informal musical knowledge and formal musical knowledge.

Recent advances in technology make the "virtual" part of the residence less of an obstacle. New websites and programs allow students to easily create and communicate their music ideas. Recently developed online notational systems can assist students in the often-difficult experience of working with standard notation while providing the opportunity to hear their work and easily revise.

Large, well-funded music programs may be able to continue to commission new works and welcome visiting composers, but the current economic climate limits opportunities for our students to gain the benefits described from these types of experiences. Additionally, geography continues to serve as an obstacle for many teachers who would otherwise like to provide experiences linking their students with the larger musical community. Many rural schools are located too far from densely populated places with communities of professional artists or large universities with composition faculty. Other schools face the obstacle of outside perceptions of their neighborhoods as unsafe, keeping otherwise willing musicians away from working with our wonderful students. It is my hope that this chapter will encourage educators to consider bringing a composer to their classroom, even if at a distance. Although the VCRP program targets middle school band students, I believe this type of program could be effective in any K–12 classroom.

References

Adolphe, B. (1999). *Of Mozart, parrots and cherry blossom in the wind: A composer explores mysteries of the musical mind*. New York: Limelight Editions.

Barrett, M. (2006). "Creative collaboration": An "eminence" study of teaching and learning in music composition. *Psychology of Music*, 34, 195–215.

Barrett, M., & Gromko, J. (2001, January). Scaffolding the creative process: Provoking the "muse that sings." Paper presented to the Ninth International Conference on Thinking, Auckland, New Zealand.

Berkley, R. (2004). Teaching composing as creative problem solving: Conceptualizing composing pedagogy. *British Journal of Music Education*, 21(3), 239–263.

Ford, A. (1992). *Composer to composer*. St. Leonard's, NWW: Allen and Unwin.

Hindemith, P. (1942). *Craft of musical composition*. New York: Schott Publishing.

Kaschub, M., and Smith, J. (2009). *Minds on music: Composition for creative and critical thinking*. Lanham, MD: R&L Education—A Division of Rowman & Littlefield Publishers.

Kennedy, M. A. (2002). Listening to the Music: Compositional processes of high school composers. *Journal of Research in Music Education*, 50(2), 94–110.

Reid, S. (2002). Creativity: a fundamental need of adolescent learners. In Sullivan, T., & Willingham, L. (Eds.), *Creativity and music education* (pp. 100–109). Edmonton, Alberta: Canadian Music Educator's Association.

Lapidaki, E. (2007). Learning from masters of music creativity: Shaping compositional experience in music education. *Philosophy of Music Education Review*, 15(2), 91–110.

McCutchan, A. (1999). *The muse that sings: Composers speak about the creative process*. New York: Oxford University Press.

Persichetti, V. (1961). *Harmony: Creative aspects and practice*. New York: W.W. Norton.

Piirto, J. (1992). *Understanding those who create*. Dayton: Ohio Psychology Press.

Piston, W. (1987). *Harmony*. (5th ed.). New York: W.W. Norton.

Strand, K. (2005). Nurturing young composers: Exploring the relationship between instruction and transfer in 9–12 year-old students. *Bulletin of the Council for Research in Music Education*, 165, 15–17.

Tsisserev, A. (1998). An ethnography of school student composition in music—A study of personal involvement in the composition process. Unpublished doctoral dissertation, University of British Columbia, Canada.

SECTION } V

Composition in University Courses

SECTION } V

Composition in University Courses

The inclusion of composition in undergraduate study is contextually influenced by institutional challenges, faculty interest and expertise, and frankly, consumer demand. To date, very few schools offer composition methods courses. There fore, music teacher-educators must generate excitement about the possibilities offered by engagement in the study of music composition. Programs successfully implemented at other institutions may serve as models that can be adapted for local use.

Video-conferencing can offer one tool for connecting varied populations engaged in composition activities. Patricia Riley describes a project in which pre-service music educators in Vermont taught students in Mexico and Japan over the Internet using video-conferencing. A second project that she facilitated involved an international partnership that allowed children in the United States and China to collaboratively create music compositions via video-conferencing. These engagements serve as models of collaborative practice and as ways of exploring cross-cultural connections that encourage pre-service teachers to try similar activities in their future classrooms.

Pre-service and in-service teachers in an urban university setting can become comfortable with leading compositional activities. After briefly discuss the changing meanings of composition in the twenty-first century, Janice Smith considers the importance of encouraging undergraduate and masters-level music educators to study composition and composition pedagogy. Integrating compositional practices in methods classes and field experiences is viewed as a best practice. Moreover, the challenges of urban teaching are considered opportunities for encouraging musical creativity, both for teachers and their students.

Although the term "composition" is associated with classical music and "songwriting" more with popular music, the two activities share similar processes and artistic intents. John Kratus describes his experiences in teaching songwriting classes to college students and provides a rationale for such courses for both music education students and for the general population of college students. The detailed outline provided at the conclusion of the chapter serves as an excellent model for others seeking to implement similar courses.

14 }

Composition in International Settings:
Broadening Pre-Service Perceptions
Patricia Riley

This chapter explores video-conferencing as a tool for connecting varied populations, as well as for developing a "world view" of educational practices within music through virtually-direct engagement. It describes projects in which pre-service music educators in Vermont teach students in Mexico and Japan over the Internet using video-conferencing, and an international partnership that allowed children from the United States and China to collaboratively create a music composition via video-conferencing. The possibilities of this medium and its usefulness in exploring cross-cultural connections will be discussed. To that end, the chapter will also look at issues of social equity and access to instruction. Finally, this chapter will suggest ways to bring in guest lecturers and performers with a variety of expertise into classrooms via technology so that pre-service teachers see the value of these experiences and become encouraged to try similar activities in their own future classrooms.

Projects described in this chapter integrate ideas of music, culture, social justice, and communication through video-conferencing. It is my hope that these integrations will serve as models for future collaborative video-conferenced projects between and among faculty, teachers, students, cultures, and disciplines. According to Gouzouasis, "video-conferencing is a powerful communications medium, and may be used in creative interactive contexts" (1994, p. 229). Kratus states that "musical communities can be formed by musical interest rather than acquaintance or physical proximity. . . . The dream of music serving as a bridge connecting the world's people is within our grasp" (2007, p. 45).

In this chapter, the project with the Mexican children serves to describe what has been learned about the video-conferencing teaching environment, and how the undergraduate music education majors and I came to realize that engaging the children in creative activities was one of the most effective teaching strategies used. The outcomes of this first project led to the second and third projects and provided a context for them. The project with the Japanese students focuses on a music composition unit delivered through video-conferencing, and the cross-cultural music composition project uses video-conferencing to connect children in the United States and China.

Project with Children in Mexico

This first project was designed to give undergraduate music education majors in the United States the opportunity to develop teaching skills as they delivered general classroom music lessons to children at a school for underprivileged children in Puebla, Mexico using video-conferencing technology. Through this interaction, the undergraduate music education majors and I sought to help the children in Mexico "gain deeper, broader, more significant musical meanings" (Reimer, 2003, p. 133); and in the spirit of social equity, strove to overcome challenges inherent in the video-conferenced classroom environment to "unselfishly . . . help others achieve the values of music for themselves (Elliott, 1995, p. 309). Many challenges were encountered and progress was slow. The experiences of video-conferenced music teaching over a two-and-a-half-year period, and the learning that the pre-service teachers (the undergraduate music education majors), the students, and I have shared serve to illustrate how the use of video-conferencing in music teaching can be utilized, improved, and employed to engage students in music composition activity. This project is examined with a research perspective in the journal article "Video-Conferenced Music Teaching: Challenges and Progress" (Riley, 2009).

The nine pre-service music teacher participants were enrolled in sections of an undergraduate elective course entitled Spanish Immersion/Video-Conferenced Music Teaching Practicum. The pre-service teachers were at various stages in their training, ranging from some who had not yet taken any pedagogy courses, to some who had completed all of the pedagogy courses, including general music methods and general music practicum courses. All of the teachers could be characterized as belonging to the American middle class, and all but two were of Caucasian ethnicity. The students in this project attended a residential elementary school for underprivileged children in Puebla, Mexico. All of the students were of Mexican ethnicity.

I served as facilitator in this project, by coordinating the video-conferencing technology and participants, providing musical materials, and supervising the planning and teaching. The video-conferenced music teaching was an extension of an in-person music teaching practicum course that I supervised in which pre-service teachers from the United States participated in a Spanish Immersion program at a Mexican university near the elementary-school project site.

The principal of the elementary school shared with me his dismay that the music instruction was occurring only for a three-week period during the early summer, and with limited groups of children. His wish was that there could be additional instruction during the majority of the school year, and that more children would be included. It was during this discussion that I proposed the video-conferencing project. The expectations were that (1) the Mexican children would receive more consistent music-learning opportunities; and (2) the American music education majors would have the opportunity to be involved in a cross-cultural teaching experience using a developing technological medium with children who would not otherwise receive formal in-school music instruction.

Each semester, the pre-service teacher(s) and I planned the lessons together, using the experiences of the prior semester to inform the process. The first teaching episode occurred in September of 2005 with four pre-service music teachers and twelve fifth-grade students. As the project continued in subsequent semesters, the number of teachers varied from one to four; and number of students from ten to fourteen. Grade levels varied from third grade to fifth grade. There was some carry-over of teachers and students from semester to semester. Teaching occurred for one half-hour approximately once every other week, with hour-long supervised planning sessions in between. Prior to this experience, most of the children at the school in Mexico had not engaged in any formal music education, although informal music experiences occurred in their homes and communities.

The video-conferencing equipment was quite basic, with a computer, i-Sight camera, audio speaker, projector, and screen at each location. A high-speed Internet connection was used, along with the computer programs i-Chat (used for the first two semesters) and Skype® (used in the remaining semesters). Language in this project was a challenge, as all of the teaching was done in Spanish. There was a facilitator, José, at the Mexican school, who brought the video equipment and set it up each time. He functioned as the teachers' "arms and legs" during the teaching episodes when needed, and also restated or translated instructions when necessary.

Each semester, a little more was learned about how to teach effectively within the video-conferenced classroom environment, and how teaching in this environment differs from an in-person environment. Teaching adjustments designed to compensate for the video-conferencing constraints of time-delay and echo included speaking a complete thought and then pausing during the echo, rather than starting and stopping as the echo occurred; waiting before gesturing in call and response activities, so that the teaching gesture occurred simultaneously with the sound the children were hearing; and not trying to sing or accompany simultaneously with the children. As the project progressed, the practicum teachers moved from focusing primarily on instruction and teaching content to quality of student learning and improved assessment; and moved away from activities focused on reading and understanding notation toward activities focused on understanding through creating music. According to Kara, one of the pre-service teachers

> I would teach the students in a way that is familiar to them, and not what is familiar to us. The whole concept of education, especially in a musical world, is that it is no longer about the teacher, it is about the students. The students should be learning concepts that are valued in their own culture, and taught in ways that are authentic to them.

Based on the reflections generated in this project, the pre-service teachers and I concluded that there are benefits and drawbacks to teaching and learning in the video-conferenced environment. Thorough planning, flexibility in teaching, cultural sensitivity, and thoughtful reflection are necessary. Teachers must work creatively to overcome difficulties caused by lack of proximity, and feelings of isolation between teachers and students. As technology and Internet connections improve, the quality of sound and picture are also improving and the time delays and echo are becoming minimized, facilitating an improving environment. Two of this project's most successful lessons featured improvisation activities. Through this, we realized that creative activities can be very successfully delivered in this video-conferencing environment, and can facilitate and enhance music teaching and learning using this medium. Based on this, it was decided to have music composition become the focus of the subsequent projects with the Japanese, Chinese, and American children.

Project with Students in Japan

This second project occurred in the spring semester of 2009, and describes an interaction between pre-service music teachers in Vermont and students at an international school in Yokohama, Japan. It is somewhat of a continuation of the project with the Mexican children, and focuses on the use of video-conferencing for teaching music composition lessons. This project is examined with a research perspective in the journal article "Video-conferenced classes: American pre-service music educators teach composing skills to students in Japan" (Riley, in press).

Participants in this project were three undergraduate college music education majors enrolled in their general music methods course, and ten seventh-grade students in their general music class. Together, the pre-service teachers developed lesson plans, taught, and reflected on two beginning melody-writing music composition lessons. The students worked two-to-a-computer-station, each equipped with a keyboard and the online music notation application, Noteflight. Each lesson was forty-five minutes in length, and was facilitated by the classroom music/technology teacher in Japan, Mr. Jones, and by me in the United States. In between the two lessons, the students worked on composing their melodies and the teachers mentored the pieces, which were sent from the students to the teachers and back again through email. The mentoring followed the guidelines established by the Vermont MIDI Project (renamed Music-COMP — Music Composition Online Mentoring Program), an online music composition-mentoring program with which the teachers had experience. The mentoring guidelines include "offer two or three suggestions without overwhelming young composers," "encourage development of material with specific suggestions," "ask questions to focus thinking," and "use phrases like: 'Have you considered' and 'I wonder if' rather than being directive." The complete mentoring guidelines can be found on the Vermont Midi Project webpage at www.vtmidi.org. During the first lesson, characteristics of melodies were examined, and the initial composition project was assigned. During the second lesson, melodic characteristics of the student compositions were discussed, revision of the compositions was assigned, and future composing was encouraged.

According to the teachers' lesson plans, objectives of the first lesson were to discuss and demonstrate elements of a well-constructed melody, including stepwise motion, emphasis on the home note or tonic, not too many skips or leaps, that it is easy to sing, and that there is repetition. The students were then to compose eight-measure compositions that include the discussed elements. In between the two lessons, the student created the compositions and received mentoring feedback from the teachers. During the second lesson, the student compositions were shared with the class and discussed in regard to the elements, and the concept of question and answer phrases was introduced.

Figure 14.1 shows an excerpt of one of the student compositions.

FIGURE 14.1 Excerpt of a student composition.

This student composition exemplified all of the elements of a well-constructed melody discussed and demonstrated by the teachers. It included mostly stepwise motion and emphasis on the tonic. It began and ended on the home note, and visited it three other times during the eight measures. The qualities of not too many skips or leaps, easy to sing, and repetition were also achieved in this piece. Based on the elements discussed and demonstrated by the teachers, the students who composed this melody were able to compose a well-constructed melody. This melody was representative of the other compositions; two of which also exemplified all five of the elements, two of which exemplified four of the elements, one of which exemplified two of the elements, and one of which exemplified one of the elements.

The following is mentoring feedback from Teacher 2 (Sally) to the student composers:

> Great job coming back to the home note throughout the composition. You did a nice job with repetition, but don't be afraid to vary your pattern a little bit. You have very good use of stepwise motion, and even though you used some larger intervals, they were still very sing-able and easy for the ear to hear. I like your second to last measure because you take your rhythm and change it a little bit into something new and different.

This mentoring feedback was also representative of the other mentoring feedback. It exemplifies several of the Vermont MIDI Project mentoring guidelines, including offering a suggestion without overwhelming young composers, encouraging development of material with specific suggestions, and using language that offers suggestions without being directive.

I believe this teaching and learning episode can be interpreted as successful. The lesson objectives were met, the students composed well-constructed melodies, and the teachers delivered mentoring according to established guidelines.

After the video-conferenced classes had concluded, the American teachers and Japanese students reflected on their teaching, mentoring, or learning experiences, answering questions posed by me. The following are a sampling of the questions and answers:

What was it like to teach students/learn from teachers in Japan/the United States using video-conferencing technology?

Teacher 1 (Debbie) stated that she was immediately interested in this project, and that she "liked the idea of being able to teach actual children, especially in Japan." She went on to write that she was "very nervous" the first time she and her co-teachers taught using this technology, because she was "not exactly sure how everything was going to go." She was afraid that the students were not going to pay attention, or that they might not value what she and her co-teachers had to say. After the teaching, she realized that this was not the case, stating "even though we weren't in the same room as the students (or even the same country for that matter!), they were very attentive and interested." Debbie concluded that she was "impressed" with how well she and her co-teachers were able to communicate with the students using this technology, that it was "cool" to teach using video-conferencing, and that it was a "very successful" experience.

Teacher 2 (Sally) had taught using video-conferencing technology in a previous semester, so was more familiar with the experience. She commented that this experience was better than her previous one because the Internet "connection was really good with the classroom in Japan." In this teacher's previous video-conferenced teaching experience, the Internet connection with the classroom was via satellite, while in the Japanese classroom it was a high-speed wireless Internet connection. The high-speed connection resulted in better quality of sound and picture, less time-delay, and fewer interruptions due to loss of the connection.

The Japanese students' statements included that they thought it was "really cool" to be taught by teachers using video-conferencing technology. They asserted that learning using this technology was "the same but in a different way." A positive aspect was that they received "lots of feedback, including that of people on the other side of the world."

How do you think learning in this environment could be useful/not useful to students?

Both teachers asserted that they thought this environment could be very useful to students. Debbie stated

> students have the opportunity to get many different perspectives through video-conferencing. . . . If you were doing a unit about Japanese music, for example, you could video-conference with someone in Japan and watch actual playing techniques, instruments, and culture. I think it is an excellent use of technology.

Sally concurred, writing "I think it is good because it is something new and exciting for kids. They are also able to get perspectives from lots of different teachers and they are shown many different teaching styles." Debbie concluded:

I feel that the good outweighs the bad in this situation. I feel that this teaching experiment was beneficial both to the students and to us teachers. I would love to be able to video teach again. I really feel that I got a lot out of it.

The positive and negative aspects identified in this second project are similar to those articulated in the earlier project with the Mexican children. Common difficulties in technology encountered include problems with the sound and picture and interruptions due to time delays. Teaching difficulties due to lack of physical proximity, and the implausibility of singing simultaneously with students again occurred. The need for thorough planning and flexibility to adjust teaching, the inability to cover as much material as in face-to-face teaching situations, the feeling of isolation between participants, and the necessity of assistance by a facilitator at each of video-conferencing site were also reinforced. Continuing positive outcomes of the video-conferenced teaching environment included student enthusiasm, interest in the cultural context of participants, the seemingly minimized sense of distance between participants, and the increased opportunities that the video-conferenced teaching environment affords students.

In this second project, some of the positives and negatives cited by the pre-service teachers are not unique to the video-conferenced teaching environment, but are issues that I have commonly observed in in-person teaching. They include enjoying the freedom to plan and execute lessons when limited guidelines are assigned, needing to have all materials ready and transitions worked out before teaching starts, and problems with getting all participants to contribute equally during group-work projects.

Pre-service and in-service teachers can incorporate these outcomes to develop and refine their own teaching skill as they plan and implement music composition lessons via the video-conferencing teaching environment. Most prominent are the need

- for thorough planning (including efficient transitions)
- to have materials organized and ready before lessons begin
- for flexibility to adjust pacing and content as lessons unfold
- to seek out and accept assistance as needed

As always, thoughtful reflection is critical to successful planning and teaching.

I feel that this second project is an example of positive interaction between teachers and students through technology, and demonstrates that music composition can be successfully taught via video-conferencing. The use of the online notation application was beneficial in this project, enabling students and teachers to share, view, and mentor music compositions directly. This alleviated one aspect of the proximity issue, and contributed to effective communication between students and teachers.

Cross-Cultural Composition Project

This third project describes a collaborative cross-cultural music composition created by children in the United States and China. It is based on the learning resulting from the project with the Mexican children, and provides insight into the use of video-conferencing technology to foster collaborations among distant students, and into the creation of a music composition cross-culturally. Participants were two 10-year-old children enrolled at the Gaoxing No. 3 Primary School in Xi'an, China, and two 10-year-old children enrolled at the Wells Village School in Vermont. China and the United States were chosen as the host countries for this collaborative cross-cultural project because of their approximate locations on opposite sides of the world, and because the cultures are generally regarded as being quite different.

The Gaoxing No. 3 Primary School is a large, affluent, well-equipped city school with four on-staff music teachers. The Wells Village School is a small, rural, moderately-equipped school whose music instruction is delivered by one part-time itinerate music teacher. These particular schools were chosen because of their accessibility to me, and the agreeability of the school administrators and music teachers to host the project. The children at both sites engaged in weekly general music classes provided by the schools. One of the Chinese children, Julia, had also participated in private piano study. All four of the children had previously engaged in limited music composition experiences within their general music classes.

Both schools contain pianos within the classroom music spaces, as well as a variety of pitched and non-pitched instruments. Instruments available for use in this project included those already at the sites, as well as Orff xylophones, a metallophone, glockenspiels, claves, maracas, an African shaker, a tambourine, a hand drum, a guiro, and a woodblock, which I provided in China. These instruments were selected because they represent a wide range of timbres, and originate from a variety of cultures and because they are similar to the instruments available at the school in the United States. The Orff xylophones, the metallophone, and the glockenspiels were provided also because they are similar to a piano, and because they are relatively easy to play.

The project occurred in April 2008 during five 90-minute sessions. I functioned as the facilitator of the music composition activity, and was the project-site coordinator in China. The project-site coordinator in the United States was the fifth-grade teacher at the Well Village School. The functions of the coordinators were: to let the children into the school, composition space, and instrument storage area; to turn on the technology equipment and establish the video-conferencing connection; to videotape the sessions; to distribute and collect all materials; and to troubleshoot any problems. On the final day, the coordinators also administered concluding interviews during which the children at both sites answered questions about the project.

Choices made in the design of this project were based on findings of related research. The decision to have the children work in pairs at each site was influenced by Marsh (1995) and Wiggins (2000); to have exploration experiences included in the design, by Ashby (1995), Kratus (1989), Levi (1991), and Marsh (1995); to have each of the barred instruments equipped with thirteen pitched bars and arranged diatonically from a lower C to a higher A with no chromatic alterations, by Kratus (2001), and to include non-traditional notation, by Auh and Walker (1999).

During the first session, prior to composing, the children at each site separately experimented with the instruments to be used and the musical elements of pitch, duration, tempo, dynamics, and timbre. At the second session the technology was initiated, and an Internet video-conferencing connection was established using the computer program Skype®. Technology equipment used were school computers; an iSight video-conferencing camera (in the United States); a video camera used as an exterior camera and a fire-wire cable to connect the two (in China); headphones for all involved; and headphone splitters. The children at each site were able to see a large view of the children at the collaborating site, as well as a smaller view of themselves, on the computer screen. They were able to hear the sounds at the collaborating site through headphones and/or computer speakers. At this second session, the Chinese and American children, translator, and facilitators were introduced. The children at both sites were told that

- they were to work collaboratively to compose original music
- they could work together on this project in whatever way they felt would be most productive
- they should put their musical ideas down on paper in whatever ways they felt would be useful to remember them
- they would have two more composing sessions on the following two days
- on the final day, they would rehearse their music composition, perform it, and answer questions about their composition and the process through which it was created.

Following this, the children chose the instruments that they would use, and started working on their composition.

At the outset of the project, it was decided by the children to work independently, each child on individual melodies, and then to share the melodies with all of the other children for feedback. The Chinese children (Julia and Susan) worked separately to create, notate, and revise their melodies, although they chose to share one glockenspiel and two mallets as they worked. The American children (Brandon and Caroline) worked separately to create and revise ideas, but worked together to notate their ideas, and helped each other remember ideas when needed. They also chose to share one melodic instrument, a xylophone, but used the instrument one at a time, passing it back and forth, and using two mallets each. Brandon and Julia decided to also notate some of the ideas of the children at the other site.

On the second day of the project, five melodies were created, one by Brandon, two by Caroline, and two by Julia, with Susan adding a jingle bell accompaniment to Julia's melody. All of the children discussed together their opinions of the melodies, and decided the order in which the melodies should be arranged.

On the following day, the melodies were reviewed and refined, and additional melodies created (one each by Brandon, Caroline, Julia, and Susan). After all of the melodies were created, all of the children discussed together their opinions of the new melodies, and decided which melodies to include and which to discard. They also discussed together the order in which the melodies should be arranged.

On the last day of work, each child collaborated with the other child at their site to add non-pitched instruments to the melodies, and then shared their rhythmic additions with the children at the other site for feedback. All of the discussion between the children of the other children's ideas was positive. Any negative discussion or discarding of an idea was of a child's own work.

The process and products of this collaborative cross-cultural music composition project were very similar to the processes and products of music composition projects within single cultures. The children explored, developed, notated, shared, revised, and arranged ideas and generally worked within a whole-part-whole format. Their music composition was tonal, with cadences on sol and do; and included rhythmic and melodic repetition, melodic development, and sequences. In the concluding interviews, the children stated that they worked together to create a composition that sounded good to them and that they were happy with. They liked working together and now regard each other as friends. Based on this, it can be concluded that this collaborative cross-cultural project was successful.

This project can serve as an example of music composition processes for undergraduate music education majors to analyze. They could discuss ways in which they might incorporate such a project with current students (practicum or student teaching), or with future students. They could brainstorm about teachers they know or might have access to, and children that they could connect to engage in a multi-site music composition project. Using available technology in their university settings to facilitate the planning process could include discussion boards and video-conferencing. They could videotape the implementation (process and products) and use the videotapes for reflection and evaluation. They could also share the videotapes with each other and their instructors for feedback and further reflection.

As stated in the introduction to this chapter, the projects discussed integrate ideas of music, culture, social justice, and communication through video-conferencing. The video-conferencing environment connected pre-service music teachers with students at a school for underprivileged children in Mexico, and at an international school in Japan. It also connected students and facilitators at two very different schools in the United States and China. According to Josh, one of the pre-service teachers in the project with the Mexican children, video-conferencing "make[s] distance obsolete and brings trained teachers to any student in the world." Providing access to certain types of instruction for those who would not otherwise have that opportunity, (formal music education for the children in Mexico, and music composition lessons for the students in Japan) is a very powerful way to include social equity in pre-service teaching curricula.

Related literature on this topic highlights the importance and relevance of this inclusion. Cochran-Smith states "teacher preparation is a learning problem and . . . there is a reciprocal relationship in learning to teach for social justice among the learning of student teachers, the learning of their more experienced mentors, and the learning of the pupils they teach" (2004, p. xix). According to Green, "to teach for social justice is to teach for enhanced perception and imaginative explorations, for the recognition of social wrongs, of sufferings, of pestilences wherever and whenever they arise" (1998, p. xlv). Ayers writes "the teacher creates an environment for learning that has multiple entry points for learning and multiple pathways to success. That environment must be abundant with opportunities to practice social justice" (1998, p. xxv).

In addition to connecting teachers and students anywhere in the world, the videoconferencing medium is rich with possibilities for connecting guest experts to classrooms, whether at the elementary-, secondary-, undergraduate-, or graduate-school levels. All that is required is a little creativity in planning, and a world of possibility and opportunity unfolds. Composers, performers, conductors, lecturers, anyone really can be sought out and contacted via the Internet, and guest appearances arranged. With just a computer, an Internet connection, and the free program, Skype®, any agreeable expert can interact virtually with, and enrich, any classroom.

Recently, my colleague who teaches the course Introduction to Music Technology asked me about inviting Sandi MacLeod, Executive Director of the Vermont MIDI Project, the music composition online mentoring program, to come into his class as a guest lecturer. Sandi agreed, and while she lives in close proximity to the university, she was to be out of state at the proposed time; so we decided to connect with her using Skype®. The students in the technology class were very positive about the experience, citing as benefits the savings in time and expense, as well as opportunity for and accessibility of interacting with experts. According to Maggie, a sophomore music education major:

> It's great to be able to hear from experts, but not have to go anywhere. We learned a lot from our own classroom. I liked being able to have a big group discussion, even though we were not all in the same place. It would be very helpful in my future classroom to have Skype®, especially if I am teaching a band, and need one of my college friends to give assistance with instruments I am not expert at.

Another similar option is to Skype® into classrooms for group observations. Even though my students and I have been engaged in video-conferenced teaching for years, the idea of video-conferenced observing had not occurred to me until I attended a session on it, "Add Contact: Guided Observations in Music Settings Using Skype®," presented by Alison M. Reynolds, Jill Reese, and Matt Clauhs at the 2011 Symposium on Music Teacher Education at the University of North Carolina at Greensboro. I was so excited by this idea, that I hurried back to my Introduction to Music Education class to try it. In this class, we normally travel together on four group observations, carpooling to schools within a fifteen-minute radius of our campus. Since this is the first music education course in the students' curriculum, I offer these group observations so that in the class session following each, we can reflect together, and I can guide the students toward the quality and substance of reflection that I deem most advantageous to their development as professionals before sending them out for the remainder of their state-required sixty hours of observation.

For the first Skyped observation, I called upon a general music teacher whom I regard as one of the best in the state, but one who works at a school too far from campus for practical travel. The teacher used the camera on her Smartboard to facilitate the Skype® connection, and I used the teaching computer in the music department's computer lab and built-in projector for our end of the connection. Following our greeting the teacher and students at the beginning of the observation, I turned on the mute button on our end so that I could point out important items that I wanted my students to notice during the observing. This added a layer of instruction that would not be possible during an in-progress, in-person observation. This observation worked out so well, that the students requested another.

For this second Skyped observation, I decided to seek out a composition lesson, since my students were in the midst of discussing various ways in which the composing National Standard could be implemented. The educator who we observed is an exemplary instrumental music teacher who was teaching a music composition lesson within the context of a music theory course. The students were composing individually in the music department's computer lab, and the teacher walked from computer to computer with his iPad, which he was using for his end of our Skype® connection, giving us a window on each student as they worked. For my students' end of the Skype® connection, we used my MacBook Pro attached to an LED projector in our regular classroom. Student comments included "it's great to 'be there' without taking up time to get there or taking up class space" (Jack); and "it is convenient for schools that are further away, so we can get a wider range of observations of how music is taught" (Carly). When asked whether the students think the Skyped environment is an effective way to observe composing, Carl stated "It is efficient and effective . . . it is a perfectly unobtrusive way to get many students into a classroom to observe." According to Bea:

> Yes, although the technology could be momentarily frustrating, we were still able to see the students' compositions, hear the compositions clearly, and hear the students talk about their pieces. Once students took out their headphones, we were able to hear as well as watch the composition process.

The above two examples of Skype®-facilitated interactions (the guest expert, and the observations) illustrate that the video-conferencing environment is not only effective in international contexts, but also can be very effective closer to home. Connections can be made between states, within states, and even within school districts. With this in mind, the possibilities become even more abundant and accessible.

Additionally, YouTube (www.youtube.com) can be utilized to bring video footage of a wealth of performances, and TED Talks (http://www.ted.com/talks) can be accessed to bring a variety of lectures into classrooms. A quick search of YouTube can yield Leonard Bernstein's *Young People's Concerts*, Igor Stravinsky conducting his *Firebird Suite*, The Beatles first US appearance on the *Ed Sullivan Show*, or Ravi Shankar performing on sitar. Easily accessible music lectures on TED Talks include *Bobby McFerrin Hacks Your Brain with Music*, *Herbie Hancock's All-Star Set*, and *Emmanuel Jal: The Music of a War Child.* The listening examples available on YouTube, and perspectives offered by these experts are an excellent resource for inspiring and influencing music composition. The quantity and variety of listening material accessible on the Internet can provide multiple examples of musical elements (melody, harmony, form, timbre, etc.) and principles (repetition and contrast, tension and release, etc.) for students to analyze and experiment with in their own composing.

In conclusion, I want to emphasize that the possibilities for connecting through the communication and video resources on the Internet are endless. It is my hope that this chapter helps encourage music education professors and the future music educators they teach to explore and embrace the unique opportunities for enhanced music composition experiences that can be accessed through video-conferencing and technology.

References

Ashby, C. L. (1995). An analysis of compositional processes used by children. *Masters Abstracts International*, 34(01), 0040. (UMI No. 1375862).

Auh, M., & Walker, R. (1999). Compositional strategies and musical creativity when composing with staff notations versus graphic notations among Korean students. *Bulletin of the Council for Research in Music Education*, 141, 2–9.

Ayers, W., Hunt, J. A., & Quinn, T. (Eds.). (1998). *Teaching for social justice*. New York: Teachers College Press.

Cochran-Smith, M. (2004). *Walking the road: Race, diversity, and social justice in teacher education*. New York: Teachers College Press.

Elliott, D. J. (1995). *Music matters: A new philosophy of music education*. New York: Oxford University Press.

Gouzouasis, P. (1994). *Video conferencing with preschool children: Mass Communication medias in music instruction*. Retrieved from ERIC database. (ED 388248).

Green, M. (1998). Introduction: Teaching for social justice. In W. Ayres, J. A. Hunt, & T. Quinn (Eds.), *Teaching for Social Justice*. New York: Teachers College Press.

Kratus, J. (1989). A time analysis of the compositional processes used by children ages 7–11. *Journal of Research in Music Education*, 37(1), 5–20. doi:10.2307/3344949.

Kratus, J. (2001). Effect of available tonality and pitch options on children's compositional processes and products, *Journal of Research in Music Education*, 49(4), 294–306. doi:10.2307/3345613.

Kratus, J. (2007). Music education at the tipping point. *Music Educators Journal*, 94(2), 42–48. doi:10.1177/002743210709400209.

Levi, R. (1991). A field investigation of the composition processes used by second-grade children creating original language and music pieces. *Dissertation Abstracts International*, Section A, 52(08), 2853. (UMI No. 9202227).

Marsh, K. (1995). Children's singing games: Composition in the playground. *Research Studies in Music Education*, 4, 2–11. doi:10.1177/1321103X9500400102.

Reimer, B. (2003). *A philosophy of music education: Advancing the vision.* (3rd ed.). Upper Saddle River, NJ: Prentice-Hall.

Reynolds, A. M., Reese, J., & Clauhs, M. (2011). Add contact: Guided observations in music settings using Skype. Greensboro, NC: Symposium on Music Teacher Education.

Riley, P. E. (2009). Video-conferenced music teaching: Challenges and progress. *Music Education Research*, 11(3), 365–375. doi:10.1080/14613800903151580.

Riley, P. E. (in press). Video-conferenced classes: American pre-service music educators teach composition skills to students in Japan. *Journal of Technology in Music Learning*.

Wiggins, J. H. (2000). The nature of shared musical understanding and its role in empowering independent musical thinking. *Bulletin of the Council for Research in Music Education*, 143, 65–90.

Pre-Service Teachers in Urban Settings: Composing Connections
Janice Smith

In this chapter I will explore the ways pre-service teachers in an urban university setting become comfortable with leading compositional activities. First I discuss the changing meanings of composition in the twenty-first century. Next, I will consider briefly the importance of encouraging undergraduate and masters level music educators to study composition and composition pedagogy by integrating compositional practices and methods classes and field experiences. Third, the challenges of urban teaching will be viewed as opportunities for encouraging musical creativity for both the teachers and their students. Finally, I will give some suggestions for building compositional partnerships between urban schools and urban universities.

While the focus of this chapter is on urban education, many of the suggestions here apply equally well to rural and suburban settings. The examples I provide are taken from my own experience and those of my students at the Aaron Copland School of Music at Queens College, City University of New York. Their schools and identities have been changed, but the stories and examples are directly from young teachers who are teaching composition in their classrooms and ensembles. Let us begin by considering the definition of composition as it is evolving in many urban schools.

Broadening the Definition of Composition

Ask most people to think about what music composition is and they will come up with ideas about writing down notes and playing instruments. Many professional musicians and composers may think one cannot compose until one understands music theory. Additionally, it assumed that one cannot compose unless one plays an instrument, preferably the piano. However, in the twenty-first century, new definitions and new practices are enabling more people than ever before to expressively create with sound. This is exactly what composers do.

The essence of music composition is meaningful organization of musical sound. While it may be true that musical experience, music literacy, and instrumental facility make it easier to manipulate or control some music materials, it is expressive sound that is the defining quality. Music experience includes listening. Many people have extensive listening experience and because of that, they also have an intuitive understanding of what constitutes a composition. They may have a very deep understanding of the components of a particular style. This depends on the depth of their perceptions and conceptions about what they listen to.

In a related manner, people are often musically literate in ways that are not encompassed by notation. Think of all the aural musical traditions that are not limited to what can be notated and how expressive those traditions can be. While our system of music notation is one of the defining characteristics of Western European art music, music was being created long before there was a way to notate it. Why, then, should it be that people need to know notation in order to compose?

Lastly, many of the issues of instrumental technique have been overcome by software programs that allow people with little or no instrumental performance experience to organize sound. To quote a well-known advertising campaign, "There's an app for that." While instrumental technique is still a useful skill, much like notation, it is no longer a prerequisite.

None of these qualities by themselves make people musically expressive. Composition is a way of expressing feeling in music by organizing sound. It is the sound—and not the ways that it is preserved—that constitutes the composition. Some musical traditions have long relied on the composer/performer's memory to preserve musical creations. Notation was a great invention in the time before recordings because it allowed the sharing of musical ideas without a performance.

However, now notation is rapidly becoming relegated to simply one of the ways people can preserve their musical ideas. In the last hundred years, recordings have become ubiquitous. While we have not usually thought of recordings as a way of composing, the advent of computer assisted composing has made recordings one of the predominant ways musical ideas—and new music—are preserved and shared.

Moreover, it is the rare individual in the early twenty-first century that does not carry a personal music device with them nearly all the time. This allows music to become an individual experience. Prior to recorded music, listening to music almost always had to be a group experience. Because cell phones can record, save, and play back sound, people can capture interesting sounds wherever they may encounter them by recording them onto their cell phones. Those sounds can the later be manipulated in ways the composer finds interesting. Composers also then have an easy way to share their work with whomever is interested in it. All of these ideas are easily adapted to urban classrooms (as well as those in other places) by virtue of the fact that just about everyone has a cell phone. So what are the implications for urban composition education? First, let us consider composers.

Encouraging Undergraduates and Masters Students to Pursue Composition

There are often students in our programs who become interested in composition once they have tried it. Occasionally, students enter our programs with compositional experience and a serious interest in combining a composition program with an education program. John Richmond's chapter in this book discusses a model for that. Until very recently music education students at the Aaron Copland School of Music were required to take a course in composition. Credit limits and increasing state mandates have forced us to combine the composition class with the arranging class in a class called composing and arranging for school ensembles. While not ideal, this does give our undergraduates a taste of composition.

Particularly in our masters programs, we have students who come into our program with undergraduate experience in composition. They often enroll in our advanced certificate program in order to obtain a teaching certificate. These students are often delighted to learn of ways to include composition in their ensembles and classes. They do come with the same biases about students needing structure and theoretical knowledge in order to compose. However, once we get them beyond the notion of compositional etudes, and into expressive qualities and principles, they become our strongest advocates for teaching composition to all students.

Occasionally, the etudes we do in class inspire them to go on and create expanded works of their own. Because they are experienced composers, their ideas and contributions often serve as models and inspiration for the students who are just beginning to compose. When these composers then obtain positions in schools, they are eager to have their students compose as well. It is often simply a case of giving them some models for how to proceed. Because they are used to composing as a solitary activity, our role as teacher educators is to provide them with examples of how to proceed with composition in large and small ensembles and groups.

Similarly, undergraduate students who have never had compositional experience are often inspired to take electives in composition after composing our methods classes. Because our faculty includes six practicing composers, it is often easy for students to arrange this. Composition is still offered as an elective class each semester following the combined composition and arranging class. For talented students private study in composition is encouraged as well.

Everyone benefits from this arrangement. Students get to expand their compositional abilities, composition classes become large enough to run on a regular basis, and composition faculty have a broader audience for their own work and their teaching. So what sorts of things are integrated into our methods classes and how does this apply to future urban teachers?

Integrating Basic Activities into Methods Classes

My own early work with composing with children was heavily influenced by the work of R. Murray Schafer in the 1970s. Consequently, I have long been comfortable with rather creative ways of engaging children in manipulating sound long before computers were available to manipulate sound waves. In our elementary methods classes we focus on creating pieces with a clear beginning, middle, and end, on allowing children to improvise, and on creating simple forms. Approximately one third of the time I spent in elementary methods is used for composition, but this is usually in combination with teaching listening skills and classroom instruments.

Students also create a compositional unit that they would be able to teach in an elementary classroom while student teaching or in their first year of teaching. They write a teaching scenario for how they imagine the lesson would proceed as well as completing a planning grid following the model we presented in *Minds on Music: Composition for Creative and Critical Thinking* (Kaschub & Smith, 2009).

Many of our student teachers subsequently teach these units during their elementary placements, even when their cooperating teachers have little composition background. Often the cooperating teachers are eager to try what our students bring to them, even if they are a little skeptical about how it may work with their students. I find it helps if I play an active role in encouraging both the student teacher and the cooperating teacher to expand a bit outside their comfort zones.

This can happen during a post-observation conference or in a separate meeting where I try to encourage them to try composing with their students. Sometimes I participate in the classroom as another adult mentor while the student teacher facilitates a composition activity. This allows me to model hands off teaching while the students work on their pieces. Teachers without training in composition often try to structure the activity too highly, so that there will be guaranteed success for their students. Often they eventually come to see that disaster does not necessarily follow from allowing students to work things out on their own. This type of freedom for the students teachers to teach composition is often much more possible in elementary settings than it is in secondary settings or in ensembles.

Sometimes following a concert, however, there is a time when ensembles have the opportunity to work on composition as a group. This can begin with something as simple as creating a setting of a folksong. In instrumental ensembles a theme and variation on a folk tune often works well, especially in like instrument sections. While this can be a noisy and chaotic class setting, the creativity and excitement it generates is well worth the time it takes to do it, even if there is never a public performance of the work. Young teachers who have had some experience composing often begin early in the year on similar assignments and perform them as part of an end-of-year concert.

Composing in choral ensembles simply requires that the teacher make a commitment to doing it once a week or some similar schedule. Usually the issues that must be taught in direct instruction include those of text setting and recognizing the value of all ideas within the group. Some choral directors actually model a process and then allow individuals and pairs to work on songs of their own, which can then be shared in composers' circles or simply with the teacher.

Composing instrumental ensembles can be a bit more complicated due to transposition issues, but some teachers from our programs are now doing exactly this. Often instrumental teachers start working with composition in a jazz ensemble or a chamber group of some type simply to get used to the process. Others dive into large ensemble work from the very beginning with the notion of completing a work of wind ensemble. Either way it takes a time commitment from the director to implement this the first time it is done. After that, composing often takes on a life of its own and it becomes an accepted part of an instrumental program. Even beginners can create short pieces. Some of my most ardent composition educators are teachers of beginning strings or beginning band. They see first-hand the strides their students make in technique and theory when they are trying to create and perform their own pieces.

In many ways, composing in urban ensembles is no different than it is in more affluent settings. However, one major difference can be the type of ensemble one is directing. One instrumental teacher with whom I worked created a very fine steel drum band. With money for arrangements always an issue, she soon learned to arrange for the group and then taught them to arrange as well. Other ensembles in urban areas often exist that do not bear any close relationship to band, orchestra, or chorus. These ensembles can also be a source of inspiration for young composers and their teachers.

In core music urban settings where instruments are often unavailable, we encourage students to begin with creating pieces that use body percussion. One of the most engaging ways to begin this process is to show a short film clip such as one called "Kiwi!"[1] or "Say Cheese"[2] without the sound and discuss what music adds to a film. Then have small groups of students create the sound effects and a soundtrack using only body percussion. Repeat the activity during the next class using only vocal sounds. This is a good place to focus on principles of composition such as unity in variety, motion and stasis, sound and silence, stability and instability, and tension and release.

At the end of the second class, assign the students the task of bringing something to class the next time that makes interesting sounds at least two different ways. Finally, repeat the original soundtrack activity, but allow the students to use body percussion, vocal sounds, and found sounds in combinations that they find musically satisfying. This introductory type of lesson often can serve as a springboard to more complex compositions such as songwriting. By practicing this type of lesson in their methods classes, students develop confidence to try it with their own students later on.

Another activity that I use in elementary methods which my students often then use in their student teaching and first years of teaching is what we call paired composition. Students work in pairs using two different sound sources of contrasting timbres and create a simple ABA composition. Sometimes these are geared toward a musical concept we have been studying such as balanced phrases, or a principle such as tension and release. At other times the directions are left completely open except for the form. Each person in the pair has to play at least one solo section and they have to play together at least part of the time. Each is allowed to choose his or her own sound and create his or her own part. It is better for the students to form their own pairs.[3]

In secondary method classes I often begin the semester by creating advertising jingles. With middle level students this should be for products with which they are familiar but preferably ones that do not already have a catchy musical slogan. In my secondary methods class I try to find products that they are not familiar with. They have to come up with descriptions that might be what the manufacturer would like to have the product convey. While this might seem too complicated for beginning composers and middle school, it is often quite successful if they have done some preliminary work with using vocal sounds, body percussion, and found sounds. Students who play instruments can be encouraged to bring them to class and use them in their work.

Our students have to play guitar in secondary methods, which leads quite naturally into songwriting experiences. Again, the emphasis is not on notating the song, but rather on text setting, chordal progressions, and tone painting. We began writing songs as soon as the class has mastered two chords. Sometimes we start with simple rounds using only one chord; however, it seems easier for music majors to at least have a tonic and dominant when they are trying to set a text. In classes, I play examples of songs that use only two chords and we sing and play them. They are often surprised to find so many two-chord songs.

We also do an exercise that leads to idea generation for topics for their songs. I ask each student to list on a piece of paper three things that they are either concerned about or that are important to them. I collect the papers, which are anonymous, and then list the topics on the board. While we could stop there, I try to come to an agreement about a topic about which the class will write a song. Once we come to agreement on a topic, we come up with a theme for the lyrics or at least a thesis statement. For example, one recent class came up with the topic of money—not surprising in this economy and for struggling students. To my surprise, the thesis statement was that money is no good if you do not have your health.

We then proceeded to write a two-line refrain, complete with melody. We brainstormed ideas for the verses and the students went home and came back for the next class with a verse and a melody. We sang each one with a refrain that been composed in class and came up with a complete song. While the quality of the ideas of the music majors are usually higher and more complicated than the ones I have received from middle school students, the process up to this point is basically the same.

My methods class students also each create a two-chord song that they must sing and play for me as part of an individual midterm. For their final, they must be able to play and sing an original song that has at least two verses and a refrain and uses at least three different chords. They have to provide me with the notated version or the melody line with chords written in above. This gives them at least the basic experience needed to lead songwriting activities in their own future classes.

Observations of Teachers Teaching Composition

As more and more of our graduates find positions teaching in nearby schools, it becomes more possible for our students to observe other teachers conducting composition activities. By offering summer classes and tuition waivers, we have been able to encourage more practicing teachers to incorporate composition activities. Consequently now I can encourage our students to make contact with these teachers and observe what they are doing. I also encourage the teachers to make active use of our students as mentors to small groups of students who are working on compositions.

In my methods classes I talk about composition circles and how to provide feedback and model appropriate comments. We also discuss ways of dealing with students who make inappropriate comments in a feedback circle. One of the most valuable aspects of this is actual hands-on experience with mentoring young composers. I have video of at least one master teacher that I show in class and I model the feedback process myself. When I have composers who are part of my classes, I have them also lead composition circles and model the behavior. They are often very good at providing appropriate feedback. This may be because they have received appropriate feedback from their mentors, or in some cases, they have received inappropriate feedback and know how that feels as a composer. In any event, our students practice the skills of providing feedback in composer circles in the methods classes before attempting it with their students.

Creative Opportunities and Cautionary Tales

There are some settings where my students have found it particularly difficult do implement composition activities. Very large secondary general music classes—over thirty students—often do not work well for composition, especially in small spaces. I suspect almost any kind of instruction is difficult in these circumstances. However, because composition requires making sounds, it is very difficult to do this in large classes in small spaces. What can be done sometimes in these settings is to do whole class activities. Sometimes these can be successful, if the majority of the students can be motivated to contribute to the task. I would be more inclined to do some sort of whole class project along the lines of creating a class musical. This would involve composing but it would also involve set design, lighting, and other aspects of musical theater. It would be more likely that students would be able to find something they found attractive about working as part of a production company.

Several urban music educators have successfully taught units on protest music that culminated in writing protest songs in small groups, which worked well in spite of large class sizes. After spending time looking at protest songs throughout history, discussing how those songs are put together and the usefulness of such things as metaphor and satire, the students are often eager to try writing a protest song of their own. The critical link here is that the students must choose issues about which they feel deeply in order to write their songs. These can be done individually, or in small groups. It is often wise to compose at least part of one as a class first to model a process. Like all composition, adequate time must be allowed for the product to emerge. Students have to be encouraged to go beyond their first ideas and to probe the musical possibilities of their ideas.

A similar project was done by one of our middle school instrumental teachers. She had her students create music for Earth Day. They brainstormed ideas for possible topics such as global warming, rain forest preservation, recycling, and waste disposal. The class then brainstormed how music for each of those topics might sound. They formed self-selected groups and attempted to write music that would capture the essence of one of the topics. These were eventually formed into a suite and performed in class.

Another urban teacher, who was herself a composer and had an undergraduate degree in composition, was eager to start a composition program at her school. However, there did not seem to be time in the schedule to create a composition class. Consequently, she began a Friday noontime composers' forum. Students would bring their lunches and come together in the band room and share their works in progress. She acted as an advisor and soon the group was given club status within her school. Eventually, space was made for music theory class, which became a composition class. She continues the noontime composers' forum. Students liked the informality of the noontime group and the chance to eat lunch with the teacher. What started out as a small group has expanded into an evening concert of student-created works.

One favorite activity for general music classes is to show a video of the group Stomp and use it as a stepping-off point for creating something similar. Part of the challenge can be to find things that are normally a part of classroom environment and use them as the sound sources. After that, sounds can be added from the outside world. I sometimes use the video as a homework assignment in methods classes. I asked the students to create a teaching guide based on the video for how they would use it in a classroom and then to write a scenario for how they think the lesson might go. This gives them practice doing this before they have to create one of their own design. To get middle-level students started with the process, it is often useful to have them try to copy the rhythms from the video. The next step then is to create their own rhythms and their own sounds.

If there is a dance program in the school, this is the perfect opportunity for collaboration. If not, secondary students are often quite inventive and creating their own choreography to accompany the sounds they have composed. Some may have had experience with the Brazilian martial art form capoeira, which incorporates music, and those students would bring those ideas to bear on this project. Other students may have dance experience outside of school. These students often become choreographers for the class projects.

Many cell phones have video capability. Usually it is not difficult to find someone who can record. It is often helpful to have someone recording as the process moves along, so that the groups can see the results of their works-in-progress and determine next steps more effectively. Even if the goal is not a public performance, videotaping a class performance and watching the film as a group is a very valuable large group experience. I enjoy seeing videos of the work of the students of my former students and occasionally have permission to share those videos with my current students. This type of partnership with a school makes the materials from the methods classes more situated and realistic to methods class students. Most of them have not been encouraged to compose in their own school experiences and some have trouble believing that it is reasonable and feasible to do so.

Possibilities for School/College Composition Partnerships

As this chapter draws to a close, I would like to suggest three ways that music departments within urban universities might consider partnering with schools to encourage the development of students' compositional skills. One of the easiest ways is to find teachers who are themselves composers and build relationships with them that allow your students into their classrooms while they are teaching composition. This is the sort of thing I mentioned above when I talked about observing practicing teachers as they teach composition and helping to mentor their students. This does require that you teach the college students how to facilitate compositional growth in students without dictating. It also means finding composition teachers who understand that composing is more than filling in the blanks and who look beyond theory exercises to student expressivity. Such teachers encourage the individual voices of students and individual expression by providing the freedom to compose.

One way of building a cadre of teacher composers is to offer summer workshops and classes in composition pedagogy. Teachers are used to taking classes in the summer and often find a composition class attractive, even if it is also somewhat scary. At our university this summer class is also paired with composition lessons provided by our composition faculty. While a one-week class can only provide a taste of what is possible in ensembles and classes, it does allow teachers to begin thinking in new ways about how to implement composition in their classrooms. Because there is a follow-up assignment where they write about how they have implemented composition in their classes, I begin to have a sense of where compositional activities are occurring. This allows me then to contact those teachers and ask about the possibility of my students observing and/or assisting.

Finally, urban universities can create composition festivals where student work can be showcased. This can be done in partnership with composition faculty, school faculty, or even private teachers. These festivals can be competitive or noncompetitive. There can be prizes or simply performances. There can be opportunities for composers to discuss their pieces or simply have them performed. Often times university students can be involved in performing works that primary and secondary students have created. Sometimes these can be for specific ensembles such as a woodwind quintet. Alternatively, the pieces can be chosen for the festival and then the necessary instrumentalists or vocalists can be assembled. The composers themselves may choose to perform their pieces. Because New York State has a statewide school music composition festival, we encourage our students and the students of our graduates to attend those sessions at the statewide conference. The more opportunities for young composers to hear their works performed and to hear the works of other young composers, the more likely it is that composition will become an important and integral part of their lives. Additionally, when colleges host such events, undergraduate music education students can hear the work of young composers and develop some sense of what to expect of the young composers they will soon teach.

Reference

Kaschub. M. and Smith, J. P. (2009). *Minds on Music: Composition for Creative and Critical Thinking*. Lanham, MD: R&L Education—A Division of Rowman & Littlefield Publishers, Inc.

Notes

1. "Kiwi!" can be found at http://www.youtube.com/watch?v=sdUUx5FdySs.
2. "Say Cheese" can be found at http://www.archive.org/details/SayChees2001.
3. See pp. 136–137 and 162–164 in *Minds on Music* for more details.

16 }

Preparing Music Educators to Facilitate Songwriting
John Kratus

Near the end of her life, my grandmother resided in a nursing home for seniors with Alzheimer's and other forms of dementia. Her mental state had deteriorated to such an extent that she spent her days repeatedly spelling the word "Sunday"— S-U-N-D-A-Y, S-U-N-D-A-Y—over and over. It was heartbreaking to observe. She still maintained her pleasant demeanor with those around her, but she had passed the point of remembering the names or even recognizing her own children. On one visit I wheeled her chair over to an old upright piano in the commons room and started singing "She'll Be Coming Around the Mountain When She Comes." She immediately sat up and started singing along with me in a surprisingly strong voice. Not only did she know the melody perfectly, she also knew all the words, remembering verses that I had never heard before. As we progressed on to sing "Goodnight Ladies" and other songs, I couldn't help but wonder, "What is there about the power of songs that ingrains melody and lyrics more deeply in the mind than the names and faces of our own children?"

Songs and Collegiate Schools of Music

One musical genre that has endured from the beginning of recorded history is the song. While the stylistic features of songs have varied across time and cultures, the structural characteristics of songs have remained remarkably consistent. Songs have lyrics, are sung by one or several persons, and are usually accompanied by one or more instruments to provide harmonic and/or rhythmic support. Songs usually have sections of music that repeat: the verse is the section in which the music stays the same while the lyrics change, and the chorus is the section in which both music and lyrics stay the same. The song may be humanity's most ubiquitous and enduring form of music.

From the lyric poetry of Athens to the troubadour songs of the Renaissance, from hymns to harvest songs, from Billie Holiday to Lady Gaga, songs have served to express the depth and breadth of human experience, imagination, and feeling. From the lullaby to the requiem, songs are and always have been the "people's music": easily performed on the instrument we all possess and readily reverberating through our memories. It is not surprising, then, that songs play a predominant role in the musical lives of today's young people, and all people for that matter. The mp3 players that so many adolescents possess[1] are loaded with songs, and, in fact, the memory size of these devices is measured in terms of the number of songs they can hold. For most young people the words "music" and "songs" are synonymous.[2] The musical world of adolescents is a landscape of songs.

Songwriting is a form of composition that is especially suitable for inclusion in music curricula for middle school, high school, and college students. Songwriting can be taught as a stand-alone elective class; as a project or series of projects in general music, choir, piano class, and guitar class; and as an after-school activity. There are a variety of reasons why songwriting appeals to students at the secondary and tertiary levels: (1) it attracts an underserved school population of musicians who play guitar, keyboard, or electronic instruments; (2) it satisfies the expressive, emotional, and creative needs of adolescents and young adults; (3) it connects to adolescents' musical culture while expanding their horizons to other musical cultures; and (4) it is a sustainable skill that can be easily carried on and developed further outside of school.

Given the pervasiveness of songs in our musical cultures, it is curious that collegiate music curricula tend to accord songs a second-class status, far below that of symphonies, operas, oratorios, concert band works, chamber music, piano solos, and other such concert pieces. The primary performance medium in colleges is the large ensemble, which does not easily lend itself to the modest performance requirements of songs.[3] Collegiate composition students are rarely taught songwriting in their studies. Songs become footnotes in musicologists' telling of Western music history, with the music of the people (songs) taking a back seat to the music of the aristocracy (orchestra), the music of the church (choir), and the music of the military (band). "Strummin'" a guitar while "singin'" a song barely qualifies as "music" in collegiate schools of music. Singing and playing your own songs can get you thrown out of a practice room.

History provides a reason for the neglect of songs in contemporary colleges of music. In the nineteenth century, conservatories sprung up across Europe to provide classical musicians to fill the burgeoning numbers of orchestras and opera companies.[4] Classical music performance at that time was a growth industry. The course of study in European conservatories enabled its graduates to take their place as orchestral and opera musicians. The conservatory curriculum focused on developing expertise on a single instrument or voice type, large ensemble, or opera experience, reading music notation using solfège, and the study of music history and literature, featuring a repertoire of European music in the classical tradition. This course of study was eminently practical for providing conservatory students with the knowledge and skills to perform in nineteenth-century orchestras and opera companies.

Two hundred years later, colleges of music employ a nearly identical curriculum for educating musicians,[5] steadfastly ignoring two centuries of change in the nature of music and musical experience. That, some may well consider, is a problem.

As a result of this anachronistic anomaly, the musicianship that pre-service music educators develop and the musical experiences they encounter in college have little in common with the song-based musical world of the students they will teach. Often the composition assignments that music students have in college are academic exercises, rather than authentic and personally expressive creative experiences. Songwriting, a form of composition that resonates with adolescents and connects to their musical world, is rarely taught in collegiate music schools.

Music teacher educators who want to prepare their students to enter twenty-first-century classrooms have a choice to make. They can either elect to wait another two hundred years or so, hoping that their colleagues on music faculties will update their nineteenth-century ways, or they can take action to teach a different kind of musicianship and pedagogy to the music teachers they educate. The remainder of this chapter is for those who wish to pursue the latter course.

A Vignette—Teaching What We Do Not Know

Several years ago I was invited to a major university to participate in a week-long summer symposium for music teacher-educators who had reputations as composition pedagogues. The group of fourteen scholars from around the world was an impressive assembly, professors who had published numerous books and articles on teaching children to compose. I felt honored to be among them. But as the week wore on, an undercurrent of tension arose among the participants over the issue of structure in the classroom. The majority of participants advocated a classroom in which students were given complete freedom to compose whatever they wished in whatever manner, and a minority of four believed that students should learn to compose, at least initially, within certain constraints.

On the last afternoon of the symposium, the group was sitting around a large conference table, planning the book to be published by the members of the seminar. In frustration over the week's tension, I asked, "How many people here have ever composed anything? I don't mean a major symphonic work. I mean anything—a children's song, a fanfare, anything." An embarrassed silence filled the room. Only four hands went up, from the four people who had advocated placing constraints in the teaching of beginners. A few awkward jokes were made, and we moved on.[6] That, some may well consider, is a problem.

I was left with the distinct impression that there was something seriously amiss in our teaching of composition to children. It is impossible to imagine an art teacher who has never picked up a brush, or a swimming coach who has never been in the water, or a chess instructor who does not play chess. How can it be that "expert" pedagogues in children's composition have never composed anything?

Teaching What We Know

I want to be clear about the point of this vignette. I am not of the opinion that only professional composers are qualified to teach composition. Many K–12 music educators are outstanding teachers of composition, and they do not compose professionally. Nor do I believe that a teacher of composition has to be the most accomplished composer in a classroom. As a teacher of songwriting I know that some of my students will become or are now better songwriters than I am. But it is simple common sense that a teacher with no personal experience in a domain can not teach that domain effectively. Consider this analogy. I have never skied in my life. Yes, I have been on snow-covered mountains and, yes, I have watched professional skiers on televised Winter Olympics, but I have never actually been on skis. In David Elliott's terms,[7] I have no *procedural knowledge* of skiing. There are no books on skiing pedagogy I can read, no skiing "methods" classes I can take that will qualify me to teach others to ski. There is simply no substitute for teachers having some level of direct, personal experience in that which they teach.

If music teacher-educators are serious about the inclusion of composition in the K–12 music curriculum, then pre-service music teachers will have to be given some authentic experience in composing. A collegiate course or unit on composition *pedagogy* does not sufficiently prepare pre-service teachers to guide their own students' composing. Neither do the voice leading and technical exercises in four or five semesters of music theory qualify one to teach composition.

I have found that college music education majors with no prior composition experience can quickly learn some of the basic elements of composition in a relatively short time. If these composition experiences are authentic and meaningful, these students often become ardent advocates for teaching composition in their own classes and ensembles. A one-semester songwriting class is much more effective then a songwriting unit within a music methods course, because a songwriting class allows students sufficient time to develop the skills of songwriting and the identity of a songwriter.[8] It can change music education majors' perceptions about musicianship, teaching, and their role within the classroom.

Starting a Songwriting Class

The idea of teaching a songwriting class came to me, as all good curriculum ideas should, from one of my students. She knew that I wrote songs and asked if she could take an independent study with me in songwriting. My first response was to smile and tell her that I did not think songwriting could be taught. As a songwriter I was an autodidact. In sixth grade I wrote funny (i.e., "funny" to an eleven-year-old boy) lyrics to existing popular songs.[9] When I was thirteen I bought my first guitar and started tentatively writing my own songs, some of which were performed by the basement band of novices with whom I played. The only feedback I got on my songs came from my bandmates and from the audiences for whom we performed. Later in my life, and in all of my years in music education at the elementary, secondary, and collegiate levels, it had simply never occurred to me that songwriting could be a skill learned from a teacher.

After I agreed to teach the independent study to the student, she asked if her friend could join her in the independent study. The friend had a friend who had a friend, and in the end I arranged to teach songwriting as a one-time-only special topics course. Eighteen students enrolled. That first semester I learned more about music teaching than my students learned about songwriting.

At the end of the course two of the students in the class dropped out of college to pursue careers as singer-songwriters. One of the two students could play only two chords on the guitar at the beginning of the semester. Her plan was to record a CD of her songs and tour colleges throughout the Midwest, performing her music and selling her CD. It floored me that a single two-credit, elective course could have such an impact on a person's life.

I should have been prepared for such an outcome, given the passion for songwriting the students had displayed previously in the course. One student in the class worked as a night guard in a dormitory and spent his entire eight-hour shift writing songs. Another student locked himself in his room for three days in order to compose and record a song. During the semester I had to frequently remind students to do their homework . . . in other classes. The obsession that many of the students in that first class developed for songwriting is something that I have seen repeatedly in later songwriting classes. Clearly, this is one form of composition that has the power to transform lives.

Since that first songwriting course, I have taught songwriting in various formats: as a three-credit special topics course, as a four-credit humanities course, and as a two-credit music course. In all cases enrollment was open to both music majors and non-music majors. The only prerequisite for the course is a statement listed online, but unenforced by audition, that students "be able to sing and play an accompanying instrument like guitar or keyboard." A few of the students who have taken the class stretched the definition of "able," but all have successfully performed the songs they wrote.

There is a pedagogical reason for including non-music majors in a course that I intend for music education majors. It is valuable for pre-service music teachers to learn that the musicianship they possess and develop in their college music classes is not the only form of musicianship that exists. Oftentimes, the students who are not music majors are the best songwriters in the class.[10] There may be a variety of reasons for this outcome, which extend beyond the scope of this paper. Regardless, it has been my experience that the education that music majors receive does not provide them with any special advantage in a collegiate songwriting class.[11]

In seeking permission to offer songwriting as a collegiate music course, I first asked the composition faculty to review my proposal. This was not a problem, since none of the composition faculty was interested in teaching such a course themselves.

A music theory professor on the college curriculum committee asked how many semesters of theory would be necessary as prerequisites. When I said "none," he asked, "Then how will they turn in their songs?" I replied, "They will sing them," and that was that.

In the next section of this chapter, I describe the approach that I have used to teach songwriting. This is most certainly not the only way, and maybe not even the best way, to teach the class, but this approach has been refined for a decade and has worked for me. What follows is a very *prescriptive* approach to the organization and teaching of a songwriting class. It is not in my nature to be so rigid about pedagogical matters, and I write this with the understanding that there are other good ways to teach songwriting. For those music teacher-educators who would like to try their hand at teaching a songwriting class, what follows could be a good starting place.

The Nuts and Bolts of Teaching a Collegiate Songwriting Class

GOAL AND OBJECTIVES

The primary goal of the one-semester songwriting class is for class members to develop and refine their ability to express themselves through songwriting. There is no single standard that all students are expected to meet, because the past experiences of the students differ so widely. About one-third to one-half of the students who have taken the course have had varying levels of songwriting experience prior to taking the class.

The course objectives are as follows:

- Develop compositional ability through the writing and performing of six songs.
- Describe artistic and cultural aspects of existing songs through the analysis of lyrics and music in two self-selected songs.
- Critique one's own songs (in writing) and the songs of others (in class discussions) in a constructive manner.
- Reflect on one's own development as a songwriter by maintaining a songwriter's journal.

The course objectives reflect the position that learning to be a songwriter includes more than compositional skill. Students also learn to analyze songs, think critically about songs, and reflect on their progress as songwriters.

COURSE ORGANIZATION

The course is divided into two components: a teacher-led section including lecture, discussion, and guided listening, and the songwriters' circle, in which students perform their songs for each other and receive feedback. When I began teaching songwriting, I assumed that I would spend about half the class time on each type of activity. My students quickly taught me that that was the wrong balance. Now when I teach the class, the teacher-led portion lasts about twenty minutes per week, and the remainder of the class time is devoted to the songwriters' circle.

The division between the two instructional formats imposes a strict enrollment limit on the course. All students are expected to perform once a week (more on this later), and each student is allotted ten minutes per week for performing and feedback. A course that meets for two 110-minute sessions per week can accommodate no more than 20 students: 20 minutes for teacher-led instruction plus 10 minutes per student for 20 students. The class I teach meets twice a week for 110-minute sessions.

The room is set up with chairs in a semi-circle. A piano for keyboard players and a chair for guitarists are at the open end of the circle. (My students dubbed the chair "the hot seat.") A music stand is available for those students who want one. Some students maintain a fierce pride in memorizing these songs and use no memory aids. Other students, especially non-music majors, are used to reading whatever notation they use from a horizontal surface like another chair.

An acoustic piano is not the ideal keyboard instrument for a songwriting class, because the dynamic level of instrument overpowers many singers. It is much better to use an electric keyboard or a microphone and amplifier for singers at the piano. Other instruments students have used effectively for accompaniment include accordion, ukulele, and computers with pre-recorded music. The new generation of instruments for iPad and other portable devices allow students to perform real-time electronic accompaniment for their songs with minimal technical expertise.

The course content and activities for the first two weeks are designed to ease students into songwriting and enable them to get comfortable performing in front of each other. Several weeks prior to the first class meeting, I e-mail students asking them to prepare to sing or play a familiar song on the first day of the class. For students who have written songs previously, they are to perform a "greatest hit." For students who have never composed a song, they are to perform a cover of a song they admire. This activity gives students an understanding of the musical tastes and interests of their fellow class members. After each performance the class applauds. Since there is no lengthy discussion after each performance, a class of 20 students can usually complete this activity in a 110-minute class.

I begin the second day of the course by discussing with the class the course syllabus, class requirements and procedures, and grading policy. Then we brainstorm about possible topics for song lyrics. This activity usually results in a sprawling list of potential topics. For the last activity the whole class writes a new verse or two to a familiar melody, like the Beatles' "Oh-Bla-Di Oh-Bla-Da." First I model the song and the class sings a verse and chorus. I solicit ideas for the topic of our new verse (typically having something to do with college life), then show students the phrase structure of the verse. The class decides on a rhyming scheme for the verse (e.g., a-a-b-b *or* a-b-a-b). Individual volunteers offer lyrics to fit each of the four lines. No ideas are discarded, and no votes are taken on the ideas given. The class concludes by singing the new verse and the song's original chorus.

The project for the following week is for each student to compose a new verse to "America" and perform it for the class. Students are assigned one day of the week on which they will perform for the remainder of the semester.

In the second week, students perform their new versions of "America." After each performance the class discusses the decisions made by the songwriter. The teacher-led content for the second week is a quick romp through practical music theory, focusing on transposition of songs from one key to another. The project for the following week is for students to select a simple text, set it to music, and perform the resulting song in class.

After this introduction to songwriting, for the remainder of the course the students' songwriting is much less guided. Once a week each student performs for the class. The performance can be any of the following: a new song, a partial song, or a previously performed song that has been revised. Over the semester, students are required to complete six songs. There are four other projects required for the class:

1. *Critical analysis projects.* Students complete two listening projects in which they must listen analytically and critically to self-selected songs. (See Appendix A for a detailed project description.) In the analysis of a song, they first learn about the context of the song via web resources, then analyze what is happening lyrically and musically in the song, and finally interpret and evaluate the song with critical listening. One of the projects is due one-third of the way through the semester, and the second project is due at the two-thirds point.

2. *Songwriter's journal.* Students maintain a journal, in which they make an entry every time they work on a song. I ask students to take a few extra minutes at the end of every songwriting experience to write down what they accomplished and how they feel about what they accomplished. They are to write at least 200 words per week. The journal can take the form of a bound book or notebook, or it can take the form of a blog or computer-based journal. Students report that at first the journaling feels intrusive, but that it soon becomes second nature. The journal provides students with a place to store their musical ideas and their reflections on their progress as songwriters. The journals are collected, reviewed, and returned at the midpoint of the semester and at the end of the course.

3. *Live performance.* Students perform their songs in public two times during the semester. Some semesters I have arranged for my class to put on concerts in dormitory lounges or coffee houses, and some semesters I have left students to their own devices. It is simply not practical for me to observe all the student performances. Students simply report to me when and where they have performed. Oftentimes groups of students from the class will participate at open mic nights together. This aspect of the

course can be the most terrifying, yet the most rewarding, for many students. I have never taught a student who felt worse about himself or herself as a singer/songwriter after performing live. In their journals, the word "epiphany" is used frequently to describe the experience of performing original songs in front of a roomful of strangers.

4. *Recording project.* The final project in the course is the creation of a CD containing 15 minutes of original music. I ask students to think of the recording as a time capsule they are creating for themselves 20 years in the future. The songs should reflect who they are as songwriters and as people at this point in their lives. Students typically record four or five songs they composed earlier in the semester. Some students produce fairly simple recordings using programs like GarageBand® or Audacity and the microphone built into their laptop. Other students have taken this project to the extreme, renting studio time in a recording studio or seeking out friends with professional quality recording equipment. By the end of the semester, students know each other quite well, and many of them perform on each other's recordings. Some students also create elaborate cover art for their CDs. For most of the students who have taken the songwriting class, this project is a labor of love. For extra credit, students can write a "review" of their CD.

COURSE TOPICS

The topics for the teacher-led portions of the course are divided into musical aspects or songs, lyrical aspects of songs, and miscellaneous aspects of songwriting. Depending on the topic, the method of instruction could employ guided listening, class discussion, or lecture/demonstration. A list of sample topics is as follows:

Musical Aspects: chords and modes, standard chord progressions, 12-bar blues, sectional forms (intro, verse, chorus, bridge, outro), phrasing, expressive use of musical elements, performance issues (breathing, projecting, arranging).

Lyrical Aspects: rhyming and alliteration; metaphor and irony; telling a story; describing a person, place or time; expressing feelings; ethical issues.

Miscellaneous Aspects: psychology of creativity, overcoming writer's block, copyrighting music, recording techniques.

The teaching technique I use most frequently is guided and active listening. For example, the use of metaphor in song lyrics can be demonstrated by analyzing the lyrics of Sting's "The Hounds of Winter." Sting uses words for light, dark, heat, and cold to describe his feelings for his lost lover. The use of standard chord progressions to unify a song is illustrated in U2's "One," which makes use of only three simple progressions throughout the song. Students are given clear directions for what to listen for and how to describe their response in writing. Then students share their results with each other.

I enlist my students in providing contemporary musical examples for in-class listening. For example, two weeks before teaching a class on telling a story in song, I ask students to bring to class recordings of story songs that they like. Then I choose from among their songs.

When I started teaching the songwriting class ten years ago, I expected to teach some musical and lyrical aspect one week and then ask students to compose a song for the following week using what was learned in class. What happened was that many students would come in the following week saying that they were moved to write some other song, one that did not use what had been taught.

Now I tell my students that my teaching is to provide them with idea generators, and that they are free to use what they wish in their songs. Sure enough, three or four weeks after I teach a lesson on telling a story, half of the new songs students perform are story songs.

SONGWRITERS' CIRCLE AND ASSESSING STUDENTS' SONGS

It is necessary to understand that the learning environment created in the classroom is the key to a successful songwriting class. Songs can be personal expressions of deep feelings, reflective of serious life passages, like the break-up with a loved one, the illness of a parent, the anger of racial injustice, and the uncertain love of a new friend. For students to feel comfortable sharing such intimate feelings, they need to feel secure and supported by the teacher and, perhaps more importantly, the other students in the class.

The set-up of the class contributes to the learning environment. When students sit in a semi-circle, they face each other, and no student sits in row two. A semi-circle obliterates the isolation engendered in classrooms with rows of desks.

The format for student performances is established early in the semester. Prior to the start of class, students are tuning their guitars and setting up any electrical equipment they might be using. They know to do this before class begins, because I ask them to do so. If it is their day to perform, they pick up a Songwriting Evaluation Sheet (see Appendix B) and complete the top of the form. When it is time to start class, I ask students to count off, which will be their order for performing. (This step eliminates the awkward silence between performances, when the teacher would ask, "Who wants to go next? Anybody? Anybody?") I sit among the students in the semi-circle.

When it is time to start the class, I call "Number 1," and the first performer hands me a Songwriting Evaluation Sheet and goes to the keyboard or the guitar chair. (For some reason, most of my students do not like to stand when performing their own songs on guitar.) The student may or may not introduce the song; it is an individual choice. If a student has a partially completed song to perform, he or she might ask the class in advance of the performance to listen for some aspect of the song and provide ideas after the performance. I do not require students to say anything about the song they are about to play, because some students are nervous and just want to get on with the performance.

While the student performs, the instructor writes comments on the Songwriting Evaluation Sheet. The comments are primarily supportive, especially at the beginning of the semester. Rather than point out faults in the song, I suggest things for the student to consider. My university does require that I give a numerical grade on student work and I do so.

After the performance, the class applauds. Even if the performance has crashed and burned, the class applauds. The applause is unconditional. The class then discusses the song and provides feedback to the songwriter, while the songwriter stays in the front of the room. After the discussion, the student returns to the semicircle, and the class applauds again.

Perhaps the most challenging part of teaching a songwriting class is guiding the feedback given the student. An unintentionally harsh word or critical comment from the teacher or a fellow student can shut down a novice songwriter. My students are not aware of it, but in my leading of the discussion and feedback, I am progressing during the course of the semester through three levels:

1. *Generically positive.* This is the type of feedback that most students give to performances early in the semester. "That was good." "That's really cool." "I really liked it." "It was really, really good." You get the picture. In a songwriting class, there is a bit of "there-but-for-the-grace-of-god-go-I" among the students. They all know that they will have their turn in the front of the room, and they want to treat each other as they hope they will be treated when it is their turn. Generically positive feedback is worthwhile at the beginning of a songwriting class, because it provides the students with a sense of security and increases their trust in other class members and the instructor. My role during this phase is to ask students to focus on what they liked in the song. Was it some turn of a phrase? Or was it the singer's expressive voice? Or the way the lyrics described her hometown?

2. *Descriptive.* The generically positive feedback increases the comfort level of students, but does not provide much specific information to the songwriter about how to improve. In the second phase, descriptive feedback, the instructor asks the class questions about the musical and lyrical characteristics of the song just performed. For example, I may ask, "What unexpected incident happened to the man in the last verse?" or "What melodic hook was used to unify the song?" or "How was the strumming in the verse different from the strumming in the chorus, and why?" These are the same kind of questions that I would ask students when doing guided listening activities in the teacher-led portion of the class. The purposes of descriptive feedback are (a) to highlight those unique aspects of the song that other class members might want to employ in their own songs, and (b) to provide the songwriter with the knowledge that his or her song is worthy of analysis. In effect the class is saying, yes, we really did notice that you sang louder in the last verse.

3. *Prescriptive.* When the class reaches the prescriptive level of feedback, it has become a master class for songwriters. Prescriptive feedback provides the songwriter with suggestions for improvement. All songwriting classes eventually get to this level, but it is not advisable to move to the prescriptive level too quickly. I once taught a jazz studies masters student, who had written over 50 songs prior to taking the songwriting course. He was an accomplished songwriter, and in the fourth week of the class I suggested to him that he experiment with substituting an A minor chord for a C major chord in one of his chord progressions. He looked up from the piano to me as if I had stabbed him. The lesson I learned is that one cannot rush the prescriptive feedback in a songwriting course, regardless of the students' background.

Songwriters' circle activities should always happen first in a class before the teacher-led activities. The reason for this is that students do not want to listen to the instructor and do guided listening when they have a song they are dying to share or are nervous about sharing.

Occasionally there will be extra time available at the end of a class, when all students have performed and all comments have been given. This is the time for the instructor to sit at the piano or in the hot seat and share a song or a work-in-progress with the class. The students will prescribe all sorts of improvements. I cannot stress enough how valuable it is for the instructor to put herself or himself out there as a songwriter and ask class members for suggestions. It is a humbling experience but one that will earn the instructor the right and the credibility to facilitate the songwriting of others.

Finding Room and Making Time

Finding the room for a one-semester songwriting course in an already overflowing undergraduate music education curriculum is more a matter of will than of time. Consider the amount of time that pre-service music educators spend in large ensembles over the course of their education. Students who begin ensemble participation in sixth grade spend about 1000 hours performing in the ensemble by the time they leave high school (50-minute classes x 5 days/week x 40 weeks/year x 6 years = 60,000 minutes). College music majors spend another 525 hours in large ensembles (60-minute classes x 5 days/week x 15 weeks/semester x 7 semesters = 31500 minutes). Music teachers spend about 1525 hours performing in a large ensemble during their education, and that is a *lot* of time devoted to one form of music-making.

Replacing one semester of a large ensemble experience with one semester of a songwriting class would have little detrimental effect on music education students' learning of large ensemble performance, while opening up to them an entirely new world of creative musical experience. Music teacher educators need to ask themselves whether the nineteenth semester of band, orchestra, or choir will prepare future music teachers any better than their eighteenth semester did. If not, then other forms of music-making, more in tune with the twenty-first century than the eighteenth century, should be included in the education of music teachers.

A college student in one of my songwriting classes once asked why she could not take the course more than once for college credit. She pointed out that students could repeat any ensemble multiple times for credit. "Why not songwriting?" she asked. Her innocent question raises a dirty secret about music learning in school ensembles. The ensemble "curriculum," such as it is, is based on the repertoire to be performed. Students learn to perform their part on each piece the teacher presents to the ensemble, and the music learning that occurs is that which is necessary to perform these particular pieces. If a student is in the same school band from tenth grade through twelfth grade, the repertoire does not become more challenging year after year, just more extensive. The twelfth grader has performed more pieces than has the tenth grader, but students' musicianship does not necessarily become more sophisticated as they continue in the ensemble, because the repertoire has to be geared toward the youngest students as well as the oldest.

In a songwriting class, the curriculum becomes more challenging over time, as the students' musicianship and songwriting ability becomes more sophisticated. That is because the curriculum for any one student is based on his or her own creative output, not on a shared repertoire among class members. As students become more experienced as songwriters, their songs reflect increasing levels of musical and lyrical sophistication. Concomitantly their perceptions of the songs of others become increasingly nuanced, and their comments to each other in the songwriters' circle grow to be more knowledgeable. For this reason, students in a songwriting class can continue to learn and develop despite having other students in the class with varied levels of proficiency. Contrast this with the more experienced students in an ensemble, who are still performing music at a level that can be performed by the novices in the ensemble. In a perfect world, students could take a songwriting class multiple times for credit, but an ensemble only once, or at most twice, before moving on to another, more challenging ensemble.

There is one final point for music teacher educators to consider regarding "finding room and making time." No amount of pedagogical knowledge of songwriting can substitute for authentic experience as a songwriter. If the next generation of music teachers is to include songwriting in their repertoire of teaching strategies, then they will have to be educated by college faculty who themselves have also written songs. Remember the vignette about the composition pedagogy experts who had never composed.

For many college music faculty members, writing a song and performing it for their students in the context of a songwriting class will be an act of courage, and rightfully so. Sharing a song based on one's own life experiences can be scary, especially if the singer is a college music professor and expected to be a highly proficient musician. Furthermore songwriting is an act that will go unrewarded by many college administrations.[12]

Music teacher-educators are products of the system that many of them are trying to change, and their own education has not provided them with songwriting experience. They are used to relying on their own personal experiences as educators in the teaching of future educators. What I am suggesting is that music teacher educators invest some quality time into banging on the piano or plunking on that old guitar in the closet, while thinking of ways to express their life experience to others. It is a daunting process, but one that will bring them closer to why they became music teachers in the first place.

Sharing a self-composed song with others is an act of courage. In a songwriting class a special magic can occur, in which students express themselves and connect to each other in ways rarely experienced in schools or elsewhere. Just a few days ago in my class a student sang a six-minute song about her 23-year-old brother, who had died in a car accident the previous week. The song alternated between the story of their maturing brother-sister relationship over the years and her anguished prayer to a god who knew best but had forsaken her. I looked around the semicircle as she finished the song. All had tears in their eyes, and some students were openly weeping. Two days later the songwriter recorded a videotape of herself performing the song, uploaded it to the Internet, and sent the link to her grieving parents. This was her way to give voice to her deep emotions, to share her pain and hope with others, in a way that discursive language never could. Her song, as difficult as it was to listen to, was a very personal gift to her audience. I wonder, are songs acts of love that we give to each other? Perhaps this helps to explain why my grandmother's songs were fixed more intensely in her mind than were the names and faces of her children.

Songs have always possessed that special magic, throughout history and across the world's cultures. Songs bind us together and are one of the deepest expressions of our individuality and our shared humanity. A high school student in a songwriting class in Illinois described this much better than I can. When the teacher of her songwriting class asked her to describe what songwriting meant to her, she wrote, "Songs can be a way for people to realize that they are not alone in this world."

Appendix A—Critical Analysis Project

MUS 210—Songwriting

Critical Analysis Project

Objective: To understand and evaluate an existing song through the critical analysis of lyrics, form, instrumentation, and arrangement.

Procedures:

- Select a recording of a song that you admire. The song and artist should be a sufficient interest and depth the warrant your study and deep involvement.
- Do some web research on at least two sites to find some background information on the songwriter's life. Be able to provide a brief bio of the songwriter and the context in which the song was written (e.g., when in the songwriter's output was the song written? Does it have any special significance related to the songwriter's life?).
- Analyze the lyrics in two ways. First look at the content or the meaning of the words. What is the song about or expressive of? Then analyze the *way* the lyrics are written. What is the rhyming scheme, if any? Is there any consonance or assonance? Are there any phrases or words used in an unusual way?
- Analyze the music by first outlining the form. Then describe the instrumentation and arrangement, and describe the sound of the singer's voice. In what ways does the music fit (or not fit) the words?
- If you are able to also analyze the harmony and rhythm, go for it!
- Finally write your personal evaluation of the song. What does the song mean to you? What, specifically, do you admire in the song? If you were to perform it or rearrange it, what would you do differently?
- Report your findings in a paper at least five double-spaced pages long. Most of the paper will be in paragraph form, but some of the analysis can be illustrated or be written in outline form.
- The project should include your paper, a copy of the lyrics, and a recording of the song.
- The project is due on October 7 and November 11.

Criteria for evaluation: Thoroughness and accuracy of the analysis, depth of evaluation, grammar.

Appendix B—Songwriting Evaluation Sheet

MUS 210: Songwriting

Name_____   Date_____
Title_____   Accompaniment_____

MUSIC
 	
    Musical sense
 	
    Organization/structure
 	
    Flow/contrast
 	
    Accompaniment	

LYRICS
 	
    Coherence
 	
    Effectiveness
 	
    Authenticity
 	
    Word play (rhyme, alliteration, turn of the phrase)	

OVERALL IMPRESSION
 	
    Relation between lyrics and music
 	
    Substance and depth	

PERFORMANCE
 	
    Clarity
 	
    Continuity
 	
    Comfort	

Grade _____

Notes

1. According to the Pew Internet and American Life Project, in 2010, 79 percent of American teens owned an iPod or other mp3 player. (Source: Lenhart, A., Purcell, K., Smith, A., and Zickuhr, K. "Social media and young adults.") http://www.pewinternet .org/Reports/2010/Social-Media-and-Young-Adults.aspx

2. College Student: I really liked that song we listened to in class today.
   Me: You mean Beethoven's Fifth Symphony?
   College Student: Yeah, the Beethoven song.

3. While writing for a large ensemble, Beethoven came to understand the power that a song can convey in the final movement of his final symphony. The "Ode to Joy" theme is introduced, not as a choral work, but as a song, with a solo singer and simple accompaniment. Beethoven dressed the theme up later in the movement, but the song itself remains one of his most enduring and recognized works.

4. M. Bruno, "Cantus in choro: A global view of choral singing," *Church & Organ*, 27–30 (2006, November/December). http://www.yale.edu/schola/Schola_CO.pdf

5. See National Association of Schools of Music Handbook, 2010–2011.

6. One year after that meeting I received an e-mail from one of the participants. She said that she had felt embarrassed at the time of my comment, because she was not one of those who raised their hands. She was writing to tell me that she had been inspired to compose several choral works and that her university's women's choir had just performed her music on a concert.

7. David Elliott, *Music Matters: A New Philosophy of Music Education* (New York: Oxford University Press, 1995).

8. Students in songwriting classes have demonstrated a remarkable ability to perceive themselves as songwriters after a single course. (Kratus, J. [2011, February]. *The role of personal expressiveness in the formation of identity among beginning songwriters.* Presented at the Suncoast Music Education Research Symposium: Popular Music Pedagogy, Tampa, FL.)

9. A song about riding the school bus set to the music of the Beach Boys' "California Girls" was one of my greatest hits.

10. Prior to the first day of class, I usually e-mail the students and ask them to prepare for the first day to sing either a song they have written or a cover song. As the students were leaving the first day of class, I overheard one music education major laugh and tell another, "Those non-majors kicked our asses."

11. I have observed many examples of this in my teaching. A voice major who had performed the lead in three operas said that singing one of her own songs in class was more nerve-wracking and rewarding than performing her opera roles. A doctoral music student, who excelled in voice and piano, wrote in her journal that the songwriting class was the hardest music course she had ever taken.

12. I was once told in an annual review letter by my music dean that a faculty artist recital of my own songs I had performed with 40 of my students would not count for merit pay, because my job was to write about and teach creativity, not to be creative!

Strategic Administrative Practices for Including Composition in Music Education

Strategic Administrative Practices for Including Composition in Music Education

Pre-service educators need spaces to practice composition pedagogy with students. As there is a paucity of school composition programs, creating opportunities for fieldwork takes strategic planning. Partnerships with K–12 practitioners can serve to create these spaces. Additionally, these partnerships may offer support to teachers who are eager to learn new techniques or work collaboratively with other educators.

John Richmond describes the origins of a composition applied major within the music education program offered at his institution. He discusses how his institution decided who should teach composition pedagogy to pre-service music education students, what courses were implied in this curriculum besides a methods class in composition pedagogy and its companion practicum, and what costs would be associated with a composition pedagogy curriculum. Once these parameters were established, the practical issues of where university students could be placed for composition practicum experiences in K–12 settings and what role the university music school might play in partnering with local districts to create employment opportunities for those with degrees in music composition pedagogy are considered. Finally, Richmond advocates for a more ambitious and inclusive agenda for music education in American schools in the twenty-first century.

Successful partnerships and workable field experiences can be constructed to benefit all the stakeholders in such a partnership. Gena Greher traces the development of several university and public school-based partnerships that she has created to allow her students to experience teaching composition in various settings while improving her own professional practice and that of the practitioners with whom she has partnered. She describes some important steps to be taken when creating and maintaining this type of partnership.

Michele Kaschub offers two strategies to address the dual challenge of preparing practitioners to teach composition, and securing field sites for pre-service teachers to practice leading composition activities with PreK–12 students. The first approach is a professional development program that prepares practitioners as composers and knowledgeable teachers of composition prior to their hosting pre-service interns. The second approach fosters collaborative partnerships between practitioners and pre-service teachers in situations where pre-service teachers have studied composition pedagogy while their host-site practitioners have not. Throughout the chapter, issues faced by music teacher-educators, practitioners, and pre-service teachers are presented as a contextual frame for the development models that focus on the critical nexus of theory and practice as composition education evolves.

17 }

"All In" for Composition Education: Opportunities and Challenges for Pre-Service Music Teacher Curricula

John W. Richmond

Introduction

The editors of this volume have asked me to describe our pre-service teacher education program that includes a concentration in music composition education. Naturally, I am pleased and flattered to do so. The considerable journey that we have begun at the University of Nebraska–Lincoln (UNL) to bring this program into being has been extremely rewarding, occasionally frustrating, and always remarkably challenging. Indeed, it remains rewarding, frustrating, and challenging today.

Readers of a book such as this will know that the traditional paths to pre-service music teacher training and certification commonly include focus on one or more of the specialties in *instrumental music* (band, orchestra, jazz ensembles, etc.), *choral/vocal music*, or *general music* (most commonly associated with the elementary school setting). Music composition has been an explicit and agreed-upon aspiration of U.S. school curricula for grades K–12 since the adoption of the National Standards for Music Education in 1994, and music composition has been a part of the deliberations of our profession for much longer than that. Nevertheless, there has been only modest progress toward the incorporation of music composition pedagogy as a focus of pre-service music teacher curricula in American colleges and universities (Reimer, 2003: 259).

A telling confirmation of this state of affairs can be inferred from the National Association of Schools of Music (NASM) *Handbook*, the document that provides the official compendium of all specialty (as contrasted with regional) accreditation standards for college and university music degree programs in the United States. In it, NASM provides explicit accreditation standards for music education degree programs leading to certification in instrumental, choral/vocal, and general music education in considerable detail (NASM *Handbook 2010–2011*, IX.L.3.c). There is no such discussion of music composition education in this section of the *Handbook*, however, other than by way of references to (1) a minimum required level of composition/improvisation competence expected of music students enrolled in all undergraduate professional music degree programs, including degrees in music education, and (2) the requirement that music education students acquire some measure of competence in arranging music for K–12 student music ensembles. Let us consider these two standards in order.

First, here is the language of the NASM standard regarding the composition/ improvisation competencies required of all music students in all undergraduate professional music degree programs.

> Composition/Improvisation. Students must acquire a rudimentary capacity to create original or derivative music. It is the prerogative of each institution to develop specific requirements regarding written, electronic, or improvisatory forms and methods. These may include but are not limited to the creation of original compositions or improvisations, variations or improvisations on existing materials, experimentation with various sound sources, the imitation of musical styles, and manipulating the common elements in nontraditional ways. Institutional requirements should help students gain a basic understanding of how to work freely and cogently with musical materials in various composition-based activities, particularly those most associated with the major field. (NASM *Handbook 2010–2011*, VIII.B.3)

The reader will notice here that the focus of this standard is on the expected competence of the music student him- or herself to learn to compose *or* improvise. There is no reference whatever to *learning how to teach others to compose*.

The current NASM standard regarding arranging skills for pre-service music education students reads as follows:

> Arranging. The prospective music teacher must be able to arrange and adapt music from a variety of sources to meet the needs and ability levels of individuals, school performing groups, and in classroom situations. (NASM *Handbook 2010–2011*, IX.L.3.b[2])

Again, the focus is on the competence of the music education student in learning how to arrange music so that K–12 students can perform it. There is *nothing* about composition pedagogy in this standard. The only other mention of music composition in the music education section of the NASM *Handbook* simply states that "institutions should provide opportunities for advanced undergraduate study in such areas as conducting, composition, and analysis" (NASM *Handbook 2010–2011*, IX.L.3.e[5]). For readers not sensitized to the nuances of accreditation language and policy, the telling word in this last quoted standard is the word "should." Because the standard reads that the institution "should provide," rather than "must provide," member institutions are under no obligation to provide ". . . advanced . . . study in . . . conducting, composition, and analysis." They simply are admonished by NASM that this is something member institutions *should* do.

The reader should not infer, nor am I implying here, that NASM is somehow averse to music teacher education programs that embrace composition education as a legitimate ambition and focus of teacher training programs. Rather, the NASM accreditation standards reflect a consensus position of the member institutions about best practices in music teaching and learning in the United States. These standards guide each member institution in the ongoing obligation of fashioning music curricula and marshaling institutional resources so as to bring these standards of best practice to life in the contexts and circumstances of each member institution.

So if NASM is *not* averse to composition pedagogy curricula situated in pre-service music education programs, how do we explain the association's silence on this question? I believe it likely is because the NASM membership in the aggregate has not yet found a reason to articulate standards about pre-service curricula in composition pedagogy for music education students. This curricular focus simply has not yet grown enough in size and reach across U.S. higher education to trigger an accreditation action for the Association. The goal of this chapter is to share one university's experience in addressing this meager state of affairs by attempting to move composition pedagogy into the pre-service music education curriculum.

The balance of this narrative will address first the set of practical questions that so often dominate discussions I have had about this curriculum when I have been asked to speak about it at professional meetings across the United States and abroad. These practical questions include:

1. Who should learn to teach music composition to children in K–12 settings?
2. Who should teach composition pedagogy to pre-service music education students?
3. Where can university students be placed for practicum experiences in K–12 settings?
4. What costs are attached to a composition pedagogy curriculum and how can university music schools and departments shoulder such costs, especially in times of diminishing funding and resources?
5. What role might university music schools play in working with local districts to create employment opportunities for music composition pedagogy specialists?
6. Are there other courses implied in such a curriculum besides a methods class in composition pedagogy and its companion practicum?

Obviously, each of these questions could occupy a chapter (or book) of its own. My answers will have to be far shorter here, but I hope they will give a general sense of the kinds of concerns that we have tried to manage, along with a few words about how we have tried to manage them. I then will close with a brief reflection on certain philosophical matters that have informed much of our work here and that speak to a more ambitious and inclusive agenda for music education in American schools in the twenty-first century.

Practical Considerations and Questions

WHO SHOULD LEARN TO TEACH MUSIC COMPOSITION
TO CHILDREN IN K–12 SETTINGS?

While some institutions often find this initial question to be a vexing one, we had the good fortune to come to a rather easy consensus about this—*all of our music education students should learn to teach music composition*. This is not the complete answer to this question, by the way, but it has been a vitally important part of the answer—one on which so much of the balance of these curricular reforms rests. Our music education faculty decided years ago that the only certification program in music that we would offer our students is a comprehensive one. Based on the traditional curriculum of pre-service teacher training, this meant a curriculum for every music education student that led to comprehensive music teacher certification—K–12 instrumental, choral/vocal, and general music education.

When the opportunity then arose to consider the question of composition pedagogy for our music education students, this meant our faculty had the challenge of finding space in the curriculum to which we could *add* this important fourth dimension for our students. More about the details of this challenging exercise of finding curricular space will follow below. Suffice it to say here that our faculty members are committed to the idea that pre-service music teacher training should be broad and inclusive. There are several justifications to support this approach in context. First, our alumni have reported that this broad preparation and comprehensive certification provided them with an important philosophical perspective of the music education profession. Understanding how all of the parts of the K–12 music education enterprise work in symbiosis provided a helpful understanding of the role any given music teacher plays in the larger scheme of things. Second, our faculty believes that earning a K–12 certification in music provides our alumni with a competitive advantage in pursuit of employment in K–12 settings that they otherwise might not enjoy. Third, our faculty has observed that first-year students, who arrived imagining that they would occupy one focus area of the music education profession, soon found themselves led in very different directions as a consequence of the breadth of the curricular exposure they experienced in the undergraduate program. Offering this comprehensive curriculum affords students the opportunity to move among the various music education specialties easily as their professional interests mature without prolonging the time and credits to the completion of degree requirements unnecessarily. Finally, the faculty has found it important to consider the demographics of Nebraska, the state that supports UNL in the work we do. A word of explanation is in order here.

Nebraska is a very large state by geography (ranked 16th in the country by area) and a very small state by population (ranked 38th in the country with a population of just over 1.8 million). Of that 1.8 million Nebraskans, over 860,000 live in metropolitan Omaha and over 300,000 live in metropolitan Lincoln (U.S. Census Bureau, State and County Quick Facts 2010). This means, of course, that nearly two-thirds of the entire population of the state is clustered in the east, leaving the balance of the population scattered across a large landmass covering two time zones.

The provision of music education programs in the public and private schools in these two urban centers resembles in many ways the typical organization of music instruction in K–12 schools across the country. Choral specialists direct choirs. Band specialists direct bands. Orchestra specialists direct orchestras. General music specialists work in the elementary schools. Persons moving from other urban centers to these two Nebraska urban communities would discover a system of schools that would seem familiar.

What has this to do with our devotion to a comprehensive approach to pre-service education and teacher certification in music education? The population in much of the rest of our state is sparse. Music teachers hired by the schools of rural Nebraska often are the only music educators in a given school or set of schools. They are the sole provider of the full range of music instruction in the community, including general, choral/vocal music, and instrumental music education. In fact, it is still possible to find one-room schoolhouses in our state. As a consequence, Nebraska needs broadly prepared music educators who are able to deliver the full range of music instruction at all grade levels and focus areas in these rural settings.

Thus, the pre-service, undergraduate music education curriculum must provide instruction for all music education students in the various families of instruments, in voice pedagogy, in general methods, choral methods, and instrumental methods. Music education students must experience placements in school-situated practicums in these various kinds of teaching settings and curricula, and must receive formative and summative assessments of their effectiveness as music educators. The music education students' sense of personal identity may align more strongly with one of these traditional specialties than another, but our faculty believes that all music education students must receive the full array of courses in support of this broad orientation to music teaching and learning. Our alumni may very well be called upon, especially in the more rural areas in our state, to teach general music to elementary students in the morning and direct the high school marching band in the afternoon, for example.

It is for these reasons that, for us, the development of a curriculum focus on composition pedagogy in the pre-service curriculum required its *addition* to the curriculum rather than composition pedagogy as a replacement for one or more of the traditional curricular foci. Composition pedagogy needed to be a fourth major focus of our comprehensive approach, a full and equal partner to instrumental, choral/vocal, and general music education. So if these traditional foci required major methods courses devoted to their respective content areas that every pre-service music education student would be required to take, then composition pedagogy would need its own required methods course, as well. If these traditional foci required practicums in the schools, then composition pedagogy would, as well (and this requirement of a composition practicum proved to be a formidable challenge, given the dearth of music composition teaching and learning being delivered formally in area K–12 schools). The rationale that supported a comprehensive approach to pre-service music teacher training (philosophical perspective of the profession, employment competitiveness, identity shift of undergraduate students from one traditional curriculum focus to another, the needs of schools in rural Nebraska, etc.) all supported the approach of *adding* composition pedagogy as a fourth full partner to our pre-service music education curriculum.

I mentioned earlier that the decision to embrace composition pedagogy for all of our music education students was an important part of the answer to the question of who should learn to teach music composition to K–12 children, but that there was more to our answer than this. The other part of the answer for us was that we believed that just as some students naturally gravitate to one of the three traditional music education specialties of instrumental, choral/vocal, or general music education, so there likely would emerge students who would naturally gravitate to music composition pedagogy. Some students surely would identify with this newly affirmed and exciting specialty in our profession.

If this were the case, then this particular kind of pre-service music education student likely would have a stronger interest in composition, likely would have some experience composing original works during their high school experience, and may have been fortunate to have been taught by a music educator who encouraged composition in the classroom or rehearsal. This student's interests would not be nourished sufficiently by a single methods class in composition pedagogy any more than a music education student with a choral interest would be nourished sufficiently by a single methods course in choral pedagogy. A choral student would expect voice lessons, voice recitals, choral ensembles, conducting instruction, musical theatre experiences, diction instruction, etc., in order to acquire the depth of sophistication and range of expertise he or she surely would want to apply day to day as an accomplished choral/vocal educator in the schools.

So too, then, the composition education student would expect composition lessons, instruction in orchestration/arranging, instruction in composition technology (notation software, sequencing programs, sampling programs, MIDI, etc.), composition recitals, and instruction in music composition for mixed media. In short, pre-service music education students who identified with composition rather than band or choir, etc., would expect a set of experiences that equipped them as composers in a manner comparable to their performance- and general-music counterparts. For this to happen, *our curriculum had to support music education students whose applied major would be composition.* And for this to happen, the composition faculty would have to be prepared to accept into the composition studios music education students in a fashion that parallels music education students in the other applied studios.

Once again, whereas this would be a source of great anxiety in many university music schools, this was not a contentious issue for us. The composition faculty seemed to recognize that music education students are often the most accomplished performers in the various performance studios. Might it not also be the case that music education students might prove to be among the most promising composers? Further, the composition faculty speculated that the music education program might afford another kind of employment outlet for young composers—an outlet too often otherwise foreclosed to them. Might the career prospects of composition music educators, able to pursue employment in K–12 schools (with salary, health benefits, retirement, etc.), then attract a new cohort of composers to our institution at a time when student recruiting is becoming ever more challenging? Our faculty believed the answer to these questions was yes.

Finally, and almost ironically, several long-serving music faculty remembered that there had been in UNL's history a few music education students who had taken composition lessons as a part of their degree programs in the past. These students had done well in the composition studio, had continued to compose beyond their degree, and had found ways to teach composition, albeit in a rather impromptu fashion, in the schools where they had found employment.

To summarize, we decided to expand the tripartite pre-service curriculum of instrument, choral/vocal, and general music education for all music education students to include an additional fourth focus in our comprehensive program of teacher preparation—composition pedagogy. All music education students would receive a methods course in music composition pedagogy, coupled with appropriate opportunities for micro-teaching experiences with K–12 students. In addition, UNL would recruit a subset of music education students whose primary interest (and even musical identity) was composition. These students would have composition as their primary applied area. They would study orchestration/arranging, would study relevant music technology, would present composition recitals, and would, in a sense, become composition pedagogy specialists. The expressed plan for this cohort of composition-intensive students was to begin the process of cultivating a cohort of composition pedagogy specialists in the K–12 profession, much as we have in the other more traditional focus areas of music education. The reader may be interested to note that at this writing, roughly a quarter of the undergraduate composition studio enrollment is made up of these music education composition students.

WHO SHOULD TEACH COMPOSITION PEDAGOGY TO PRE-SERVICE MUSIC EDUCATION STUDENTS?

Should it be music education professors with an enthusiasm for composition teaching? Should it be composition professors with an interest in (or in some cases tolerance for) music education students and young composers in K–12 schools? Should it be public school teachers who are open to collaboration with both university specialists?

Because we have on our faculty a music education professor with a longstanding interest in questions about composition pedagogy through a music education lens (Moore, 1986; and Moore, 2003), our first and ultimate choice was to turn to him for the design and delivery of our methods course in composition pedagogy. However, as discussions among our faculty unfolded in both formal and informal settings, other music education professors expressed interest in being a part of this course design and other courses that seemed promising (a course in songwriting, for example).

We also had to decide about the role and scope of music technology in music composition pedagogy first for music education pre-service undergraduates and second for the K–12 students with whom our undergraduates would work. Again, our lead professor in this area has considerable expertise and years of experience in music technology, so an instructional design supported by and infused with music technology made sense for us (Moore, 1994).

Finally, our music education faculty considered the possibility of organizing the methods course in a team-taught manner involving both music education professors and composition professors. While we have not implemented this team-teaching approach yet, it remains an interesting and compelling option that all parties agree may have important potential. This is becoming more viable in one sense, now that several music education majors are students in the composition studios. Music education students are now known and respected by our composition faculty. Our composition faculty members quite naturally are becoming invested in the success of these young composition music educators.

WHERE CAN STUDENTS BE PLACED FOR PRACTICUM EXPERIENCES IN K–12 SETTINGS?

Given the dearth of music composition teaching and learning in American schools, and also in Lincoln, Nebraska schools, the question of where to place pre-service university students for practicum experiences with K–12 students remains an ongoing challenge. Nevertheless, our faculty embraced the wisdom of Confucius that "a journey of a thousand miles begins with a single step" and looked for a single public-school partner with whom to collaborate in providing a site from which to launch our composition pedagogy initiative. Lincoln North Star High School, one of six public high schools in the Lincoln Public Schools, proved to be that school and their music teacher proved to be that dedicated collaborator, who was encouraged by a supportive high school administration and district music supervisor. A number of important lessons have emerged from our early work together.

First, university music education students, as well as the high school students they serve in these composition practicums, are, for the most part, novice composers. Both groups are on a journey to acquire "a rudimentary capacity to create original or derivative music" (NASM *Handbook 2010–2011*, VIII.B.3). University students and high school students find themselves to be co-learners about the art and techniques of music composition. Second, our decision to employ composition technology means that sharing work and the "rendering" of music compositions for sharing and feedback in a classroom or on the web are at once easier and more reliable. Third, composition by way of technology allows the professor, the university students, and the high school students to archive their work for a variety of purposes in the future (keeping revisions of compositional products, maintaining research on compositional products and processes, sharing compositions with family and friends, sharing student works with other faculty in support of in-service education, etc.).

Our next goal is to grow the number of collaborative sites from this one high school program to additional high schools, and to add middle schools and elementary schools, so that our university students can have the opportunity to work with a broader range of ages, interests, and backgrounds. We expect to be able to do this with greater ease as more of our music education alumni, all of whom now are receiving instruction in composition pedagogy, are placed in this school district and others in the region after they graduate—alumni who understand the value of music composition in the curriculum for their students and who are able to partner with us to expand and enrich composition activities for students.

FINANCES

What costs are attached to a composition pedagogy initiative and how can university music schools and departments shoulder such costs in times of diminishing funding and resources? In our experience thus far, costs can be calculated in terms of technology, time, space, and political capital. I will provide a few words of annotation about each of these. Please understand that each of these matters could fill a book. I wish to avoid burdening this narrative needlessly. Suffice it to say that an important aspect of this planning process requires careful budgeting of the resources necessary to pursue this initiative successfully.

The resources needed to support this initiative fall into the following categories:

- Technology—this financial cost may be large or small, depending upon the university music school's decision to employ technology robustly or not in the service of composition pedagogy and also depending upon the music school's ongoing investments in such things. If, for example, the institution already maintains a music-enabled computer lab with suitable composition and sequencing workstations, there may be no additional money needed to utilize this resource in support of a composition pedagogy curriculum. If the K–12 schools at which the composition pedagogy practicums are housed likewise have computer labs that are capable of music computing, then the new resources needed for this aspect of the curriculum may be relatively small (software and a few music-peripheral devices).

    As an aside, the management of these financial costs appears to be shifting now as some universities are undergoing a change of philosophy regarding the provision of open-use computer labs of all kinds. In short, universities are phasing them out (Terris, 2009). So many students are arriving on college campuses with smart phones and laptops in hand that the open-use, general-purpose labs are seen as no longer needed. Some universities are taking the additional step of requiring incoming students either to arrive on campus with a specific computer configured with specific software for the program of study into which they are matriculating, or the institution simply is selling them the required hardware and software through the university bookstore. Finally, grant monies to support the innovative use of instructional technology remain a viable way to leverage new resources in support of these kinds of initiatives. As an example, in 2010 alone, our music education faculty secured more than $100,000 to fund music technology and music composition pedagogy efforts.

- Time—the time required to launch a fourth focus in pre-service music teacher training is, at least in our experience, considerable and, unlike the technology, is a *net* cost. Whereas one might see the additional financial costs of the technology required for a composition pedagogy program to be minimal, inasmuch as money already is being invested in music technology that can be conscripted in the service of this additional curricular task, the time needed to plan and put into action a new curriculum represents a time commitment that does not overlap other time investments in curriculum planning, especially when composition is not replacing another of the more traditional music education program foci. Here are a few examples of the time investments an initiative like this will require:
  - The music education faculty will need time to decide *if*, and then *how*, music composition pedagogy will become a part of the pre-service experience. The faculty will want to review the professional literature on composition pedagogy, schedule formal meetings to discuss issues and questions, and engage in lots of informal conversations as means of moving toward a consensus position.
  - The music education faculty will need time to identify and enlist possible partners among the public schools in the region so that practicum sites can be prepared.
  - The music education faculty and the composition faculty will need time to discuss, and then come to agreement about, the role, if any, that the composition faculty will play in the education of the pre-service music education students.
  - The music education faculty will need to brief their institutional administration (chair, dean, or director) to explain what they wish to do and enlist support. They also likely will need to seek curricular approvals through the normal processes of the institution (departmental and college curriculum committees, etc.). The time

required to accomplish this will expand in proportion to the ambitions of the proposal—the simple adding of an elective composition-pedagogy workshop in the summer will be relatively straightforward, while a major adjustment to the music education pre-service curriculum will take more time for planning and approvals.

- Space—the costs in terms of space have both a literal and a metaphorical dimension in these discussions. When speaking literally, the costs of space refer to the possible need for a classroom, lab, or other facility in which composition instruction can take place as elegantly as possible. If, for example, the faculty wishes to deliver a course on composition pedagogy in the music school's computer lab, the music education faculty must determine if the facility is suitably equipped to support the curriculum as conceived. The school administration then must determine if the lab space is available at a time when the new course or courses can be delivered and the students would have time in their daily schedules to take them.

  The metaphorical meaning of space refers to the pressures being felt across higher education to deliver degrees in a prescribed maximum number of quarter- or semester-hours. Music education curricula tend to be very congested, with many required courses and few if any electives. If the faculty decides, as UNL did, to add a fourth focus area in the pre-service music education curriculum, they must determine if it possible to do so without offending these credit hour limits—limits sometimes required by state statute. At UNL, the music education faculty decided to make all credit hour adjustments *within* the music education curriculum itself. This approach then "liberated" three semester hours in the existing curriculum, two of which then were reinvested in the fourth composition methods course. This approach, in effect, added the desired fourth course while concurrently generating a net reduction in hours to degree.

- Political capital—in Nebraska, music education certification is available for the three traditional focus areas. So long as the curriculum attends to those three music education foci, certification is not implicated adversely by the addition of this fourth focus on composition. This proved to be the case regarding our accreditation with NASM, as well. We made this innovative program and its virtues conspicuous to our accreditation visitation team. In that it added to the curriculum and exceeded NASM standards, it was not a concern in our reaccreditation application.

  However, not all states have policies that permit this kind of flexibility. Music education professors eager to explore this approach in their own institutions will be wise to sort through the certification and accreditation implications. Even in those states that direct music education students to seek a single certification in only one specialty, I suspect it will be possible to blend a traditional focus (general music, for example) with composition pedagogy and thereby soften, if not eliminate, political exposure.

TRANSITIONING FROM UNIVERSITY TO EMPLOYMENT

What role might university music schools play in working with local districts to create employment opportunities for music composition pedagogy specialists? With the exception of fine arts magnet schools, it is difficult to name any K–12 schools in the United States that routinely employ music educators with a focus on composition teaching—colleagues who teach children how to compose music as their full-time teaching assignment. Because this is so, it seems hard to know where and how to begin to build such programs. Professionals in the other areas of music education know that sustained, rigorous study of music requires a kind of feeder system. Bennett Reimer, a long-time champion of composition education in the schools, reminds us of how complex composition education is and should be, but does not really get at this very tough question of how to start (Reimer, 2003). How might a courageous school board and visionary set of school principals launch a composition program and keep a music composition educator fully engaged throughout the school day and school year?

Rest assured that I have no delivered wisdom and only few hunches about all of this. I do think that, of the many approaches I have considered and discussed with colleagues, the model that seems most promising to me is that of the itinerant music teacher, serving a number of schools each day. This way of teaching music has enjoyed great success for string educators over the years and I suspect it could be used with good effect for composition education, too (see Daniel Deutsch's chapter in this book for a helpful example of this composer-educator-as-itinerant-teacher approach).

Under such an approach, a single composition education specialist could be hired full-time to teach a few hours each day in an elementary school, a middle school, and a high school. In effect, a school district could hire a single composition education specialist and launch a composition program in which this one teacher cultivates her own "feeder system." As music composition "catches on," the demand for multiple sections of the several levels of music composition teaching may recommend the augmenting of that faculty.

We have begun these discussions with our local district music supervisor. We have not put forward a proposal to the school board yet, but we have had some lively talks about how this might work and what the challenges would be given our local context at this time.

COURSE OFFERINGS

Are there other courses implied in such a curriculum besides a methods class in composition pedagogy and its companion practicum? The short answer to this question is yes. Taking the advice of such national leaders as John Kratus from Michigan State University and Peter Webster from Northwestern University, we decided to offer some trial elective courses in music songwriting for our music education students, both during the regular school year for our pre-service under-graduates and also during the summer for our in-service graduate students. Early feedback from our students has been very encouraging. We also offered a new course on vernacular performance pedagogy for our pre-service music education students. In support of this effort, our school purchased two full sets of rock-band instruments so that our music education students could learn about how to form and rehearse rock bands with students in schools. The school produced a student recital of these student "lab" rock bands during the school day at a time in the schedule when the entire student body could attend. The students performed cover tunes and original songs as required elements in this end-of-term concert. Our music education faculty went so far as to secure smoke machines and light trees in order to provide an authentic context for the performances of our teacher/per-former/composer *vernacularists*.

Some members of the music education faculty since have incorporated questions about composition pedagogy, vernacular music, and related questions into their own research agenda, thereby nurturing the synergies of teaching and research that institutions such as ours should have as hallmarks of their professional enterprises (Bazan, 2009; Bazan, 2011; Woody, 2007; Woody & Lehmann, 2010). Other attempts by our faculty to share this work have included a public performance on campus in which the music education faculty organized themselves into a rock band and performed "cover tunes," thereby modeling the very sorts of creative engagements our pre-service students and their students are seeking to cultivate in music teaching and learning in our region.

Composition Pedagogy and Pre-Service Music Education Curriculum—Looking Ahead

This chapter has been an attempt to look at the structural and institutional challenges involved in a decision to infuse composition pedagogy into the pre-service music education curriculum at our university as a way to say to the profession that, at least in our experience, it can be done. This chapter has not been an effort to summarize best ways to teach composition to children and adolescents. I have made no attempt to synthesize the important research literature that continues to emerge from so many distinguished and devoted scholars who are examining these important questions every day. Our own modest progress at UNL owes much to the richness of their work, much of which is presented in chapters of this book and elsewhere (Hickey, 2003; Kaschub & Smith, 2009; Webster & Williams, 2006). This chapter also is an invitation, of sorts, for music education faculty at other institutions to explore ways that they could join us in giving systematic attention to composition education instruction for pre-service music educators. There are a number of reasons, both philosophical and sociological, why I think it is now time to move aggressively to do so.

First, it remains true today as it has for decades that U.S. students elect to take the music instruction we offer in schools less and less the longer they are enrolled in school. This is not, however, because children and adolescents become less and less interested in music over time. Rather, it is because the excellent curriculum we provide in orchestras, bands, and choral music is deeply interesting and compelling to some, but not most, of America's young people. This reality also is born out in our culture well beyond the borders of the schoolhouse. In a paper I presented to the Mayday Conference on Music Education and Ethics, I explored at some length the "disconnects" between the music we teach and the music our culture consumes. I wondered, with my esteemed colleagues at that professional meeting, about questions of cultural relevance and resource constriction as we endeavor to chart a strategic future for university music schools (Richmond, 2010). Recent reports document that the classical music of the European tradition and concert jazz make up less than 5 percent of the music consumed by our culture (CD sales, music downloads, concert tickets, etc.) (Midgette, 2010). At this writing, and unimaginable as this would have been to ponder even a decade ago, the Philadelphia Orchestra—one of America's "big five" professional orchestras—is seeking protection from its creditors in bankruptcy court (Yu, 2011).

The reader must not interpret these remarks as a condemnation of ensemble education. This is a story of enormous success and a real source of pride in the history of American music education. As a choral educator myself, I have no desire to reduce or minimize the importance of ensemble education in our schools. From all appearances, roughly 20 percent of American high school students will continue to be interested in ensemble education as they have been for more than 150 years.

Rather, it is a simple acknowledgement that American adolescents are engaging in music composition, vernacular music performance, song arranging, and digital media at impressively high numbers and at high levels, but they are doing so without the help of the portion of the American music education community employed in K–12 schools. These students are teaching themselves, they are seeking instruction from YouTube videos, they are seeking out each other as peer tutors, but they are not getting much systematic help from us (Green, 2002). But they could. And they should. The musical traditions to which these young composers are situated are nearly all vernacular and driven by commercial influences. But they need not be. Were the music education to respond to students' composition interests, surely the profession could introduce students to so many more of the world's music composition traditions than are possible when unbridled commercialism is the only influence to which students are exposed.

Finally, one of the most compelling features about music composition as a vehicle for music teaching and learning is the clear invitation such pedagogy provides for musical decision-making by students. While it is true that ensemble education has matured greatly in recent years, it also remains true that musical decision-making in ensemble settings is the province of the teacher more often than it is the student. In fact, how can school bands, orchestras, choirs, and jazz groups of any size function at all and not descend into chaos unless the conductor/educator is bringing about musical consensus and, for lack of a better word, *ensemble*?

Independent musical decision-making may be the most lofty aspiration music educators can have for their students. Surely we desire as a music education profession to see our students outgrow us—to know that they are capable of making informed, thoughtful, compelling musical choices. It is hard for me to imagine any kind of musical education that encourages music decision-making more than music composition. It is likewise difficult to imagine a time in our history when we have been better positioned than today, in terms of a robust research literature, a powerful instructional technology, and a clear understanding of the desire students have to participate in these creative musical engagements.

I invite the profession to consider ways, appropriate to the local contexts and constraints in which teacher-training programs may find themselves, to embrace the opportunities to equip pre-service music educators to become composer educators, and to expand the agenda of music education in the schools. Our children will flourish as these important learning opportunities expand.

References

Bazan, D. E. (2011). *Training pre-service teachers to teach through popular music.* Full paper presented at the 2011 Suncoast Music Education Research Symposium, Tampa Bay, FL.

Bazan, D. E. (2009). *An exploration of after-school popular music programs.* Full paper session presented at the 2009 Annual Conference of the American Educational Research Association, San Diego, CA.

Bazan, D. E., & Woody, R. H. (2009). *Preparing future music teachers to teach through popular music.* Best practices poster session presented at the 2009 Society for Music Teacher Education Symposium (SMTE), Greensboro, NC.

Green, L. (2002). *How popular musicians learn: A way ahead for music education.* Burlington, Vermont: Ashgate.

Hickey, M., ed. (2003). *Why and how to teach music composition: A new horizon for music education.* Reston, VA: MENC: The National Association for Music Education.

Kaschub, M., and Smith, J. P. (2009). *Minds on Music: Composition for Creative and Critical Thinking.* Lanham, MD: R&L Education—A Division of Rowman & Littlefield Publishers, Inc.

Midgette, A. (2010). Classical artists such as Hilary Hahn chart big on Billboard with little sales. *Washington Post* (January 30, 2010).

Moore, B. (1986). Music composition and learning style: The relationship between curriculum and learning. Unpublished dissertation, University of Wisconsin–Madison.

Moore, B. (1994). Technology in middle school: A powerful potential. In J. Hinckley (Ed.), *Music at the Middle Level.* Reston, VA: MENC: The National Association for Music Education.

Moore, B. (2003). The birth of song: the nature and nurture of composition. In M. Hickey (Ed.), *Why and How to Teach Music Composition: A New Horizon for Music Education*. Reston, VA: MENC: The National Association for Music Education.

National Association of Schools of Music (2011). *Handbook 2010–2011*. Reston, VA: National Association of Schools of Music.

Reimer, B. (2003). *A Philosophy of Music Education: Advancing the Vision*. Upper Saddle River, NJ: Prentice-Hall.

Richmond, J. W. (2010). Cultural relevance, resource constriction, and ethical leadership: Envisioning a strategic future for university music schools. Unpublished paper delivered to the Mayday Conference on Music Education and Ethics, Montclair State University.

Terris, B. (Dec. 6, 2009). Rebooted computer labs offer savings for campuses and ambiance for students: new gathering places for laptop users help colleges save on upkeep. *Chronicle of Higher Education*. Online. Available: http://chronicle.com/article/Computer-Labs-Get-Rebooted-as/49323/.

U.S. Census Bureau, State and County Quick Facts 2010. Online. Available: http://quickfacts.census.gov/qfd/states/31000.html.

Webster, P. R. & Williams, D. B. (2006). *Experiencing music technology*, 3rd edition. Belmont, CA: Thomson, Schirmer.

Woody, R. (2007). Popular music in school: Remixing the issues. *Music Educators Journal*, 93(4), 32–37.

Woody, R., and Lehmann, A. (2010). Student musicians' ear playing ability as a function of vernacular music experiences. *Journal of Research in Music Education*, 58(2), 101–115.

Yu, J. (2011). Philadelphia Orchestra declares bankruptcy. In *DP.com*, the website of the Daily Pennsylvanian. At http://www.dailypennsylvanian.com/article/philadelphia-orchestra-declares-bankruptcy, April 24, 2011.

18 }

Creating School-University Partnerships to Enhance Learning
Gena R. Greher

Introduction

If you were to take an informal survey of your college students' musical back-grounds, you would more than likely find that their first memory of learning to play music has more to do with learning the symbol system surrounding the study of music than with the actual music itself. Recapturing my students' initial curiosity about making music is the focus of why I began collaborative partnerships between our university and our local schools. This chapter will detail the genesis of two partnerships that began quite differently: one from an administrator's invitation and one from a teacher's invitation. While these partnerships began with very different goals and organizational structures, there are many commonalities that need to be considered when entering into what is essentially a collaborative arrange-ment, where each stakeholder may have different goals that need to be negotiated, ideally through a flattened hierarchy. At the heart of both of these partnerships is the desire to provide my students with the kinds of teaching experiences I was fortunate enough to have had as a graduate student in music education as a Teach-ing Artist (TA) with the Creative Arts Laboratory (CAL) at Teachers College Columbia University[1]. This experience sowed the seeds for my future research and involvement with school university partnerships, in my case particularly with regard to helping teachers and future teachers teach with technology. I will present an overview of some of the projects we engaged in, provide guidelines for setting up and maintaining a partnership, as well as offer tips for how to prepare your students for the experience.

For most students, the formal study of music will often shift the focus away from the visceral and aural sensation that made music a pleasurable experience in the first place, toward a more visual and more abstract endeavor. Hardly anyone remembers just *playing around with sounds*. Kaschub's and Smith's (2009) reminder that ". . . notations, either invented or codified, are representations of music—not actual music (p. 52)" is often at odds with what our students experience in many of their college music classes. In fact, many music students who are classically trained find the act of making music without some form of sheet music in front of them to be a very intimidating prospect. Yet were you to place these students, or even veteran music teachers in the role of a "sound explorer," in much the same manner as one might advocate for younger students, you can almost feel their excitement at rediscovering their own musicality and musical intuitions at the most basic level. However, they first need to get over the initial shock of actually having to create the music from nothing more than a germ of an idea, and then perform it in front of their peers.

As Gardner (1993) suggests in *Creating Minds*, childhood is the time for exploration. Those who are given discovery opportunities accumulate what he refers to as "creative capital." He goes on to state that students who are raised in a more restrictive environment are less likely to retain the curiosity to probe, discover, and conceptualize new phenomena (1993). Bamberger (2003) proposes that even at the college level, students possess musical instincts that in the proper environment can be developed and nurtured. Based on her findings Bamberger (2003) believes we need to encourage "compositional action-based projects," and encourage students' critical listening, improvising, experimenting, and reflecting on their decision-making (p. 34). In my own experience, a required college composition class was less about the *act of creation* and experimentation than it was about seeing how well we absorbed *the rules*. The idea of creating music to express one's feelings and thoughts through sound was a concept that was never discussed.

For my college students, this newfound sense of discovery within the world of sound alters how they think about music, how they hear music, how they perform music, how they create music and most profoundly, how they will eventually teach music. As much as all students need to engage in musical exploration through improvising and composing, pre-service music teachers in particular need to explore the various ways of imparting these concepts to others. In addition, having a setting where these novice music teachers can experiment with concepts and ideas with younger students can go a long way toward helping them work through the challenges of teaching music through composing and improvising.

Contextualizing the teaching and learning process for pre-service music teachers can involve altering how you evaluate student learning to a total reenvisioning of the curriculum, so that teaching and learning activities mirror the types of activities students might engage in outside of school. There is a great deal of research to suggest much of our system of education separates skill development (which is more easily measurable) from understanding. This often leaves students feeling disconnected from what is being studied (Brooks & Brooks, 1999; Bruner, 1977; Dewey, 1938; Lave & Wenger, 1991). Composition projects provide a context for encouraging students at all levels of development to think like a composer (Copland, 1988). While we can certainly contextualize the act of composing by infusing our music teacher education classes with a variety of relevant and engaging composition exercises, it is the *teaching of composition* in an actual school setting that can provide a richer framework for students who are learning to teach.

In a typical methods class you might place your students in the role of the teacher through hands-on micro teaching assignments with their classmates. This activity provides these novice teachers with a practical application of what they are learning and discovering through readings and discussions. However, by placing these pre-service music teachers in an actual school with actual students as part of the process of learning why and how to incorporate composition in the classroom, the learner/teacher dynamic begins to take on a whole new dimension. They immediately feel the tensions inherent in merely teaching the subject, which is a natural default orientation where one reverts to teaching *about* music. How well your students understand their students and how to engage them in an interactive exchange of ideas will greatly impact the success of their lesson. This act of *teaching the child*, along with the appropriate subject content, is where developing partnerships with schools can provide enormous advantages for the pre-service music teacher. In a school-based context, issues of socialization regarding both teacher and students, teacher identity-formation, as well as the effects of the school environment on the learning process, will begin to surface (Bresler, 2001; Burton & Greher, 2007; Conkling, 2004; Conkling & Henry, 2002).

There is no doubt that embedding school-based experiences within the methods classes is definitely extra work for the university professor, the music education students, and the teacher. It involves a great deal of collaboration, flexibility, communication, and time. These experiences underscore for the university students the importance of connecting with the students they are teaching while keeping the university professor more connected to what is actually happening in the schools.

Teaching and Learning in Context

We have several music outreach projects on our campus that can provide teaching opportunities for our students who seek them out. However, I was looking for a more systematic approach that would involve all our music education students in order to provide a means for merging theory to practice well in advance of their student teaching experience. An invitation to work with our demonstration school's PreK–4 students came from the Dean of our Graduate School of Education and the Director of our demonstration school. This was an opportunity to test the viability of embedding field experiences into the methods classes through a school-university partnership.

The first issue that arose was how to fit this into an already crowded schedule without necessarily taking time away from the methods class. Quite honestly, giving up class time was not a viable option since we only met two days a week. Adding an extra day to the schedule required some negotiation with the students. Normally, as part of the course requirements, these students would be required to spend twenty additional hours observing in schools, which was always problematic for most of the students to complete in time. By counting the time they would spend in the classroom as well as some of their preparation time, we had an almost even exchange. By actually immersing them in the *doing* of teaching in addition to observing music teachers in action, it was my belief this partnership opportunity would ultimately provide them with greater insight into the realities of working in a school environment.

Through a seed grant from our university, we were able to create a small music lab of five computer workstations and set up a weekly schedule for the university students to teach the classes in grades K–4. At the outset the focus of this particular partnership was on teaching music and technology in a child-centered setting, as well as providing the demonstration school students, who are representative of our city's diverse immigrant community, with more arts and technology experiences than they were currently receiving. We developed a project-based curriculum around the school's philosophy of experiential and activity based learning. We used a thematically focused, interdisciplinary curriculum incorporating a rich variety of materials that encouraged reading and writing across the curriculum.

Working with second-, third-, and fourth-grade classes, our Fairytale Project was created to support the students' literacy development through music-making and music creation. Students reimagined and/or retold their favorite fairytales and created their own drawings, which were scanned and uploaded into a simple movie program. This was accompanied by their narration as well as music they created through a basic looping program. At that time we were using *Super Duper Music Looper*, a fairly intuitive program.

THE FAIRYTALE PROJECT OVERVIEW

Before introducing the technology, our college students along with several of our graduate teaching assistants (TAs), went into the classrooms and initiated some simple music and listening activities along with discussing several popular fairy tales. They let the elementary students tell the story as a group discussion, and the TAs modeled how to tell a story from different points of view. The elementary students were then asked to retell the story from a new perspective; either from a specific character's perspective or by putting the story in a new setting[2]. They were asked to think about each character's attributes and create drawings to go with their interpretation.

At this point the elementary students were introduced to the concept of musical motif and were asked to think about what type of instrument and what kind of music would best represent each character. Using a looping program, students began to explore different sounds to create a musical motif for each of their story's characters. The drawings were scanned, narration was recorded, and all the elements were imported into a simple movie-editing program for their final presentation. The elementary students were learning to use the looping software through purposeful explorations. Both the college students and the graduate TAs observed the various groups of elementary students listening carefully and discussing the qualities of the different musical loops with each other as they began to craft their motifs by editing and layering the loops.

At the completion of the project, the director of the demonstration school asked each of the college students involved with this project to write about their thoughts on the project's benefits to the elementary students. It was also requested that they ask each of the elementary students what they thought about this project and what they learned. In addition to their weekly class meetings, the college students kept journals of their experiences each week, along with web-board discussions to reflect on the progress and problems encountered. At the end of the year there was a showing of student work to parents and their peers, as well as representatives from the university, the city, and the school board.

Throughout this experience the college students were learning how to:

- Devise listening activities to spark their students' imaginations
- Guide the students through the composing process, rather than telling them what to do
- Trouble-shoot student conflicts
- Properly label and save computer files

As suggested by one music education student's journal, "As an educational experience this was more real than anything that I could be taught in a methods or pedagogy class. I got to understand first hand the classroom dynamic between students and teachers . . . ."

Success Is in the Details

By all accounts this was a successful partnership. While finding a school or teacher to start a partnership with has its challenges, the real work is in the development, planning, and implementation of the collaboration. It is important to stress from the outset that each partnership is going to be different and will be context-specific (Abdal-Haqq, 1989; Burton & Greher, 2010; Lieberman & Miller, 1990; Sedlak, 1987). We each drew from experiences collaborating with colleagues both within and outside of our respective fields. Our experiences with setting up and maintaining this particular partnership underscore much of the literature on school-university partnerships (Bresler, 2002; Burton & Greher, 2007; Conkling, 2004; Conkling & Henry, 2002; Goodlad, 1991; Lieberman & Miller, 1990; Rice, 2002; Peters, 2002).

We each had articulated clear goals from the outset. Though our individual rationales for starting this partnership were different, our overall goals were in sync with each other's. It was clear to everyone involved that we were aiming for a high-quality experience for all of our students in line with our state's curriculum frameworks. We had support from our respective administrators and we each respected each other's expertise. The director of the school and the university course instructor engaged in a partnership of co-equals. We maintained regular communication with each other and were proactive in our planning. Consideration for the people who worked in the school was paramount and we did not make unrealistic demands on time, resources, and attention. Since this school did not have a dedicated full-time music teacher, we were careful to plan this in such a way as to not add to the workload of the classroom teachers. Consequently, we received and maintained their support in our endeavor.

I was very clear from the outset with my students that we were guests in this school. When I provided this opportunity for my students I also made clear they were to treat this experience as a professional commitment by dressing professionally, meeting with each other regularly in their groups to carefully plan their lessons, and being prepared and dependable. They were reminded that if they did not show up, it would not only negatively impact their teaching team, but it would seriously disappoint the classroom students. We began their experience with an orientation session from the school's director about the school, its philosophy and culture, what the student body is like, and ways to deal with issues should they arise.

In this particular partnership, teams of undergraduate students were paired with a graduate student mentor to help with the teaching, planning, and feedback. As a result of this collaboration, all involved music education students had an opportunity to experience a classroom environment reflective of the theories and philosophies they had been reading about, and to work with elementary school classes as part of a team of their peers. They were learning how to apply technology-based composition projects in a classroom and keep the students engaged, while getting instant feedback on their teaching from their students, the graduate students, their professor, and their peers. Perhaps the most important aspect of this particular school setting was the opportunity to work with a diverse population in an urban setting. This helped to dispel many of the negative stereotypes that are so prevalent in the media.[3]

Shifting Focus

Since these partnerships were originally created as technology partnerships, our project-based approach to learning included a large concentration of composition projects. The objective for our partnership approach was, and is, to shift the focus from teaching *about* technology to *thinking with* technology (Doering, Hughes, & Huffman, 2003). A parallel argument could be made that through composition activities we can shift the focus from teaching *about* music to *thinking with* music. Despite a technology focus, the reality is that these partnerships are teaching as much about lesson planning, sequencing, pacing, classroom management, the importance of building relationships, and those intangible factors that promote or hinder learning as they are about teaching composition and technology.

We are linking theory to practice as the students experience many of the situations that in past classes they might have only read about. Instead of creating lesson plans as a paper-and-pencil mental exercise—that I, as their professor, would merely comment on—they are planning lessons they actually have to implement. Additionally, they have to reflect on what did and did not work and why. There is nothing like a room full of students to provide feedback on whether or not the lesson plan and your execution of that plan worked. It is a sobering experience, to say the least. For the professor it is a major reality check on how well the students can actually apply what they are learning, as well as how well they can think on their feet while they are under the pressure of being in a classroom with real students.

What began with one campus-based demonstration school partnership has now morphed and expanded into several schools within our community across a variety of music methods classes in our music education program. We realize that the student teaching practicum often does not provide opportunities for creative activities. Consequently a central component in all our partnerships is for our pre-service music teachers to learn strategies for engaging students in creating music through composition and improvisation activities.

However, unlike the traditional student teacher practicum, school-university partnerships are about more than just the education of the pre-service teachers (Abdal-Haqq, 1989; Clark, 1999). Since there are multiple stakeholders involved, these partnerships have to function on many levels and provide benefits to all involved (Goodlad, 1991). On one level the goal in these particular partnerships is to instill in pre-service music teachers a comfort level for working with the complexities of technology, as well as encouraging a culture of musical composition as something everyone can engage in. This can be particularly daunting if they themselves have never had these experiences in their own schooling, or their experiences were less than positive ones.

On another level, we are either in the classroom of a veteran teacher or a novice teacher who may not be thinking about technology as a tool to unleash creative thinking. For the veteran teacher, if her/his view of musical composition is one that is narrowly defined as something that can only be accomplished after students have had a sufficient amount of traditional theory classes, how might we transform this teacher's practice through the inclusion of composition activities? For the novice teacher who may in fact be one of our recent graduates, how might we provide the extra support and feedback needed to encourage this teacher to continue to take creative risks through composition activities in the classroom? Given the challenges for teachers of performance demands from the administration and parents, along with the limited exposure to their students that is typical for arts educators, these partnerships can serve as a much needed site-specific form of professional development. For the new teacher in particular, it also adds a mentorship dimension.

Teachers in Partnership—Developing Relationships

Professional development is generally top-down and instigated by district adminis-trators. For the most part, these scatterings of one-shot workshops lack the fostering of in-depth understanding. Oftentimes these workshops are schoolwide and promoted to illuminate the latest trend or next new idea in school reform. There is often little regard for what the individual teacher needs most and little probability these workshops will provide teachers with a deeper understanding of the new material being presented. Professional development of teachers is rarely focused on sustained professional growth (Burton & Greher, 2007, 2010; Conkling & Henry, 2002; Darling-Hammond, 1997; Greher, 2011; Henry, 2001; Myers, 2003). Another factor specific to music teachers is their relative isolation within their building. Unless the professional development is district-wide, other than at conferences, there is little opportunity to interact with other music teachers to share ideas.

In an interesting twist on school-university collaboration and professional development, the next collaboration I will detail is one that was instigated by the classroom teacher, and was driven mainly by her needs and interests. An experi-enced high school general music teacher approached me with an idea that she felt would be mutually beneficial. She had recently had her computer lab updated. Though quite at ease teaching keyboarding classes, this high school music teacher believed she was completely out of her comfort zone with digital media and reached out to me for ideas. At the time, I was looking for new secondary student teaching sites that had music technology labs. What began as a simple informal conversation about developing a new course and providing each other with resources in fact turned into a rich model for ongoing professional development, music teacher education, and school-university collaboration.

We began our partnership with a very loose informal arrangement. The semester before she was to initiate a digital audio course she agreed to let my methods students observe and teach a music technology unit based on whatever concepts she was working on with each of her classes. My students would get practical experi-ence at the secondary level well before beginning their student teaching. This arrangement also provided them with feedback from the high school students and the classroom teacher. In return, the classroom teacher would gain insight into the types of composition and multimedia projects we were doing at the university. During the following semester, when several other students did part of their student teaching with her, the relationship that developed between this teacher and my students was one that was highly interactive and collaborative, so that the teaching and learning was reciprocal in nature.

At that same conference a year later she gave a presentation on digital audio, using as examples many of the composition projects my students introduced in her classes. While she was teaching my students about teaching, they were teaching her about digital audio. She learned to take risks and involve her students in listening, analyzing, and creating. In this case, the embedded nature of the teaching and learning that took place in her classroom was closer to that of a Professional Development School (Darling-Hammond, 1997a, 1997b; Holmes Group, 1986, 1990) and the student teacher took on more of the teaching artist role closer to that of the Creative Arts Laboratory (Pogonowski, 2001). The teaching and learning was a reciprocal teaching/learning loop.

A year later our technology in music education class was redesigned to align with her digital audio and piano class. We made sure to find a common meeting time that worked with both of our classes. The fact that I had a long established relationship with the arts supervisor in our local school district went a long way toward helping her make the needed scheduling changes. While this was and is a partnership built from the ground up, having administrative support for these types of endeavors is a critical factor in both the development and maintenance of a partnership through all of the inevitable personnel shifts and budget crises that affect schools. Unlike the more formal top-down approach to professional development, this model takes an informal approach with a flattened hierarchy driven by the needs of the teacher and the university professor. There is the same concentration on peer-to-peer learning that is advocated for students, and it was observed that the teacher involved was more willing to take risks in this context (Burton & Greher, 2007, 2010; Conkling & Henry, 2002; Darling-Hammond, 1997a, 1997b; Henry, 2001; Myers, 2003).

A Teaching and Learning Feedback Loop

Over the course of the semester we undertook many projects that were designed to help teach the college students and the high school students various technology programs through a variety of composition projects. For the digital audio class, all the students were asked to create several cell phone ringtones. The purpose of this was to introduce the students to a basic looping program along with creating their own loops from scratch. The college students and the high school students were asked to create individual ringtones to reflect some aspect of their personality they wanted to share with us. In addition, they were asked to collaborate on a ringtone for the university professor and the classroom teacher. This turned out to be a good ice-breaker for the class in terms of learning a little bit about everyone's personality and interests in a non-threatening manner.

One of the many challenges of this particular assignment was the fact that our university music lab is a Mac lab and the high school's was a PC lab. This necessitated discussions on universal file formats and how to save and play back files on different operating systems. After the ringtone project we had a short film-scoring project as an introduction to the larger scale cartoon-scoring project, which they were going to undertake collaboratively as their final project.

For the large scale scoring project a vintage cartoon was downloaded from www. archive.org. The original sound was stripped from the movie file and groups of students were assigned different sections of the cartoon to score. These sections would then be edited together for the final presentation that was to take place at the university. We had several classes where we analyzed a silent movie clip for what might be taking place, what the mood might be and how we might depict that musically, and what the pacing of the video clip was. I showed examples of the same video clip with different types of music to demonstrate how the various musical excerpts could alter the perception of what might be happening. We also looked for spots in the video that might benefit by some type of sound effect or musical emphasis. The students were required to use a combination of loops and original recordings and sounds. By the very nature of the fact that different groups of students were composing different sections of the cartoon, it was interesting to see how the very different musical personalities eventually fit together.

For the piano class, there was a methods book the classroom teacher was using where the students were allowed to practice on their own and perform for the teacher through headphones in order to move up to the next piece in the book. To add a little interest to this class the college students were given MIDI files of TV Themes to arrange via a notation program for their high school partner to learn. This required the university students to assess the abilities of their partners and seriously pare down the MIDI arrangement to an entry-level composition that still maintained some interest for the student.

Each college student was required to create a duet in order to play along with their partner so that the high school student might not feel like they were being put on the spot. This had the side benefit of putting both the college and high school students on a level playing field, since most of the college students were not keyboard majors. As one of the high school students observed, "They get to get over their fright of playing in front of people . . . We get to learn new songs that we want to learn."

Eventually the student pairs collaborated on creating an original blues composition. The college students were asked to create a presentation on the blues and perform some examples for the high school students as an introduction to the blues. They then worked on a collaborative composition using a notation software program. In this case the college students were working with a different notation program than the high school students. This meant that everyone needed to remember to save their files as MIDI files so their compositions could be opened on each other's computers. This sometimes presented the students with some formatting issues once they opened the file through another program. However, with notation programs such as Noteflight[4], which is a web-based program modeled on social networking sites, it is now easier than ever for students to collaborate on a composition.

The high school students welcomed the opportunity to show off their compositions for their college partners as well as hear what their partners created. What was interesting in this partnership is that both the college students and the high school students were learning to use the technology and both were being asked to compose in an atmosphere that felt more collaborative than a top-down student/teacher relationship. As one high school student commented, "I like being at the same level as the college kids . . . they were pretty much at the same learning level as us." Another student commented that, "The class goes by a lot faster when they're here. You know how they say time flies when you're having fun."

The Benefits of Teaching in Context

This partnership with our technology class is now going into its sixth year. Though the partnership is set up so that we always go to the high school on our designated meeting days, we have the final project presentation at the university to make the experience seem more special for the high school students. It is designed as a day-long trip during which they get to attend a general methods class and participate with a different group of college students. In addition, they get a tour of the university and music building from one of our admission's officers, have lunch in the cafeteria, and give their final presentations.

The sustained presence of the university students in the high school teacher's classroom provides many opportunities for her to observe her students' reactions to new creative activities, as well as providing her with fresh new instructional ideas. In this class both the high school students and the college students have generally been thrown into projects and collaborative relationships and asked to reflect on experiences and how they think learning is taking place. As one college student reflected, "I learned that you can often count on the students to teach each other in such a setting. Really, that is probably the most effective and meaningful method of learning, anyway."

This collaboration provides an added benefit in that the college students are now observing the high school students in the learning process and beginning to understand the importance of supporting students' intuitive thinking as suggested by both Bruner (1997) and Bamberger (2003). One of the university students wrote in his journal that, "What always surprises me is how much these kids already know . . . I can never assume that I know more about a particular subject than a high school student."

Before we began the collaboration with the local high school, I was viewed by the high school music faculty as just another ivory tower professor who was out of touch. My sustained presence in the school, interacting with the students and often teaching many of the classes alongside the music teacher, has made a positive impact on our personal dynamic. This experience also keeps me connected to the next generation of students.

Student journals and teacher feedback suggested that all parties felt this partnership was meaningful for all involved. Yet it was not until the following semester, when we were not in the school, that I realized the biggest payoff. I was getting regular updates from the music teacher regarding the creative composition projects she was instituting in her classes on her own. She was sending files of her students' finished projects, where the students reedited downloaded cartoon footage into public service announcements or commercials with original music.

These experiences confirm the importance of getting students into meaningful classroom experiences early in their education and not just as observers. This helps pre-service music teachers understand the importance of connecting with their students. The composition activities helped them see first-hand the importance of intuitive thinking in the learning process, as well as how powerful peer-to-peer learning can be. As previously stated, they get instant feedback on their teaching from the students, as well as suggestions from both the classroom teacher and the university professor. As a side benefit they also get to interact with a diverse population and realize they have more in common than they previously thought.

For the classroom teacher, these experiences have allowed her opportunities to take risks in involving her students and encouraged her to implement composition projects in her classes. These experiences also provide the music teacher with a window into how her students react to the various opportunities and reflect on what she might have done differently. Many music teachers welcome the opportunity to mentor college students in their classrooms. While the teachers provide mentorship they are also learning new ideas from these students, in much the same manner as the students are learning from the teachers. This model often provides opportunities for each of the stakeholders to apply new ideas in a collaborative, non-threatening environment. In the current culture of high stakes testing, most professional development is a top-down hierarchical series of one-shot infusions of information that is rarely relevant for music teachers. In contrast, a school-university partnership such as those described here can serve to provide sustained professional development suited to the needs of the individual teacher.

For university faculty, the importance of establishing relationships with the wider school community cannot be overstated. Unlike the traditional student teaching practicum, which is a relationship that was clearly developed to serve the needs of the university and its students, a school-university partnership should serve the needs of all the stakeholders. As previously mentioned, you will rarely find two partnership situations that are identical, yet the common denominator in establishing and maintaining a successful partnership relates to the relationships that develop between the university faculty and the local community, and more specifically, the music teachers. As suggested by Bruner (1977), the acquisition of skills and the development of understanding should not be mutually exclusive endeavors. Yet much of a music education course sequence is a series of exercises in compartmentalized learning of facts devoid of context. By participating in partnerships, the process of learning to teach becomes a more holistic practice.

References

Abdal-Haqq, I. (1989). *The Nature of Professional Development Schools. ERIC Digest 4–89*, ERIC Document Reproduction Service No. ED316548.

Bamberger, J. (2003). The development of intuitive musical understanding: A natural experiment. *Psychology of Music* 31(1), 7–36. doi: 10.1177/0305735603031001321.

Bresler, L. (2001). Agenda for arts education research: Emerging issues and directions. In *Enlightened advocacy: Implications of research for arts education policy and practice*, ed. M. McCarthy. College Park, MD: University of Maryland.

Bresler, L. (2002). Out of the trenches: The joys (and risks) of cross-disciplinary collaborations. *Bulletin of the Council for Research in Music Education*, 152, 17–39.

Brooks, J. G., & Brooks, M. G. (1999). *In search of understanding: The case for constructivist classrooms*. Alexandria, VA: Association for Supervision and Curriculum Development.

Bruner, J. (1977). *The process of education*. Cambridge, MA.: Harvard University Press.

Burton, S. L., & Greher, G. R. (2007). School-university partnerships: What do we know and why do they matter? *Arts Education Policy Review*, 109(1), 13–24. doi: 10.3200/AEPR.109.1.13-24.

Burton, S. L., & Greher, G. R. (2010). Research meets reality in school/university partnerships: An analysis of two diverse school-university collaborations. In M. Schmidt (Ed.), *Collaborative action for change: Selected proceedings of the 2007 Symposium on Music Teacher Education*, 155–181. Lanham, MD: Rowman & Littlefield.

Clark, R. W. (1999). "School-university partnerships and professional development schools." *Peabody Journal of Education*, 74(3 & 4), 164–177.

Conkling, S. W. (2004). Music teacher practice and identity in professional development partnerships. *Action, Criticism and Theory for Music Education*, 3(3), 1–15. Retrieved December 30, 2007 from http://www.maydaygroup.org/ACT/php/v3n3 .php.

Conkling, S. W., and Henry, W. (2002). "The impact of professional development partnerships: Our part of the story." *Journal of Music Teacher Education*, 11(2), 7–13.

Copland, A. (1988). *What to listen for in music* (4th ed.). New York: Penguin Books.

Darling-Hammond, L. (1997a). *Doing what matters most: Investing in quality teaching*. New York: National Commission on Teaching and America's Future.

Darling-Hammond, L. (1997b). What matters most: 21st century teaching. *The Education Digest*, 63(3), 5–11.

Dewey, J. (1938). *Experience and education*. New York: Touchstone.

Doering, A., Hughes, J., & Huffman, D. (2003). Preservice teachers: Are we thinking with technology? *Journal of Research on Technology Education*, 35(3), 342–362. Gale Document Number:A100131603.

Gardner, H. (1993). *Creating minds: An anatomy of creativity seen through the lives of Freud, Einstein, Picasso, Stravinsky, Eliot, Graham and Gandhi*. New York: Basic Books.

Goodlad, J. I. (1991). School-university partnerships. *Education Digest*, 56(8), 58–61

Greher, G. R. (2011). Music technology partnerships: A context for music teacher preparation. *Arts Education Policy Review (AEPR) Symposium on School University*

Partnerships. 112(3) Eds. Burton, S. L., & Greher, G. R. Washington, DC. doi:10 .1080/10632913.2011.566083.

Henry, W. (2001). Music teacher education and the professional development school. *Journal of Music Teacher Education*, 10(2), 6.

Holmes Group. (1986). *Tomorrow's teachers*. East Lansing, MI: Author.

Holmes Group. (1990). *Tomorrow's schools*. East Lansing, MI: Author.

Kaschub, M., & Smith, J. (2009). *Minds on music: Composition for creative and critical thinking*. Lanham, MD: Rowman and Littlefield.

Lave, J., & Wenger, E. (1991). *Situated Learning: Legitimate peripheral Participation*. Cambridge, England: Cambridge University Press.

Lieberman, A., & Miller, L. (1990). Teacher development in professional practice schools. *Teachers College Record*, 92(1), 17.

Myers, D. (2003). Quest for excellence: The transforming role of university-community collaborations in music teaching and learning. *Arts Education Policy Review*, 105(1), 5–12.

Peters, J. (2002). University-school collaboration: Identifying faulty assumptions. *Asia-Pacific Journal of Teacher Education*, 30(3), 14. doi: 10.1080/1359866022000048394.

Pogonowski, L. (2001). *The creative arts laboratory professional development model*. New York: Teachers College Columbia University.

Rice, E. H. (2002). The collaboration process in professional development schools results of a meta-ethnography, 1990–1998. *Journal of Teacher Education*, 53(1), 55–67. doi: 10.1177/0022487102053001006.

Sedlak, M. W. (1987). Tomorrow's teachers: The essential arguments of the Holmes group report. *Teachers College Record*, 88(3), 314–325.

Notes

1. The Creative Arts Laboratory (CAL), established in 1994 at Teachers College Columbia University, is a professional development model based on the premise that integrating the arts into the school curriculum facilitates teachers' capacities to help students make connections across subject matter areas. http://www.tc.columbia.edu/centers/cal/CreativeArtsLaboratory.html

2. Good examples of fairy tales told from a different character's perspective are *The True Story of the Three Little Pigs* [Paperback] by Jon Scieszka and *Once upon a Fairy Tale: Four Favorite Stories* [Hardcover], Starbright Foundation (Author).

3. The demonstration school was eventually merged with another school in the city, where we have doubled the size of the computer lab and where the current music teacher is one of the original graduate student mentors. This is an ongoing partnership.

4. www.noteflight.com

19 }

Advancing Composition in Music Education through Strategic Professional Development
Michele Kaschub

Introduction

In this chapter I will describe two strategies used at the University of Southern Maine to address the dual challenge of preparing practitioners to teach composition and securing field sites for pre-service teachers to practice leading composition activities with PreK–12 students. The first professional development program prepares practitioners as composers and knowledgeable teachers of composition prior to their hosting pre-service interns. The second approach fosters collaborative partnerships between practitioners and pre-service teachers in situations where pre-service teachers have studied composition pedagogy while their host-site practitioners have not. Throughout the chapter, issues faced by music teacher-educators, practitioners, and pre-service teachers will be presented as a contextual frame for the development of these and other models that focus on the critical nexus of theory and practice as composition education evolves within the profession.

Challenges and Opportunities

The field of school-based music education is in an intense period of self-reflection (Kratus, 2007; Williams, 2007). Ruminations unfold on multiple levels ranging from individual practitioners to those responsible for teacher education to those who steer and state future visions for the profession (Jorgensen, 2011; Shuler, 2011). Though such contemplations continue, one outgrowth of recent acute reflection is an emerging focus on composition and its role in music education.

Curricular movements encompassing the 1960s and early 1970s focused on introducing composers and new music to school-aged children, but very few of America's children were engaged in creating original music in their own right. While MENC had published Wiggins' *Composition in the Classroom: A Tool for Teaching* in 1990, it was not until the advent of the *National Standards for Arts Education*   **319**

(NSAE) in 1994 that the call to engage children in composition experiences (presented in a less intimidating form in the phrase "composing and arranging") was clearly made. Even with the prominence of the NSAE document and its subsequent influence on the development of state and local curricula, promptings to teach composition have been treated more as a nagging whisper than a prophetic push toward the future that we now inhabit.

For some practitioners, composition seems an insurmountable challenge (Bell, 2003; Strand, 2006). Few report any instances of being asked to compose when they themselves were students or as part of their teacher education programs. Trained as though the concepts of "performer" and "musician" are synonymous, music teachers rarely have prior experience upon which to base their actions as facilitators of students' compositional learning. This leaves many school children undereducated and falsely indoctrinated. Introduced to composers and their works through stories, posters, and recorded products, school children who have not been invited to compose their own music believe composers to be old, white, long-haired men who literally write notes on staff paper while seated at pianos (Glover, 2001). Thus, music education creates the next generation of people who do not consider themselves "creating musicians" though they may regularly create music with their voices, traditional instruments, or through the endless array of highly portable technologies introduced over the past decade.

Music teacher educators face challenges similar to those of practitioners. Today's college professors were prepared for teaching careers before, or alongside, those who are currently school-based practitioners. Like practitioners, many music teacher educators have never composed or led music composition lessons and activities in general music or ensemble settings. Complicating matters further, music teacher educators are charged with preparing teachers not only to meet, but also to shape, the future of music education—a future in which individual musicianship, including the ability to create original music and apply it across multiple technologies through varied media, already plays a significant role.

Given current circumstances, music teacher educators have the opportunity to assume the mantle of responsibility in the areas of self-education and professional leadership. In the area of self-education, this text provides a solid introduction to historical contexts, future visions, research, teacher preparation models, and lessons learned and shared by those blazing paths in this area of professional growth. This text, however, is not enough. Music teacher educators also need to embrace their inner composer and compose. There is great joy to be found in exploring and shaping musical sounds—a joy that is sometimes forgotten in the myriad tasks of administering college level programs. Similarly, music teacher educators should get into the field and interact with children who are composing. Children are fabulous teachers, enthusiastic in their playful and purposeful explorations of music and candid to a fault about how teachers can help or hinder their work. It is through these interactions that music teacher educators become ready to guide the learning of practitioners and pre-service teachers in the area of composition pedagogy.

Music teacher educators must exert leadership in creating points of access for pre-service and practicing music educators. Programs offering undergraduate music teacher education need honest appraisal and curricular restructuring. While it is easy to report that students compose in music theory classes, these exercises are rarely more than etudes for demonstrating theoretical understanding and usually lack expressivity and intent. Also, they fail to make the point that composition can occur prior to the study of music theory. Composition, as one of five direct experiences people can have with music (sing, play, compose, improvise, listen), deserves highly focused attention in courses where a PreK–12 spectrum of philosophy, research, child development, curriculum planning, methods of implementation, assessment, and evaluation are all addressed. To do less is to do a great disservice to both teachers and their future students.

Practitioners, too, need opportunities to study music composition and its pedagogy. PreK–12 music teachers have the power to bring about significant change in educational practice because they serve dually as the experience point for school children and the connective tissue between college classrooms and "the real world" for teachers-in-training. While traditional means of professional development are highly valuable and appropriate for practitioners, other models are also worthy of exploration.

Pre-service teachers who have completed course work in composition methods are uniquely positioned to function as collaborators with practitioners. Possessing an understanding of composition pedagogy that practitioners may not have, but still needing guidance in the day-to-day interactions that occur between teachers and students in school-based settings, pre-service teachers are able to offer advanced content knowledge in the area of composition pedagogy while completing their internships. The knowledge of setting and students that practitioners hold, partnered with the pre-service teachers' understanding of composition methods, can allow both teacher and intern to gain valuable teaching insights while maximizing the quality of engagement experienced by students as they explore composition.

School children play the most important role in the web of music education. The efforts invested in examining the profession and its future direction, the reflection performed by teachers, the hours spent wrestling with credit hour limits versus the sheer number of hours in the day, and even the step-by-step planning that goes into creating a single ten-minute composition activity, are all undertaken on their behalf. Yet, it is their voice—literally the things that school children say to us about their music-making and the things that they do as they create their music—that offers us the clearest direction for our efforts. Children love to make their own music. They discover who they are and how music works in the process. The results can be quite wonderful. Indeed, it is children who provide the motivation for music education to evolve.

In order to meet the needs of children and to help them discover who they are as music-makers, the profession of music education must take strategic action to create professional development opportunities that meet the needs of practicing and pre-service teachers. Like a spiderweb of delicately spun threads, these challenges and solutions are intertwined such that individual strands are mutually dependent. Professional development opportunities, too, must be woven such that they advance opportunities for all stakeholders.

Strategy 1: Composing Together

INTRODUCTION AND PROGRAM OVERVIEW

It is vital for music education as a whole to provide professional development to teachers who were not given the opportunity to study composition methods as part of their formal pre-service education. Workshops and other short-duration learning opportunities for professional development typically help teachers amass a collection of instructional strategies or specific activities, but often fail to meet the long-range needs of teachers (Duling, 1992). To be adequately prepared to lead learning in an unfamiliar content area, teachers must develop foundational understandings in philosophy, research, child development, curriculum planning, teacher-student interactions, assessment, and evaluation as they pertain to the new area of teaching and learning. Further, teachers need direct experience with new activity first as music makers, and then as music teachers, in order to fully comprehend the educational, musical, and human value of the experience that they will share with students.

Composing Together, the first program of its kind in the United States, was initiated in 2007 at the University of Southern Maine. Since its inception, the nine-credit certificate of advanced study has sought to provide highly-focused professional development in composition pedagogy. The program is open to any student possessing an undergraduate degree in music and requires no prior formal training in composition. Collaboratively developed by the author with Janice P. Smith of the Aaron Copland School of Music, Queens College, CUNY, the program requires the completion of three course-levels focusing one each on beginner, intermediate, and advanced child composers as encountered in PreK–12 music classrooms, private and group lessons, computer laboratories, and rehearsal settings.

The initial challenge was convincing the first cohort to take a chance on a course focused on something they had never done and were not sure they wanted to do. Aside from that, the most substantial challenge was to create a course that allowed teachers to overcome their fears and concerns about learning to compose and about teaching composition. Personal fears typically stem from a lack of personal experience with composing, hesitancy to define oneself as a composer, and the fear of not knowing what to say to help a child move forward with a composition. Professional concerns address curricular issues such as knowing what to expect of children at different levels of development, finding time to fit composition into existing curricular plans, executing lessons with children of highly varied skill and prior experience, and uncertainty about how to determine and prove that children are learning. All of these concerns, and many others, are easily addressed.

In designing the intensive week-long courses, particular attention is given structures that blend foundational direct experiences with music with the discovery of conceptual and pedagogical knowledge. Every class member takes applied lessons in composition and participates in community-building activities where individual composers share their works. Additionally, class members engage in the same compositional activities that would be used with children, first to experience the lessons and then to deconstruct and analyze the organization of the lesson. Key elements such as the student experience, teacher experience, and learning that resulted from the engagement are carefully examined and used to inform future lesson design.

The second major component of the week's work is the creation and sharing of materials that are ready to use as soon as practitioners return to school. One set of materials is created and shared by the course instructor. These pieces serve as experiential cornerstones and provide models for deconstruction. Some materials are highly successful, while others may be offered with conceptual or structural flaws so that teachers can learn to gauge what makes an effective composition lesson. The second set of materials are created by the practitioners and tailored to suit their students, curriculum, and instructional timeframes. Careful attention and feedback is given to materials created by teachers so that they feel confident about using their own lessons with their students in the upcoming school year.

In designing courses to meet the professional development needs of practitioners it is important to remember that teachers are goal-oriented. They can be impatient and somewhat rigid in their pursuit of the right way to get a job done. While both direct and observational learning are valuable, teachers are almost always hands-on learners. They learn by doing, teaching, and evaluating the efficacy of their instruction. They are greatly concerned with the outcomes of student learning and reflect both formally and informally on observations drawn from both projected and actual practice. To maximize the efficiency of this work, teachers need a strong conceptual foundation, a focused plan for implementation, and a system of ongoing professional support.

ESTABLISHING FOUNDATIONS

The knowledge and beliefs held by practitioners influence every decision they make as they work with children. Just as the foundation of a building is designed to withstand the loads placed on it, so do the foundational knowledge and beliefs of teachers support the weight of the myriad decisions they make as they design lessons and interact with children. Teachers who possess robust underpinnings are more likely to respond positively to the challenges of teaching composition than those who are uncertain about the value of composition or who know very little about children's compositional capacities (Kaschub & Smith, 2009). For this reason, a significant amount of time within Composing Together is invested in exploring why composition should be taught and what is currently understood about children's compositional processes and products.

The ability to succinctly express why composition is important within both general and specific music education offerings comprises a critical aspect of professional development. In order for practitioners to passionately pursue any teaching in music, they must be aware of their professional convictions and personal philosophies related to music education (Reimer, 1989). Teachers with little or no experience in composition may exclude it from their classrooms because they think it is too specialized, or possibly unimportant since it was not part of their own musical experiences. Practitioners must be invited to consider composition's relationship to singing, playing, improvising, and listening and must also determine composition's value within an overall music education program. Further, for teachers looking to introduce composition courses or programs in schools where none have existed, the ability to outline the value of composition in terms of its importance to children, community, culture, music, and school greatly increases the odds of such programs and courses becoming available to students.

One of the most pressing questions asked by program participants is, "How do I know if the students can do that?" This question is initially addressed by consulting existing research and then confirmed in practice. Critical inquiry into the work of young composers assumed significant forward motion in the early 1980s. With more than three decades of dissertations, published studies, articles, and numerous literature reviews available for those interested in gaining a general overview of what is known about young composers, the chasm between research and practice can easily be bridged. Practitioners should encounter research or research summaries that focus on young composers and their development, individual, and group working configurations, process and products, materials, instruments, technologies, task structures, and even the role the teacher plays in facilitating and providing feedback. Information gathered from studies addressing these areas provides important background information for determining appropriate curricular objectives and learner outcomes.

In addition to the conceptual foundations forged through philosophical inquiry and the review of research, practitioners also need to develop a personal frame of reference for the act of composing. Class members take two or three private composition lessons with a professional composer during each level of the Composing Together program. These lessons help practitioners develop their own composition skills, experience the role of student, and study how a professional composer views composition and approaches the teaching of composition within the context of the studio lesson.

In addition to private study, practitioners participate in composer circles. These assemblies are gatherings where composers share their work and provide feedback to each other within a supportive community of creative musicians. During the weeklong course, each practitioner not only practices giving feedback and receiving feedback, but also fills the leadership role in facilitating the circle to learn how to establish a safe and supportive environment for open and candid discussion of compositional work.

DEVELOPING TEACHING FOUNDATIONS

As philosophical, research, and experiential foundations are forged, attention is given to the structures that rise from these foundations. Curriculum planning, approaches to developing composition capacities with composers of various levels of previous experience spanning PreK–12 settings, strategies for providing meaningful feedback, and systems for assessing student work are introduced. These components advance conceptual knowledge and prepare teachers for the interactions they will have with their students.

Questions related to curriculum structures weigh heavily on teachers. Individual lesson planning, in particular, is a significant priority for those eager to introduce composition in their classes. In the first level of the Composing Together program, the planning process involved in creating stand-alone composition activities tailored to student needs garners significant attention. However, these individual activities are quickly reframed as starting points for the creation of thematic units, as unit design and implementation is a goal that teachers can successfully attain in their first year of including composition. Practitioners who experience success with thematic units return to the second level of course work eager for guidance in developing specialized courses of study and, in some cases, programs paralleling instrumental and choral music programs. The progression from single activities, to units, to courses, and to programs corresponds nicely with the growth of student interest in composition. Composition programs are easy to create, but difficult to implement as a whole curriculum at once because the crucial component of the program—the young composer—needs time to develop and mature.

One of the most daunting tasks that teachers face when engaging students in composition activities is providing meaningful feedback. Practitioners need to rehearse this teacher-student communication while others listen and provide insight as to how the teacher's words may be heard by the student. Feedback is always meant to be helpful, but a student's composition is a highly personal creation. Comments offered innocently can inflict emotional wounds because students view their compositions as reflections of themselves. Every comment may be construed to be about the composer, not just the composition. In many cases, the most valuable feedback that teachers can provide occurs in the form of a question. Carefully phrased questions allow the composers to gain further insight into their own thinking processes, intentions, and musical choices. The ability to ask probing questions without implying that there is a single correct answer, or a specific answer that will satisfy the teacher, requires constant attention and practice to become habitual.

In addition to designing composition activities and offering feedback as students compose and share their compositions, practitioners are also required to provide evidence of learning. This evidence is usually drawn from an assessment of process and product artifacts. Within the Composing Together program, practitioners learn that three compositional artifacts are necessary for assessing student work: a performance and/or recording of the work, a score, and the composer's explanation of the piece (Kaschub & Smith, 2009). These three data sources allow teachers to determine the composer's intent, what was accomplished, and what intentions may have been hampered by a lack of personal performance or social interaction skills.

Students come to composition with different skill sets and varied prior experiences with music and composition. Multiple levels of skills and understandings are to be expected and should be valued within composing communities. Baseline, formative, and summative assessments with distributed representation from the perspectives of teacher, peer, and the composer himself or herself contribute to the process of ascertaining individual growth as well as programmatic value. As compositions are a unique and personal outgrowth of the composer, teachers should always explain to students the criteria and methods that will be used to assess their work.

GROWING COMMUNITIES

Open and honest communication between all members of a composing community is critical to the health and success of the collective. Practitioners must create and grow two communities simultaneously in order to fully support the growth of composition in music education. The first community belongs to the students and is additionally inhabited by teachers, performers, and professional composers when they are invited to join. The second community is one built of practitioners engaged in facilitating composition study with students. Over time, overlap of these two communities can create an opportunity for significant expansion.

Communities of learners are typically thought of as within-school programs. Such communities are comprised of students within a particular class, across a specific grade level, throughout a school building (another layer of community), or even across the full spectrum of a PreK–12 music program. Successful communities begin with small groups of interested students and expand as compositions are shared, professional composers are brought in as models, experts, or consultants, or as performers are engaged to premiere works. In each case, expansion of the community introduces others to the work of young composers and allows young composers to gain valuable feedback from a range of knowledgeable musicians. These interactions foster future growth of the composers and further expansion of the community.

Complimenting student-based communities are practitioner-based communities. One of the most significant benefits of studying composition with a group of practicing teachers is that practitioners face many of the same challenges and understand similar things about working with children of a particular age or skill set. Most teachers are eager to share materials and recognize the value of using other teachers as sounding boards for project ideas. Teachers participating in intensive composition pedagogy programs bond strongly over even a single course and establish contacts and plans for collaboration that help to sustain their work even when they are faced with unexpected challenges.

Practitioner communities offer ongoing professional support in that teachers can design and share lessons, gather feedback from colleagues, exchange materials and plans, teach each other's lessons, and provide valuable feedback and reflection on aspects of pedagogical practice. Within the Composing Together program, professional development is inherent to each cohort. Current efforts now focus on establishing linkages between cohorts so that more expansive communities of practitioners can be built. It is these teachers who will set an agenda for composition within district and state music education associations and create increased opportunities for young composers to grow and share their work.

In helping practitioners learn to guide and facilitate composition in PreK–12 settings—an activity that is new to them and for which they may have little natural comfort—each unique approach must be honored. Careful consideration must be given to the effectiveness of the materials chosen, lessons designed, the activities outlined, and the reflections and projections made as teaching unfolds. Practitioners with varied backgrounds and experiences bring as much to our classrooms as they take away. They have incredible insights to the daily learning and activities of school-age children. As each practitioner seeks to meet the needs of his or her students, that teacher is also engaged in a construction of self in which personal philosophies are being reshaped and modes of operation are being adapted to fit the requirements of composition teaching and learning.

MENTORING PRE-SERVICE TEACHERS

Teachers seeking professional development through the Composing Together program eventually mentor pre-service teachers in much the same way that they would guide those interested in teaching listening in classroom settings or leading ensemble rehearsals. Yet, these mentors are anything but ordinary exactly because they are highly knowledgeable and experienced in the area of composition education. Their classrooms and rehearsal halls represent rich learning environments for other practitioners, pre-service teachers, and PreK–12 students.

Teachers engaged in composition education are prized mentors for student teaching interns, but are also of value to undergraduate students as they study composition methods or explore composition's role in courses where composition is not the primary focus. Choral methods students may be able to observe a teacher leading students in the creation of warm-up exercises or full pieces. Music education majors studying classroom management will find no environment more challenging than one which features twenty-five third-graders engaged in small group composition with pitched and non-pitched classroom percussion instruments! As music education evolves and composition's role within school-based music programs becomes more apparent, practitioners who can model effective and engaging practices in composition will play a crucial and vital role.

Strategy 2: Collaborative Partnerships

Preparing practitioners to teach composition before they take on a student teaching intern is the ideal situation. Practitioners gain new skills and have time to refine their methods and strategies for application before they welcome novice teachers into the classroom. Yet, we should not halt the forward motion of music education or the practicum work of interns because there are few practitioners ready to hold them. Rather, we need to reframe the mentor-mentee relationship to strategically accomplish a broader professional development goal. As music teacher educators work to create courses for practitioners, they must also create courses for undergraduates. These two approaches allow for constructive overlap and bridging in the profession and allow children to experience composition even as their teachers build their compositional and educational foundations.

FROM MENTORSHIP TO PARTNERSHIP

Through much of the 1980s, mentor-teachers filled the role of daily advisor, instructor, and student teacher evaluator (Timperly, 2001). With the 1990s, practitioners were additionally guided to encourage student teachers to reflect on their own practices as a source of self-knowledge (Atterbury, 1994; Barry, 1996; Gromko, 1995) while still providing emotional support and career advice. The promotion of self-reflection and an increasing awareness of personal development through the process of teacher socialization continued to evolve through the first decade of this century. This evolution has further expanded to the point where mentees are expected to develop a sense of self rather than becoming mere carbon copies of the mentor-teacher.

In this ongoing expansion of responsibility, practicing teachers play an increasingly critical role in the preparation of novice teachers (Beck & Kosnik, 2002; Lane et al., 2003). Experienced practitioners are being asked to adopt new ways of working with pre-service teachers as teacher education programs seek access to authentic contexts of practice (Brown, 2002). Indeed, many believe experiences built on classroom immersion to be the critical component in music education students' ability to define themselves as *real teachers* (Conkling, 2004; Roberts, 2004). Yet, how can practitioners convincingly fill the role of expert when they are not confident in their own abilities as teachers of composition?

Clearly the traditional role assumed by mentors is not fully accurate or appropriate for teaching and learning in composition in most cases at this time. Therefore, the role of both contributors must evolve in appreciation of the fact that both mentor and mentee can be learners as well as leaders. Reframing the mentor-mentee relationship as one of collaborative partnership recognizes that both "expert" and "novice" partners possess different types of knowledge, but undertake their "task simultaneously, thinking together over demands and tackling complexities" (UNESCO, 2000). Partners contribute their unique knowledge, skills, and understandings to a collaborative act of learning that involves "shared creation and/or discovery" (UNESCO, 2000).

The creation of collaborative partnerships for composition education presents an opportunity to evoke change in the profession. Change, however incremental, remains a multifaceted task. Music teacher educators will need to market the collaborative concept to practitioners and administrators by outlining the clear benefits of composition study. Host practitioners, some who may have previously acted as expert-mentors, will need guidance in playing their new mentor-plus-learner roles. Further, music teacher educators will need to develop opportunities for partners to learn and teach together.

In the collaborative partnership, practitioner and pre-service teacher help each other create knowledge. Partial success rests on the practitioner's ability to limit mentoring to areas of expertise while remaining an open partner in the exploration of new pedagogical knowledge and content. This openness must be meet by the pre-service teacher's willingness and ability to share conceptual knowledge related to composition. With these contributions in place, collaborative efforts at composition lesson design effectively join theory (pre-service teacher's content knowledge) with knowledge of the learner (teacher's situated knowledge of practice) so that both partners can develop and enhance their overall teaching skills.

DESIRABLE CHARACTERISTICS IN HOSTS AND PRE-SERVICE COLLABORATORS

It is a challenge to find practitioners who are willing to welcome college students into their classrooms to experiment with teaching methods and content not used by the host. In typical hosting arrangements, practitioners may enjoy the personal and professional rewards of imparting knowledge, advice, and experience to those newly entering the profession. They also realize that hosting necessitates changes to yearly plans, curricular units, and even routine day-to-day operations. In opening the door to a pre-service teacher eager to lead composition study, host teachers also welcome a new personality with unique interpersonal skills and a few unfamiliar expectations. More importantly, the host welcomes new skills and understandings along with an additional set of eyes and ears that can be invaluable when generative music-making activities are first introduced.

Teachers who are simply amazing with children are not always equally amazing with pre-service teachers. College students are adults caught between school and entrance to the workforce. They learn differently, have more deeply established expectations, and may even represent a generational shift within the profession. Their teaching "mission" within music education may vary significantly from that of their host who was trained at an earlier time (Goodson, 2006). Practitioners selected to engage in this model of collaborative partnership must be leaders not only in the sense that they can convince others to follow them, but in the way they allow others to develop their own sense of leadership. Mentors of this type foster the development of future teachers because they have the vision to imagine new ways of teaching and the confidence to enact that vision.

Host collaborators must be committed to the idea and value of true collaboration. They must understand that tenacity and perseverance are critical components in the development of pre-service teachers, but they must also accept the novice teacher at their point of personal development with measured patience as they journey forward together.

The ability to empathize with the pre-service teacher about topics and experience relevant to the "new" status is necessary, but so is the ability to suggest possibility in the face of failure. Pre-service teachers thrive when their experienced hosts practice transparency as they describe the thought processes involved in creating lessons, leading instruction, questioning students to guide their learning, assessing growth, and all of the other tasks and behaviors that teachers are regularly called upon to employ in the act of teaching. Most importantly, experienced hosts need to project optimism for future events when critical reflection reveals flaws in practice.

Just as there are characteristics that indicate the likely success of host partners, so are there traits that pre-service collaborators should strive to exhibit. Successful novice teachers must be able to clearly and succinctly describe their working style and habits as well as express what they know and what they would like to learn during the partnership. They must be willing to actively engage in the processes of teaching and interact dynamically with students. Pre-service teachers must be able to set goals, ask for specific feedback, and be mindful listeners during exchanges with their collaborative partners. Additionally, they must be willing to try new things and be flexible when the unexpected occurs. Above all else, in order to be viewed as a partner of value, they must be professional in all manner of dress, timeliness, preparation, and execution of tasks and responsibilities.

ESTABLISHING A COLLABORATIVE RELATIONSHIP

The roles of teacher and learner must shift fluidly within and between collaborators for a successful partnership to be attained. There are times when practitioners hold the managerial knowledge that can move a class of students forward in an activity. Similarly, there are times when pre-service teachers may hold content knowledge or produce a pedagogical approach to composition that is new to the host. Balancing power within partnerships allows for the introduction of new teaching skills and practices for both contributors. Every interaction, plan, activity, and reflection holds clues to improving the quality of the experience for all involved.

Practitioner and pre-service teachers should meet to discuss the specific goals and objectives of their relationship. They should specifically discuss:

- What learning outcomes are desired for students engaged in composition activities?
- How will the practitioner and the pre-service teacher collaborate to bring these goals about?
- How will the two teachers partner to design and implement lessons?

- What types of feedback will they provide to each other and how will it be provided? Are there guiding questions that help equalize the relationship (which is not equal in that it occurs in the practitioner's classroom with the practitioner's students). What efforts will be made to equalize this relationship?
- How will this relationship contribute to each person's professional growth?

It is important to remember that it takes time to learn to be a good collaborator. Both partners must be open to suggestion and question. One common situation arising in collaborative partnerships finds the pre-service teacher in a position where they would like to question the status quo. It is easy for pre-service teachers to fall into the trap of compliance as the host's approach is assumed because adoption of practice is easier than challenging a teacher of greater experience. Yet, practitioners often value just these types of questions. Such inquiries allow teachers to examine their work anew while providing additional insight to their collaborative partner's perceptions and beliefs.

STRATEGIES FOR COLLABORATIVE TEACHING

Collaborative partnership utilizes the varied skill sets of both practitioner and pre-service teacher to jointly share responsibility for planning, implementing lessons/activities, and monitoring the growth of students. It is difficult to present a narrative snapshot of this process because it varies from day to day, classroom to classroom, and partnership to partnership. When fully operational, a partnership is a dynamic process of constant adaptation. There is continual assessment of student progress, reconfiguration of teaching responsibilities, and a constant evolution of instructional strategies that respond to learner needs. There are several strategies for collaborative teaching that partners can explore together as they design and implement composition learning engagements for students.

Accent and Highlight. In this mode of instruction, one teacher presents information while the other poses questions to determine student comprehension or application ability. The second teacher places an "accent" on particularly important points of information or experiences by drawing additional attention to particular concepts or percepts. Accented partnership works well when the primary goal is sharing information, critical and analytical listening, or when skills of craftsmanship (Kaschub & Smith, 2009) are being addressed. Partners must carefully plan teaching episodes within this model so that critical accent points are clearly identified before the lesson begins, although other notable ideas and experiences may arise and be addressed as the lesson unfolds.

Circulate and Support. One teacher leads the main class activity while the other teacher circulates around the room helping individuals or teams of students. This mode of instruction works well when students are in a large group. The circulating or floating teacher is passive; offering help, but not distracting from the lead-teacher. Partners exploring this mode need to switch roles regularly so that neither teacher becomes "just the helper" in the eyes of the students. It is also important to note that having multiple adults in motion in a room can be a considerable distraction. Authority is commonly situated with one teacher and confusion may arise when two teachers are in play. In the circulating support model, the lead teacher will most likely control the pacing of instruction and maintain students' attention while the floater teacher addresses minor disruptions or helps to return to task students who may briefly lose focus.

The Composer's Help-Desk. Activities that feature individual or small group work often benefit from partnerships that involve a lead and a fixed teacher. In this mode of instruction, one teacher presents the task to the students and then circulates through the room, monitoring individual or group work, while the other teacher runs a help-desk. Some additional motion may be observed in this format as students move from their working area to the help-desk, but students are also more likely to get answers when they need them. Both teachers are active and equal in this model, though they perform slightly different tasks.

Instructional Duet. Just as musical duets feature the equal partnership of two performing musicians, so are instructional duets characterized by two teachers presenting information, asking questions, monitoring student progress, and providing feedback in equal measure. Teachers working in this mode interact easily with each other and truly collaborate in the facilitation of learning. Instruction shifts periodically so that one teacher takes the lead while the other monitors the students' learning, and then emphasis may shift. This model works particularly well for large and small group instruction and allows partners to engage in teacher-to-teacher role play to model compromise, polite and respectful disagreement, and peer feedback so that students may use these skills within their compositional teams.

Reduced Ratio. One of the major challenges in composition pedagogy is that of providing appropriate feedback tailored to the unique needs of each individual composer. While composition can certainly unfold within full classrooms and large ensembles, the presence of a second teacher makes possible teaching arrangements where the teacher-to-student ratio can be enhanced. In reduced ratio teaching, students are divided into two groups or into smaller groups to be divided between the two teachers. The teachers present the same information and engage students in identical activities, but work with fewer students so that there is a greater opportunity for every voice to contribute to the conversation as learning unfolds. This model also allows teachers to compare notes as they reflect on the multiple facets of a particular lesson plan and its implementation—in effect doubling the experience of the teachers.

TRUST AND FEEDBACK

One of the key factors influencing the development of new teaching skills is access to meaningful feedback related to teaching performance. In fact, this is one of the support structures that pre-service teachers specifically identify as imperative to their education (Conway, 2002; Killian & Dye, 2009; Stegman, 2007). In order for broad teaching skills to be further developed by pre-service teachers and for practitioners to gain a deeper understanding of composition pedagogy, both partners must be willing to provide feedback to each other. This requires a significant level of personal and professional trust.

Recently scientists have begun to understand how interpersonal attachments occur at the biochemical level. When collaborators feel good about themselves, dopamine, serotonin, and norepinephrine, the neurotransmitters that power the frontal cortex, stimulate brain activity so that new networks are created (Zull, 2002). These new networks include information about the social interaction as well as information exchanged within it. Thus, opportunity, experience, and meaningful feedback within a trusting relationship "stimulate the brain to grow, organize and integrate" (Cozolino, 2002, p. 213).

Meaningful feedback alone, however, is insufficient to spur this important brain growth. Social interaction, through dialogue with eye contact, is required in order for feedback to have the greatest impact. When a meaningful connection is made, the processes of asking questions, reformulating statements, summarizing what has been said, listening for and respecting silent thinking, and listening reflectively (Zachary, 2000) can be utilized to their full potential. Teachers introduced to these five techniques report an increased awareness of other teachers' needs to analyze and assess their own teaching before being offered solutions (Evertson & Smithey, 2001).

Teachers engaged in developing new content knowledge, teaching skills, or broader understandings of teaching and learning as it relates to particular students and contexts, benefit from feedback addressing organization of lesson activities, appropriate implementation of new material, effective use of instructional time and materials, pacing, positive teacher-to-student and student-to-student interactions, and the overall fluidity and nature of the classroom environment and functional structures. The presence of this type of open and honest feedback between collaborators makes it less likely that either will revert to the mere survival strategies and more likely that reflection necessary for future growth will take place.

REFLECTION AND STRATEGIC ACTION

Reflective teaching is a form of action. Its execution requires a critical analysis of all aspects of teaching coupled with a purposeful plan to alter and improve future practice. As Sgori has noted, the learner's "journey is essentially a journey inward. The only vehicle on which the journey can be made is trust" (1998, 26.) The trust established between collaborative partners as they learn and teach together allows for constructive feedback to become the foundation for active change in practice.

Apfelstadt observes that, "Learning to teach is an evolutionary process" (1996:5) in which change may be incremental or monumental. In this evolution, reflection plays a critical role. Pre-service teachers in well-structured methods courses are invited to view education from multiple perspectives. They are challenged to explore the foundations of teaching and they are engaged in a critical examination of historical and current practices. These activities are intended to prepare new teachers to meet the changes that they will experience over the course of their careers.

In field-based work, pre-service teachers need to continue this interrogation of practice as they are immersed in the contextual experience of school. It is through such practices that pre-service teachers continue to construct their teacher-identities and develop their personal philosophies. Within collaborative partnerships, pre-service teachers may draw upon these skills to examine their teaching practices, but they rely on practitioners to model when these techniques should be applied.

Practitioners need to explicitly model how they reflect on their own perceptions, beliefs, experiences, and practices. This includes openly discussing with pre-service teachers how their impressions change over time. While not all reflection leads to immediate shifts in thinking or practice, longer periods of reflection, time away from teaching, and recurrent experiences of a similar nature may amass to allow the "big picture" to assume focus over time. New perceptions and emerging beliefs coupled with strong foundations and a plan to try lessons and activities differently allow for purposeful, informed teaching to transpire.

DYSFUNCTIONAL PARTNERSHIPS

The rich relationship that evolves between most collaborative partners does not, unfortunately, form between all practitioner/pre-service matches. Some practitioners turn out to be anything but collaborative. Rather, they are impatient and unwilling to share their expertise, classroom, or students with pre-service teachers. Similarly, pre-service teachers who are consistently unprepared, unwilling to ask questions, and who fail to either make their needs known or show initiative are viewed as incompetent and draining by their hosts.

Most non-collaborations stem from mismatched expectations, conflicting goals, power struggles, non-complimentary personalities, territorial issues, and the failure of one or both parties to follow through on professional commitments. Pre-service teachers are not only learning to teach, but also to act as professionals. The importance of attending meetings, arriving on time for work, and having materials and lessons prepared well in advance of the class where they are to be used signals reliability, and in turn, trustworthiness. Professional behavior by both partners is necessary for a sense of mutual respect to develop. Without effort to build and maintain this level of interpersonal professional interaction, partnerships will quickly collapse.

BROAD BENEFITS

Implementation of the collaborative partnership model of professional development addresses multiple challenges in music education. Practitioners expand their repertoire of skills as collaborators and as teachers of a new content area within music while pre-service teachers gain access to authentic teaching experiences. Pre-service teachers prepared to lead composition activities in partnership with teachers who have little formal training in composition pedagogy are able to assume a leadership role and strengthen their perception of themselves as teacher-leaders.

Most fittingly, students benefit immensely from successful partnerships as they encounter new ways of interacting with music and with each other as they engage in composition activities. As generative music projects are introduced by the pre-service and host-teacher, students learn that the act of creating original music is as accessible to them as are the acts of listening to the music of others or performing works created by other composers. This expanded view of music and music-making more aptly reflects music as it is practiced beyond school walls and in the lives of children.

LOOKING FORWARD

The Composing Together and Collaborative Partnership models offered in this chapter are but two of the many ways that music teacher educators might assist practicing and pre-service teachers in preparing to lead composition study in PreK–12 settings. Both models offer practitioners without prior experience in composition pedagogy access to new knowledge and understandings that they can use with their students. Moreover, both models also prepare practitioners to serve as bridges between college courses and classrooms as they host pre-service teachers and grant them access to direct experiences of teaching.

These models, and the many others offered throughout this text, demonstrate the power of music teacher educators to shape education at multiple levels. In designing and delivering professional development opportunities that simultaneously engage colleges, PreK–12 schools, practicing teachers, pre-service teachers, and students, music teacher educators can spur communities to embrace composition's vital role in music education.

References

Apfelstadt, H. (1996). Teacher education: A process of becoming. *Journal of Music Teacher Education*, 6(4). doi: 10.1177/105708379600600102.

Atterbury, B. W. (1994). Developing reflective music educators. *Journal of Music Teacher Education*, 3, 6–12.

Barry, N. H. (1996). Promoting reflective practice in an elementary music methods course. *Journal of Music Teacher Education*, 5, 6–13.

Beck, C., and Kosnik, C. (2002). Components of a good practicum placement: Student teacher perceptions. *Teacher Education Quarterly*, 29(2), 81–98.

Bell, C. L. (2003). Beginning the dialogue: Teachers respond to the national standards. *Bulletin of the Council for Research in Music Education*, 156: 31–42

Brown, M. (2002). Mentors, schools and learning. *EQ Australia*, 2, 17–19.

Conkling, S. (2004). Music teacher practice and identity in professional development partnerships. *Action, Criticism, and Theory for Music Education*, 3(3).

Conway, C. (2002). Perceptions of beginning teachers, their mentors, and administrators regarding preservice music teacher preparation. *Journal of Research in Music Education*, 50, 20–36.

Cozolino, L. (2002). *The Neuroscience of Psychotherapy: Building and Rebuilding the Human Brain*. New York: Norton.

Duling, E. B. (1992). The development of pedagogical-content knowledge: Two case studies of exemplary general music teachers (Doctoral dissertation, Ohio State University, 1992). Dissertation Abstracts International, 53(06), p. 1835.

Evertson, C. M., and Smithey, M. W. (2001). Mentoring effects on protégé classroom practice. *Journal of Educational Research*, 93(5), 294–304.

Glover, J. (2001). *Children composing 4–14*. UK: Routledge.

Goodson, I. (2006). Teacher nostalgia and the sustainability of reform: The generation and degeneration of teachers' missions, memory, and meaning. *Educational Administration Quarterly*, 42(1), 42–61.

Gromko, J. E. (1995). Educating the reflective teacher. *Journal of Music Teacher Education*, 3, 8–13.

Jorgensen, E. R. (2011). *Pictures of Music Education*. Bloomington: Indiana University Press.

Kaschub, M., and Smith, J. P. (2009). *Minds on Music: Composition for Creative and Critical Thinking*. Lanham, MD: R & L Education—A Division of Rowman & Littlefield Publishers, Inc.

Killian, J. N., and Dye, K. G. (2009). Effects of learner-centered activities in preparation of music educators: Finding the teacher within. *Journal of Music Teacher Education*, i(1), 9–24.

Kratus, J. (2007). Music education at the tipping point. *Music Educators Journal*, 94(2), 42–48. doi: 10.1177/002743210709400209.

Lane, S., Lacefield-Parachini, N., and Isken, J. (2003). Developing novice teachers as change agents: Student teacher placements "against the grain." *Teacher Education Quarterly*, 30(2), 55–68.

Macfarlane, B. (2011). Professors as intellectual leaders: formation, identity and role. *Studies in Higher Education*, 36(1), pp. 57–73. doi: 10.1080/03075070903443734.

MENC (1994). *National standards for arts education*. Reston, VA: Music Educators National Conference.

Reimer, B. (1989). *A Philosophy of Music Education*, 2nd edition. New York: Prentice Hall.

Roberts, B. (2004). Who's in the mirror? Issues surrounding the identity construction of music educators. *Action, Criticism, and Theory for Music Education*, 3(2).

Sgroi, A. (1998) Teaching learning partnerships in the arts. In I. M. Saltiel, A. Sgroi, & R. G. Brockett (Eds.), *The Power and Potential of Collaborative Learning Partnerships*. San Francisco, CA: Jossey-Bass, pp. 23–32.

Shuler, S. C. (2011). Music education for life: The three artistic processes—paths to lifelong 21st-century skills through music. *Music Educators Journal*, I, 9–13. doi:10.1177/0027432111409828.

Stegman, S. F. (2007). An exploration of reflective dialogue between student teachers in music and their cooperating teachers. *Journal of Research in Music Education*, 55(1), 65–82.

Strand, K. (2006). A survey of Indiana music teachers on using composition in the classroom. *Journal of Research in Music Education*, 54(2), 154–167.

Timperly, H. (2001). Mentoring conversations designed to promote student teacher learning. *Asia-Pacific Journal of Teacher Education*, 29(2), 111–123.

UNESCO (2000). Definitions. Retrieved June 15, 2011 from the UNESCO website http://www.unesco.org/education/educprog/lwf/doc/portfolio/definitions.htm.

Wiggins, J. H. (1990). *Composition in the classroom*. Reston, VA: Music Educators National Conference.

Williams, D. A. (2007). What are music educators doing and how well are we doing it? *Music Educators Journal*, 94(1), 18–23.

Zachary, L. J. (2000). *The Mentor's Guide*. San Francisco, CA: Jossey-Bass.

Zull, J. E. (2002). *The Art of the Changing Brain*. Sterling, VA: Stylus.

SECTION } VII

Moving Forward

20 }

Enacting the Vision: Creating and Sustaining Meaningful Composition Programs

Betty Anne Younker

Introduction

This chapter includes an examination of composing within an undergraduate music education experience, specifically as a musical action and as an approach to constructing a life in music learning and teaching. Suggestions for engaging undergraduate music education students in such experiences and the types of support needed are presented. A vision of a future in which composing is a major aspect of the undergraduate music education experience concludes the chapter and the book.

Influences from the Past

From whence did we come? How have we become defined as a profession? What are the characteristics that identify the profession? Descriptive and informative accounts have been published, to which we refer when informing students of our heritage as framed by definitions and characteristics (e.g., McCarthy & Goble, 2005; Mark, 1996). Our roots in performance-based practices—with nods to conducting, as found in orchestral, choral, and band settings with the Western European art form serving as the canon—has solidified much of what is taught as well as has informed how we engage students in music-making. The role of the student in performance-based settings was typically one that was subservient to the conductor and teacher, thus viewed from a hegemonic stance, and excluded as a contributing member during technical and musical decision-making processes (e.g., Gould, 2008). While attention in recent years has been given to how students are engaged in ensembles, and as a result some changes have occurred, there is still much concern about the absence of students' critical engagement as informed, thinking musicians whose engagement includes a quality felt experience.

Listening as an engaged musical experience, as well as an integral part when performing and conducting, became explicit due to the work of Frances Clark who, during the 1930s and 1940s, offered guided listening experiences in conjunction with the new and ever-growing fund of LP materials. This was in response to the growing performance- and competition-based music education directed by utilitarian values, much of which was supported by the music business industry. This work continued at the University of Illinois by a variety of music educators, including Bennett Reimer, who wrote extensively on the experience of engaged and creative listening (2003). Subsequent writings viewed listening as part of the performing and conducting experience in addition to a "stand alone" experience, while others viewed musical experiences as all-encompassing of everyone who contributed to a musical occurrence (Small, 1998). The desire of "musicking," the act of music action, was to experience successful musicking or quality musicking, that is, to experience the richest experience possible given what one has in one's context and fund of experience.

The 1950s and 1960s witnessed the profession examining how students were involved, which was primarily through performing, and with what kind of music, which was primarily with the canon from the Western European art form. Symposia such as the 1968 Tanglewood Symposium called for music educators to involve students in music-making that included composing and improvising, and with diverse music from around the world and of varying genres and styles. Technology was viewed as an instrument through and with which music could be composed (Mark, 1996). The call was to add on to what already existed in the undergraduate curriculum—to include more content. This call to "add on" continued with a variety of curricular and school vision documents as put forth by MENC, including the standards as found in the national standards documents (1994). Students were to engage in a variety of musical actions including performing, listening, reading and writing, composing, critiquing, and improvising. Again, however, the call was about what students were to do in addition to what was already expected.

While one could argue that in response to such calls, music programs across the country have grown beyond the performance-based traditional settings to include garage bands, iPhone orchestras, composers who compose with and for acoustic instruments, composers who compose with and for technology, composers who mix acoustic and technological instruments, sound engineers, jazz bands, musical theatre ensembles, opera productions, show choirs, marching bands, pep bands, glee clubs, guitar clubs, and so on and so forth, the majority of experiences during the undergraduate degree program occurs in large ensembles, chamber music, and studio lessons with a very specific repertoire and master/apprentice engagement. There are multiple educators in these settings who engage students in critical inquiry in and with music; however, the focus is mainly on the content of repertoire and performance as the goal. One could also argue that engagements in multiple settings as listed above just might reflect the same experiences as those that involve specific repertoire and reflect master/apprentice engagement. So while the content has increased, the quality and kind of engagements experienced remain the same.

The crux of the issue, then, is that we need to shift our thinking beyond what is taught to how students are engaged and what those experiences feel like—the quality of the felt experience. We need to get beyond packaging, distributing, and standardizing content and teaching and learning. We need to unpack how students are engaged when they rehearse, practice, perform, discuss, memorize, analyze, evaluate, write, discriminate, and identify music as well as think and apply information about music. We also need to unpack why and how informed choices are made about when to abide by rules that govern musical decisions as well as why and how choices are made that expand or discard the rules.

The shift, therefore, needs to include systemic changes; to continue to add on to what is already experienced is to contribute to the system. It does not address changes in quality and the felt experience. Examining what organizes the experiences, and how organizers can engage students in fluid, dynamic, and dialectical thinking requires systemic changes. Such changes affect and relate to the system as a whole—the whole body as distinct from having a local effect. This differs from a systematic change, one that is carried out in a methodical and organized manner, and uses a method or system for organization in a deliberate and regular manner in accordance with a system of taxonomic classification. Systemic resembles life; systematic resembles how things are organized and standardized.

To organize undergraduate experiences based on systemic changes resembles life that evolves through critical and creative examination. It remains closed temporarily as decisions are evaluated only to reopen as experiences are encountered with imagination and curiosity. Systems tend to close and become formalized. Evaluations may require change, but only within the system and in relation to local concerns. The overall structure, therefore, becomes institutionalized and quite possibly calcified. The former resembles philosophical inquiry while the latter, ideological cement blocks.

For this chapter, it is through the lens of systemic changes that "composing" a life is viewed. Bateson (1989) wrote about "composing a life" in which themes of cooperation and competition, symmetry, and complementarity occur throughout. Bateson writes about how lives are composed by discovering the shape of how each is created in the process of living as opposed to travelling toward a vision already defined.

Taking chances, improvising, and innovating are part of the shaping of life, one that is continuous in its growth as redirection of life occurs. During this evolution, that which is familiar is recombined into new understandings within contexts of interactions and responses. Such evolution does not occur a-contextually or locally, but contextually to the whole—thus reflecting systemic changes. The experience offers balance and diversity and involves the dialectical pull of tension and release. It involves that which is familiar and unfamiliar as we intersect with situations that cause us to stop and reflect (Dewey, 1938). It requires imagination and taking risks as "curiosity seekers" (Allsup, 2011).

So how might "composing a life" as an undergraduate music education student be felt while learning and teaching in and about music—while experiencing music— while musicking? How might such experiences make explicit the responsibilities of maintaining and transforming ourselves, and those with whom we engage in music? How might such experiences make explicit the responsibilities of examining through a critical lens why we might maintain, or why and how we must transform that which defines and characterizes the profession?

This chapter is less about what students should learn and what kind of music in which they should engage and more about how students need to be engaged. It is more about how dispositions of curiosity, imagination and openness, fairness, trust, and responsibility, as well as engaging in reciprocal and dialectical relationships, are all core to engagements in music and life. These dispositions and engagements can be reflected in multiple acts of musicking, including composing. It is the act of composing that will serve as the focus, specifically as a musical action and as a process to experience learning during one's music education.

A Theoretical Framework

Four democratic principles will frame the approach to composing an undergraduate life in music education and composing as a musical action. They include: sound reasoning, fairness, responsibility, and reciprocity. I turn to Dewey (1916, 1938), Giroux (2001), Rawls (1999), and Kozol (1991, 2005) for guidance. Dewey's influence on those who have written and presently write about issues related to learning and teaching is widely felt. Many of his core ideas have been clarified, built upon, and implemented. Giroux's writings are helpful, particularly his contributions about citizenship education, which are broad and deep, and concise and clear. Rawls' examination of issues related to social democracy—in which citizenship education is critical—is all-encompassing and thorough. In addition, he draws on Dewey, amongst other writers, and delves extensively into what it means to live and work in circles where justice in educational settings is expected, implemented, and evaluated on a continuous basis. To focus on such principles allows us space to consider the breadth and depth of musicking that music education students experience and the level of marginalized thinking that occurs in such experiences, both in terms of musical actions and engagement.

Sound reasoning involves logical thinking when finding results or drawing conclusions. As one thinks through a problem or situation in a logical fashion, one identifies the issue, diverges while generating solutions, converges on a solution, and evaluates while implementing the solution(s). Because one never accepts what is or what was without constant critical reflection, one becomes involved in a cycle that is recursive (Dewey, 1916; 1938). This disposition to engage in critical reflection avoids dogmatic and ideological thinking, thus challenges the status quo. Reasonableness involves being capable of making rational judgments. We, as humans, are capable of making rational judgments; it is a human condition. The consistency and level of being reasonable as we interact is a result of many things, including expectations and quality of education within family, schools, and larger communities.

Kozol (1991, 2005) identified two critical characteristics of educative interactions (he uses Dewey's definition of educative; that which contributes to growth) as fairness and responsibility. To be fair is to afford spaces for those invested voices to be heard as decisions are made. With this voice, however, comes a responsibility to be informed, fair, and reasonable. There is a responsibility, an ethical duty, on the part of those who educate and are educated to guide students in their growth as rational thinkers. It is also the responsibility of the educators and those being educated to acquire the necessary knowledge and understanding to think logically, and make informed decisions and rational judgments. Without knowledge and understanding, we make decisions and render judgments based on ignorance—a characteristic that often results in behavior that is intolerant and discriminatory, dogmatic and ideological. To be effective when educating, we need to assess our students so that we recognize who they are, understand what they know and have experienced, and realize what they need to understand and experience so that they can be fully involved in their musical communities. The obligation to treat others without harm, with fairness, and to be just in our dealings (Rawls, 1999) requires a critical mind and value for citizenship education (Giroux, 2001).

Finally, an overarching necessary characteristic is reciprocity. Dewey (1916) defines reciprocity as "a mode of associated living, of conjoint communicated experience" (p. 87). This experience would counter hegemonic experiences in which one is a master, the podium "determines," and a methodology or theory "prescribes." Engagement that involves reciprocity would be experienced as learning and teaching, and guiding and following, as informed and reflective individuals give back in meaningful ways to the community. The experiences afford spaces for growth and transformation of the individual and community to deeper levels of understanding.

Bowman (2007) causes us to pause as he reminds us that just providing and adopting such characteristics globally is more about injustice than it is about justice. What might appear to be fair in one context based on one's opinion might be completely unfair in that or another context. How words are actualized and experienced across contexts needs careful consideration. As a result, this requires us to ask questions other than what is typically asked when examining educational experiences. It might be less about defining and acting upon the definitions and more about dispositions that are needed to discern what is just and for whom, when, and where. Examining the "how" in situated contexts and desired dispositions of those who successfully engage in such a process is critical when identifying characteristics that support educative spaces.

Dewey (1938) reminds us that such principles can afford spaces at the center of our thinking for students as the decisions are made about what will be covered and how the students will be involved as reflective participants. The need, then, is to examine *who* is in our environments, and *why*, *how*, *where*, and *what* we teach. In these described communities, students can be transformed through active engagement that requires flexibility, adaptability, curiosity, and imagination (e.g., Dewey, 1938; Donovan, Bransford, & Pellegrino, 1999; Eisner, 1998; Goodlad, 2004).

As students experience composing a life and composing as a musical action, they can be guided to approach each with dispositions that reflect (at least) the four principles as outlined above. In composing, one can value rights, including the right to be treated based on sound reasoning, as well as fairly and justly, and without harm; and to have access and a voice that critically examines traditions within one's community. With these notions of being, composing can be approached with understanding and value of the codes and rules and yet with opportunities to perfect, expand on, or discard those rules, thus allowing for creations to evolve from the inside-out. Students are engaged in decisions about why and when to maintain or transform that which is and can be, whether rules are to be adhered to or not; and how choices are informed and critically evaluated. Such engagements can nurture students to be "curiosity seekers" (Allsup, 2011) and doers in musicking (Small, 1998). The need to know the composer's intent is critical but as Allsup suggests, the composer is now a "guest" and "advisor" as the student and teacher work through decisions about the performance. In turn, the performer becomes a "guest" as the listener structures the listening experience. This allows for open-ended experiences in which imagination and possibilities are in the foreground of the enactments. It allows for reasonableness, integrity, and responsibility to what is given as part of the tradition and what is either refined or transformed.

Composing: A Brief View of What We Know

Earlier pioneers in the field include Wiggins (1992, 2003), whose examples and results of engaging students in group composition activities in elementary general music settings provided insights for those who were curious. Programs such as Yamaha: Music in Education provided possibilities through keyboards and structured activities. Paynter and Aston (1970) and Schafer (1975) offered ways to engage students of all ages in composition-like activities with Schafer's approach being identified with ones that purported found sounds, exploratory experiences, and as much focus on the experience (process) as the ultimate product.

Historically, there have been calls for inclusion of composition in K–12 settings (e.g., the Tanglewood Symposium). However, there was minimal direction for music educators at the university level about pedagogical considerations when engaging students in composition, nor was there direction about gaining experience in composition in order to guide such music-making. Music educators at the collegiate level bring a fund of performing, conducting, and listening experiences, but typically not composing experiences. The influence of the Tanglewood Symposium document is found in NAfME publications, including the National Standards (1994) in which ways to engage students were articulated, one including composition. The *Young Composers Project* that occurred in the late 1950s and early 1960s brought composers into classrooms for the purposes of creating music for ensembles and guiding students in composition-based activities, but again guidance about pedagogy and composing experiences were minimal at best.

What was absent in these documents and activities was direct attention to undergraduate music education programs and *how* to engage students in composing activities. What received attention was on *what* should be taught. This also was, and still is, evident in composing activities as outlined in the various methodologies and approaches that have influenced the field, e.g., Kodaly methodology, Orff pedagogy and Music Learning Theory. While informative, the content is bound culturally and stylistically and offered in prescriptive manners that can close down notions of imagination and curiosity. Two publications have begun to address these issues (e.g., Hickey, 2003, Kaschub & Smith, 2009) but much remains to be understood, particularly for the undergraduate student experience.

Integration of composition into a music education sequence is more than adding yet another course or requiring composition activities within existing courses as found in typical music education degree programs. While either or both of these approaches could be beneficial and involve students in composition across multiple semesters, it would not be as effective as an interwoven fund of experience that engages students in composing. As one can consider composing a life as articulated by Bateson (1998), one could consider composing an undergraduate experience through performance, listening, conducting, *and* composing. Just as performance, conducting, and listening are integral experiences across the undergraduate degree program, so could composing be. Just as students experience and understand the role of performing, conducting, and listening in music-making, so would they begin to understand the role of composing in music-making.

Since the 1980s there has been a body of research dedicated to processes and strategies as made explicit by students while composing, all of which has been informative. The field, however, has yet to incorporate the ideas into undergraduate curriculum mainly because we as the faculty have not experienced such processes, nor have, for the most part, the undergraduate students. This body of research includes but is not limited to insights about (1) utilization of processes and strategies when asked to compose a piece of music (Barrett, 1996; Bunting, 1987; Burnard, 2000a/b; Christensen, 1993; Citron, 1992; Daignault, 1996; Hickey, 1995; Levi, 1991; Sundin, McPherson, and Folkestad, 1998; Wiggins, 1992; Younker, 2000a/b); (2) strategic processes identifiable within a developmental progression as exhibited by "novice" and "expert" composers (Colley, Banton, Down, & Pither, 1992; Davidson & Welsh, 1988; Younker & Smith, 1992, 1996); (3) time spent on differing composing processes (Ainsworth, 1970; Kratus, 1989); (4) the role of creative thinking in composition (Burnard & Younker, 2002; Younker & Burnard, 2002); and (5) pedagogical, assessment, and curricular issues related to composition (e.g., Hickey, 2003; Kaschub & Smith, 2009; Paynter & Aston, 1970; Schafer, 1975; Wiggins, 2003; Younker, 2003).

In addition, educators have investigated and created musical environments in which musical decisions are mainly student-directed, often composition or rock-based settings as opposed to the more traditional large-ensemble-based settings (e.g., Green, 2002; Jaffurs, 2004). These music educators have reminded us of the importance of examining music education programs, i.e., what constitutes a program and how students are engaged in learning. What do these experiences "feel" like and what is the quality of engagement?

This body of literature can inform us as we integrate such roles and processes in our classroom as students analyze, discuss, evaluate, create and re-create music. Publications such as these have offered insights about why and how to incorporate composition and can guide the profession. What is needed, however, are models that represent comprehensive inclusion of composing as a musical action throughout the undergraduate experience as well as reflections of composing a life as one who engages in music-making in mindful and open ways.

Moving Forward: One Vision for the Inclusion of Composing

Following are ideas viewed through the theoretical framework of democratic principles and within the metaphor of "composing a life." In this next section, I will offer ideas for including composing across an undergraduate music education degree program. The reader is cautioned that while these ideas have been articulated in a variety of conversations in formal and informal settings with colleagues in music education and across disciplines as found in schools of music, what is offered is theoretical; thus, yet to be implemented and experienced. The author invites you to open your mind to imagine what is yet to be experienced and thus understood, but is believed to be possible.

When constructing a curriculum that includes the aforementioned characteristics as described above, fundamental questions should *guide* the construction: (1) How do we want our students to "feel" during their undergraduate experience, as well when they move on to become contributing members to the musical communities and communities at large? (2) How should students be engaged while experiencing the program? (3) What might those engagements be? Structures that can *facilitate* and *guide* interactions and critical involvement could include: (1) What, why, and how (knowledge- and process-centered) with a focus on connecting across disciplines and examining relevance to ensure that transfer is transparent. (2) Who, how, and why (learner-centered), with a focus on what the student brings to the experience, and how to ensure relevancy is consistent, and notions of caring and spaces for intellectual play are afforded. (3) Evidence (assessment-centered) to assess the kind of learning that occurred within the context of the experiences with a focus on evidence of the quality of the experiences (Bransford et al., 2005).

WHAT IS EXPERIENCED?

Typically speaking, we hear ourselves advising performance majors to "get through the first two years of the core curriculum" so that by the time one reaches third and fourth year, one can indulge in more options. Often times, students enter first year already knowing the rules and closed-bound systems so continuing to follow the regime of "taking care of business" is natural and comforting. Once the student reaches third year, he or she either takes the reigns, imagining the possibilities while exploring other interests in addition to what is required in the performance degree program, *or* appears increasingly uneasy about what life is all about. For the latter type of student, the notion of being able to choose and follow whatever interests are appealing or to even imagine what might be appealing is minimal at best. These are the students who realize that they do not know what they want to do after graduation. They have acquired an infliction called "senioritis." A third group of students continues to focus and hone their performance craft while completing requirements for the next degree—often in business, arts administration, medicine, law, or "part two" of their second major, taken in addition to performance.

What of the music education students? They move through the core curriculum during their first two years, in addition to beginning what is required for the music education degree. By their third and fourth year, their course of study becomes more refined and focused as they concentrate on an instrumental or choral/vocal track while completing a course or two on the other track. Their experiences become or stay just as closed-bounded because they are regulated by a variety of accrediting bodies, state regulations, and university requirements. Often times, however, if we examine each individual accrediting body, regulation, and requirement, it is revealed that there are varying levels of closed-bounded nooses; it is the combination of all that binds students to an experience. Due to the quantity of courses and content, to which the profession has added, in response to the calls of previous decades, curriculum to ensure students are knowledgeable about technology; world music; special learners; jazz; popular music; composing, improvising, performing, reading, writing and critiquing in all of the areas; the need for content to be delivered via rule-governed, packaged, prescriptive means is quite evident (The length of this sentence is deliberate to feel the burden of the undergraduate degree program!). What if music education students (and all students in music degrees) experienced a more fluid and dynamic first two years during which the process was in the foreground and content less burdensome? This would reflect what Pink (2006) describes as more the conceptual age and less the information age. What would that feel like?

Possibilities: Examining New Wine in New Bottles

What follows are descriptions of courses taken during the undergraduate music education experience. The content has been intentionally less prescriptive about set content and more focused on how students could be engaged.

COURSES ACROSS THE SCHOOL OF MUSIC

For understanding in and about composing, students would take composition lessons in addition to performance lessons and belong to a chamber group as required by the degree program. For students to be afforded time to engage in multiple years of chamber music, a balance of credit hours involving large and small ensembles would be required. The requirements for the group would be to learn and perform music relevant for that group and works written by the students in the group. Compositions would reflect knowledge and rules followed, extended, and discarded, as understood in music theory and history classes. Students would respond to each others' work, thus constituting a "working" group for each student composer. The notion of closure (converging) and opening (diverging) would be reinforced as ideas are offered and responded to throughout the process. The integral role of peer interaction in collaborative group processes has been made explicit in the talk of children while composing (Macdonald & Miell, 2000a/b) and deemed a valuable process in collaborative group processes across ages and musical tuition.

Music history choices would include what is currently offered in addition to what is typically offered to non-majors (e.g., jazz, musical theatre, music of other cultures, rock and roll, popular song writing). Students would be required to complete a certain number of credit hours but not all would be required to complete the same courses. Representations of understanding (Eisner, 1998) as forms of assessment in the classes would include composing a life as lived in the era—politically, socially, culturally, and musically, with knowledge of stylistic and aesthetic characteristics as well as political, social, and cultural ramifications. Students would bring to life a composer through writing papers, providing lecture recitals, engaging in debates that would reflect political and cultural issues of the time, creating scenes that would reflect life as experienced by the composer while engaged in composition.

Election of music theory courses would reflect music history choices. Representations of understanding include composing utilizing the rules that govern the style, genre, and culture as well as bending, extending, or discarding the rules; these representations would be the means for how students would be assessed. Students would continue to assess themselves and others as they engaged in performances of their own and others' compositions, and to respond thoughtfully by representing understanding about choices made with regard to knowledge acquired.

Piano classes would require students to acquire skills through learning repertoire necessary to function in K–5 music classes and choral settings found in middle and high schools. Students would also be required to transpose, arrange, and compose in the style of music as reflected in the repertoire. Knowledge from theory classes and composing lessons would be utilized in the arranging and composing experiences.

MUSIC EDUCATION COURSES

Introduction to music education classes would involve unpacking musical experiences and understandings acquired by students thus far. Reflections on their leadership roles taken on before entering university would be expanded to identifying and describing dispositions and attributes of successful leaders who nurture, guide, and lead as needed. These characteristics would be compared with those of educators and musicians who students have had in previous years, as well as in their current year. Who are the models and how do those mentors emulate educative environments? How did those models and mentors contribute to their identity as it was shaped through musical experiences accumulated before entering schools of music? What are the values that shape their identities as musicians and leaders in their past and current musical worlds? What dispositions and attributes as musicians and musical leaders will contribute to their evolving educator identity?

The conversations in the introduction class should continue to examine and re-examine what is valued as music and music-making and how future judgments about what constitutes music and music-making should be informed and reasoned. Experiencing and reflecting on the above should occur throughout all of their engagements in subsequent music education classes.

Continuation of music education courses incorporating the traditions of what characterizes our profession and possibilities would be based on the foundations of performing and composing. One such course would be in music technology, in which students would learn about software through editing, arranging, composing, and improvising, and gain insights about mashups, raps, re-mixes, a cappella forms of the song. Identifying how music is evaluated in terms of quality and criteria relevant to the style and genre would be made explicit. While students cannot learn all styles and relevant criteria, focusing on selected styles could enable them to gain a deeper understanding about the characteristics of those styles and in turn, understand notions of craftsmanship and expressiveness that characterize quality within the style.

Other courses would cover that which has influenced the field and what has been not included. Examinations can occur through composing and performing in rule-bound activities as prescribed by the approaches and methodologies as well as combinations and rejection of such rules. What would be the opposite boundary of the given rule?

Non-music electives would include but not be limited to psychology, sociology, political science, humanities, critical theory, and arts policy content-based courses during the four years. The content of these courses could be interwoven throughout conversations in music education to make explicit the context and role of, as well as issues related to, music-making. Students would not necessarily have to take the same courses at the same time but rather would be bearers of information for others in the course who in turn, would carry those beginnings of understanding as they would take the course. Such a diverse fund of experiences would enrich the class as students and faculty members would shift in the roles of learner and teacher.

OVERALL CONSIDERATIONS: THE BIGGER PICTURE

In each of the areas, quantity of representations is less important than depth and breadth of understanding as reflected in each assignment. Experiences of imagining and curiosity are paramount. Experiences shape spaces for students to explore, identify, analyze, compare, synthesize and evaluate responsibly, processes necessary in music-making, including composing, and as one composes a life. There is an understanding of reciprocity in the relationships between student and teacher, student and music, student and composer, and student and student. For such relationships to develop, levels of trust, honesty, and fairness are critical, as are openness to spaces for voices to be heard.

Other conversations need to continue about making explicit what they are experiencing in practice rooms, large and small ensembles, studio classes, composing and performing lessons, juries and recitals. What are the processes involved? What is the role of such experiences in music-making and what insights are gained? The unpacking, identifying, analyzing, and synthesizing, evaluating, and the practice of plunging back into diverging and exploring must be constant processes throughout the musicking and the reflecting on music. As students create and recreate, the roles that they experience would become explicit. These roles would include, but are not limited to, those as encountered by sound engineers, composers, performers, critics, conductors, theorists, historians, teachers, and students in fluid and dynamic fashions. Finally, growth in musicking, that which is successful and of quality, should and can occur throughout the experiences (Small, 1998).

Challenges Embraced by "Curiosity-Seekers"

The conversations that will have to occur at undergraduate curriculum meetings amongst music education faculty and with colleagues across departments in schools of music are multifaceted. The first is about the responsibility of music educators to experience music as broadly and deeply as possible. As noted earlier, because of the quantity of music and ways in which music can be experienced, we cannot expect future students to know the breadth and depth of content, and experience the multiple forms of music-making. We can, however, expect students to experience with imagination and curiosity while doing *something* with what knowledge and skills are acquired. It is the doing of *something* that is critical, as noted above (e.g., Dewey, 1938; Goodlad, 2004; Pink, 2006). In addition, we can expect students to engage democratically reflecting the principles as outlined above. Finally, we can nurture habits of mind to imagine that which we do not know and provide spaces for courage to grow, which is needed to embrace the unknown and the messiness of living (Jorgensen, 2008).

A second conversation should illuminate how musicianship/musicking can evolve through performing *and* composing with the disposition to imagine throughout that evolution. The point is not for K–12 music educators to "create" composers any more than it is for them to "create" performers; the point is to engage K–12 students in ways in which the creation and re-creation of music is experienced in environments that reflect the characteristics as made evident in this chapter with the focus on the felt experience and not just on the content covered.

A third conversation is needed to make explicit that which is in place, but not utilized by music education students because of the closed-bounded, rule-governed models of the undergraduate curriculum. Schools of music currently offer much of what has been suggested in this section. Music education students, however, often do not have access to such offerings. A critical examination of that which we think binds us (beginning with National Association of Schools of Music, since other accrediting bodies refer to and acknowledge NASM guidelines) will reveal that degree programs as devised at the institutional level are often more binding than the accrediting body. As a result of such an examination we might view curriculum as more open-ended as students progress through the program so that they can engage with what is being learned, and thus be metacognitively involved during the learning. For example, the directive is not "You need to read music" but rather the question is, "Do you need to read music to become functional musical participants in [x] musical culture?"

A fourth conversation must be continued with those in the field. The challenge is to find field placements in which composition is offered in addition to performance-based experiences. The understanding is that not all programs will offer both; thus, it is necessary to seek out diverse settings in which to place music education students. One model, as made explicit by Tobias (2011), is to engage summer masters students in composing experiences, as they will, in turn, engage their students during the next academic year. It could be that the undergraduate students' notions of music-making might be more solidified because they have just come from traditional music settings. The teachers in the field are dealing with the current generation's music, which is experienced in informal settings and which provides first-hand insights about what is current. With the pace of technology and fusions of musical styles and genres as currently experienced, the generation span has shortened considerably. We in university settings must be open about learning from the undergraduate students as they become informed in composing. We can approach the experience with the same dispositions and attributes expected of our students; that is, being responsible to reciprocity, trust, openness, fairness, imagination, curiosity, and being just and reasonable.

Final Thoughts

Bourne (2007) ends her book with the following paragraph:

> Students in our world deserve a chance. If they receive only limited opportunities to experience and express joy anywhere else, than let it occur inside the music class. The music teacher constructs an environment where all children are welcomed, they know what's expected of them, they are encouraged to achieve, and they know someone cares about their existence. That's the heart. The teacher also creates a learning climate of rigor, challenges and new

awareness. That's the art. Both are necessary and are channeled by the teacher's ability to inspire and see the positive potential in each student. Together, they bring results that feed two souls—the music teacher and the child. What could be better than that? (p. 144)

As we construct communities of learning, it is our duty to structure learning and the environment with sound reasoning, fairness, responsibility, and reciprocity at the core. In the context of this chapter, engagements that embrace these characteristics afford educative growth through composing. The profession continues to examine how and why students are engaged with music and each other. It is through careful scrutiny that beliefs and assumptions are examined and challenged. It is only through such scrutiny that informed decisions can be made about structure, content, and processes that define music programs in university settings. Ultimately, the goal is to be doing the best we can with what we have and have acquired. That is a process that is cultivated and honed with each fund of experience.

References

Ainsworth, J. (1970). Research project in creativity in music education. *Bulletin of the Council for Research in Music Education*, 22, 43–48.

Allsup, R. (2011). The compositional turn in music education. Keynote address presented at the *Leaders in Music Education* conference, The University of Western Ontario, London, Ontario, May.

Barrett, M. (1996). *Children's aesthetic decision-making: An analysis of children's musical discourse as composers*. Doctoral dissertation, Monash University, Australia.

Bateson, M. C. (1989). *Composing a life*. New York: Grove Press.

Bourne, P. (2007). *Inside the music classroom: Teaching the art with heart*. Dayton, Ohio: Heritage Press, A division of the Lorenz Corporation.

Bowman, W. (2007). "Who's Asking? (Who's Answering?) Theorizing Social Justice in Music Education." *Action, Criticism, and Theory for Music Education* 6/4: 1–20. http://act.maydaygroup.org/articles/BowmanEditorial6_4.pdf.

Bransford, J., Derry, S., Berliner, D., Hammerness, K., & Beckett, K. L. (2005). Theories of learning and their roles in teaching. In L. Darling-Hammond & J. Bransford (Eds.), *Preparing teachers for a changing world: What teachers should learn and be able to do* (pp. 40–87). San Francisco, California: Jossey-Bass.

Bunting, R. (1987). Composing music. Case studies in the teaching and learning process. *British Journal of Music Education*, 4 (1), 25–52.

Burnard, P. (2000a). Examining experiential differences between improvisation and composition in children's music-making. *British Journal of Music Education*, 17 (3), 227–245.

Burnard, P. (2000b). How children ascribe meaning to improvisation and composing. *Music Education Research*, 2(1), 7–23.

Burnard, P. & Younker, B. A. (2002). Mapping pathways: Fostering creativity in composition. *Music Education Research*, 4(2), 245–261. Paper co-presented at *The Second International Research in Music Education Conference*, Exeter, England, April, 2001.

Christensen, C. B. (1993). Music composition, invented notation, and reflection in a fourth grade music class. Paper presented at the *Symposium on Research in General Music*. University of Arizona, Tucson.

Citron, V. (1992). Where's the eraser?: Computer-assisted composition with young music students. Paper presented as part of a panel, *The computer as catalyst: Creating opened-ended music tasks to foster musical thinking from kindergarten through conservatory* (Vicki Citron, Harold McAnaney, & Larry Scripp). ATMI Conference, San Diego.

Colley, A., Banton, L., Down, J., & Pither, A. (1992). An expert-novice comparison in musical composition. *Psychology of Music*, 20, 124–137.

Daignault, L. (1996). *Children's creative musical thinking within the context of a computer-supported improvisational approach to composition.* Unpublished doctoral dissertation, Northwestern University, Evanston, IL.

Davidson, L., & Welsh, P. (1988). From collections to structure: The developmental path of tonal thinking. In J. A. Sloboda (Ed.), *Generative processes in music: The psychology of performance, improvisation, and composition.* New York: Oxford University Press.

Dewey, J. (1916). *Democracy and education.* New York: The Free Press, A division of Simon and Schuster, Inc.

Dewey, J. (1938). *Experience and education.* New York: Collier Books, Macmillan Publishing Company.

Donovan, M. S., Bransford, J. D., & Pellegrino, J. W. (Eds.) (1999). *How people learn: Bridging research and practice.* Washington, DC: National Academy Press.

Eisner, E. W. (1998). *The kind of schools we need.* Portsmouth, NH: Heinemann.

Giroux, H. (2001). *Theory and resistance in education.* Westport, CT: Bergin & Garvey.

Goodlad, J. I. (2004). *Romances with schools.* New York: McGraw-Hill.

Gould, E. (2008). Devouring the other: Democracy in music education. *Action, Criticism, and Theory for Music Education* 7(1), 29–44. http://act.maydaygroup.org/articles/Gould7_1.pdf

Green, L. (2002). *How popular musicians learn: A way ahead for music education.* London, England: Ashgate Popular and Folk Music Series, Ashgate Publishing.

Hickey, M. (1995). *Qualitative and quantitative relationships between children's creative musical thinking processes and products.* Unpublished doctoral dissertation, Northwestern University, Evanston, IL.

Hickey, M. (Ed.) (2003). *Music composition in the schools: A new horizon for music education.* Reston, VA: MENC The National Association for Music Education.

Jaffurs, S. (2004). The impact of informal music learning practices in the classroom or how I learned how to teach from a garage band. *International Journal of Music Education: Practice*, 22(3), 201–218.

Jorgensen, E. (2008). *The art of teaching music.* Bloomington: Indiana University Press.

Kaschub, M., and Smith, J. P. (2009). *Minds on Music: Composition for Creative and Critical Thinking.* Lanham, Maryland: R&L Education—A Division of Rowman & Littlefield Publishers, Inc.

Kozol, J. (2005). *The shame of the nation: The restoration of apartheid schooling in America.* New York: Three Rivers Press, an imprint of the Crown Publishing Group, a division of Random House, Inc.

Kozol J. (1991). *Savage inequalities: Children in America's schools*. New York: Harper-Collins.

Kratus, J. (1989). A time analysis of the compositional processes used by children ages 7 to 11. *Journal of Research in Music Education*, 37(1), 5–20.

Levi, R. (1991). Investigating the creative process: The role of regular musical composition experiences for the elementary child. *Journal of Creative Behavior*, 25(2), 123–136.

Macdonald, R., & Miell, D. (2000a) Creativity and music education: The impact of social variables. *International Journal of Music Education*, 36, 58–68.

Macdonald, R., & Miell, D. (2000b) "Musical Conversations: Collaborating with a friend on creative tasks." In R. Joiner, K. Littleton, K., D. Faulkner, and D. Miell (eds.), *Rethinking Collaborative Learning*, pp. 65–78. Free Association Books.

Mark, M. (1996). *Contemporary music education* (3rd edition). New York: Schirmer Books: An Imprint of Simon & Schuster Macmillan.

McCarthy, M. S., & Goble, J. S. (2005) The praxial philosophy in historical perspective. In David J. Elliott, *Praxial music education: reflections and dialogues*. New York: Oxford University Press.

NAfME (1994). *The school music program: A new vision*. Reston, VA: Music Educators National Conference.

NAfME (1994). *National standards for arts education*. Reston, VA: Music Educators National Conference.

Paynter, J., & Aston, P. (1970). *Sound and silence*. Cambridge: Cambridge University Press.

Pink, D. H. (2006). *A Whole new mind*. New York: Riverhead Books.

Rawls, J. (1999). *A theory of justice* (revised edition). Cambridge, MA: The Belknap Press of Harvard University Press.

Reimer, B. (2003). *A Philosophy of Music Education: Advancing the Vision* (3rd Edition). Englewood Cliffs, New Jersey: Prentice-Hall.

Schafer, R. M. (1975). *The rhinoceros in the classroom*. Canada: Universal Edition.

Small, C. (1998). *Musicking: The meanings of performing and listening*. Hanover, NH: Wesleyan University Press.

Sundin, B., McPherson, G., & Folkestad, G. (1998). *Children composing*. Sweden: Lund University.

Tobias, E., Van Klompenberg, A., and Reid, C. (2011). Reflecting on the transformative potential of digital and participatory culture in music education. Paper presented at *Mountain Lake Colloquium for Teachers of General Music*, May.

Wiggins, J. H. (1992). *The nature of children's musical learning in the context of a music classroom*. Unpublished doctoral dissertation, University of Illinois at Urbana-Champaign.

Wiggins, J. H. (2003). A frame for understanding children's compositional processes. In M. Hickey (Ed.), *Music composition in the schools: A new horizon for music education* (pp. 141–165). Reston, VA: MENC.

Younker, B. A. (2000a). Thought processes and strategies of students engaged in music composition. *Research Studies in Music Education*, 14, 24–39.

Younker, B. A. (2000b). Composing with voice: Students' strategies, thought processes, and reflections. In B. A. Robetrts (Ed.), *The Phenomenon of Singing*, Proceedings of the International Symposium, St. John's, Newfoundland, Canada. pp. 247–260. Paper presented at *The Phenomenon of Singing International Symposium* II, St. John's, Newfoundland, Canada. June, 1999.

Younker, B. A. (2003). The nature of feedback in a community of composers. In (M. Hickey, ed.), *Music composition in the schools: A new horizon for music education*, pp. 233–242. Reston, VA: MENC The National Association for Music Education.

Younker, B. A., & Burnard, P. (2002). Composing realities: Problem finding and solving in the musical worlds of student composers—an international perspective. Paper co-presented for the roundtable session of Focus Area III: Across virtualities and realities at the *ISME 2002 World Conference in Music Education*, Bergen, Norway, August.

Younker, B. A., & Smith, W. H., Jr. (1992). Modeling the thought processing structure of high school and adult expert and novice composers. Poster presented at the poster session at the annual meeting of the *Music Educators' National Conference*, New Orleans, LA: April.

Younker, B. A., & Smith, W. H., Jr. (1996). Comparing and modeling musical thought processes of expert and novice composers. *Bulletin of the Council for Research in Music Education*, 128, 25–36.

CONTRIBUTORS

Randall Everett Allsup is Assistant Professor of Music and Music Education at Teachers College Columbia University. His research focuses on the problems and promises of pluralism, democratic learning environments, teacher preparation, and democratic and moral philosophy. He is past chair of the International Society for the Philosophy of Music Education (ISPME). He serves on the advisory boards of the *Bulletin of the Council for Research in Music Education, Finnish Journal of Music Education*, and *Music Education Research*.

Bruce Carter is Assistant Professor of Music at the University of Maryland. His current qualitative work explores intersections of social justice and music education. He has authored chapters in several books and articles in journals such as *Music Educators Journal, American Educational Research Journal*, and the *Bulletin of the Council for Research in Music Education*.

Richard Dammers is Associate Professor of Music Education and Chairperson of the Music Department at Rowan University. His research interests include comprehensive musicianship and technology in music education. Prior to teaching at Rowan, he was a music teacher (band and technology) and the Fine Arts Facilitator in the Ladue School District in suburban St. Louis. He has authored articles in the *Bulletin of the Council for Research in Music Education, Contributions to Music Education*, and *Update: Application of Research in Music Education*.

Daniel Deutsch has been Director of the student composition program in the Three Village Central School District (Stony Brook, NY) since 1990. As the founding chairperson of the New York State School Music Association composition/improvisation committee, he has helped to lead a major initiative in the fields of composition and improvisation in New York. He was appointed the first chairperson of the Council for Music Composition of the National Association for Music Education (2011–2014) and also serves as national chairperson of the NAfME Student Composers Competition. He has presented many sessions on teaching composition at educational institutions and at national, division, and state conferences, and his articles on composition pedagogy have been published in music education journals. He studied music at Yale University (BA, *magna cum laude*), Stony Brook University (MA), and Columbia University (DMA). His awards include the National Endowment for the Arts Composers Fellowship Grant, grants from Meet The Composer, Columbia University's Rapaport Composition Prize, and two Harvard Club of Long Island Distinguished Teacher Awards.

Gena R. Greher is Associate Professor of Music at the University of Massachusetts Lowell where she teaches undergraduate and graduate music classes. Her research interests focus on: integrating multimedia technology in urban music classrooms, the effects of school-university partnerships on music teacher education, as well as a music technology intervention program for teens on the autism spectrum. Her National Science Foundation–funded research at the intersection of music and computer science has resulted in several publications, conference presentations, and the creation of new interdisciplinary coursework with her colleagues in both music and computer science. Before entering the education profession, she was an award-winning music director in advertising, where she worked for several multinational advertising agencies producing jingles and underscores for hundreds of commercials.

Alice M. Hammel earned her DMA (music education) from Shenandoah University, and her MME (music education) from Florida State University. Her teaching responsibilities include faculty positions at James Madison, Christopher Newport, and Virginia Commonwealth Universities. She also teaches privately and in an urban elementary school. She has presented at numerous state, division, and national conferences, and has published widely in journals. She published (with Eugenie Burkett) an online course, *On Music and Special Learners* (Connect for Education), and a text (co-authored with Ryan Hourigan) for Oxford University Press, *Teaching Music to Students with Special Needs: A Label-free Approach.* Her works are often included and cited in resources published by MENC. These resources include *Spotlight on Teaching Special Learners* and *Readings in Diversity, Inclusion, and Music for All.* Her research interests include students with special needs, urban music education, and early-childhood education. She is chair of the students with special needs section for Virginia Music Educators Association.

Maud Hickey is Associate Professor of Music Education at Northwestern University. Her research focuses on children's compositions and improvisations, as well as on using technology to facilitate these processes. Dr. Hickey's recent work involves using composition and improvisation with at-risk students. She has authored chapters in several books and her articles have appeared in journals such as *Music Educators Journal, General Music Today, Journal of Research in Music Education*, and *Research Studies in Music Education.* She has also edited the MENC text *Why and How to Teach Music Composition.*

Michele Kaschub serves as Professor of Music and Coordinator of Music Teacher Education & Graduate Studies at the University of Southern Maine School of Music. Her teaching responsibilities include courses in music education philosophy, research, and curriculum, as well as PreK–12 choral/vocal methods and composition methods. Her publications include articles in a variety of national and international journals and chapters in several books. She has presented clinics, papers, and workshops at multiple state, national, and international conferences. She has recently coauthored *Minds on Music: Composition for Creative and Critical Thinking* (Rowman & Littlefield, 2009) with Janice Smith. In addition to her work with music teacher education and composition, Michele also serves as the Artistic Director/Conductor for the Lyric Choir of The Boy Singers of Maine and as President of the Maine Music Educators Association.

Alexander P. Koops is Assistant Professor of Music and Director of Undergraduate Music Education at Azusa Pacific University. He specializes in instrumental music with a particular interest in how composition can be used to enhance students' understandings of music in band and orchestral settings. His recent research has focused on instrumentalists in middle school settings.

John Kratus is Professor of Music Education at Michigan State University, where he teaches courses in secondary general music, music education foundations, songwriting, research techniques, psychology of music, and philosophy of music education. He has published widely in the fields of creativity, composition, and curriculum development, and has presented his ideas to audiences around the world.

Sandi MacLeod has served as Vermont MIDI Project coordinator since 1996 and was a founding member of the project. This nationally acclaimed music composition and online mentoring project now includes hundreds of students in Vermont schools, as well as pilot projects in schools in six other states. She has also been able to partner with universities to allow undergraduate students to experience web-based mentor-mentee interaction with school-based composers.

Michael Medvinsky is a K–12 general music teacher in the Brandon School District in Michigan and lecturer in music education at Oakland University. He uses technology to support learners in composing music in styles most familiar to them and then engages them in exploring the less familiar. He has engaged in cross-disciplinary teaching that connects music learning experiences to aspects of the general curriculum and has taught choral music, instrumental music, and world drumming ensemble. Mr. Medvinsky has written for the *Michigan Music Educators Journal* on his approach to cross-disciplinary teaching and on bringing popular music into the classroom. He has been an invited presenter for Michigan school districts, countywide in-service programs, and the Michigan Music Conference, and has regularly hosted both in-service and pre-service music teachers as observers in his classroom. He is president of a professional development organization affiliated with Oakland University that offers workshops in inquiry-based music education practice aiming to foster independent musicianship and learner agency among music learners. He is also a region representative to the Michigan Music Educators Association.

John W. Richmond is Professor and the Director of the School of Music at the University of Nebraska–Lincoln. His research focuses on arts education policy, legal issues in arts education, and the philosophy of music education. He is published in such respected journals as the *Journal of Research in Music Education, Research Perspectives in Music Education, Arts Education Policy Review,* the *International Journal of Music Education,* the *Journal of Aesthetic Education,* and the *Choral Journal.* He is a Founding Director of the *Suncoast Music Education Forum,* the Founding Editor of the *Florida Choral News,* and served as the Conference Director for the 1994 World Conference of the International Society for Music Education (ISME). He edited the Policy/Philosophy Research Section of the second edition of the *New Handbook of Research in Music Teaching and Learning* (Oxford University Press, 2002), and also wrote the chapter on "Law Research and Music Education." He recently completed four biographical entries and an institutional article for the new AmeriGrove Project and is under contract for a chapter for the upcoming *Oxford Music Education Handbook* (Oxford University Press).

Patricia Riley is Associate Professor and Coordinator of the Music Education Program at the University of Vermont. Previously she taught at The Crane School of Music (SUNY Potsdam), and for twenty years in the public schools of New Jersey and Vermont. Dr. Riley has published in *Music Education Research, Update: Applications of Research in Music Education, Research and Issues in Music Education, Visions of Research in Music Education,* and *Teaching Music*. Her research interests include student music composition, cultural studies, technology, and assessment.

Janice P. Smith is Associate Professor of Music Education and undergraduate coordinator of music education at the Aaron Copland School of Music, Queens College, City University of New York. Her teaching responsibilities include courses in music education philosophy, general music methods, and composition pedagogy. She has presented at numerous state, division, and national conferences and has published articles addressing composition in music education and working with unpitched singers. She is the research chair for the New York State School Music Association. In addition to various book chapters in edited publications dealing with urban education and/or composition pedagogy, she is the co-author (with Michele Kaschub) of the book *Minds on Music: Composition for Creative and Critical Thinking* (Rowman & Littlefield, 2009).

Sandra L. Stauffer is Professor of Music at Arizona State University. Her studies of children and young people as composers and her research on music teacher preparation can be found in the *Bulletin of the Council for Research in Music Education,* the *Journal of Research in Music Education, Research Studies in Music Education, The Mountain Lake Reader,* and *The Orff Echo*. She also has collaborated with composer Morton Subotnick in the development of his creative music software for children.

Katherine Strand is Associate Professor of Music at Indiana University. Dr. Strand specializes in classroom composition, action research, and integrated arts curriculum development. Her articles have appeared in *Music Education Research,* the *Journal of Research in Music Education,* the *Journal of Music Teacher Education,* the *Bulletin of the Council for Research in Music Education, Arts Education Policy Review,* the *Philosophy of Music Education Review, General Music Today, Music Educators Journal,* the *Indiana Musicator,* and *Teaching Music*.

Peter R. Webster is the John W. Beattie Professor of Music Education & Technology at Northwestern University. Dr. Webster is the author of Measures of Creative Thinking in Music, an exploratory tool for assessing music thinking using quasi-improvisational tasks. Coauthor of the book and DVD Experiencing Music Technology (Thomson/Schirmer, 2006), he has also authored over seventy book chapters and articles on technology, music cognition, and children's creative thinking in music and its assessment. He also serves as an editorial board member for the *Journal of Research in Music Education, Journal for Technology in Music Learning, International Journal of Education in the Arts, Research Studies in Music Education,* and the *Asia-Pacific Journal for Arts Education*.

Jackie Wiggins is Professor of Music Education and Chair of the Department of Music, Theatre, and Dance at Oakland University. Known for her expertise in constructivist music education theory and practice, she has composed with music learners for more than forty years and studied children's compositional process as a researcher for more than twenty years. Author of *Teaching for Musical Understanding* (1st edition, 2001, McGraw-Hill; 2nd edition, 2009, CARMU) and *Composition in the Classroom* (1990, MENC), she has made more than two hundred presentations, including keynote addresses on four continents, and published numerous book chapters and journal articles on constructivist music education practice, the nature of musical understanding, and creative process in the music classroom. Wiggins currently serves on the editorial boards of the *Bulletin of the Center for Research in Music Education, Research Studies in Music Education*, the *International Journal of Education and the Arts*, and the *Asia-Pacific Journal for Arts Education*.

Betty Anne Younker is Professor of Music Education and Dean of the Don Wright Faculty of Music, The University of Western Ontario, London, Ontario, Canada. Her research interests include the philosophy and pedagogy of music education, and critical and creative thinking. Publications include articles in a variety of national and international journals, and chapters in several books, while paper presentations have occurred at multiple state, national, and international conferences. Before appointments at the university level, Dr. Younker taught in public schools in band, choral, and general music settings. In addition, she has taught studio flute, working with beginning to university-aged students. Presently she is a member of the 2012 College Music Society program committee and serves in other capacities for the CMS as well, continues to serve as a consultant for a NASM working group, and serves on a variety of editorial boards.

INDEX